Intimate Labors

Intimate Labors

Cultures, Technologies, and the Politics of Care

Edited by Eileen Boris and Rhacel Salazar Parreñas

Stanford Social Sciences
An Imprint of Stanford University Press
Stanford, California

Stanford University Press
Stanford, California

Printed in the United States of America on acid-free, archival-quality paper

Library of Congress Cataloging-in-Publication Data

Intimate labors : cultures, technologies, and the politics of care / edited by Eileen Boris and Rhacel S. Parreñas.
        p. cm.
    Includes bibliographical references and index.
    ISBN 978-0-8047-6192-5 (cloth : alk. paper)—ISBN 978-0-8047-6193-2 (pbk. : alk. paper)
    1. Women—Employment—Social aspects. 2. Intimacy (Psychology)—Economic aspects.
3. Interpersonal relations and culture. 4. Women employees—Labor unions. 5. Sex-oriented businesses. 6. Work—Social aspects. I. Boris, Eileen, 1948– II. Parreñas, Rhacel Salazar.

    HD6053.I65 2010
    306.3'6082—dc22
                        2010006263

Typeset by Thompson Type in 10/14 Minion Pro.

Contents

ACKNOWLEDGMENTS

WE WOULD LIKE TO THANK EVERYONE who made possible this work on *Intimate Labors*. Eileen Boris is grateful for the generous gift of Blair Hull, who endowed the Hull Chair, which she holds. She also thanks the UCSB Academic Senate and her research assistants Janiene Langford and Jason Stoler. Rhacel Salazar Parreñas thanks the extraordinary staff support provided by Billie Gabriel at UC Davis and Rosanne Neri and Jean Wood at Brown University. At Stanford University Press, the enthusiastic support of our editor Kate Wahl has made all the difference, Joa Suorez has provided remarkable editorial assistance, and Margaret Pinette has saved us from numerous errors as only a superb copyeditor can. This project also benefits from the comments shared by two anonymous reviewers.

Most of all we are indebted to the talented scholars in this collection. Such intellectual community that crosses disciplines is precious, and we look at this volume as a beginning rather than an end in an ongoing and ever expanding conversation. The labor that went into editing this book was a true collaboration. We especially thank each other!

This book builds on a conference we co-organized in 2007 at the University of California, Santa Barbara, which was funded by the UC Labor and Employment Research Fund; UC Humanities and Research Institute; UCSB Interdisciplinary Humanities Center; UCSB College of Letters and Science and Division of Social Sciences; Hull Chair in Feminist Studies; UCSB Center for the Study of Work, Labor and Democracy; UCSB Instructional Grants; and the College of Humanities, Arts, and Culture Studies at UC Davis. We further thank Elizabeth Tandy Shermer for her outstanding organizational skills and Tanya Paperny for her design work, as well as the staffs of the UCSB Department of Feminist Studies and ISBER (Institute for Social, Behavioral, and Economic Research).

We dedicate this book to the women closest to us. Eileen Boris dedicates this book to her sister Rhonda Boris, the one who cares, and Rhacel Salazar Parreñas dedicates this book to her two sisters in academia, Celine Shimizu and Juno Parreñas, and her friend Malou Babilonia. Finally, we both dedicate this book to intimate workers everywhere.

CONTRIBUTORS

Rene Almeling is Assistant Professor of Sociology at Yale University. She recently finished an appointment as a Robert Wood Johnson Foundation Scholar in Health Policy Research at the University of California, Berkeley/UCSF. She is completing a book on egg and sperm donation, and she has started a new research project on how gendered ideas about bodies shape the presentation of and response to genetic knowledge.

Elizabeth Bernstein is Assistant Professor of Women's Studies and Sociology at Barnard College, Columbia University. Her publications include *Temporarily Yours: Intimacy, Authenticity, and the Commerce of Sex* (University of Chicago Press, 2007); and *Regulating Sex: the Politics of Intimacy and Identity* (Routledge, 2005), coedited with Laurie Schaffner.

Eileen Boris is Hull Professor and Chair of Feminist Studies at the University of California, Santa Barbara, where she holds affiliate appointments in History and Black Studies and directs the Center for Research on Women and Social Justice. Her publications include *Home to Work: Motherhood and the Politics of Industrial Homework in the United States* (Cambridge University Press, 1994); *The Practice of U.S. Women's History: Narratives, Intersections, and Dialogues* (Rutgers University Press, 2007), coedited with S. J. Kleinberg and Vicki Ruiz; and *Caring for America: Home Health Workers in the Shadow of the Welfare State* (Oxford University Press, forthcoming), coauthored with Jennifer Klein.

Laura Briggs is Associate Professor and Head of Gender and Women's Studies at the University of Arizona, where she holds affiliate appointments in History, Anthropology, and Latin American Studies. Her publications include *Reproducing Empire: Race, Sex, Science, and U.S. Imperialism in Puerto Rico* (University of California Press, 2002); *International Adoption: Global Inequalities and the Circulation of Children* (New York University Press, 2009), coedited with Diana Marre; and *The Politics of Transnational and Transracial Adoption* (Duke University Press, forthcoming).

Dorothy Sue Cobble is Professor of History and Labor Studies at Rutgers University, New Brunswick, New Jersey. Her publications include *Dishing It Out: Waitresses and Their Unions in the Twentieth Century* (University of Illinois Press, 1991); *Women and Unions: Forging a Partnership* (Cornell University Press, 1994); *The Other Women's Movement: Workplace Justice and Social Rights in Modern America* (Princeton University Press, 2004), which won the 2005 Philip Taft Book Prize and other awards; and *The Sex of Class: Women Transforming American Labor* (Cornell University Press, 2007).

Ariel Ducey is Associate Professor of Sociology at the University of Calgary. She is now researching the use of new medical devices in urogyneacology and how consulting firms shape health care systems. Her publications include *Never Good Enough: Health Care Workers and the False Promise of Job Training* (Cornell University Press, 2009).

Kimberly Hoang received her M.A. in Sociology from Stanford University and is a Ph.D. candidate in Sociology at UC Berkeley, where she works with Raka Ray. Her dissertation addresses the stratification of sex work in Ho Chi Minh City. She is the author of "Vietnamese Immigration and Incorporation in the United States since 1975," forthcoming from ABC-CLIO in 2012.

María de la Luz Ibarra is Associate Professor of Chicana and Chicano Studies at San Diego State University. Her articles focus on Mexican migrant women employed as care workers. She currently is writing a book entitled *Extending Kinship: Mexican Women and Transnational Elder Care*.

Miliann Kang is Assistant Professor of Women's, Gender, Sexuality Studies and affiliated faculty in Sociology and Asian/Asian American Studies at the

University of Massachusetts, Amherst. Her book, *The Managed Hand: Race, Gender, and the Body in Beauty Service Work* (University of California Press, 2010), won the Sara Whaley book prize from the National Women's Studies Association. Currently, she is researching work-family issues for Asian American women and the ways that gender and race influence motherhood and career paths.

Jennifer Klein is Professor of History at Yale University. She writes on health care, pensions, Social Security, labor politics, and long-term care. Her publications include the prize-winning *For All These Rights: Business, Labor, and the Shaping of America's Public-Private Welfare State* (Princeton University Press, 2003); and *Caring for America: Home Health Workers in the Shadow of the Welfare State* (Oxford University Press, forthcoming), coauthored with Eileen Boris.

Premilla Nadasen is Associate Professor of History at Queens College, CUNY. She is an activist and a scholar who writes and gives public lectures about women's history, social policy, and grassroots organizing. Her publications include *Welfare Warriors: The Welfare Rights Movement in the United States* (Routledge University Press, 2005), winner of the John Hope Franklin Prize. She is currently writing a book on domestic worker organizing.

Rhacel Salazar Parreñas is Professor of Sociology at the University of Southern California. She is the author of numerous essays and books on gender, migration, and globalization, including *The Force of Domesticity: Filipina Migrants and Globalization* (New York University Press, 2008). She is currently writing a book on the labor and migration of Filipina entertainers in Tokyo's nightlife industry.

Seemin Qayum is a historical anthropologist and the author and editor of several works on nationalism, elites, and gender in modern Bolivia. She has been a consultant to national and international organizations in the fields of environment, development, gender, and culture. Her publications include *Cultures of Servitude: Modernity, Domesticity, and Class in India* (Stanford University Press, 2009), coauthored with Raka Ray.

Raka Ray is Sarah Kailath Chair in India Studies, Chair of the Center for South Asia Studies, and Professor of Sociology and South and Southeast Asian Studies at the University of California, Berkeley. Her publications include *Fields of Protest: Women's Movements in India* (University of Minnesota Press, 1999); and *Cultures of Servitude: Modernity, Domesticity, and Class in India* (Stanford University Press, 2009), coauthored with Seemin Qayum.

Ellen Reese is Associate Professor of Sociology at the University of California, Riverside. Her publications include *Backlash against Welfare Mothers: Past and Present* (University of California Press, 2005); and *The Wages of Empire: Neoliberal Policies, Repression, and Women's Poverty* (Paradigm Publishers, 2007), coedited with Amalia Cabezas and Marguerite Waller. She is currently writing *They Say Cutback; We Say Fightback! Welfare Rights Activism in an Era of Retrenchment.*

Becki Ross is Chair of Women's and Gender Studies at the University of British Columbia, Vancouver, where she holds a cross-appointment in Sociology. Her publications include *Burlesque West: Showgirls, Sex, and Sin in Postwar Vancouver* (University of Toronto Press, 2009).

Kalindi Vora is Assistant Professor of Ethnic Studies at the University of California, San Diego. She held a UC Presidential Post-Doctoral Fellowship at the University of California, Berkeley. She is currently working on a book manuscript about relations of interdependence and exchange between India and the United States with the working title *Life Support: The Transmission of Vital Commodities between India and the U.S.*

Jane Ward is Associate Professor of Women's Studies at the University of California, Riverside. Her publications include *Respectably Queer* (Vanderbilt University Press, 2008) and several articles on queer politics, masculinity, and sexuality.

Viviana A. Zelizer is Lloyd Cotsen '50 Professor of Sociology at Princeton University. She has published books on the development of life insurance, the changing economic and sentimental value of children, and the place of money in social life. Her publications include *The Purchase of Intimacy* (Princeton University Press, 2005).

Intimate Labors

Introduction

Eileen Boris and Rhacel Salazar Parreñas

ONE OF THE MOST STRIKING FEATURES of contemporary global capitalism is the heightened commodification of intimacy that pervades social life.[1] We not only seek to buy love, but also express devotion through goods and depend on services to fulfill obligations or display closeness to others. So did nineteenth-century Victorians in Britain, the United States, and throughout the British Empire. Our historical moment is distinguished by both the intensification of commodification and the subsequent crowding out of indigenous and alternative ways of being. But the monetization of daily life and the privatization of public goods still generate resistance in the broadest sense. People seek solace and joy on their own terms and develop collective challenges to their understanding of the good life.

Against the colonization of the intimate, this volume focuses on the proliferation of labors, both paid and unpaid, that sustains the day-to-day work that individuals and societies require to survive—and flourish. It moves us through the expanding service economy into the crevices of what appears as most private and thus most hidden, even if such locations reflect cultural definitions of the shameful or personal. It reveals acts of love and work for money to be interconnected. That is, the essays in this collection examine the social construction of commodified intimacies, or, more precisely, the intersections of money and intimacy in everyday life, by looking at the ways that intimacy as a material, affective, psychological, and embodied state characterizes such labors. Intimacy occurs in a social context; it is accordingly shaped by, even as it shapes, relations of race, class, gender, and sexuality. And the work of intimacy constitutes intimate labors.

But what intellectual work does the linking of *intimate* and *labor* perform? The joining of such terms denies the separation of home from work, work from labor, and productive from nonproductive labor that has characterized capitalist globalization. Intimate labor encompasses a range of activities, including bodily and household upkeep, personal and family maintenance, and sexual contact or liaison. It entails touch, whether of children or customers; bodily or emotional closeness or personal familiarity, such as sexual intercourse and bathing another; or close observation of another and knowledge of personal information, such as watching elderly people or advising trainees. Such work occurs in homes, hospitals, hotels, streets, and other public as well as private locations. It exists along a continuum of service and caring labor, from high-end nursing to low-end housekeeping, and includes sex, domestic, and care work. Against a scholarship that considers nurses, nannies, home aides, cleaners, prostitutes, and hostesses apart from each other, we explore intimate labor as a useful category of analysis to understand gender, racial, class, and other power relations in the context of global economic transformations.

Through the category of "intimate labor," we consider various occupations—usually subsumed under the often discretely examined categories of care, domestic, and sex work—as sharing common attributes. Each of these labors forges interdependent relations, represents work assumed to be the unpaid responsibility of women, and, consequently, is usually considered to be a non-market activity or an activity of low economic value that should be done by lower classes or racial outsiders. These activities promote the physical, intellectual, affective, and other emotional needs of strangers, friends, family, sex partners, children, and elderly, ill, or disabled people. They comprise tasks for daily life, including household maintenance (cooking, cleaning, washing, shopping) and personal existence (bathing, feeding, turning over, ambulation). They rely on clean sheets and swept rooms. They involve bodily and psychic intimacy: manipulating genitalia, wiping noses, lifting torsos, and feeding mouths, but also listening, talking, holding, and just being there. The presence of dirt, bodies, and intimacy, however, helps to stigmatize such work and those who perform it.[2]

Characteristics that sociologist Paula England and economist Nancy Folbre attribute to care work apply to the broader arena of intimate labor: "The worker provides a service to someone with whom he or she is in personal (usually face-to-face) contact"; "the worker responds to a need or desire that is directly expressed by the recipient"; and, perhaps to a lesser extent, the service "develops the human capabilities of the recipient."[3] These criteria seemingly exclude hotel housekeepers and private household servants, but the lines between tending people and tending their homes are fluid. Home health aides spend a good portion of their time cleaning, cooking, and straightening up, tasks that are essential to enabling an elderly or disabled person to remain at home in dignity. The hotel housekeeper, who has "to get on my knees to clean the bathroom" and provide additional "creature comforts" for guests, produces pleasure and comfort even if she works when the receiver is not present and provides indirect care.[4] In sum, the labors of cleaners and housekeepers revolve around the intimate and the bodily, belonging to those intimate labors associated with unpaid tasks done for the household and its members by wives, mothers, daughters, and previously slaves.

What Is Intimate Labor?

These chapters capture a wide range of intimate labors and complicate the space-time continuum under which such work occurs. They include fleeting encounters and durable ties. Regardless of temporality, these labors all rely on the maintenance of precise social relations between employers and employees or customers and providers. Brief encounters under the rubric of intimate labor might comprise nail manicuring, bill collection, street prostitution, and sperm donation. Intimate labors that depend on durable relations might include various forms of sex work, such as bar hostessing and escort service; child and elderly care; domestic work; and various forms of health care. Through ethnography and history, scholars are determining if a job is a form of intimate labor rather than merely drawing a line without considering case studies of actual labor.

The category "intimate labor" places in a continuum the discretely examined categories of care, sex, and domestic work. These forms of labor are quite varied and diverse. In our discussion, care work entails not only the tending of the elderly or the sick as described by María de la Luz Ibarra or the watching of children as discussed by Ellen Reese but also the care of transgender subjects. As Jane Ward illuminates, care work can embrace the "gender labor" of feminine partners who bolster the masculinity of their transgender female-to-male partners with their performances of femininity. Likewise, sex work comes in diverse forms and would include the labor of sexually titillating customers in hostess clubs, as seen by Rhacel Salazar Parreñas; the street work of transgender sex workers, as presented by Becki Ross; fleeting encounters between working-class prostitutes and their customers, as recorded by Kimberly Kay Hoang and Elizabeth Bernstein; but also the purchase of the girlfriend experience, also analyzed by Bernstein. Lastly, domestic work entails not only cleaning but also various forms of care work that are performed inside the home, as Ibarra and Eileen Boris and Jennifer Klein suggest. Even domestic labor makes social relations that involve forms of intimacy, as Seemin Qayum and Raka Ray found for Kolkata and New York and Premilla Nadasen, for Atlanta. Notably, there are porous boundaries between these various work categories. Sex workers do a great deal of care work, and likewise domestic workers provide care.

Attentiveness appears as a key to understanding intimate labor, but this does not necessarily entail face-to-face interactions. The work of tending encompasses a wide range of activities from taking care of one's reproductive needs—for instance, the provision of children through adoption or the giving of an orgasm via sex—to tending to bodily care—from the provision of a manicure by a working professional, as Miliann Kang shows here, to the giving of a sponge bath to an elderly patient. It includes the upkeep of homes as well as people. Tending need not entail face-to-face encounters because technological advancements facilitate communication across time and space. Attentiveness could entail tending to the materials and objects that improve the quality of our lives. Ariel Ducey magnificently points to this in her description of the ways hospital workers ensure the comfort of their patients by adjusting equipment, regulating the hot water tap, and supplying them with adequate toiletries.

Intimate labor stands alongside other conceptions. In this volume, Dorothy Sue Cobble speaks about "personal service workers" interchangeably with "intimate workers." Intimate labor might not involve face-to-face interaction, though many types of personal service work do entail intimate labor. At the same time, not all types of interactive service occupations would fall under the rubric of what we mean by "intimate labor." A fast-food worker, a stamp dispenser at a post office, or a concierge in a hotel need not do intimate labor. However, bill collectors could arguably be categorized as intimate laborers because their work requires them to know intimate details about another person that could be embarrassing to that person if known to others. Building from Viviana Zelizer's theorizations on the purchase of intimacy, intimate labor would lead to "knowledge and attention that are not widely available to third persons."[5] The knowledge generated by intimate labor would include "such elements as shared secrets, interpersonal rituals, bodily information, awareness of personal vulnerability and shared memory of embarrassing situations."[6]

Some forms of labor clearly fall under the rubric of intimate labor more than others. Why would a bill collector in India, as described by Kalindi Vora in this volume, engage in intimate labor while, let us say, a concierge in a five-star hotel in San Francisco, as described by sociologist Rachel Sherman, would not necessarily do so?[7] A sex worker is clearly an intimate laborer because, after all, intimacy is a euphemism for sexual intercourse.[8] Likewise, a domestic worker because of access to the intimate space of the home and knowledge of its inhabitants' habits would be an intimate laborer. But what makes a nail salon worker an intimate laborer? And how do the labor of foreign adoption and the construction of good and bad motherhood, as considered by Laura Briggs, advance the formulation of intimate labor?

Intimate labor involves tending to the intimate needs of individuals inside and outside their home. Our intimate needs would include not just sexual gratification but also our bodily upkeep, care for loved ones, creating and sustaining social and emotional ties, and health and hygiene maintenance. Meeting one's intimate needs would include not only child care but also the bearing of children for others, as Briggs astutely points out in this volume. Under this definition, work that is as wide ranging as prostitution, nail salon work, surrogate mothering, and housecleaning would be considered intimate labor. Intimate labor also refers to work that exposes personal information that would leave one vulnerable if others had access to such knowledge. Such work would arguably include bill collection, domestic work, elder care, various forms of therapy, and prostitution.

Doing Intimate Labor

Our formulation of intimate labor builds from a rich feminist literature on women's work. Enhancing our conception of intimate labor are previous discussions on the labor processes of reproductive labor and emotional labor.[9] In this section, we situate our discussion of intimate labor in feminist discussions of women's work. We wish to distinguish what we mean by intimate labor from emotional labor, a concept that many of our contributors draw from when explaining specific intimate labor processes, and reproductive labor, a category that one would argue also encompasses the provision of sex, care, and domestic work, which are the three types of discretely examined occupational categories that we wish to bring together in this volume. By distinguishing intimate labor from these other forms of labor identified in the literature, we wish to further contain our definition of intimate labor. Moreover, we wish to clarify that not all forms of interactive service occupations would be forms of intimate labor.

The process of intimate labor is not uniform. As we noted earlier, intimate labor in some cases entails face-to-face labor, and in other cases it does not. In this volume, our contributors introduce various labors constituted as intimate labor including for example the work of "gender labor" identified by Ward and "entertainment work" highlighted by Parreñas, which refers to the labor of sexually titillating customers via song, dance, and conversation in hostess clubs. These examples show that intimate labor manifests in different forms, requires different labor responsibilities, and entails diverse labor processes.

In many situations, intimate labor would entail emotional labor but not always. Coined by the sociologist Arlie Hochschild, the term *emotional labor* refers to a form of face-to-face labor in which one displays certain emotions to induce particular feelings in the client or customer.[10] Emotional labor relies on the manipulation of one's emotions. Various intimate laborers do emotional labor, including bill collectors who must act stern or empathetic so as to pressure customers to pay their bills, hostesses and high-class prostitutes who must display emotions of joy and love to heighten feelings of specialness among customers, and domestic workers who must suppress their emotions so as not to make their employers uncomfortable.

In explaining the process of performing emotional labor, Hochschild draws from the work of Konstantin Stanislavski to distinguish "surface acting" and "deep acting." In "surface acting," one merely pretends to be the character. For instance, a domestic worker would pretend to feel grateful that her employer offered a hand-me-down of furniture instead of a raise at the end of the year. In contrast, in "deep acting," one embodies the traits and emotions of his or her character, becoming the actual character. In this scenario, the domestic worker would feel genuinely happy to have received old furniture instead of a salary increase. According to Hochschild, emotional labor often results in "emotional dissonance" for workers unable to feel the emotions they must display but who have no choice but to feign them.[11] Those suffering from emotional dissonance are more likely to be persons in low-status occupations who are without "status shields" against the poor treatment they may experience at work from those with greater access to money, power, authority, or status in society. Thus, domestic workers, street prostitutes, and bill collectors are those more likely to suffer from emotional dissonance. Hochschild's notion and discussion of emotional labor gleans insight into the labor process of intimate workers, as their performance of their work often relies on the manipulation and control of their emotions. However, emotional labor is not a prerequisite or requirement in intimate labor. In many cases, intimate laborers need not regulate their emotions. Sperm donors, considered by Rene Almeling in this volume, and surrogate mothers do not engage in emotional labor, though their jobs may involve emotional labor that would occur in private and not public spaces. Lastly, emotional labor is not always the central marker that defines the experience of intimate laborers. Emotional labor may be an aspect of the job for, let us say, a housecleaner or a nail salon worker, but it need not be a significant aspect that defines the job.

Another way to characterize intimate labor is to define it as work that involves embodied and affective interactions in the service of social reproduction. According to sociologist Evelyn Nakano Glenn, social reproduction encompasses the "array of activities and relationships involved in maintaining people both on a daily basis and intergenerationally." She defines reproductive labor to include "activities such as purchasing household goods, preparing and serving food, laundering and repairing clothing, maintaining furnishings and appliances, socializing children, providing care and emotional support for adults, and maintaining kin and community ties."[12] Political economist Isabella Bakker provides an even more expansive definition that includes the biological, including "the conditions and social constructions of motherhood"; labor force replication, including "subsistence, education and training"; and "provisioning of caring needs," including aspects "wholly privatized within families and kinship networks or socialized to some degree through state supports."[13] Not all of this work entails relation and emotional labor, closeness or touch, but a considerable amount does. Social reproduction refers not only to the care of others but also to the care of the self.

Care and domestic work are clearly included in the wide definition offered by Glenn, but not sex work. Bernstein (in this volume) would expand our understanding of reproductive labor to include sex work. After all, reproductive labor refers to the labor needed to sustain the productive labor force.[14] In this age of late capitalism, Bernstein argues that overworked professionals now pursue paid sexual liaisons not only for human connection but also for emotional satisfaction. What distinguishes reproductive labor from intimate labor? The idea of reproductive labor comes out of a political economic and Marxist tradition that calls attention to the behind-the-scenes labor of women and the poor that became defined as unproductive of exchange value.

Such is hardly the case when the more affluent pay for children, as Briggs shows, or those on welfare pay for child care, as Reese discusses. The idea of intimate labor more often focuses on the personal or the daily praxis of intimacy, which, as we underscore in this book, is increasingly commodified in late capitalism.

Commodification of Intimacy

Intimate labor remains a primary source of livelihood, which women increasingly gain by being paid for it in the marketplace rather than through performing it within a heterosexual marriage in exchange for support. The commodification of intimate labor raises feminist contentions over the relationship of "care" and the economy. Some bemoan an increasing commodification of the intimate. Others, including the authors in this volume, insist that relations of intimacy already involve the exchange of money. Contributors interrogate the intersections of commerce and intimacy from multiple perspectives, mapping historical shifts in and the changing nature of women's work; social meanings of gender, race/ethnicity, class, and sexuality in intimate labor; implications of intimate labor for worker empowerment and self-organization; and the porous boundaries between the paid and unpaid labor of women.

This volume goes beyond the usual debates on intimate labor. We seek to avoid the binary trap of exploitation versus agency that plagues discussions on sex work and reject the dualistic formulation of domestic work as either viable employment or an antiquated relation of servitude better relegated to precapitalist societies or noncapitalist social relations. Some view the responsibilities of care work as belonging in the private sphere and best performed by family, especially women. Others argue care work is a potentially rewarding occupation for women. A similar split over the view of sex work as viable employment or its labeling as only oppression characterizes conversations regarding a range of sexual labors. It is perhaps even more contentious than contentions over paid and unpaid domestic work.

A split between radical feminists and sex-positive feminists distinguishes the scholarship on sex work.[15] Radical feminists view prostitution as a form of violence against women; the commodification of the female body becomes the ultimate symbol of patriarchal masculinity.[16] They argue that either economic coercion or psychological damage from rape or sexual abuse underlies the entrance of women into prostitution.[17] Liberal feminists and/or sex-positive feminists question the obliteration of agency by radical feminists as well as their conflation of sex with love, that is, the view that commodification contaminates the purity of sex. In contrast, these activists and scholars acknowledge multiple meanings in sex work. Above all else, sex work becomes a form of labor in which the worker sells not her body but her service.[18] Some may disdain the job of servicing sex, but others may find it rewarding. As Laura Agustín describes such reactions, some view that "they perform an art, a therapy or a rite" when performing sex work, while others "feel selling sex is analogous to typing or running a machine and see benefits from being called sex workers."[19]

Avoiding these usual dichotonomies, the essays in this volume see intimate labor as work situated in the labor market—both formal and informal—and subject to market forces and ideological views on gender, ethnicity, race, and sexuality, and structural constraints. Two central themes underlie our cross-disciplinary discussion. One underscores the significance of the social, cultural, political, and economic structures that shape the characteristics and dynamics of intimate labor. These essays chart the history of intimate labors in light of the rise and devolution of welfare states, women's labor force participation, family formation, the expansion of sex work into new industries, and development of institutions for young, elderly, ill, and disabled people. Intimate labor thus serves as a springboard not only for understanding women's labor market activities but also as a key lens for examining the impact of macrostructural forces of economic globalization and the neoliberal state. By using the term *neoliberalism*, we refer to the rise of unfettered markets brought by the deregulation of corporations and financial institutions, privatization and the concomitant decline of social welfare, and the imposition of free trade policies. Cast in the name of individualism, neoliberalism has resulted in the curbing of labor unions, the diminishment of social programs, and the loss of social democratic policies. As a number of these chapters underscore, it has also intensified the responsibilities of women at home and on the job, particularly through the compounding of their intimate labor.

Simultaneously, larger macroeconomic processes spur the formation of "new" forms of intimate labor. The advent of "time-space compression" heightens the sex tourism industry, and business travel forces the transfer of care from unpaid work within to paid work outside the home. Hence, this collection situates intimate labor processes in globalization. It asks: what types of intimate labor does the global circulation of goods, ideas, and peoples encourage? What forms of inequalities do the practices and processes of intimate labor engender and maintain? How do practices of intimate labor reflect larger structural inequalities and cultural processes in national and transnational contexts? Intimate labor emerges as a mechanism that maintains and reflects socioeconomic inequalities. These inequalities are displayed and negotiated in social interactions in private spaces as well as public settings that are central to the operation of global capitalism, for instance airports and business hotels. How does the performance of services in these settings reflect inequities of race, class, ethnicity, and gender? How are such inequities negotiated, resisted, and maintained in the performance of intimate labor?

Second, the essays in this volume advance the debate among feminist theorists over the relationship between "care" and "economy." For some, these terms stand in for the "hostile worlds" of love and money, an inscription of separate sphere ideology with gendered attributes repackaged: Women give care, men earn money. These theorists lament an increasing commodification of aspects of life that normatively they contend should be beyond the market, such as tending to dependents, usually defined as the frail, ill, and young.[20] Philosopher Virginia Held typifies such argument in regarding "caring work as enabling those cared for to know that someone values them" and for "expressing social connectedness, . . . contributing to children's development and family satisfaction, and . . . enabling social cohesion and well-being," all outside of market norms. Likewise economist Susan Himmelweit defends caring labor as a special kind of work involving relationship and emotional attachment so that "much of the quality of our lives would be lost if the imposition of inappropriate forms of market rationality turned such work into mere labor." By such criteria, the attentiveness of a flight attendant, the touch of a sex worker, or the comfort making of a maid would fall outside caring labor, leaving the field to nursing and related health occupations, child and elder care, and personal support services.[21]

Others—and here we place ourselves—claim that commodification already has entered into relations of care, while still others point out that relations of intimacy already involve the exchange of money. The wages of intimate labor suffer from social expectations about what women should undertake out of love, kinship, or obligation. As England and others have found, most "interactive service work" occupations with care at their core pay less than jobs with equivalent skill, sex composition, and educational requirements, and care work that evokes mothering has an even greater wage penalty. Additional factors also lessen the wages of intimacy: "the labor intensive nature of the work, the inability of recipients to pay, and the intrinsic motivation of some workers."[22]

To express their findings in another way, when intimacy becomes employment, it loses status as a labor of love and becomes regarded as unskilled work that anyone can perform because women have undertaken such activities without payment. Call this the devaluation thesis: double devaluation because of the lack of pay and the "nature" of the doers. Those who have performed such paid jobs are of lower status, often men and women of color and/or recent immigrants. Though such jobs need not be women's or black or immigrant women's work, historically they have been; indeed, men who engage in them experience the costs of racialized feminization. Characteristics of the worker have continued to define the skill and value of the work.[23]

To navigate these debates, the authors in this volume seek to understand what happens when intimate labor enters the marketplace and becomes paid both in terms of working conditions and the value of the worker herself. The collection as a whole brings together research on racialized and gendered labors not usually thought about together, creating an interdisciplinary dialogue among scholars from women's studies, ethnic studies, history, and humanistic sociology. This interdisciplinary approach helps unpack the social, cultural, political, ideological, and representational definitions of work and worker and shows how embodied identities based on gender, race, nation, and class shape the meaning of intimate labor. The following chapters define intimate labor; interrogate its significance and the meanings of the experience vis-à-vis market participation and global economic processes; evaluate relations of race, class, gender, sexuality, and citizenship; consider popular representations; and analyze challenges and struggles in organizing those who make their livings through touch, closeness, and personal attentiveness, another name for care.

Notes

1. Hochschild, 2003.
2. Palmer, 1989.
3. England and Folbre, 1999, 40; England, Budig, and Folbre, 2002, 455.
4. Cleeland, 2004.
5. Zelizer, 2005, 14.
6. Ibid.
7. Sherman, 2007.
8. Zelizer, 2005, 14. She enumerates the definition of intimacy as provided by the *Oxford English Dictionary*.
9. Brenner and Laslett, 1989; Glenn, 1992; Hochschild, 1983.

10. Hochschild, 1983.

11. Ibid, 90.

12. Glenn, 1992, 1.

13. Bakker, 2007, 541.

14. Parreñas, 2000.

15. Laura Agustín describes this divide when she states: "Under some circumstances, a worker's control may be so radically diminished as to approximate slavery or indentured servitude. For abolitionist critics of prostitution, such cases serve as compelling evidence that the commercialization of sex is an inherently abusive transaction. From the perspective of prostitutes' rights advocates, on the other hand, what makes prostitution abusive in some but not all instances is a question of the conditions under which the *work* takes place (the relations of production) rather than the terms under which the *sex* takes place (for money, love, or pleasure). These two very different perspectives have produced opposing strategic responses" (Agustín, 2007, 131).

16. Pateman, 1988.

17. Barry, 1995: 9.

18. Chapkis, 1997.

19. Agustín, 2007, 73.

20. England, 2005; Hochschild, 2003; Williams and Zelizer, 2005, 362–363; Zelizer, 2005, 20–26.

21. Held, 2002, 21–22; Himmelweit, 1999, 37.

22. England, 2005, 383; England, Budig, and Folbre, 1999, 460.

23. Glenn, 2000, 84–86; Glenn, 1992; MacDonald and Merrill, 2002, 75.

Remaking the Intimate
Technology and Globalization

BOTH TECHNOLOGY AND DISTANCE as barriers to intimacy dominate our utmost assumptions of relationships. Considering it cold, rational, and emotionless, we assume technology to be the antithesis of intimacy. Likewise we consider distance to be the polar opposite of intimacy. The chapters in this part look not at how technology and distance challenge intimate relations but instead at how they redefine them. Without doubt, unprecedented developments in technology have transformed the contours and dynamics of the intimate labor of care, domestic, and sex work. Likewise, globalization—while long argued by scholars as being nothing new—more than ever challenges us to sustain social relations across far distances. Even the maintenance of families with members across nation-states has increasingly become the norm in the global South due to the rising trend of labor migration in contemporary globalization.[1]

With technology, however, distance has become less of a strain in preserving intimacy, allowing people to respond to the global demand for their movement across nation-states. Additionally, up close, when it comes to care and reproduction, technology has disrupted set ideas of what is "natural," challenging notions of biological parenting with the production of test-tube babies and use of surrogate mothers. But, as Ariel Ducey well shows in this volume, technology does not necessarily diminish intimacy but only changes its dynamics.

Yet technology and globalization can make intimacy a vehicle for inequality. The political economic challenges brought by neoliberal privatization of social welfare and deregulation of labor standards encourage the use of technology to expand the pool of affordable labor to meet the intimate needs of the middle and upper classes in advanced, capitalist nations. Surrogate parenting is more affordable to arrange in Central America than, let us say, the

American Midwest. Hence we see the rise of what Laura Briggs calls "offshore (re)production." Likewise, residents of the United States need not invest in the infrastructural development of their medical education system as they could instead encourage hospitals to recruit registered nurses and doctors trained in a foreign country. The making of new forms of intimate labor is a window to the construction of race, class, gender, and sexuality in the state, the family, and labor market. Moreover, the making of new forms of intimate labor becomes a vehicle for aggravating relations of inequality. Technology and globalization, Kalindi Vora astutely analyzes in her chapter, have for instance added the commodity of emotions as a resource extracted from the global South to North.[2]

In our query on how technology and globalization redefine intimacy, we ask not only about how intimate relations have changed, as Ducey examines in her reading of the impacts of technology on care relations in the hospital, but we also acknowledge the emergence of new forms of intimate labors. Some of these new forms of labor include call center work, gender labor in the making of transsexual identity, surrogate mothering, and sperm and egg donation. All of these forms of labor not only redefine intimate labor as we know it but also introduce different dynamics to the labor process. We see this for instance in transnational parenting, in which we observe not only a change in the meaning of parenting but also transformations in the work entailed in it. With advancements in communication technology, close relations such as parenting can now be sustained without physical contact. No longer is intimacy limited to face-to-face interaction. Moreover, time and space are less of a hindrance to intimacy.[3] While rapid advancements in technology enable the maintenance of intimacy across great distances, they do compound the time people would need to dedicate to sustaining closeness through the greater use of computer-mediated communication, including e-mail, online chats, and text messaging. The reliance on technology to maintain intergenerational relations across distance does not ease the work but creates a new set of requirements. This development should come as no surprise. After all, technology too often has meant "more work for mother." As historians Rose Schwartz Cowan and Susan Strasser have demonstrated, labor-saving technologies in the home coincided with the increase in standards of housework, expanding the hours of domestic and care work.[4]

The chapters in this part delve into two sets of discussions. First, they consider the ways technology has transformed intimate labor, adding to what we know as work by creating new forms of intimate labor, as Ducey addresses in the cultivation of objects by health care professionals to enhance treatment of patients, Jane Ward demonstrates in terms of the "gender labor" by femme partners that female-to-male transsexuals (FTMs) depend on to bolster their masculinity, Rene Almeling describes in the practice of sperm and egg donation, Vora shows in the work of call-center operators, and Briggs theorizes in her discussion of the production of children for foreign adoption. Second, these chapters show how sociocultural inequalities of race, class, gender, and nation become magnified in the intimate labors engendered by technological breakthroughs in reproduction, communication, and sexuality. In interpreting these "new" forms of labor, the chapters underscore the ways that technology facilitates the enmeshing of social, political, and economic systems of inequality with intimate labor.

Looking at how objects and affect reshape relations between patients and health care professionals, Ducey questions the idea that technology inevitably results in growing alienation. As she notes, objects and technologies do not dismantle but instead are embedded in networks of personal relations. For health care providers, the provision of care requires the "care" of objects and equipment including wheelchairs, feeding tubes, and blood glucose meters. Such objects in fact allow workers to upgrade their occupation, while at the same time they expand the ways the workers perceive the care of patients to go beyond direct interaction.

Technology not only enforces inequalities between groups, but it also exacerbates relations of economic inequality among nations. The outsourcing of call centers to India and the Philippines results in lower operation costs through lesser wages. Vora examines the intimate labor of center agents to illustrate the emergence of new forms of worker displacement. Calling attention to the outsourcing of "affective resources" or "affective commodites," she identifies emotions as a new commodity purchased by consumers to enhance their lives in the United States at the cost of the alienation of the worker in India. Alienation results not necessarily from emotion's commodification but from its displacement. The provision of emotion comes at the risk of call center agents occupying a different temporal scale from those in their vicinity, resulting in the loss of their social networks and sources of emotional support.

Mixing cultural studies with political economy, Briggs uncovers the tangled web between a perceived crisis in reproductive labor in the global North and transnational adoption. Her focus on changes in motherwork as well as its commodification reveals the differential value of intimate labor depending on who performs such work and in which settings. Within the United States, amid the return of social welfare to the family, church, and other nongovernmental institutions, panics over motherwork have portrayed poor women of color as bad mothers for endangering their children through reckless behavior, while well-to-do mothers faced their own form of policing through ideologies of intensive mothering.[5] Meanwhile, the growth in women's labor force participation left the work of social reproduction undone. Delayed childbearing for middle- and upper-class, predominantly white, women has resulted in a decline in fertility and a rising demand for domestic labor that the dirty wars and economic dislocations of Latin America have provided a double solution: the availability of babies for adoption and women migrants—perhaps the mothers of such children—for household and care work. Changes in the global economy, then, not merely link the Guatemalan infant, her migrant mother, and forty-year-old white adoptive mother but further depend on shifts in reproductive labors that these types of world players engage in.

As Briggs suggests, the varying degrees of access groups have to reproductive technologies mirror sociostructural inequalities. Technology has resulted in the greater control of reproduction by some groups and the lesser control by others. Middle-class individuals in advanced capitalist nations have gained greater control of their reproduction and a plethora of solutions to infertility, including in vitro fertilization, surrogate mothering, and sperm and egg donations. In contrast, less privileged individuals are not just denied access to these advancements in technology but penalized by reproductive technology developments—a prime example being the history of the forced sterilization of poor women around the world.[6]

In her metaphorical analysis of the passive egg and active sperm, anthropologist Emily Martin has explained how our utmost understanding of biology is rooted in sociocultural notions of gender.[7] In line with this argument, Almeling illustrates how the intimate labor of egg and sperm donations reflect sociocultural constructs of gender that construct women as altruistic donors and men as income earners. Through studying infertility clinics, she found that gendered cultural notions of parenting—selfless motherhood and distant fatherhood—shape the process of donation. Women appear to engage in gift giving, while the contribution of sperms becomes constructed as a source of income.

Ward's discussion of the caring work of femme partners of FTMs likewise illustrates the reinforcement of gender inequalities in and through intimate labor. FTMs depend on their partner's femme labor of being the "girl" to reinforce their masculinity. The reproduction of gender emerges in various forms of femme labor, including cooking, nursing, and sexual performance itself. Looking at femme labor as caring work, Ward reminds us that "gender is reproduced through routinized forms of care work," even in queer relationships; the burden of care remains with women even in situations of transgression.

Overall, the chapters in this part show how technology has created new forms of intimate labor that remain situated in sociocultural, political, and economic systems of inequality. They also challenge narrow understandings of work as employment by expanding our framework of what constitutes labor, even as they probe the depth of intimacy as itself a variable set of practices redefined by self as well as technological refashioning.

Notes

1. Parreñas, 2005.

2. Hochschild, 2002. Arlie Russell Hochschild makes a similar argument as Vora, describing the migration of domestic workers as the extraction of love from the global South to the global North.

3. Parreñas, 2005; Constable, 2003.

4. Cowan, 1985; Strasser, 2000.

5. Roberts, 1997; Hays, 1996.

6. Briggs, 2002.

7. Martin, 1987.

2 Technologies of Caring Labor

From Objects to Affect

Ariel Ducey

IN THE LITERATURE on caring labor, technology has arguably been viewed as non-essential to caring relations or a barrier to them—when technology is considered at all. There is certainly evidence from health care settings to support such a perspective: Nursing home patients, for example, can often be found summarily parked in front of televisions, "nursebots" threaten to substitute for human interaction, and bureaucratic forms and information systems recognize only those activities amenable to the calculation of productivity and profit.[1] All of these undermine caring labor, especially when it is understood as a "face-to-face service that develops the human capabilities of the recipient."[2]

Yet a conception of caring labor that does not make face-to-face or human interactions so central would hew more closely to what frontline health care providers do and the more varied part technology plays in their work. Caring labor, more broadly conceived, enhances capacities to affect and be affected—arguably for those who provide care as well as those who receive it. Some recent radical political theorists have therefore opted to call it "affective labor"—meaning laboring practices that produce "first and foremost a 'social relationship,'" according to Michael Hardt, or "produce collective subjectivities, produce sociality, and ultimately produce society itself," in Maurizio Lazzarato's words.[3] This conceptualization suggests the wide array of situations and settings in which affective labor takes place. It also rightly brings to the foreground that sociality is actively produced and that those who produce it do labor of the most necessary kind.

Michael Hardt and Antonio Negri, however, have further argued that affective labor is one face of "immaterial" labor—which generates the cultural, informational, and symbolic aspects of commodities. The process of affective labor may be corporeal, they acknowledge, but its products are "intangible, a feeling of ease, well-being, satisfaction, excitement, or passion."[4] In so doing, they have written technology out of the story of caring (and affective) labor. By depicting caring labor as unique because of its nontechnological or immaterial character and acknowledging only its corporeal elements, they not only create a partial image of the process of caring labor—one that offers little resistance to the gendered notion of caring labor as primarily emotional and innate—but also disguise material shifts in the nature of contemporary sociality and strategies for governing bodies, subjects, and populations.[5]

This chapter draws on concepts of objectualization and affective technologies to suggest how technology might be theorized in relation to caring labor in a way that is felicitous to what caring laborers do and the political and economic forces that shape their work. While these concepts involve different notions of technology, they share in making it integral to human relations and the laboring practices that enhance capacities to affect and be affected. Their relevance is especially apparent in the world of health care work, in this case in the New York City hospitals and health care facilities where, beginning in the mid-1990s, "restructuring" policies premised on neoliberal principles of an expanded role for markets and profit making drove health care politics and policy. Theories of objectualization and affective technologies both attempt to reimagine changes arguably linked to the rise of neoliberalism, changes often characterized as entailing increased individualization and the retraction of traditional social forms and structures, such as the state, that previously anchored identity and social order. Certainly in New York City's health care sector, as politicians attempted to withdraw the state from its role in subsidizing and regulating health care, one of the few new programs they were willing to support was hundreds of millions of dollars to train health care workers for the jobs of the market-based future—and thereby shift responsibility for any deterioration in working conditions and patient care that accompanied the market onto individual workers.[6] Yet the concepts of objectualization and affective technologies draw attention to how technology—literal objects on the one hand and new techniques and practices of governing on the other—destabilizes a simple story of growing alienation and exploitation in health care under neoliberalism and caring labor in restructured health care institutions.

Karin Knorr Cetina has conjectured that the corollary of individualization and the withdrawal of older, traditional social and institutional forms has been the heightened importance of relationships with objects, "an increasing orientation towards objects as sources of the self, of relationship intimacy, of shared subjectivity, and of social integration." Therefore, we have not seen a "loss of texture for society" but "what the texture consists of may need rethinking." "Postsocial" society, Knorr Cetina argues, is not asocial or nonsocial but characterized by new kinds of relations that have not previously been considered social.[7] This is most apparent in the case of the knowledge objects of expert and scientific cultures, for instance in the biologist Barbara McClintock's relationship to maize, and plants more generally, which was marked by desire, bondedness, and moral in addition to epistemological dimensions. The nature of McClintock's attention to her plants enabled her to see (in the visual and imaginative senses) the possibility of the exchange of genetic information between chromosomes well in advance of colleagues using techniques regarded as more technologically sophisticated.[8] Knorr Cetina argues such relationships with objects are characterized by a wanting or lack. Knowledge objects indicate both what is missing in our understanding of them and what we should be wanting to know about them—unlike objects that are tools, which raise no questions, or are commodities, from which we can be alienated. Knowledge objects are continually unfolding in conjunction with our own subjectivity and epistemic powers. Moreover, these relationships are neither solely cognitive nor necessarily the source of positive emotional ties; they can be imbued with ambivalence and distance, as well as elements of power and domination.

The implications of this argument for cultures, relations, and institutions of caring are several.[9] Knorr Cetina draws attention to the possibility that the type of things or beings in a relationship does not determine the quality of the relationship—that is, whether that relationship can be intimate or, more specifically, caring. Care can be extended to things, just as people can be treated like tools or commodities. Although objects are not usually considered the focus of concern in institutions and relationships that provide care, the objects that figure in such institutions can arguably become the source of intimate and caring relationships in their own right or the basis of unfolding awareness and what Bruno Latour would call increasingly articulate bodies.

My own fieldwork in health care settings presented examples of the centrality of objects to the daily lives of health care workers, including their sense of themselves and their ability to provide caring labor—even for nursing assistants, who are usually viewed as providing the most hands-on and least technological aspects of care, whose jobs would seem the least tied to a world of things. For instance, everyday tools and devices took on some of the dimensions of knowledge objects when they became problematic, when they ceased to be simply "ready-to-hand" and transparent.[10] On one unit I observed, a "step-down" unit between acute and long-term care, both showers on the floor were unusable—one was broken, and the other had no hot water. The nursing assistants were required to offer showers to their patients every other day, but the patient charts left space only for the nursing assistants to record whether a shower had been given or "offered but refused." Unsurprisingly, there was no space for the nursing assistants to write "shower not working" or "cold shower refused," and the unit supervisor told all the staff in a meeting that she did not want this information documented anywhere. Yet it was the nursing assistants who would face questions and blame if patients were not showering regularly. So, one resourceful nursing assistant in the meeting related, in detail, a procedure that a maintenance staff person had explained to her for coaxing hot water out of the shower, which required knowing what time of day there was most likely to be hot water and fiddling with the water nozzle in a particular way. Nursing assistants and nurses were often likewise absorbed in getting wheelchairs, feeding tubes, scales, and blood glucose meters to work right. These objects sometimes required more time and attention than what might typically be imagined as caring activities, such as conversations with patients. And while some of this attention was that of frustration at routine malfunctions, it could also be the source of experimentation and innovation, eliciting skills and accomplishments that made their work richer and more interesting. Such frontline health care providers were continually adjusting, and adjusting themselves to, the objects and equipment around them.

Knorr Cetina also suggests objects may become an "embedding environment for the self," that is, they constitute contexts and settings for belonging,[11] which is arguably why missing or malfunctioning objects had an impact on the sense of self and security of health care workers who needed them. I watched one nursing assistant tell a patient who had been vomiting that the unit was out of toothpaste. She made do and gave the patient a lemon-scented glycerin toilette and a bowl of water instead but felt personally at fault for not being able to provide toothpaste. The nursing assistants at another facility were similarly chagrined that they had to tell diabetic patients the hospital had stopped carrying sugar-free ice cream. One male nursing assistant pointed out to me, while helping a patient shave in the shower, that the hospital razor blades were useless because they were purchased at ten for ninety-nine cents.

One nurse, sitting at the nurses' station doing paperwork, said with some irritation to those around her, "How can we work without scissors?" Even though outcomes for patients do not seem to hinge on these objects, they are nonetheless important to health care workers because they are the things that can make patients feel better when so much else is going wrong; they can have a disproportionate effect on how patients perceive the care they receive. And frontline staff, like nursing assistants, are most likely to bear the emotional consequences of patient dissatisfaction. These gaps in a world shaped by objects, or holes in the workers' embedding environments, support Knorr Cetina's thesis about the significance of object environments to belonging and identity. These staff are made to feel through objects—in this case incomplete and inadequate—that their work and their needs are not very important.

The perspective I am moving toward therefore foregrounds objects and technologies, such that they are the structure on which sociality, and the caring labor that produces it, hangs. As a heuristic device, we could conceive of relationships—even those with and between people—as entering into and negotiating a framework of objects and technologies, rather than objects and technologies being incorporated into a network of personal relations. The dynamic is more accurately one of ongoing and mutual construction between objects and subjectivities, but the heuristic puts objects on the same plane as interpersonal relations and matters of individual motives and decisions. Objects are intertwined with caring relations—they are not just intermediaries in them. Objects may be artificial, or constructed, but their evolution, effects, and meaning are not entirely given at the beginning.

Furthermore, the technological infrastructure on which care hangs includes not only specific objects and devices, but—in a more Foucauldian vein—mechanisms, techniques, and technologies of power. The latter create and/or foster the objective conditions for not only enhancing affective capacities but also channeling such capacities into behaviors and expressions that support existing structures of power and domination. In the case of caregiving in formal health care settings, such techniques and practices include, for instance, public and private policies on wages and immigration that influence who will be more likely to find him- or herself performing caring labor (namely women and the poor) and on what terms. Such policies create obdurate realities—a network of practices, advice, bureaucratic procedures—and even condition how those people will feel about the caring labor they are doing.

This observation alone is not new. Existing institutional structures and practices, and material conditions and contexts, shape how human potentials and relations are actualized. Ideas and ideologies inform this process as well. What appears to be new, however, is the attempt to subject the capacity to affect and be affected to ruling relations, via technologies aimed at an affective level. As Brian Massumi argues, the "affective modulation of the population" is "now an official, central function of an increasingly time-sensitive government," seen, for example, in the color-coded terror alert system created after 9/11—which was intended to create a perpetual level of readiness to the threat of terrorist attack and therefore has never dipped below yellow, or "elevated."[12] According to Massumi, there are two levels "at play" in any event: that of intensity, a state of suspense, of potential disruption; and that of semantics and semiotics, of language, narrative, and expectations. These two levels resonate with one another; their vibrations are sometimes dissonant and other times harmonious. Affect is "their point of emergence" and "their vanishing point," where the vibrations between the levels either emerge as something actual or fade into the virtual. Affect therefore shadows every event. It is the source of the unexpected, of the unmotivated, of surprise. The level of noncognitive intensity is autonomous from what emerges in consciousness, but it is nonetheless the realm of potential from which any cognitive realizations will be drawn. Cognition—the realm of language and decision-making—reduces intensity, converting suspense into expectation.[13] To intervene in affect, as does the terror alert system, is therefore to attempt to control or modulate how intensity becomes expectation, action, and decision.

The training industry for health care workers that emerged in New York City in the 1990s could also be construed as a means of affective modulation, especially (but not only) in the ubiquitous talk of the market in, and the incorporation of workers' bodies into, "soft skills" training seminars. As I have examined more closely elsewhere,[14] in New York City during the 1990s, private hospitals and 1199/SEIU United Health Care Workers East, the union representing frontline workers in those hospitals, leveraged billions of dollars from state and federal officials to prepare for presumably radical changes underway in the health care sector. The newly elected Republican governor and mayor favored policies that shifted patients from Medicaid (the state's single largest budget expenditure) into managed care plans and forced hospitals to behave as if they were in a market by, for instance, bidding competitively for payment rates from private insurers. Such changes threatened the sizeable proportion of hospitals' revenue that either came from or was guaranteed by the state, and hospital leaders used this environment to argue that wage increases were inconceivable, layoffs inevitable, and restructuring along the lines used in the corporate sector the only way to save themselves. Dennis Rivera, then president of 1199, opted to partner with the leaders of the private hospitals to fight the new policies. The partnership was not without contradictions for the union and its members, and its chief result was a health workforce training industry to which the state claimed it had contributed $1.3 billion by 2005.[15]

The most common training programs were for "multiskilling" (that is, training nursing assistants to take on some of the tasks of nurses), individualized upgrading, and "soft skills" training—the single largest category of spending and my focus here. Tens of thousands of New York City hospital workers were sent to training seminars in areas such as customer service, communication skills, team building and teamwork, cultural diversity, conflict resolution, and leadership training.[16] In 2001 and 2002, I observed such courses in three settings—a communication skills program at a private hospital, a "retreat" on teamwork and customer service for employees of a public hospital, and in-services at one of the city's largest (and recently unionized) home health care agencies. In those courses, an infrastructure of techniques and practices to mold and redirect the affective capacities of the allied health workforce took shape.

By affective capacities, I do not mean emotions and feelings, which these courses sometimes addressed. For instance, the courses directed frontline health care workers to take responsibility for managing the emotions of others and subordinate their own feelings to the larger cause of getting along. The longest section in the communication skills course was on anger management, during which the instructor advised participants not to "stuff" their anger but to express it—only with "respect and calm." In this sense, such courses very much recall the training for flight attendants documented by Arlie Hochschild thirty years ago. In the in-services for home care workers, participants were told to imagine their patients as family members, or themselves as patients in the future, just as airline managers told flight attendants to think of the cabin as their living room. They also resembled the training Hochschild observed in their demand that workers align their emotions, bodies, and behavior to the goal of profit making.[17] Instructors I observed asked health care workers to compare their hospitals to Microsoft, McDonald's, Disneyland, and Singapore Airlines, and themselves to Donald Trump and Bill Gates. Patients became "customers" or "clients" and clinical services "product lines." Private consultants, some new to the world of training altogether and others possessing proprietary training packages they had long offered to private businesses, created presentations tailored for what they saw as the "untapped market" of health care.

Perhaps unsurprisingly, much of this soft skills training conveyed that the responsibility for ensuring high-quality care lies with those on the shop floor. The problems course participants raised—shortages of staff and supplies, too much paperwork, and too little time with patients—had all been exacerbated or created by restructuring reforms, which were largely means of lowering costs by shifting as much work as possible onto the least-paid workers. When instructors considered these conditions at all, they were framed as problems the workers themselves could change—if they demonstrated qualities of responsibility and self-management. As the communication skills instructor succinctly put it, "the most fertile area for greater control lies within the self." A lack of supplies and staffing were part of the cold, hard realities of a market-driven health care sector for which the workers needed to prepare themselves. What were in workers' control, on the other hand, were their attitudes and willingness to work together as a team, both of which could potentially improve the hospital's image and "customer" satisfaction. The communication skills instructor took such logic an additional step and argued that improved customer satisfaction might, in turn, create more business for the hospital and therefore the revenue necessary for supplies and greater staffing levels.

Yet sometimes participants' skepticism of such messages forced the instructors to shift gears. In the communication skills class, participants questioned the instructor's command to "give themselves enough time" to get their work done. They felt the main problem was not their time-management skills but continual understaffing. When the instructor of the retreat asked participants to write an advertisement for their hospital and read them aloud to each other, one nursing assistant had to stop reading hers after the line "anyone is welcome—good credit, bad credit" because the laughter was so loud. The ad cleverly imitated a type of advertising directed only at poor communities, in which businesses offer guaranteed loans to even those with bad credit for outrageously high interest rates. (Or consider ads for renting furniture on credit, which are never seen in affluent neighborhoods.) The participants' laughter suggested that if they saw the hospital as a business, it was as one that serves and suckers the poor at the same time. The nursing assistant's "ad" pointed out that the hospital could not in fact shape its "clientele"; the public hospital could not deny someone care on the basis of his or her ability to pay. The camaraderie in the room this advertisement produced came at the expense of the hospital and course instructor's message.

In light of such resistance, to the extent the course instructors could channel health care workers' commitment and engagement into loyalty to their employer or a market-based health care system, they had to do so at a level that was not explicit and not even predictable. If they were to be effective—from the perspective of control—it could not be simply or primarily at the level of ideology. Whether or not planned, it seemed to me that those who taught and developed these courses hoped participants would not think about them too much. The courses were not meant, in the end, to be taken literally or consciously evaluated and assessed. Emotions and feelings are affectivity made conscious or actualized, and in these course instructors sought to move beneath consciousness.

For example, the training courses focused not on the working conditions and stresses workers faced but on the future changes to their work that would be caused by the presumably inevitable introduction of market mechanisms into health care. The "market" was held up in a pure, idealized form as something always in the future, something for which health care workers must always be prepared. As Massumi says of the "threat" signaled by the terror alert system, it "bore precious little content," and the "alerts presented no form, ideological or ideational." The threat was neither specified nor named—no one was told (if it was even known) the source, nature, and location of the threat. Threat exists only in the future, yet "its future looming casts a present shadow, and that shadow is *fear*."[18] The market, too, cast a shadow of fear in the training seminars and became a placeholder for almost any change to the nature of health care imaginable. Given this lack of content or form, the market was something for which these workers could never, in the end, prepare. Rather than working through reason or emotional appeal, therefore, the courses functioned by habituating workers through fear to expect—and accept—anything at all imposed in the name of the market.

The courses were at points even indifferent to their manifest (conscious, measurable, observable) effects, including the specific emotions they evoked. At the retreat, the instructor had the participants play Pictionary, in order, she said, to unite team members with a common goal—"to win." During the game, however, the overwhelming emotion in the room was that of stress and tension. None of the participants had played Pictionary before, and some were clearly intimidated by it. Not only was there a sense of competition with other teams, but there was tension even within teams because various members caught on to the game more quickly than others. The emotions evoked hardly seemed conducive to improved workplace relations. The exercise created an environment in which emotions were set loose with no means of containing or directing them. I asked the instructor later about the logic behind having the group play Pictionary. She said,

> I thought Pictionary is a very interactive game, and also part of psychology is you ask people to draw their feelings, and how they express themselves is how they're feeling, so it also brings them to a lower level where they're not thinking, they're not analyzing data, they're just doing it spontaneously, and we want some spontaneity.

Though partially a rationalization of the exercise, her comment did seem to pinpoint how the game worked. The exercise could not be called effective in terms of conventional outcomes because it was, as Massumi says of the terror alert system, an attempt to "capture spontaneity" and habituate participants to the techniques of affect modulation.[19] The instructor spoke of drawing out the participants' feelings, but she was not, in fact, much interested in their specific feelings—only in triggering action. As one pharmaceutical marketer told medical anthropologist Emily Martin about the purpose of prescribing combinations of multiple drugs—"cocktails"—to those with manic depression, it is not necessarily to achieve a state of equilibrium but "a sort of mania or hyper-alertness."[20] Playing Pictionary was not so much a game in emotional management as in emotional provocation, tapping into a realm of virtual energy and hoping it would, in its openness, be amenable to managerial and ideological control.

Agnosticism or ambivalence is intolerable in a biopolitical regime based not on discipline and control but on the possibility of increasing capacities of a population—to be productive, to be "healthy" rather than not sick, to make live rather than merely let live.[21] Under such a regime, alienation or disengagement is more troubling than hostility or resistance—the latter are, at least, active positions. Much of the training I observed seemed targeted to produce any kind of engagement, and thereby risk resistance, for the chance to appropriate that energy and channel it into greater productivity and commitment to paid labor. Such training, now part of the "texture" of sociality, is a piece of an infrastructure for the explicit and continual modulation of moods and capacities that remake sociality.

The same type of modulation was evident in the handling of the bodies of course participants. At the end of the long training day, the retreat instructor led an exercise in which she asked three participants to leave the room with her for a few minutes. When they came back, she had them stand in a line in front of the class, with their arms around each other, and asked a fourth participant—who had remained in the room—to join them at the end of line. She then asked the four people in the line to close their eyes and silently count down from one hundred. When they opened their eyes, the instructor asked the fourth participant, on the end of the line, to raise her free arm. The instructor pressed down on her arm and observed that it was stiff and firm. She then asked the group to again close their eyes and count down from one hundred. This time, when she pressed down on the fourth participant's raised arm, the instructor commented that it was loose and free. She asked the fourth participant how she was feeling. "Kind of sad," she replied. A fleeting look on the instructor's face showed this was not the answer she hoped for, but she proceeded undeterred. The instructor revealed that she had told the group of three to think of something bad the first time and something happy or pleasant the second time. So, the fourth participant's arm was more loose and free the second time supposedly because she had picked up on the bodily energies of those physically connected to her.

Thus, the lesson was, apparently, about how emotions and moods are physically embodied and can be directly transmitted through touch (though the instructor did not elaborate much on the purpose of the exercise). My impression, as with the Pictionary exercise, was that the instructor hoped to bypass conscious reasoning and articulated emotions (which, after all, could be the source of much trouble for the instructors and hospital management) and gain access to and channel a sort of collective energy more directly. The focus on the bodies and energies of the workforce is significant; the trainer recognized that workers' dissatisfaction with their work is embodied, so that a more direct route to adjust their attitude toward their work might be through their bodies or through the precognitive level that conditions which emotions or attitudes can be expressed.

As Bruno Latour has pointed out, bodies are "interfaces" that become more and more distinct as they learn to be affected by more and more elements of the world. And it is through "artificial setups"—what I have been calling objects, technologies, techniques, and practices—that bodies become more sensitive to differences of the world, more articulate. These setups are not merely vehicles through which subjects become more aware of an exterior world—they are extensions of bodies and parts of the world that allow for more, and open-ended, propositions about the world, for becoming more sensible to differences.[22] While Pictionary may be a crude setup, it suggests that the instructor recognized that, to be effective in her assignment, she needed to capture something other than workers' hearts and minds, which it turns out are not easy to manipulate, especially under conditions of overwork and exploitation. How can people be motivated to care—about their jobs, their patients, their employers—when all objective indicators suggest there is little care for them? Affective interventions, techniques, and technologies are the contemporary mode of governance in a society that is anchored by injustice and inequality that is, arguably, increasingly apparent and difficult to rationalize. The training programs described here aimed to intervene in affect, which shadows but is independent of consciously modified emotions or feelings. As Patricia Clough has put it, "even when appealing to the human subject," affective technologies "aim to affect the subject's subindividual bodily capacities, that is, capacities to be moved, to shift focus, to attend, to take interest, to slow down, to speed up, and to mutate."[23] Or, as Massumi has argued about the U.S. color-coded terror alert system, it was meant to trigger readiness at a "presubjective" level.

These dynamics—objects becoming embedding environments of the self, governmentality that is focused on affective modulation—are not limited to settings of institutionalized health care and can elicit reactions and emotions other than care.[24] Yet the way in which objectualization and affective modulation intersect with institutions and relations of caregiving is particularly important because care produces society itself. When the processes of objectualization and affective modulation change caregiving, it raises concerns about whether the "care" produced is genuine or meaningful and therefore capable of producing "society itself." In my view, however, this concern also leads to a knot of motives and perceptions that is impossible to untie: What do health care providers really feel? What drives them to do their work? We might focus instead on the seeming reality that acceptable and effective care has long been provided by people with a range of motivations. Gabrielle Meagher has argued that the basis of good care in situations of paid caring labor need not be feelings of affection, like those we typically expect in familial and unpaid caring relationships (though, of course, those relationships, too, are more complex than is often acknowledged).[25]

The "technology" of affective modulation in the soft skills training I observed is troubling because it seeks to align care with bureaucratic and commercial ends, but it does not predictably produce superficial care compatible with profit making. The shift toward techniques of affective modulation is an acknowledgment of the complexity of social life and therefore governing, or the impossibility of a correlation between "official speech or image production and the form and content of response." Affective techniques address "bodies from the dispositional angle of their affectivity, instead of addressing subjects from the positional angle of their ideations."[26] Such an angle, however, entails risks. In some moments, soft skills training courses triggered a form of collective solidarity and heightened awareness of the unjust demands made of frontline health care workers.

Objectualization, similarly, could create new solidarities or even a greater range of caring interactions—including those with objects. Health care workers are sometimes inspired by the objects around them to invest more in their jobs, to learn more, and to challenge themselves. The objects and technologies become reasons for doing the work and doing it well. Relations with objects are integral to helping patients. It is perhaps not surprising that computer designers are experimenting with machines and interfaces that encourage greater emotional reflexivity. They recognize that emotions are an emergent property of bodies and interactions, so the technologies—which might have applications in health care—are designed not to narrow or control emotions but to enhance their richness and complexity.[27] In this way, we might imagine technologies or techniques that create more fertile conditions for the emergence of care, which multiply—rather than classify and reduce—the motives and emotions compatible with caring relations.

According to Latour, the normative position of those who study science (and caring or intimate labor!) might be "the more mediations the better."[28] The more artificial setups, the more chances there are to become more articulate, more sensible to differences, and more capable of affecting and being affected. This implies a different conception of the possible relationship between care and technology than that of interference or incompatibility, whether the setups are objects like nursebots or soft skills training. Still, technologies, objects, and techniques may block the capacity to affect and be affected, especially for certain bodies and subjects, which a complete normative position must recognize as well. So too it might not always be desirable to be "open" to affecting and being affected.[29] In particular, the demand that workers remain ever ready for, and open to, the effects of the market can lock them into a disposition of fear, while those who stand to profit from these workers' labor in turn frame them as fearsome because they are underprepared and threaten the survival of health care institutions. Fear, Sarah Ahmed points out, "works to restrict some bodies through the movement or expansion of others."[30] Endless preparation for, and fear of, the market forecloses imagination and preparation for other sorts of futures, and in the world of health care imagined alternatives are urgently needed. Yet it is not technology that stands in the way of the actualization of care—technology will likely rather prove to be an essential ally in that process.

Notes

1. The example of televisions is from my experience in health care settings. On nursebots, see Folbre, 2006; on patient charts and how activities such as talking to patients are excluded from them, see Diamond, 1992. Some examples in this chapter have also appeared in my previously published work. See Ducey, 2009, especially chapter 5, "More than a Job"; Ducey, Gautney, and Wetzel, 2003.

2. England, Budig, and Folbre, 2002: 455, 459.

3. Hardt, 1999; Lazzarato, 1996: 138.

4. Hardt and Negri, 2000: 292–293.

5. Hardt and Negri may downplay the technological aspects of affective labor because it does not readily fit their political message—that precisely because of its immaterial character, those who do such work are less dependent on capitalists to provide the "means of production" and thereby freed from a fundamental constraint on the possibilities for the formation of alternative solidarities and economies.

6. For a discussion of the universal appeal of job training to politicians, see Lafer, 2002.

7. Knorr Cetina, 1997: 23, 27.

8. Keller, 1983.

9. Knorr Cetina, 1997: 2.

10. Objects do not have the same status all the time and may circulate among the states of knowledge object, tool, and commodity (Ibid.: 10).

11. Ibid.: 24.

12. Massumi, 2005: 32, 35.

13. Massumi, 2002: 26–27, 32–33.

14. Ducey, 2009.

15. Commission on Health Care Facilities, 2005.

16. Other major areas of spending were on computer skills training and, by the end of the 1990s, training more nurses. See Ducey, 2009: chapter 3.

17. Hochschild, 1983.

18. Massumi, 2005: 32, 35.

19. Ibid.: 33–34.

20. Martin, 2006.

21. Foucault, 2003.

22. Latour, 2004. Latour provides evocative examples of how bodies interface with artificial setups, but see also Wissinger, 2007 on the case of fashion models.

23. Clough, 2004.

24. On affective modulation in other contexts see, Clough and Halley, 2007.

25. Feelings of affection may very well arise between caregivers and those for whom they care, but "these feelings are not—or even cannot be—a necessary basis for good quality care." Meagher argues there are a number of other possible motivations to care, such as the bond of a contract, a sense of professional duty, or compassion, which enable "good enough" care (Meagher, 2006).

26. Massumi, 2005: 33, 34.

27. See, for instance, Boehner et al., 2007; Sengers et al., 2008.

28. Latour, 2004: 219.

29. Lisa Blackman raises important critical questions about how, in much recent work on affect, the "subject" is considered in a generic mode and all movement/becoming is uncritically considered desirable (Blackman, 2008).

30. Ahmed, 2004.

The Transmission of Care

Affective Economies and Indian Call Centers

Kalindi Vora

"THE BANGALORE BUTLER is the latest development in offshore outsourcing," announces Steve Lohr in a *New York Times* article, referring to the growth of long-distance customer service into the realm of personal assistants and primary and secondary school tutors.[1] The *Bangalore butler* is a compelling phrase, redolent with a fantasy of the luxury of British colonial India, where brown men in crisp white uniforms and turbans served meals on silver platters to smartly dressed colonials, allowing them not only to get their work done in an unmanageable Indian environment but to experience indulgence and pleasure. The image is apt because the outsourcing of personal care and assistance creates the potential for middle-class Americans to use more of their time as they please without sacrificing the feeling of having personal attention and service.

Indian workers occupy particular positions in the international division of labor as a result of the material conditions India inherited from the British colonial period, as well as from its postcolonial economic and political history. Indian workers are also figured by an economy of imagination and desire that is interlaced with these histories, part of what allows for a spark of recognition on hearing the phrase *Bangalore butler*. In the past fifteen years, as innovations in telecommunications reached a level that allowed affordable real-time interaction with service workers abroad, English-speaking middle-class college graduates in India became the appropriate source of inexpensive service labor for industries relying on English-enabled customer service. This work is cheaper for U.S. corporate entities than in-country labor both because of the international strength of the dollar and because of the maintenance of a de facto lower level of life necessities for the Indian worker—the material reality behind the lower cost of living and cheapness of Indian labor. What the phrase *lower cost of living* might mean in material terms is rarely interrogated with regard to relative quality of life, a fact that allows this international division of labor to extract and invest the value produced by Indian service workers into the lives of people living in the United States, where households and vitality become a repository for the accumulation of surplus value produced in India. I argue that, in these terms, Indian lives are cheapened because the majority do not hold a position in the world economy that allows them to accumulate the surplus value they produce. This is exported through outsourcing contracts and other forms of labor extraction.

Though it doesn't have the same ring to it, the Indian call center agent is a figure closely related to that of the Bangalore butler. By reviewing ethnographic descriptions of the particular mode of production in customer-service call centers and the effect of this work on the call center agents, I examine how commodities such as attention, concern, and human communication produced by the call center agent carry value and at what cost to the worker they are produced. The transnational nature of the interactions between agents and customers means that the value produced by this work is invested into distant groups and societies, rather than the immediate communities of the workers, resulting in a net flow of affective resources to consuming nations at the expense of producing nations like India.

To explore the interiority of the production of affective commodities, alongside more sociological material I include a reading of loneliness and alienation in the play, *A Terrible Beauty Is Born*, written and performed as a monologue in English by Arjun Raina, a former call center agent and accent trainer in New Delhi. Performed for a small number of audiences at theater festivals in India and Europe, as well as on a few American college campuses as part of South Asia–related events, the play exposes some of the compromises made in the lives of call center agents. Juxtaposing narratives from this play with ethnographic narratives allows me to address the material conditions of call center work as well as the interiority of the subjective experience of this work. This method has proven successful for pointing to Durkheimian "social facts" that occur in intimate everyday interactions as represented in the affective and imaginative content of such narratives.[2] Also, by examining the affective content of everyday interactions and experience in call center work, we can look at this labor as an archive itself, along the lines of Ann Cvetkovich's argument that there are cultural archives embedded in the ephemera of everyday life, insisting on histories of feeling that would be otherwise invisible. I read the play *A Terrible Beauty* as demonstrating some of the ways that the production of different types of use values in the everyday interactions of call center workers is entangled with complex social relations as service work is transmitted to consuming nations outside India. This play also points to particular forms of alienation experienced in call center work and to the nature of social relations embedded in affective commodities. After reviewing both ethnographic and fictional narratives of the lives of call center workers, I suggest that affective labor produces value through the capacity of human vital energy as a creative force to be invested directly into other human beings, thereby supporting their lives. This understanding of value relies on a Marxist view of commodity relations but does not follow the discipline of the value chain where capital is realized through the circulation of the commodity.

Technological Mediation and Call Center Subjectivities

Ethnographic material on call centers produced by labor sociologists points to the ways that management and quality control technologies shape not only the culture of the workplace but also the very subjectivities of the call center agents.[3] The call center industry in general regulates the pace and nature of work both through computer-regulated communication technologies, such as dialing software and fully automated call volume, and through statistical and other more direct forms of performance monitoring. Technologies of virtual surveillance and the constant threat of the call center leaving the locality not only create a stressful work environment but also produce a "machinic subjectivity" where workers must reorganize themselves as subjects to protect their personalities from their communication work while projecting a false persona and keeping up with the pace of the computer dialing system.[4] The monitoring function built into the dialing software tracks the average length of calls as well as time spent by agents off their phones, among other factors. These statistics are then presented to agents to discipline their calling practices so that they more closely conform to company quality standards as measured by statistical goals. In his ethnography of Idaho call centers, Donald Winiecki argues that these statistics shape the very subjectivity of agents through how they imagine themselves and their work. At the same time, he gives examples of ways that experienced agents manipulate their behavior to "trick" the monitoring system into recording favorable numbers while they create extra time between calls to do their necessary work, to find job satisfaction through substantive customer interactions that take longer that they are supposed to, and to take breaks without the constant strain of rushing to keep up their statistical goals.

When a call center agent in India calls a customer in America, the caller and the customer must be transmitted in the form of data. The Indian agent becomes a projection of herself, with a new name, new training in accent neutralization, and unwieldy cultural knowledge of the country being called. The customer becomes a "profile," chosen by dialing software specific to the call center industry. The software that manages this digitalized interaction chooses profiles based on algorithms that determine the highest match rating between the profile and the type of call being made, such as sales or collections. In his ethnography of call center workers near New Delhi, sociologist A. Aneesh suggests that the interactions between agents and customers are postsocial interactions between two sets of spectral life forms. He calls these projections of the agent and the customer their "data forms."[5] The production of the data form of the call center agent relies largely on his or her own affective labor. The agent must acquire a sufficient volume of fluency in the foreign culture he or she is calling to react appropriately and credibly to customers in their own cultural context. For example, agents must acquire the habit of showing culturally authentic emotions on the phone: feeling sorry for a customer who relates a misfortune and keeping a smile on his or her face during the conversation. These efforts affect the data form of the agents in ways that translate into the production of value for their employers.

In addition to the affective work of producing their data doubles, the time difference between India and North America means that call center agents are required to do the daily work of managing the friction created by waking up when others are winding down their days, missing social engagements, religious rituals, and the other everyday interactions that constitute sociality. Using interviews from fieldwork in Gurgaon, a New Delhi industrial suburb, Aneesh produces a composite call center agent from his interviewees, whom he names Bharati. She explains that as time passes after she starts her job, her daytime social world becomes increasingly less relevant, until at some point she realizes she has experienced something like social death.[6] Though she quits her job on this realization, the skills she acquired to achieve and produce her data form as a call center agent—a neutral accent and her knowledge of American geography, work processes, and people—are of no use to any other industry. Within six months she joins another call center.

The data form of the call center agent turns out to be more useful to the global economy than her "real" form. Most of the college-educated middle-class youth employed by call centers profess their lack of interest in call center work yet are attracted by the pay and the idea that this is something they can do to earn money for a few years while they find a "real job."[7] In truth, when an agent tries to leave the call center industry he or she finds that the skills used in call center work are employable only in other call centers. The real form of the agent, the one who can't find a job elsewhere, is revealed to be flawed in terms of market demands. The transformation of the agent into her data form requires the suppression of her real form and yet results in the enhancement of the real form's life chances because it gives her access to global flows of capital and labor demands. As the figure of Bharati indicates, the agent realizes that it is only through her data form that she can secure insurance of her future life chances. Her nondata form can contribute only by reproducing the life of her data form. While it appears in interview material, the affective cost of the labor of producing multiple forms of oneself is difficult to track ethnographically because there is not a quantitative method of measuring the output of affective labor. A reading of the experience of call center work in Arjun Raina's play *A Terrible Beauty Is Born* points to the unique nature of the worker's alienation and the types of social relations that form through and sometimes in spite of the commodified nature of communication.

Affect and Alienation in Call Centers:
Loneliness in *A Terrible Beauty Is Born*

In the play *A Terrible Beauty Is Born*, the main characters are formally linked only through a relationship of debt and demand for repayment, but the narrative reveals other layers of social relationships they unknowingly share. It features two narrators: Ashok (whose call center alias is John Small), a customer service agent who makes collection calls for a U.S. department store from a New Delhi call center; and Elizabeth, a social worker, mother, and wife who lives in a small town four hours outside of New York City with her husband. The narration in the play alternates between Elizabeth and Ashok, who recount the history of their interactions as they lead up to the present. The events of the play take place a few weeks after the events of September 11, 2001. The play begins with Elizabeth's recounting of the way that John Small became involved in her search for her daughter after the attacks of September 11.

Arjun Raina performs the monologue dressed in a suit and standing next to a laptop, which he uses to play video images of himself performing the role of John Small at his call station. This mode of performance emphasizes the split between Ashok, in whose voice the story is told, and John, who speaks

from the laptop with a trained American accent. John Small is described as an
agent in the collections department of a call center for a big U.S. department
store as speaking with an "African American accent":

> And when my transport [the shuttle to work] picks me up . . . John Small . . .
> comes alive and blabbers away . . . speaking only in English . . . and with an
> African American accent . . . on call.[8]

His calls are made exclusively to customers who are late in paying their account balance with the store. In the play we see that in the production of
affect—including support, kindness, attention, and the structure of desire
that organizes the coherence of existence—value flows primarily in one direction: from India to the United States. There is excess in the social relations
between the Indian agent who assumes an American identity and the African
American family from whom he is trying to collect, but this excess is not lib-
eratory in the way Michael Hardt and Antonio Negri might imagine in their
formulation of a global commons constituted by immaterial labor.[9] The content that carries through his conversations with Americans over and above
that required for his work haunts Ashok's relationship to the United States
and to his work, but it does not figure explicitly in the narrative. The characters recognize that they have shared interests, but these interests are based on
false premises because John's social location and identity are false.

As Elizabeth begins her narration, she reflects back to the time when she
received her first call from John, just moments after the attacks on the World
Trade Center have occurred. He is aware of the attacks, but the call center (located in India, but pretending that it is in the United States) is still operating:[10]

> JOHN: How are you doing today? . . . Isn't it terrible . . . What's happening in
> New York . . . ?
> ELIZABETH: Yes, John, it's terrible out there . . . and for me personally . . . I
> have a daughter in New York . . . and we have no news of her . . . we're really
> very worried . . . so . . . what's this about, John?
> JOHN: Yes, Elizabeth . . . this must be very tough on you. . . . I apologise . . . for
> bringing up your account matters at this moment . . . but I've got a job to do . . .
> and I am trying to do the best I can . . . to try and serve you well, ma'am . . .

John's acknowledgment of the attacks is similar to the acknowledgment of
American holidays and other social niceties that are built into the scripts read
routinely by call center workers. John must express the same particular type

of dismay at the calamity that Elizabeth feels because he is supposed to be an American calling from America. This is what makes him successful at his job. We see John's reaction to the calamity and not Ashok's. He is doing a certain type of labor to participate in structures of crisis reaction and suffering that aren't his own because he does not live in the United States. However, as later becomes apparent, John does identify with America in a way he finds distressing and damaging.

The identity work of the call center employee functions to maintain a fantasy of social relations that exist within a shared cultural sphere. The fear is that customer realization of the foreign nature of the caller will disrupt the anticipated effect of customer service, that of a sense of the close proximity of support whenever it is needed. India does not feel close, and Indian accents do not make the agent seem accessible. For this reason, customer service work in India requires training in both cultural knowledge and the accent of the area being served. The sense of security in a given product or brand that is supported by customer service as well as the work of soothing and reassuring used to manage negative feelings in customers are two products of this work, which raises the question of whether customer service is productive in itself or rather simply allows for the maintenance of a system of economics and power that already exists, thereby reproducing it.

In addition to producing a variety of commodities and subjectivities, structures of affective labor, such as the global division of service and care work, create affective conditions that characterize certain populations of workers and not others. The character of John/Ashok in *A Terrible Beauty Is Born* lives a life characterized by a specific type of loneliness. The play portrays the experience of separation from Ashok's immediate society that occurs as a result of his call center job. He works during the night and experiences insomnia as he tries to sleep through the day when everyone else is carrying on with his or her life. Even the access he has to people's private lives in America as he calls them at home after their workday does not allow Ashok to feel integrated with that society. He gains entry only through the imagined persona he inhabits, which allows the people he calls to accept him as someone like themselves. The better he becomes at his job of collection calls, which hinges on his ability to impersonate an American, the less connected he is to either Indian or American society. In the reflections of Bharati, the composite call center agent profiled in the introduction, we can see that such loneliness can reflect a type of social death, where the producer of affective commodities becomes cut off from the source of her own social reproduction through relationships with other people and society in general.[11]

Just before he begins his shift, and as the attacks are happening in the United States, John finds out that his co-worker, a woman whose call name is Magda (we never learn her real name), has committed suicide. He briefly reflects on how she was too soft for the job, how some male customers she called would ask for sexual favors and otherwise mistreat her, and how manufacturing the appropriate persona to collect debts put a terrible strain on her. In their first conversation, Elizabeth eventually engages John to help her search for her estranged daughter in New York, but Ashok's own loss is never mentioned. He must exist only in the world of the American calls, to the point where he himself must believe in his adopted character. As a result, the people receiving calls are spared the work of participating in the suffering in which he and his co-workers are engaged. This is one way to think about affective labor, and the different affective structures that some must participate in or may be spared from participating in. Part of the work John must do to successfully collect late payments is to convince himself that he is indeed the person he is pretending to be, and thus, when he hears of the suicide, he drowns himself in activity, calling more customers than ever before. In this other version of himself there is no room to think about the suicide or what it implies about his work.

John's reaction to his co-worker's suicide indicates something about how the value produced by affect is carried or embodied in affective commodities and how it can be accumulated by some and lost by others. John/Ashok must provide the concern that allows him to do his job while repressing sentiments about his co-worker and the relationship of their work to her suicide. This is an activity that supports the continued success of the American department store for which he makes collection calls and undermines the agents' ability to discuss the implications of their colleague's suicide and react to it. Not only is it impossible to perform his job while acknowledging its costs as represented by Magda's death, but there is simply no social space within the pace and structure of the telephone interactions, regulated by the clock within the dialing software, to mourn. This is an example of how the affect of mourning and its political potential are made "unnecessary," channeled instead into the company's interest. The time and space for acknowledging the costs of call center work is segmented from the actual time and space of the work by John/Ashok's need to inhabit separate versions of himself. Ethnographic descriptions of the social spaces call center workers share after their shifts indicates that these spaces are dominated by the need to numb the mind overtaxed by the speed of work interactions and rest the faculties of social interaction.[12] We can imagine that even in such a work-related social space, John/Ashok would find it difficult to connect with other workers in a way that formed a political consciousness around Magda's death. The style of the play, alternating between monologues by Elizabeth and Ashok, and the inward nature of the narratives convey a space of aloneness that is never pierced, the only change being the content of that inner space—John or Ashok.

Elizabeth knows very little about the life of her daughter, who left home years before the events of the plot. She knows that her daughter recently bore a child and that she claimed to work in the World Trade Center. Speaking from about a month after her initial call from John on September 11, 2001, she describes how she had given her daughter a copy of her credit card, for which John is a collections agent, to use for necessities during a time of financial hardship. During the course of the conversation, she realizes that John has access to her daughter's spending records and recruits him to track this record for any new activity or patterns. We are never privy to his thoughts or feelings about these actions, as we hear about them only through Elizabeth's account of the story. Through her retrospective narrative we hear that John calls during the next few weeks to inform her of when and where the card has been used, reporting that the daughter goes to the same Manhattan ice cream parlor every week at the same time. Elizabeth and her husband then take a bus into New York, planning to try to meet their daughter at the ice cream parlor.

The type of loneliness that results from the alienation of other human beings into whom one has invested affective energy is a kind of loneliness that is more tangible than other types of alienation because it fits a common social understanding of a type of being alone that is undesirable. Any conception of the "the good life" includes the existence of specific needs and the ability to fill those needs in a way that does not entail suffering; yet, in the scope of political economic thinking, affective needs are not often accounted for. However, needs are not stable, and, in fact, the generation of always new necessities is at the core of the operation of capitalist accumulation. The relative cheapness of someone's labor and life when compared to others in this scheme therefore reflects only the "outlawed necessities" that maintain this cheapness.[13] Thinking from within a space already reorganized by capitalism, Marx imagines the good life against different aspects of capitalism's alienation. One type is the separation of productive life activity from the living of life because the work one performs as labor-power is used in a narrowed way for the purpose of securing necessities through the wage. Marx calls this self-estrangement: "[Under capitalism] Life appears only as a means to life."[14] This is opposed to "being" one's life activity.[15] One becomes aware of this productive activity, which Marx sees as fundamentally human, as something that does not belong to oneself, making it a form of suffering. The content of this activity, what I would call vital energy, is also lost in a second form of alienation. The object produced by alienated activity is invested with one's vital energy yet leaves the immediate world of the person who produces it. Losing a world where one lives surrounded by objects in which one's own energy, or the energy of persons with whom one knowingly has a relationship, is invested is a loss that Marx imagines in the life of this worker. This entails a third type of alienation, the lack of a feeling of contributing to the overall wealth and well-being of a community.[16]

The alienation produced by affective labor in call center work entails a type of aloneness that generally occurs even as the agent interacts with a string of other people in their data forms. The customer is not necessarily required to produce affect. He or she can just hang up the phone. This does not mean exchange cannot happen, just that the structure of call center work is not organized to produce affective commodities that support the agent. However, as a result of the tension between the structure of call center work and the structure of the rest of Indian society, agents most often lose access to the means of meeting their immediate affective needs in their everyday lives yet are expected to continue to produce affect on the job.

Gray Economies of Affect:
The Transmission of Other Use Values

The channels of communication that are a form of capital in the call center industry serve to transmit interactions that create relations supporting company goals as well as excessive relations that create use values outside the capitalist framework in the lives of agents and customers. For example, Donald Winiecki relates an ethnographic narrative of an employee who found a way to "buy time" by manipulating some calls to be shorter than his management's goals. He would then save this "extra" time to have satisfying interactions with other customers and feel that he had actually helped them. This behavior maintained his average call time, the crucial statistical measure of his productivity, while allowing him the freedom to find job satisfaction. At the same time, he avoided making his calls so short as to create higher expectations for decreased average call times in the future. This preserved his ability to "trick" the system into letting him do his job in a way that was personally satisfying.[17]

In *A Terrible Beauty is Born*, history infects John Small's imagined place in American society, and we see that it is a basic component in the structuring of affect and imagination as social relations. A moment in the play that reveals the complications of both pleasure and dangerous excess in John's entrance into American social structures is found in the account of his training in American language and culture. Ashok describes the experience of learning about America to better inhabit his caller identity:

> The first month and a half of training is all about the way Americans live, eat, sleep . . . how they buy groceries, how they earn and spend money. . . .
>
> All these details help us understand . . . empathize with their situation . . . empathy is a very important part of our work . . . then the customer trusts us . . . that helps us do our job better. . . .
>
> This really helped me succeed with my work. . . . It helped my calling persona stay stable . . . I mean even if the customer was shouting at me, cursing me . . . I would just imagine what John Small would do and then that would immediately help me find a way out. . . . Soon I found John Small being able to handle all situations . . . It was a good feeling. . . .
>
> But then I found I was carrying my work back . . . to this old, forgotten city. . . .
>
> I mean all night I would be imagining the life of each of the calls I was making . . . When you called someone in America you couldn't escape that . . . often you'd hear . . . the TV in the background . . . people talking . . . parents scolding their children . . . couples fighting . . . you could imagine the life in those apartments . . .
>
> All night my imagination would be alive with the sights and smells of America . . . And I would carry them back . . . to my home . . . to my room. . . . At moments little details in my room would change, transform, start looking different. . . . American . . . in a way . . .

Here John/Ashok hallucinates a blurry mixing of the world he has to imagine to do his job successfully and the actual physical reality of his room in Old Delhi. The play shows us that the labor necessary to become a convincing part of the affective and imaginative structure of American society, undertaken as a form of waged labor, can lead to contagious fantasies where histories play themselves out in new terrains, out of the control of their originary social relations. Such relationships cannot be simply constrained to the realm of the economic. Ashok's situation lends a new cast to Marx's assertion that the commodification of labor power results in a "loss of reality" for the worker, and an impoverishment of the worker's "inner world."[18] In addition to the loss of access to the objects he produces as well as his own labor, Ashok loses the ability to relate to a history that has been thrust on him by the economics of globalization. The more he successfully lives, in continuing and succeeding with his call center work, the more he alienates life.[19]

In an example of another type of transmission between American history and the Indian call center, Ashok's recounts his experience with one of his accent trainers, an African American woman who helps the trainees by pointing out that they are all trying to speak white American English, whereas in reality there are many Americas and English is spoken there with many different accents. To illustrate this diversity she has them read poetry written by black American poets, including "To a Dark Girl" and "We Wear a Mask" by Paul Lawrence Dunbar. The first poem praises the beauty of the "dark girl," who is strong even while carrying the history of slavery. In regard to the second poem's theme of wearing a "mask of smiles" to hide suffering and pain, the smiles being described as "a debt paid to human guile," Ashok/John says, "This was great stuff for us . . . reading all these wonderful words . . . we had a feeling we were being cared for . . . a strange feeling . . ." This strange feeling of care is of great importance to understanding how affective commodities carry value and how they are transmitted both to and from Indian call center workers. The investment of value in a life, here through the affective commodity of concern and attention as found in Dunbar's poems, improves the quality of that life. For the reader or audience of the play, there are resonances between these separate histories, of people under slavery in America and Indians in contemporary call centers. The greater part of Ashok's labor in producing John Small is of masking the life of Ashok from the people he calls, the cost of which is the separation of himself from the time and space in which he can address his co-worker's suicide or parse what is real and imagined in his life in Old Delhi, where the world of John Small is not supposed to follow him. Ashok's language and accent training is also a training in the history of oppression and abjection in America, a history into which it is suggested that the call center worker is being initiated. However, when that history is probed, it yields comfort and care from an unexpected place, to unexpected people. In training to be appropriate producers of affective needs for Americans (cultural fluency and idioms that will yield the necessary trust and respect to induce debt payment), these trainees also gain entrance into other structures of affect built to support those who have been exploited, revealing informal affective economies that shadow the formal economy of affective labor.

Conclusion: The Productivity of Affective Labor

Technology has allowed data, in the form of code, to become a highly mobile form of currency that can keep pace with the temporality of transnational electronic capital. Even service labor, which intuitively speaking would seem to rely on the presence of another physical being for its completion, participates in electronic capital in the form of personality data doubles. Code becomes a dominant form of currency in the current moment of global capital, and access to this currency, like access to cash currency for people whose lives are structured by debt, begins more and more to dictate not only people's desires and imaginations of their own lives but also the choices they may or must make to secure a future. As Aneesh's figure of Bharati illustrates, it is not only for a wage that code becomes currency. Bharati realizes that it is only in her data form that she can secure the means of subsistence. Her nondata form can contribute only by reproducing her data form.

The loss of consuming power by the producers of affective commodities, represented by the alienation of Ashok and Bharati in ways specific to their work, is an essential part of how "surplus" is created for export. Globalized demands for labor provided Bharati the option of using her affective labor to produce a data double to take advantage of the apparatus that would transmit that labor to the United States. Such an apparatus does not exist to provide her with affective necessities. This manufactured surplus is then invested into lives that exist separately from the social sphere and existence of those who produced it. This produces a deficit on the model of the care deficit described by Rhacel Salazar Parreñas.[20] In a sense, all labor operates as a type of biocapital, where the product of human vital energy is consumed to promote the well-being and future life chances of someone else. However, one of the important differences is that the exchange of *affective* commodities is not mediated by the embodiment of that energy into a commodity. Even with physical commodities, access to consumption of the vital energy they contain, and therefore the means to a secure and comfortable life, is restricted more in some places than others. The goal of identifying the productivity of affective labor is both to make it visible as well as to point to the flow of value represented in the lives of its producers and consumers.

Affective labor produces value in a way that incurs a tangible loss on one side of its exchange as a commodity and a tangible gain on the other. To argue that affective labor is productive, and not merely reproductive, asserts that value is created by such actions as the adopting of a concerned tone by a call center collection agent or by the comfort offered by the reassurance that someone will become responsible for a customer's concern. Attending to this form of production requires acknowledging the centrality of labor that is often invisible in both cultural and formal economic terms. As is clear through its lack in Ashok's conditions in *A Terrible Beauty Is Born* and in what Aneesh calls the social death of the call center agent, affective labor produces life in a tangible way.

Depending on the type of work under discussion, affective labor can produce other conditions in addition to the commodity, for example loneliness, as discussed above. Marx argues that all productive labor under capitalism produces the devaluing of the material world in general. In reference to industrial production Marx says, "With the increasing value of the world of things proceeds in direct proportion the *devaluation* of the world of men. Labour produces not only commodities; it produces itself and the worker as a *commodity*."[21] We can extend this to specify that the more affective commodities are produced, the more devalued the affective world becomes in general. This can be conceptualized through the alienation of affect that comes with its increasing role as a commodity, as well as the fact that the more affect commodities are produced, the cheaper each one becomes individually. In this sense, no matter how valuable Ashok's production of concern and attentive assistance is to Elizabeth in terms of her increased well-being and future security, it is only "worth" as much as his wage in rupees. However, as the suggestion of gray economies of affective exchange is intended to imply, the instability of use value means that, outside of the market, this concern and attention may have a different kind of value and cost to Ashok; and, even in the reproduction of the commodified affects of the agent, we see the potential to produce social change alongside this reproduction.

The idea of what makes a good life is in many ways subjective, but it results from the balance of needs and the ability to fill those needs in a way that does not entail suffering. The cheapness of someone's labor and life in this scheme therefore reflects only the "outlawed necessities" that maintain this cheapness.[22] Ashok's inability to mourn his co-worker and Bharati's inability to even want to connect to the rest of the social world are examples of the unavailability of necessary affective resources. If part of the drive of capitalism-based cultures is to increase the numbers of hours a day that human activity is spent doing labor that produces capitalist value, it is important to identify value produced by affective labor, often performed in nonpublic spaces accomplishing ends that do not reveal themselves in objects, and to distinguish this as additional to that produced by more visible waged work.

Affective labor produces surplus value, but it also serves to compensate and rehumanize the worker who must believe in his or her future possibilities to continue selling labor power. In this sense, affective labor produces life that can be consumed and transformed into capital through its expenditure as labor power while it also serves to compensate and "rehumanize" the worker as more than a commodity, "creating the illusion that he is an individual with unique characteristics and a real personality."[23] The work of making people "feel better," the primary product of customer service, is therefore central to the continuing existence of capitalist processes. If customer service work is located more and more heavily in the global South, then it becomes the work of people in "places like India" to restore to humanity those who live in the West. One consequence of this work is the making invisible of the worker's own humanity. The work of making consumers "feel better" can contribute to a consumer's life chances in the sense of their access to a socially valued life with the possibility of a future. Ashok's response to Dunbar's poetry in *A Terrible Beauty Is Born* suggests that there are also economies of affect that do not simply reproduce the system that evacuates value from India and deposits it in the United States. The restoration of the worker's sense of humanity and future possibility can be viewed here as a type of biocapital smuggled against the flow of value from global South to North and invested in the lives of those who are supposed to produce such commodities rather than consume them. When we attend to the work of reproducing biological life through affective labor, rather than allowing it to remain invisible, we can expand the notion of biocapital to identify the investment of Third World affect into the future life chances of people living in the West, as well as acknowledging systems of life-support that use the same currencies of programming code and electronic transmission, yet do not simply reproduce life as it is defined and sustained within capitalist culture and production.

Notes

1. Lohr, 2008.
2. Gupta, 2005.
3. Aneesh, 2008; Winiecki, 2007; Taylor et al., 2002.

4. Experimental Chair on the Production of Subjectivity, 2007.

5. Aneesh, 2008.

6. Ibid.: 11.

7. Ibid.: Ben Addelman et al., *Bombay Calling.*

8. Arjun Raina, *A Terrible Beauty Is Born,* 2004: 15. Unpublished play in author's possession. Permission to use excerpt granted to author by playwright on December 7, 2006.

9. Hardt and Negri describe the sphere of immaterial labor, including affect, as a realm that is being incorporated into capitalist systems but is not yet fully incorporated. Because this realm represents resources that can be used to produce social life, they view it as a sort of global commons, under enclosure but still available for alternate uses and end. I argue that problems of access and outlawed needs preclude the sharing in common of these resources (Hardt and Negri, 2004).

10. Raina, *A Terrible Beauty Is Born,* 2004, in author's possession.

11. The situation of social death as a result of unmet affective needs points to Spivak's suggestion of "affectively necessary labor" (Spivak, 1984).

12. Ethnographic work on call centers indicates that work-related social life involves drinking, smoking, and dating in a paradigm that is imagined as "Western." The film *Bombay Calling* in particular indicates the fatigue and need for escape that dominates the after-work bar scene among young call center agents.

13. Hennessy, 2000.

14. In Tucker, 1978: 75.

15. Ibid.: 76.

16. Note: Some distinguish this as two forms, the alienation of social relations and the alienation of species life (Ibid.: 77).

17. Winiecki, 2007: 352–353.

18. Marx and Engels, in Tucker, 1978: 72.

19. Ibid.: 101.

20. Parreñas, 2005.

21. Marx, in Tucker, 1978: 71.

22. Hennessy, 2000.

23. Ibid.: 110.

4 Foreign and Domestic
Adoption, Immigration, and Privatization
Laura Briggs

THOSE OF US WHO STUDY "soft" subjects like family or reproduction are often thought of as working on something altogether unrelated to the "hard" politics of neoliberal globalization. While feminist scholars have often commented on the ideological production of the difference between public and private in the nineteenth century, we have less reliably noticed that this line between public and private is a battlefield whose location has moved and changed. In the midst of the free-market fundamentalism that has gripped us since the late 1970s, intimate labor acts as a mediator between the privatization of government functions—pensions, the military, prisons, health care, and welfare, to name a few—and the expanding realm of the "private" space of the family, where children, the elderly, the sick, and those with mental illness are increasingly cared for, particularly in the absence of a shared social cost of that care. My goal here is to sketch what a companion piece to David Harvey's *Brief History of Neoliberalism* would look like from inside families—for we live our economic situations in households rather than abstract places like markets. I tell the story of neoliberal globalization from the perspective of the migrating mother–child dyad and the U.S. households where some work and others are raised.[1] This story illuminates something of the place of intimate labor in contemporary globalization.

Three figures frame this discussion: a Guatemalan infant, displaced from her birth family through adoption to the United States; a twenty-something Guatemalan woman, let's say the mother of that child, separated from her natal family and her other children through migration to the United States, where she works as an undocumented nanny; and a U.S. white woman in her forties, not wealthy, but certainly middle-class. Multiple acts of labor connect these figures. The infant cost its adoptive parents in the neighborhood of $30,000, including payments to lawyers, Guatemalan foster parents, and those who procured visas and passports for the child. The child's mother, in contrast, is valued at very little in terms of what wages her labor power can command and what her life was worth, crossing first Mexico and then the Arizona desert, where women are three times more likely than men to die.[2]

While we dwell on this unfairness, we might recross the border into Guatemala and notice how this Guatemalan infant is valued. She is racially minoritized, a member of one of a dozen distinct indigenous Mayan groups; her existence, we could say cynically, is the result of the failure of the genocidal campaigns of the state in the 1980s and 1990s.[3] If her birth mother had placed her with relatives, it is doubtful they could afford the fees and supplies required to send her to school; she might well find herself working for slender wages indeed by the time she was six or seven. If she did not have relatives, the virtual absence of child welfare system in Guatemala would mean she might, at best, be raised in a church-based orphanage for several years, perhaps later to join the massive population of street children, sniffing glue or doing low-paid work, including sex work.[4] Adoption to the United States serves as a privatized welfare system for the ferociously neoliberal Guatemalan state, which is bitterly fitting, given the U.S. role in defeating other visions of the state in Guatemala.[5] Her mother, although equally racially minoritized, would have what we might say is a higher social value, measured by her ability to earn wages or by the fact that she would be less likely to die of treatable disease or malnutrition than an infant separated from her family.

In puzzling out how the fact of borders reverses the relative value of these two human lives, it is clearly important to set them in relationship to different but interlocked problems of domestic labor and value in middle-class, largely but not exclusively white, U.S. American families. To offset declining real wages among men, increased numbers of heterosexual mothers entered the labor force, setting off what many saw as a gendered labor crisis at home.[6] Women were still doing most of domestic labor and fighting with their husbands about it. At the time, many feminists thought that, to resolve this crisis, men were going to have to do more child care and housework—women's wages were becoming a nonnegotiable part of domestic economies. It turned out, though, that there was actually another way of negotiating this problem for middle-class families: delaying childbearing until a time when a mother's wages would presumably be higher[7] and then hiring a nanny from outside the United States, as her wages would be significantly lower than those a middle-class U.S. woman could earn.[8] This is a risky reproductive strategy, as both partners' fertility declines as they age, most conspicuously for women beyond the age of thirty, more or less exactly the moment when she might be getting established in a career. Rising ages at reproduction for women have led to increased rates of impaired fertility,[9] which have been countered in part through transnational adoption. Thus, although overall adoption rates in the United States have declined since the 1970s,[10] we have a conspicuous growth in transnational adoption—and those who can engage in it are increasingly wealthy.[11] This narrative is also relevant for lesbian and gay families, who, while they might not have a specifically gendered labor crisis at home, are nevertheless caught up in the same problem of managing domestic and waged labor in the context of child rearing and a structural "infertility."

At the end of the twentieth century, growing numbers of households in the United States included domestic workers; these are increasingly likely to be middle-class, rather than wealthy, households, and the workers are most likely to be of Latin American origin or ancestry.[12] This situation had the effect of shifting the crisis of reproductive labor either economically downward in the United States—to bring the "who's watching the kids?" question to a greater number of working-class and/or Latino households in the United States or to carry it across nation boundaries, as mothers leave young children in their home countries to support them by doing domestic work elsewhere. Rhacel Salazar Parreñas and others have called this a "cost of reproductive labor" question. If a growing number of middle-class households in the United States are relying on labor from elsewhere because they can pay less than U.S. women earn, it is equally true that migrant women who leave their children in home countries are relying on the lower cost of reproductive labor outside the United States or Europe.[13] It is a form of "offshore (re)production" that has been, at once, crucial to other forms of globalization, including the superheating of the U.S. economy, and, to a significant extent, ignored in discussions of globalization.

Here, I am interested in a particular genealogy of how these bodies, families, and labor came to be differently valued. First, I explore how "moral panics" around race and parenting render some children less desirable than others. Second, I suggest, related hysterics around parenting have turned middle-class parents into guardians of their children and rendered "security" a keyword of the family as much as of the state. Finally, I am interested in how transnational adoption from Latin America emerged in the 1970s and 1980s, in conjunction with those nations' dirty wars. Taken together, I suggest, these three developments begin to account for the peculiar story of the relative values of the Guatemalan woman and child I introduced earlier in this chapter.

Moral Panics and Neoliberalism

There never was a golden age before neoliberalism in the United States when reproductive labor was understood to be our common, social concern, to be supported by the state and a wider community.[14] However, there were moments that seemed to offer the promise of something different: "mother's pensions" in the 1920s and a concern for migrant mothers and children in the 1930s during the New Deal.[15] In the 1960s and 1970s, feminism and the welfare rights movement advocated wages for motherhood and housework and day care centers and other support for reproductive and domestic labor; and they had some successes.[16] By the Jimmy Carter administration of 1976 through 1980, a White House conference on the family was suggesting that government had a responsibility to help families because, for the first time, a majority of mothers of young children were in the paid labor force.[17]

Beginning with the 1980 presidential campaign focus on "welfare cheats," the Reagan and then Bush (père) administrations sought to shut this space down. They began by demonizing working-class black, Latino, and indigenous women and children as unworthy of help, plagued by personal irresponsibility, moral and intellectual inferiority, and other unattractive personal characteristics. Then they moved on to white and middle-class families, particularly mothers and children, as potentially *just like* the demonic working-class Latino, black, and Native families, irresponsible and with damaged children, if they accepted government assistance. In place of such moral failings, neoliberals offered personal responsibility and security. In this context, "crack babies," fetal alcohol syndrome, and child car seats and bike helmets became major public policy issues.

As I have written elsewhere, the invention of the "crack baby" in the 1980s was part and parcel of the civic disenfranchisement and sanctioned impoverishment of black and Latino people in the United States in the Reagan and Bush I administrations, accomplished by identifying them as producing bad families. At the same time, it gave many people, who in an earlier generation might have adopted domestically, new anxieties that helped propel transnational adoption.[18] While the "crack baby" hysteria never particularly affected the white middle class, fetal alcohol syndrome (FAS) did double work: First it demonized Native American mothers, and then it turned on (usually white) middle-class mothers.[19] Together, "crack babies" and FAS provided a cover story for neoliberal decimation of the social contract between the state and its most vulnerable citizens, by producing a case for the belief that personal, private irresponsibility was illegitimately making outrageous claims on the public purse. It insisted that fetuses needed to be protected from dangerous mothers who would kill them. Privatization in this instance meant giving up on commitments to racial egalitarianism in education and employment, attributing worsening racial differences in income and well-being to biology and poor prenatal environments that created children damaged from birth— that is, biologically inferior.[20] It also provided the context in which, five years later, Newt Gingrich could urge that the state should take the children of welfare mothers and put them in orphanages, completing the cycle of the attack on wages for motherhood: Not only was no one entitled to state support for raising their children, but, if they asked, they deserved to lose their children.

The debate over FAS had divergent effects, producing in essence two racialized classes of mothers and children. One set of effects was very much like those produced by the "crack baby" crisis, a racialized underclass that was understood to be stunted from birth; television and print media produced features that decried the child abuse and even "genocide" perpetrated by Native women, including a weeklong segment on NBC in 1989 entitled *Incident at Pine Ridge*. Pregnant alcoholic women, mostly Native American, went to jail to "protect" their fetuses, notwithstanding physician objections about the absolutely appalling fetal outcomes for women in prison. Mothers lost their children at birth to the foster care system; the number of Native children in foster care increased 25 percent in the late 1980s.[21] Native American children with developmental problems were overdiagnosed with FAS: A 1994 genetic study on reservations in Arizona found that from half to two-thirds of the children diagnosed actually didn't have it but instead suffered from Down syndrome or some other developmental problem.[22]

The other set of effects, however, was that the debate terrified (mostly white) middle-class women who didn't drink very much. Historian of medicine Janet Golden has traced how the syndrome devolved from a problem diagnosed in the children of alcoholic women who drank an average of ten drinks a day to a warning to all pregnant women not to drink at all. Knowledge that alcohol was dangerous to fetuses, combined with medical uncertainty about how

much alcohol caused fetal defects, Golden argues, emboldened some researchers, public health officials, and the media to claim that any alcohol use at all
during pregnancy constituted fetal child abuse.[23]

Whether or not moderate drinking can cause negative fetal outcomes,
good reason exists to be suspicious that the entire discussion was overblown
from a public health perspective. FAS is difficult to diagnose, raising questions about all claims about its prevalence; indeed, it appears to be quite rare.
Even among alcoholic women, the likelihood of bearing an infant with FAS is
about 5 percent. Addressing poverty, inequality, and violence might be more
effective in preventing FAS than blaming women who binge drink: More recent studies have suggested that alcohol is damaging to the fetus only when
the mother is malnourished, stressed, exposed to environmental toxins, and/
or smoking. FAS is so often an issue related to adoption because, according to
some studies, *most* of the mothers that gave birth to infants affected by FAS
were dead within a few years as a result of violence or alcoholism.[24] However, as political scientists Jean Reith Schroedel and Paul Peretz point out,
"Between 1989 and 1991 . . . the *New York Times* devoted a total of 853.5 column inches to fetal abuse . . . by pregnant women's use of illegal drugs and/or
drinking. During the same period there was not a single column inch dealing
with adverse birth outcomes due to the physical abuse of women."[25]

The National Security Family

"Yuppie mothers," as they were called in the 1980s, were never demonized in
the way black or Native mothers were. Still, for them, the 1980s was a period of
intensified anxiety over child vulnerablility. In contrast to the reassuring Dr.
Spock, who told mothers that if they listened to their children and their own
common sense, all would be well, mothers in the 1980s got Richard Ferber
and T. Berry Brazelton. The new advice books warned of multiple dangers of
bad parenting, urged disciplined approaches to making your child sleep alone
and potty train, and stressed the need to educate yourself about developmental guideposts. Such books considered how to evaluate your child's development, set boundaries, discipline, provide consistency, and fulfill the need for
enrichment through piano lessons and soccer, as well as engage in careful
monitoring of school work—all without overdoing it and stressing out your
fragile child, which carried its own dangers.[26] This decade's emphasis on parenting as something learned and something that took tremendous amounts of
time, thought, and work was not a product of an expansion of leisure. With

the decline in real wages, even middle-class mothers were increasingly in the workforce, relying on day care at younger ages and on children's good sense to care for themselves after school.[27] Mothers had to accomplish more intimate labor in less time.

The 1980s also marked the emergence of a host of new anxieties about child death and disability. In 1984, uncorroborated reports of poisoned Halloween candy inaugurated an era in which parents were to go out trick-or-treating with their children. Stranger-kidnapping and sexual abuse generated countless news stories, although the far more common, intrafamilial sexual abuse never got much play. Mothers Against Drunk Driving identified a new threat specifically against children. Responding to other worries, public safety campaigns brought new laws in the 1980s mandating that children wear bike helmets and seat belts. Very young children were to ride in expensive child safety seats.[28]

Narratives about protecting vulnerable children vastly expanded the private sphere at this time of rising labor force participation. Rather than taking the increase in middle-class children's unsupervised time to be normative, these narratives invoked guilt and fear. They insisted that it actually required more work than previously to raise children, more time, thought, and concern. The 1980s expansion of *the private* was at once an attack on feminism and the incursion of neoliberalism, replacing belief in public services with private, familial labor. At precisely the moment when there might have been a widespread demand for publicly funded day care, for example, day care became seen as a dangerous place where children were routinely sexually abused. Just when mothers most needed them, sturdy, self-reliant children disappeared.

A radical agenda of privatization was, of course, the heart of neoliberalism in two senses. First, there was the "privatizing" of government responsibilities, such as a military activity, for the benefit of business (like Blackwater). Second, there was the process of delegating to families and churches many of the post–New Deal functions of government, such as supporting single mothers with children. Together, these embody the domestic and international goals that Grover Norquist memorably phrased as making government small enough to drown in the bathtub. To accomplish these goals, neoliberal ideologues needed to build a broad consensus that middle-class domestic space was *not* going to shrink in the wake of women's move into the formal workforce but, on the contrary, was going to expand.

Transnational Adoption

It is not surprising that an explosion of interest from the United States in transnational adoption developed at this time. Middle-class domestic space had grown increasingly important. Efforts to manage home and work were resulting in a steady advance in the age at which women were having their first child. Moral panics about "crack babies" and fetal alcohol syndrome left many who in an earlier generation might have adopted children from U.S. foster care leery about potential disabilities and the racial politics of doing so.

In the new neoliberal order, manufacturing plants began to move easily and repeatedly to wherever poverty was the greatest and Third World workers appeared to be interchangeable. Babies entered this world as similarly mobile, and adoption likewise followed gradients of poverty and civil disruption. Just as wars in Korea and Vietnam had produced first waves of transnational adoption, now adoption followed in the wake of advancing neoliberalism and civil war. Between 1973 and 1983, the number of intercountry adoptions to the United States doubled.[29] Most were still from South Korea, but Latin American countries were growing as a source and collectively formed the overwhelming majority of non-Korean adoptions. In the late 1970s and the 1980s, the most significant Latin American sending countries were Colombia, Peru, Guatemala, Chile, and Paraguay[30]—all of them nations that in the 1980s had right-wing governments with close ties to the United States, engaged in civil war against leftist insurgents that included massive human rights violations against civilian populations.[31]

In Latin America, during the dirty wars of the 1970s and 1980s, adoption followed the advances of these militaries and paramilitaries. Activism by human rights groups like the Asociación Pro Búsqueda de Niñas y Niños Desaparecidos in El Salvador and Todos por el Reencuentro in Guatemala, alongside the better-known Madres de la Plaza de Mayo, has made it increasingly clear that child kidnapping as a tactic of political terror also happened throughout the region, followed by adoption, sometimes within the country but also to the United States and Europe.[32] For Latin American human rights groups, adoption in the region has a very different meaning than it generally does in the United States. Networks of organizations of family members of those disappeared span Latin America and Europe: Comadres, Comité de Madres y Familiares Cristianos de Presos, Desaparecidos y Asesinados "Padre Octavio Ortiz—Hermana Silvia" (known as CODEFAM) and Comité de Familiares Pro Libertad de Presos y Desaparecidos Políticos de El Salvador "Marianella Garcia Villas" (known as COMFAC), for example. Court cases from Argentina to El Salvador have used the disappearance and adoption of children as the major—sometimes the only—prosecutable dirty war crime. Where amnesty laws and regimes of impunity have foreclosed many possibilities of legal action against war criminals, kidnapping followed by adoption is an ongoing crime, not covered by retrospective amnesties.[33] As a result, organizations of parents of disappeared children and the grown children themselves have emerged as some of the most important groups in Latin America's prodemocracy movements that demand legal accountability for war crimes.

But the really significant numbers of adoptions occurred after the wars, as "markets" were "opened." In Guatemala—the country with the highest per capita adoption rate in the world until it was shut down in 2009[34]—adoptions increased after the Peace Accords in 1996 and the subsequent growing presence of U.S. businesses and NGOs (nongovernmental organizations). After staying relatively constant at 400 adoptions to the Unites States per year, in 1997 there were 788; in 1998 there were 911; and then rates quickly shot up, with 3,783 Guatemalan adoptions to the United States in 2005.[35]

Debates about international adoption in other Latin American nations provided an opportunity for emergent coalitions of human rights advocates to pass laws favoring the rights of children, sharply curtailing transnational adoptions in most nations by the mid-1990s.[36] But in Guatemala, the country where neoliberalism perhaps has advanced the farthest, those who kidnapped children and disappeared them into adoptions during the war were restored to power after 1999 and continued to oppose the implementation of international human rights frameworks as a violation of parents' rights to do whatever they want with their children, at least until 2009 (at this writing, there is a moratorium on transnational adoption from Guatemala, but adoption proponents continue to advocate for a lifting of all or most restrictions). Despite wave after wave of reform, each a tacit admission that perhaps all was not well before, many still regard the Guatemalan adoption system as, in the words of one human rights lawyer, as "a nest of corruption."[37]

While curtailing international adoption in other Latin American countries has not by any means ended the exploitation of children of the popular classes—its not clear how substituting adoption by wealthy nationals for adoption by wealthy foreigners was going to change that—neither does it mean that all was well with adoption from Guatemala. International adoption was the result of the tremendous destruction of social networks that would have allowed families and communities to place their children closer to home, with relatives or friends, if they were unable to raise their own children.[38] Adoption consists of a set of state-to-state agreements to allow visas and to implement a legal framework (adapted from the United States) in which children can be legally estranged from their birth parents. This mixture of formal and informal social and economic connections significantly requires women's intimate labor as midwives, intermediaries, and foster care workers. International adoption further depends on the networks between rich and poor women built through service work, including domestic service, all of which contribute to the production of "adoptable" children.

Adoption is above all the neoliberalization of child welfare. As states abandon public services like subsidized health care and staple foods—whether by ending Aid to Families with Dependent Children (AFDC) and shrinking Medicaid in the United States or by adopting structural adjustment programs in Latin America—they have placed impoverished children in privatized families, rather than provide state services to support them with their birth families. U.S. Speaker of the House Newt Gingrich made this memorably clear when he announced his intention in 1994 to take the children of welfare mothers and put them in orphanages. It was the unannounced policy of militaries in Latin America when they kidnapped the children of "reds" and raised them in their own families or shipped them off to Europe and the United States. It has been and perhaps will continue to be the informal policy of Guatemalan elites to try to offload the problem of the miserable health, education, and even survival rates of the children of the poor by exporting one out of every twenty babies born in Guatemala to the United States. That facilitators make a tremendous amount of money by turning the child into a quasi-commodity itself is a side benefit.

Migrating Women

Finally, I want to turn to neoliberalism's best-known story, one central to my analysis: the ways that changes in Latin America have transformed families, resulting in increased pressure to send some members out of the country to earn wages for family survival. In the 1980s, Ronald Reagan and Margaret Thatcher pushed for changes in what the World Bank demanded of debtor nations. These structural adjustment policies (SAPs) required a radical shrinking of governmental spending on things like agricultural subsidies, health, and education. Although few Latin American states ever had a highly developed social infrastructure, the virtual elimination of state supports was devastating for working-class people, peasants, and indigenous people, especially women and children. Women in heterosexual families remained largely responsible for school fees, household food costs, and health care expenses, all of which soared.

Free trade arrangements proved disastrous for commodity-producing nations, sending the price of basic foodstuffs through the roof, thus leaving many feeling that they had to leave the country to earn a living.[39] After the civil war ended in 1996 in Guatemala, unemployment exceeded 50 percent by some counts, while title to land ownership, never clear, became extremely unstable. Promises by the government as part of the Peace Accords to undertake land reform have gone largely unfulfilled, leaving vast numbers of rural people, particularly indigenous people, landless. What isn't taken away from the people is often rendered unusable through contamination, toxic waste, and lack of irrigation or potable water. Combined with the genocidal campaign in the highlands and the abandonment of plantation agriculture even by multinationals like United Fruit, these transformations continue to drive people to the cities; half of Guatemala's population is now urban. But in the cities everything must be bought with cash—and there is precious little waged work. As a result, Guatemala has some of the worst economic and health outcomes in the hemisphere.[40]

We have many rich ethnographic accounts of how mothers decide to migrate and leave their children behind, and from them we learn of the centrality of questions of children's well-being in the decision *to* migrate. Although mothers worry about entrusting the intimate labor of care to their children's grandmothers, aunts, and neighbors, they are equally concerned with supplying their children with clothing, food, school fees, and health care. The overwhelming reason women give for leaving their children is their inability to provide them with these things, given inadequate opportunities for waged labor in their home countries. Neoliberalism has contributed to growing inequalities between rich and poor, the decline in government subsidies for these specific kinds of things, and the increased monetarization of everything—which is to say, everything costs money, making opportunities to get by through subsistence agriculture or nonwaged work in the informal economy increasingly difficult. Migration has become a pretty reliable way to know your children will have the necessities of life.

The insight that the intimate labor of housework and childcare have a monetary value and that private and public economies are intricately interconnected—harkening back to the analysis of socialist feminism of the 1970s—then yields a rich account of migration, adoption, and domestic labor. We need this transnational, female, and feminist account of intimate labor to fully understand how neoliberalism has expanded the realm of the "private," and how the resources no longer being provided by the state are being replaced with ever more intricate and multinational solutions to the problem of re-production. But a macrostructuralist account like this one does not explain why middle-class U.S. households hire Latin American women to do household labor or adopt Guatemalan babies, nor why Guatemalan women migrate or relinquish their children for adoption. Human beings are too various and unpredictable for that. Nevertheless, it does describe the historical, material contexts in which individuals do or do not make these choices and characterizes some of the things that make them likely during this post–Cold War moment in vigorously neoliberal states like the United States and Guatemala. Privatization has meant the expansion of "the private" for some and its virtual evisceration for others. We have understood neoliberalism to be about states and economies, but it is at least as true to say it is a story about families tied together by intimate labors.

Notes

1. Duggan, 2003. Harvey, 2005.

2. McCombs, 2007.

3. The Guatemalan Truth Commission report called it genocide; see Comisión para el Esclarecimiento Histórico, 1991.

4. Guzmán, 1999; Ovando, 1998, 1999; Sandoval, 2000; Lara, 1996, 1998; "Comunidad Internacional Solicita a Guatemala Conceder Más Atención a Problemática Infantil," 1996; "No Se Protege a Los Niños," 1996.

5. Hübinette, 2005; Grandin, 2005.

6. Hochschild, 1989.

7. Women's age at first child has been climbing steadily since 1970, actually increasing almost every year, from 20.1 in 1970 to more than 25 in 2002. It has increased more and faster for white women than for black women, with women "of Hispanic origin" in the middle. This would be consistent with it being a strategy for maintaining middle-class status, as more white women than black or "Hispanic" women are middle class rather than working class. In 2002, the *average* age of first birth for all white women was almost 27—getting surprisingly close to ages at which fertility is difficulty. See Chandra et al., 2005.

8. Hochschild, 2003; Hondagneu-Sotelo, 2001.

9. Although there is not, we should note, an "epidemic" of infertility, as has been widely and hysterically reported in the press, which Faludi comments on in *Backlash* (1991). Impaired fertility is part of normal aging. Rates of actual infertility are declining (Chandra et al., 2005).

10. Stolley, 1993.

11. U.S. Department of State, 2002.

12. Hondagneu-Sotelo and Avila, 1997; Hondagneu-Sotelo, 2001. The Bureau of Labor Statistics in 2006 counted 37.2 percent Latino or Hispanic "maids or housekeeping workers" and 19.9 percent African American. It recorded no nannies, but "childcare workers" were 17.3 percent Latina and 17 percent black (U.S. Bureau of Labor Statistics, 2000; 2007).

13. Parreñas, 2005.

14. Koven and Michel, 1993.

15. Kozol, 1988.

16. Ehrenreich, 2001; Orleck, 2005; Kornbluh, 2007.

17. Stearns, 2003; Collins, 1994; Dill, 1988; Glenn, 1994.

18. Briggs, 2006.

19. Armstrong, 2003: 173.

20. Krauthammer, 1989.

21. Plantz, 1988.

22. Erikson, 1995; Hoyme, Hauck, and Meyer, 1994.

23. Golden, 2005.

24. Armstrong, 2003: 7, 82.

25. Schroedel and Peretz, 1994.

26. Apple, 2006.

27. Cheever, 1995.

28. Levitt and Dubner, 2006.

29. The number of intercountry adoptions rose to 7,350, still a small number relative to 2006, when about 20,000 were adopted (Rule, 1984).

30. Ibid.; Evan B. Donaldson Adoption Insititute, 2003.

31. See, e.g., Grandin, 2004; Stern, 2004; Tate, 2001; Cornell and Roberts, 1990; Guillermoprieto, 1990; Amnesty International, 2003.

32. Personal communication with Jon Cortina, pro-Búsqueda, July 2005; also, Liga Guatemalteca para Higiene Mental, 2008; and see also Flynn and McConahay, 2002; "Aún En Busca De Los Niños Que La Guerra Se Llevó," 2006.

33. The lawyers at la Asociación Pro Búsqueda los Niños y Niñas Desaparecidos helped me understand why this was so critical (Interviews with Marta López Santiago and Jacinta López Santiago, Union Victoria, Guatemala , July 10, 2006; with Zaira Navas, Attorney for Pro Búsqueda in San Salvador, El Salvador, 2005). The Mexican

magazine *Proceso* has also been covering this unfolding story (Dalton, 2003a, 2003b, 2005; Izquierdo, 2002).

34. Selman, 2009.

35. U.S. Department of State, 2002.

36. Fonseca, 2009.

37. Benítez, 2007.

38. On the destruction of social networks, see Green, 1999.

39. Oxfam, 2003.

40. U.S. Central Intelligence Agency, 2009; Instituto Latinoamericano para la Educación y Comunicación and UNICEF, 2000; Hendrix, 1997; Tucker, 2007.

Selling Genes, Selling Gender

Egg Agencies, Sperm Banks, and the Medical Market in Genetic Material

Rene Almeling

IN THE TWENTY-FIRST CENTURY medical market in eggs and sperm, commercial agencies recruit young women and men to produce gametes for clients who are using reproductive technologies to conceive children. In egg donation, once a donor–recipient match is confirmed, the donor takes hormones for about six weeks, first to synchronize her menstrual cycle with the recipient's and then to stimulate egg production. Outpatient surgery is performed to remove the eggs, which are mixed with sperm, and, if fertilization occurs, the embryos are implanted in the recipient's uterus. The American Society for Reproductive Medicine (ASRM) estimates that one to two percent of women undergoing treatment will require hospitalization for ovarian hyperstimulation, and fewer than one patient in a thousand will require major surgery due to complications of egg retrieval. Compensation to egg donors varies substantially, both within particular agencies and in different regions of the United States, but the national average is around $4,200.[1]

Egg donation is physically invasive and risky in a way that sperm donation is not, but sperm donation restricts a donor's activities for a much longer period of time. Men sign a contract and agree to produce sperm samples once or twice a week for at least one year, and each visit must be preceded by two days of abstinence from sexual activity. Each bank has several small rooms for donors furnished with sinks, chairs, and pornographic magazines. Across the hall is the laboratory, where technicians process the sample, after which it is frozen and stored in the bank's offices until purchased by recipients for use in artificial insemination. In contrast to women, who are paid regardless of how many eggs they produce, men are paid only for samples deemed acceptable based on sperm count and quality, things that can be negatively affected by stress, sickness, or having abstained for fewer than forty-eight hours. Much less variation occurs in sperm donor compensation. All donors within a particular bank are typically paid the same, usually between $50 and $100 per sample.

While biological differences between women and men affect the process of donating reproductive material, the products for sale in this medical market, eggs and sperm, are parallel bodily goods in that each contributes half of the reproductive material needed to create an embryo. Furthermore, there are organizational similarities in how commercial agencies have developed stages in the donation process: Staff advertise to recruit gamete donors, employ a wide range of criteria to screen applicants, generate individualized donor marketing materials to facilitate matches with recipient clients, and monitor the process of egg and sperm production before compensating donors.

It is the very fact that these reproductive cells are produced by differently sexed bodies that allows for a comparative analysis of the extent to which the market in eggs parallels the market in sperm. In each stage of the donation process, from recruitment to compensation, how similar are procedures at egg agencies and sperm banks? If there are systematic differences, are these explained by biological differences between women and men? Or, given that this is an open market in genetic material, are differences shaped by mechanisms theorized in microeconomics, such as the supply of and demand for egg donors versus sperm donors? Because the intent of those purchasing gametes is to have children, do gendered cultural norms associated with motherhood and fatherhood influence the procedures at commercial donation programs?

To answer these questions, I collected qualitative interview and observational data between 2002 and 2006 at two egg agencies, Creative Beginnings and OvaCorp, and two sperm banks, CryoCorp and Western Sperm Bank (all pseudonyms), located in the western United States. Using these data, I analyze how ideas about cells and bodies, supply and demand, and motherhood and fatherhood interact to shape the commodification of eggs and sperm in medicalized donation programs.

The Market in Eggs and Sperm

Whereas Creative Beginnings has been open for just a few years, OvaCorp was one of the first agencies in the country to expand its assisted reproduction services to include egg donation. Both sperm banks have been open for more than twenty years, but CryoCorp is one of the largest in the country, while Western Sperm Bank is a smaller nonprofit program with roots in the feminist women's health movement. Despite institutional differences like tax status, size, and date of establishment, the staff in each program perceive their role to be service providers to recipient clients. To maintain their businesses, they must recruit "sellable" donors who provide "high-quality" gametes to recipients who "shop" different egg agencies and sperm banks.

Economic language permeates their talk, yet egg agency and sperm bank staff are very aware of being in a unique business. They discuss "people-management" strategies and point out that they are not "manufacturing toothpaste" or "selling pens." They also consistently refer to the women and men who produce genetic material as "donors" who "help" recipients, and they refer to the donor–recipient exchange as a "win-win situation." This confluence of economic logic with altruistic rhetoric develops through each stage of the donation process and results in bodily commodification that occurs in very different ways for women and men.

Recruiting "Sellable" Donors

Programs advertise for donors in a variety of forums (college newspapers, free weekly magazines, radio, and websites), hold "donor information sessions," and encourage previous donors to refer friends, roommates, and siblings. Sperm bank advertisements highlight the prospect of financial compensation. They often include cartoonish illustrations of sperm, and some even joke that men can "get paid for what you're already doing." CryoCorp and Western Sperm Bank are located within blocks of prestigious four-year universities, and such advertising is directed at cash-strapped college students. The marketing director of CryoCorp, which requires that donors be enrolled in or have a degree from a four-year university, explains that the location was a deliberate choice because "the owners of the sperm bank thought that that was a good job match, and it really works out well for the students. They're young and therefore healthy. They don't have to make a huge time commitment. They can visit the sperm bank anytime." Nevertheless, the staff at both banks lament difficulties in recruiting men and offer hefty "finder fees" to current donors who refer successful applicants.

In contrast, Creative Beginnings receives several hundred applications from women each month, and OvaCorp receives more than a hundred each day. The egg agencies adorn their advertisements with images of plump babies and appeal to the joys of "helping" infertile couples; some do not even list the amount donors will be paid. The director of Creative Beginnings explains the impetus behind her marketing strategy: "We appeal to the idea that there's an emotional reward, that they're going to feel good about what they've done, that it's a win-win situation, that they're going to help someone with something that person needs, and they're going to get something they need in return." Indeed, both agencies report that "young moms are the best donors [because] they pay the best attention and show up for appointments" because they understand the importance of a child to recipient clients. While the sperm bank staff explicitly acknowledge that donors are most interested in a "job," egg agencies are far more likely to reference altruism, even as they also note that donors will get "something" in return.

When a potential donor calls or e-mails a program for the first time, the staff initiate an extensive screening process by asking applicants about their age, height:weight ratio, family health history (including physical, mental, and genetic disease), and social characteristics. Guidelines for age and height:weight ratios are issued by ASRM and are stringently followed by egg agencies to select donors who will respond well to fertility medications. Some screening standards are based on biomedical guidelines for genetic material most likely to result in pregnancy, but many reflect client requests for socially desirable characteristics. For example, both sperm banks have height minimums of five feet eight inches or five feet nine inches. Even some of the nominally biomedical factors are better understood as social characteristics, as in this description of screening standards by Western Sperm Bank's donor manager:

> We have to not take people that are very overweight because of a sellable issue. It becomes a marketing thing, some of the people we don't accept. Also height becomes a marketing thing. When I'm interviewing somebody to be a donor, of course personality is really important. Are they gonna be responsible? But immediately I'm also clicking in my mind: Are they blond? Are they blue-eyed? Are they tall? Are they Jewish? So [I'm] not just looking at the [sperm] counts and the [health] history, but also can we sell this donor?

Likewise, in explaining the screening process for women applying to be donors, the office manager for Creative Beginnings says that "this is a business, and we're trying to provide a service." Later that day, her assistant notes that recipients "basically go shopping, and they want this and they want that."

OvaCorp's donor manager also emphasizes social characteristics, including educational level and attractiveness, in describing what makes a donor "sellable":

You will find that a donor's selling tool is her brains and her beauty. That's a donor's selling point, as opposed to she's a wonderful person. That's nice. But bottom line, everyone wants either someone that's either very attractive, someone very healthy, and someone very bright. That's her selling point/tool. That's why I also work with women who don't have children, because I get a higher level of academia with a lot of our single donors because they're not distracted by kids.

Research on how recipients select donors suggests that staff are responding to client interest in attractive and intelligent donors whose phenotypes are similar to their own.[2] At the same time, according to the director of Creative Beginnings, the staff are responding to recipients who "want to know that the person donating is a good person. They want to know that person wasn't doing it for the money, that person's family history is good, that person was reasonably smart, that they weren't fly-by-nights, drug abusers, or prostitutes." Intersecting with gendered expectations about egg donors having, or at least expressing, altruistic motivations, are class-based concerns in defining "appropriate" donors.

Sperm banks, in comparison, expect donors to be financially motivated, and the staff speak directly about responsibility rather than couching it in terms of altruistic motivations. Western Sperm Bank's donor manager explains:

Aside from personality, the other thing that makes me fall in love with a donor is someone that's responsible. It is so rare to get someone that's truly responsible, that comes in when they're supposed to come in, or at least has the courtesy to call us and say, "I can't make it this week, but I'll come in next week twice." Then of course the second thing that makes him ideal is that he has consistently very high [sperm] counts, so I rarely have to toss anything on him [i.e., reject his sperm sample]. And then, I guess the third thing would be someone that has a great personality, that's just adorable, caring, and sweet. There are donors, that their personalities, I think ugh. They have great [sperm] counts, they come in when they're supposed to, but I just don't like them. That's a personal thing, and I think, huh, I don't want more of those babies out in the world.

While egg agencies and sperm banks are interested in responsible women and men who fulfill their obligations, donors are also expected to embody middle-class American femininity or masculinity. Staff expect egg donors to conform to one of two gendered stereotypes: highly educated and physically attractive or caring and motherly with children of their own. Sperm donors, on the other hand, are generally expected to be tall and college educated with consistently high sperm counts.

In terms of other characteristics, egg agencies and sperm banks work to recruit donors from a variety of racial, ethnic, and religious backgrounds to satisfy a diverse recipient population. In fact, race/ethnicity is genetically re-ified to the degree that it serves as the basis for program filing systems. During a tour of CryoCorp, the founder lifted sperm samples out of the storage tank filled with liquid nitrogen, explaining that the vials are capped with white tops for Caucasian donors, black tops for African American donors, yellow tops for Asian donors, and red tops for donors with "mixed ancestry." All four programs complain about the difficulty of recruiting African American, His-panic, and Asian donors, and Jewish donors are in demand for Jewish clients.

The final phase of recruitment involves reproductive endocrinologists, psychologists, and geneticists or genetic counselors, who serve as professional stamps of approval in producing reproductive material for sale. Applicants are examined by a physician and tested for blood type, Rh factor, drugs, and sexually transmitted infections. Both egg agencies require a psychological evaluation and the Minnesota Multiphasic Personality Inventory, but nei-ther sperm bank requires that donors be psychologically screened. All four programs require donors to prepare a detailed family health history for three generations (and thus do not accept adoptees); in some programs, this history is evaluated by genetic counselors or geneticists, who might request specific genetic tests.

In this, the first stage in the process of donating genetic material, there are structural similarities in that both egg agencies and sperm banks expend funds to advertise for donors, employ a range of medical and social standards to garner "sellable" donors, and "invest" in medical and genetic screening. But comparing how staff evaluate both the donors and their genetic material in terms of marketability reveals how gendered stereotypes shape the definition of "high-quality" eggs and sperm. Despite findings in the psychological litera-ture that both egg and sperm donors report a range of altruistic and financial motivations,[3] egg agency advertisements appeal to women's altruism while men are informed of a job opportunity. In the screening process, both women and men are screened for infectious and genetic diseases, suggesting parallel concerns raised by the exchange of bodily tissue, but "girls who just want to lay their eggs for some quick cash" are rejected, while men are expected to be interested in making money.

These gendered assumptions about donor motivations correspond to traditional gendered definitions of parenthood in which mothers are selfless caregivers and fathers are distant breadwinners.[4] This link between reproductive cells and cultural understandings of motherhood and fatherhood is made especially clear in the psychological evaluations, which are required only of egg donors. Part of each session is devoted to evaluating the psychological stability of the potential donor, but women are also asked how they feel about "having their genetics out there." Sperm banks do not require that men consider this question with a mental health professional, suggesting that women are perceived as more closely connected to their eggs than men are to their sperm.

The vast majority of women and men applying to be donors at commercial fertility programs are not accepted. Both sperm banks reject over 90 percent of applicants because of the need for exceptionally high sperm counts, required because freezing sperm in liquid nitrogen significantly reduces the number that are motile. Both egg agencies estimate that they reject over 80 percent of women who apply. In short, donor recruitment is time intensive, rigorous, and costly. As staff sift through hundreds of applications, the initial framing of egg donation as an altruistic win-win situation and sperm donation as an easy job shapes subsequent staff–donor interactions, from constructing individualized donor profiles to the actual production of genetic material for sale.

Constructing Donor Profiles

Once applicants pass the initial screening with program staff, they are invited to fill out a "donor profile." These are lengthy documents with questions about the donor's physical characteristics, family health history, educational attainment (in some cases, standardized test scores, GPA [grade-point average], and IQ scores are requested), as well as open-ended questions about hobbies, likes and dislikes, and motivations for donating. Once approved by staff, egg donor profiles, along with current pictures, are listed on the agency's password-protected website under the woman's first name. The donor then waits to be selected by a recipient before undergoing medical, psychological, and genetic screening. In contrast, sperm banks do not post profiles until donors pass the medical screening and produce enough samples to be listed for sale on the bank's publicly accessible website. Sperm banks are much more concerned about donor anonymity, so men's profiles are assigned an identification number and do not include current photographs. Both banks do offer a "photo-matching service," in which recipients pay staff to select donors with specified phenotypes.

Profiles serve as the primary marketing tool for both the program and the donor. For donation programs, posted profiles represent the full range of donors available and thus are used to recruit recipient clients. The director of Creative Beginnings explains that she would prefer not to have profiles on the website because she thinks they are impersonal but that she needs them to be "competitive" with other programs. For donors, the profiles are the primary basis on which they will be selected by a recipient. Typically, recipients also consult with staff about which donors to choose; in rare cases, egg recipients will ask to meet a donor, but under no circumstances are sperm recipients allowed to meet donors. If a donor's profile is not appealing, recipients are not likely to express interest in purchasing that donor's reproductive material.

This explains why programs spend a great deal of energy encouraging applicants to complete the questionnaires and, in the case of egg donation, to include attractive pictures. During an information meeting for women interested in egg donation, the staff of Creative Beginnings offer explicit advice about how donors should appeal to recipients:

ASSISTANT DIRECTOR: The profile really gives recipients a chance to get to know you on another level, even though it's anonymous. It feels like it's personal. It feels like they're making a connection with you. They want to feel like it's less clinical than just looking it up on the Web site, and they want to see which girl best suits their needs. It's about who looks like they could fit into my family, and who has the characteristics that I would like in my offspring? You can never be too conceited or too proud of your accomplishments because they really like to feel like wow, this is a really special and unique person. And they want to feel like they're helping you just like you're helping them. They know that money is a good motivator, but they also want to feel like you're here for some altruistic purposes. So I always say to let your personality show, but also you can kind of look at the question and think, if I were in their position, how would I want somebody to answer that question? I don't want you to be somebody that you're not, but think of being sensitive to their needs and feelings when you're answering them. That's the big portion of it. The picture is another portion. We always ask for one good head and shoulder shot. It's whatever is your best representation, flattering, and lets you come out.

DONOR ASSISTANT: You don't want something where your boobs are hanging out of your top [laughter]. These people are not looking for sexy people.

ASSISTANT DIRECTOR: We get girls who send in pictures from their homecoming dance, but everybody takes those pictures where they're half-wasted and they've got their drink in one hand and their cigarette in another. Recipients don't need to see it. It's like your parents, ignorance is bliss.

Egg donors are encouraged by agency staff to construct properly feminine profiles for the recipients, who are continually referenced as an oblique "they" who will be reading the donors' answers and making judgments about their motivations. Although it is important for the "girls" to let their "personalities" shine through, the recipients do not necessarily need to know about their flaws, like wearing revealing clothing, drinking, or smoking.

If a donor's profile is deemed unacceptable by staff, or if she sends in unattractive pictures, agencies will "delete" her from the database. Creative Beginnings's office manager explains, "We have to provide what our client wants, and that's a specific type of donor. Even though [the recipients] may not be the most beautiful people on the face of the earth, they want the best. So that's what we have to provide to them." In contrast, sperm recipients are not allowed to see photographs of donors, and thus men's physical appearance is not held to the same high standard as women's.

Sperm bank staff will take extra time with donors who discuss only financial motivations in their profiles, but they are much less explicit about the need to appear altruistic. This dynamic is clear as Western Sperm Bank's donor manager explains how she came to understand the importance of profiles:

> [Prior to this job,] when I worked on the infertility side, women would come in with their little donor vials. Some of them would show me the [donor profile and say] doesn't he sound wonderful? And of course this is all they've got. This is their person, this little sheet. So [the bank's screeners] will look at [the profile] and if someone's sort of negative, to really question the donor. Do you really mean that money is the only thing for you? And if it is, we are honest enough to just leave it that way. But a lot of times [donors will] say, well, it's not just the money, it's also. [So the screeners will say] why don't you rewrite this little portion to reflect that also? The new [screeners] became more conscious and willing to put in the effort to make more complete answers because they did care about what was presented to the recipients, to give them a fuller image of what the person was like.

While egg agencies specifically use the terms *help* and *altruism* in advising donors about profiles, the sperm donor manager does not specify what other motivation the donor is expected to have besides financial compensation. He is only supposed to revise the profile with the "also" in mind.

Egg agencies and sperm banks use donor profiles to recruit clients, and recipients who select particular women and men based on details about eye color, family health history, favorite movie, and SAT scores begin to think of the donor as that profile. But donors are not producing unmediated texts that travel from keyboard to website display. Gendered cultural norms, formalized through organizational processes, result in expectations that women reflect altruistic sentiments beneath an attractive photograph, while sperm donors are vaguely encouraged to provide a "fuller image." While the recipient is actually buying eggs or sperm, this genetic material becomes personified through the donor profile, and it is this gendered, commodified personification of the donor that the recipient is purchasing.

Matchmaking and Fees

Donor profiles are used to attract recipient clients to a particular program, and a match is made when a recipient chooses a specific donor. In egg agencies, a recipient chooses a particular egg donor, who then is medically and psychologically screened before signing a legal contract with "her couple." In sperm banks, there is a limited "inventory" of sperm vials from each donor, and this supply is replenished as men continue to donate throughout their yearlong commitment to the bank. The vials are listed in the bank's "catalogue," so a recipient who calls to place an order is advised to choose two or three different donors to ensure that at least one will be available for purchase.

Matches are the primary source of income for agencies and banks, and the staff work hard to confirm them, but egg agencies find some donors easier to match than others. OvaCorp's donor manager, leafing through a profile she had just received, says, "I can tell when I can match a girl quick":

> Well number one, she's attractive. Number two, she has a child, which is a huge plus. I mean look [shows RA picture and profile]. And the kindest woman. She has a really good background. See, definitely it's not for the money. She makes 65 grand a year. Great height and weight. Obviously Hispanic, and I start reading a little bit about her, and she has phenomenal answers about why she wants to do this. She's given the couple total leadership, and that's wonderful. She can travel because she's in Texas. So she'd be an easy match. Young, 26, young child. There's definitely proven fertility. 5'7", 110 [pounds]. She's Caucasian enough, she's white enough to pass, but she has a nice good hue to her if you have a Hispanic couple. Educated, good family health history. Very outgoing. Easy match. Easy match.

This stream-of-consciousness perusal of a donor profile reveals the intersection of sex and gender with race and class in defining popular donors. The donor's own child attests to her body's ability to create pregnancy-producing eggs. Her relatively high salary and eloquence on the page demonstrate her altruism. And her "hue" makes her phenotypically flexible to match either Caucasian or Hispanic recipients.

If a donor is not currently available, as is the case with many of the most popular donors, then an egg recipient can "reserve" her for a future cycle. If a sperm donor's vials are "sold out" for that month, recipients can be placed on a waiting list. Sperm recipients also have the option of creating a "storage account," in which they buy multiple vials of a particular donor's sperm to guarantee its availability if they do not become pregnant during initial inseminations.

For each visit to the bank in which they produce a sample deemed acceptable based on sperm count and quality, men are paid $75 at CryoCorp and $50 at Western Sperm Bank (the latter is a nonprofit that charges less for sperm). Sperm samples that do not pass the banks' requirements are discarded, and the donor receives no compensation. Acceptable samples are usually split into several vials, which are cryogenically stored at the bank until purchased by a recipient. One of the sperm banks charges a minimal fee to register clients with the bank ($50), but sperm vials all cost the same amount of money in 2002: $215 at CryoCorp and $175 at Western Sperm Bank.

CryoCorp, one of the largest sperm banks in the country, lists 125 donors on its website and distributes approximately 2,500 vials every month. Western Sperm Bank lists thirty donors and serves just 400 recipients each year. Creative Beginnings lists more than 100 egg donors on its website catalogue and had twenty-three active donor–recipient matches in the summer of 2002. OvaCorp, one of the largest egg agencies in the country, catalogues nearly 500 donors and had more than 100 active matches that summer. Both egg agencies charge recipient clients an agency fee of $3,500 in addition to the donor's fee and her medical and legal expenses.

In direct contrast to the set amount paid to sperm donors, the final stage of confirming an egg donation match is negotiating the donor's fee. First-time donors are paid the least, around $4,000; with each additional cycle, especially if it results in a pregnancy, the fee will increase. At OvaCorp, highly educated donors command higher fees, and, due to the difficulty in maintaining a diverse pool of donors, both egg agencies often increase the fee for donors of color. If recipients are perceived as wealthy, the staff will often ask for a higher donor fee, as when an assistant mentions that "gay men, single men have a lot of money, and they think nothing of seven, eight thousand dollars."

In this stage of the process, a donor's attributes, encapsulated in the profile and extolled by staff, are used to generate income for the programs through matches, but the economic valuation of women's eggs is more intimate than that of men's sperm. Women are paid to produce eggs for a particular recipient who has agreed to a specific price for that donor's reproductive material. At the same time, staff tell recipients the "donor would love to work with you," while they inform donors that the recipients just "loved you and had to have you." Thus, egg agencies structure the exchange not only as a legalistic economic transaction but also as the beginning of a caring gift cycle, which the staff foster by expressing appreciation to the donors, on behalf of both the agency and the agency's clients.

OvaCorp's donor manager explains, "We have the largest donor database. The reason is we treat them like royalty. They are women, not genetics to us. A lot of times a couple doesn't meet them, so we want them to feel our warmth, feel the reality that we're so grateful for what they're doing for us, as well as because they're making our couple happy." Likewise, CryoCorp's marketing director notes, "We have to walk that tightrope and make sure the donors are happy, because if we don't have happy donors, then we don't have a program, and yet make sure the clients are happy as well [laughs], so we're always mindful of that." But in the sperm banks, a "happy donor," whose reproductive material is purchased by many different recipients months after he has produced it, is not predicated on being placed in the position of "loving" and "being loved by" extremely grateful "future parents."

Producing Genetic Material: Job or Gift?

In each of the four programs, staff identify the donor's responsibilities as being like those in a job; but, in the case of egg donation, it is understood to be much more meaningful than any regular job. At the information meeting for potential egg donors, the director of Creative Beginnings explains, "You get paid really well, and so you have to do all the things you do for a normal job. You have to show up at the right time and place and do what's expected of you." Her assistant adds, "If you really simplify the math, it's $4,000 for six weeks of work, and it's maybe a couple hours a day, if that. And to know that you're doing something positive and amazing in somebody's life and then getting compensated for it, you can't ask for anything better than that."

Agency staff simultaneously tell potential donors to think of donation "like a job" while also embedding the women's responsibility in the "amazing" task of helping others.

Indeed, women who attempt to make a "career" of selling eggs provoke disgust among staff, in part because they violate the altruistic framing of donation. Egg agencies generally follow ASRM guidelines limiting women to five cycles, recommendations designed to minimize health risks. However, it is not concern for the woman's health that the OvaCorp donor manager expresses in this denunciation of one such egg donor: "She's done this as a professional. It's like a career now. I said, there's something about that girl. Then I called [the director of another egg agency], and she's like 'oh yeah, why's she calling you? I won't work with her anymore, she worked with me eight times.' I said eight times?! She's got four kids. She's on the county. Yeah, I remember that name."

Sperm banks also limit the number of vials from each donor. The focus, however, is not on the donor so much as efficiently running a business without offending the sensibilities of the bank's clients. CryoCorp's CEO explains:

> There's an ongoing debate of how many vials should you collect from any one donor. If you have ten donors and collect 10,000 vials from all of them, and you have to replace one [donor because of genetic or medical issues], it's taken a hit to your business. If you wind up with 10,000 donors and only collect ten vials from every single one, you're inefficiently operating your business. You need to figure out what that sweet spot is. But then there's the emotional issue from a purchaser. If a client knows that with x thousand vials out there that there could be 100 or 200 offspring, what's that point where it just becomes emotionally too many? With my MBA hat on, we are not collecting enough vials per donor because we're not operating as efficiently as we should. With my customer relations consumer hat on, we're collecting the right number of vials because clients perceive that it's important to keep that number to something emotionally tolerable. At what point do you say that's just not someone I want to be the so-called father of my child because there's just way too many possible brothers and sisters out there?

Given the extensive investment required to screen gamete donors, one would expect programs to gather as much reproductive material as possible from each donor. Instead, women are discouraged from becoming "professional" egg donors, and men are prevented from "fathering" too many offspring.

In keeping with the focus on altruism in egg donation, the staffs of both OvaCorp and Creative Beginnings encourage recipients to send the donor a thank-you note after the egg retrieval. This behavior is not present in the sperm banks. In many cases, egg recipients also give the donor flowers, jewelry, or an additional financial gift, thereby upholding the constructed vision of egg donation as reciprocal gift giving, in which donors help recipients and recipients help donors. The director of Creative Beginnings explains that if recipients ask her "about getting flowers for the donors, I ask them not to do that because flowers get in the way. The donor's sleeping, and she's not thinking about flowers. If you want to get a gift, get a simple piece of jewelry because then the donor has something forever that she did something really nice."

In egg donation, the earlier stage of fee negotiation gives way to an understanding that donors are providing a gift, to which recipients are expected to respond with a thank-you note, and many choose to give the donor a gift of their own. In sperm donation, men are far more likely to be perceived as employees, clocking in at the sperm bank at least once a week to produce a "high-quality" sample. Indeed, this framing of donation as job leads some men to be so removed from what they are donating that when a new employee at Western Sperm Bank excitedly told a donor that a recipient had become pregnant with his samples, she said it was like "somebody hit him with this huge ball in the middle of his head. He just went blank, and he was shocked." During his next visit, the donor explained, "I hadn't really thought about the fact there were gonna be pregnancies." The donor manager describes this state of mind as "not uncommon." These gendered portrayals of selfless motherhood and distant fatherhood fit a very traditional pattern: Women donating eggs are expected to reproduce well-worn patterns of "naturally" caring, helpful femininity, guiltily hiding any interest they might have in the promise of thousands of dollars, while this same emotional labor[5] is not required of men donating sperm.

Conclusion

Neither the biological differences between women and men nor the economic law of supply and demand fully explain the medical market in genetic material. It is not just that individual women have fewer eggs than individual men have sperm, or that eggs are more difficult to extract, that results in both high prices and constant gift-talk in egg donation, but the close connection between women's reproductive bodies and cultural norms of caring motherhood. In contrast, men are much more difficult to recruit but are paid low, standardized prices because sperm donation is seen as more job than gift. As a result, both eggs and egg donors are more highly valued than sperm and sperm donors in this medical marketplace, where it is not just reproductive material but visions of middle-class American femininity and masculinity, and more to the point, motherhood and fatherhood, that are marketed and purchased. More broadly, this comparison of how different kinds of bodies are valued demonstrates that bodily commodification is not a generic social process. It can be expected to vary by sex and gender, race, and class, as economic valuations intertwine with cultural norms in specific structural contexts.

Notes

This is an abridged version of "Selling Genes, Selling Gender: Egg Agencies, Sperm Banks, and the Medical Market in Genetic Material." *American Sociological Review*, 72:3 (June 2007), pp. 319–340, edited.

1. Covington and Gibbons, 2007.
2. Becker, 2000.
3. Schover, Rothman, and Collins, 1992.
4. Chodorow, 1978; Hays, 1996.
5. Hochschild, 1983.

6 Gender Labor

Transmen, Femmes, and Collective Work of Transgression

Jane Ward

IN 2004, I TOOK a newly out bisexual woman friend of mine to a queer bar in Los Angeles. She had little experience with queer subculture, but that night at the bar she met a trans-identified guy, an FTM, and went home with him to have sex. As for myself, like many queer femmes who witnessed and supported the explosion of transgender identification among dykes in the early 2000s, I had become conversant in the politics and erotics of transgender alliance. In fact, in the eyes of my neophyte friend, my two brief relationships with FTMs made me an expert, and her mentor in all things genderqueer. The next day, as planned, she called to tell me about the previous night's events. To my surprise, she sounded ashamed and disappointed as she reported that everything had gone well until the moment when she had naively referred to her lover's cock using the word *plastic*. His instantly cold response made her feel rejected and underskilled. After recounting all of the details, she said, "Why didn't you tell me about this? Why didn't you tell me that I was supposed to treat the dildo like a *real* body part? Why didn't you teach me about transgender cock?" Regrettably, having forgotten my own queer training, I responded, "Wasn't it *obvious*?"

Yet by the end of our conversation we had clarified what we both already knew. Of course it is not obvious how to interact with queer bodies and genders, just as we do not naturally or automatically know how to engage normative genders and their accoutrements. Successfully recognizing and affirming the gender of the other—whether the normative or transgressive other—involves a significant amount of training, study, and practice—which, like all forms of work, can be very pleasurable, theatrical, and dynamic, or it can be tedious, failure ridden, and compulsory.

This chapter takes femme–FTM sexual relationships as a point of departure to consider gender itself as a form of labor or to illustrate how gender
subjectivities are constituted by various labors required of, and provided by,
intimate others. My analysis focuses on examples of work that women do in
relationships with transgendered men, specifically the work that they do to
validate and celebrate their partners' masculinity and to suppress the complexity of their own gender and sexual subjectivity in the service of this goal.
Though numerous theorists have accounted for the ways in which gender is
constructed, performed, and disciplined, such approaches have yet to fully
theorize the relational and feminized labors that reproduce gender and nurture new genders (or new gender formations) into public and private beings.
These collective labors are distinct from the repetitive and involuntary acts
that constitute the subject or that take form as unwilled labors of the *self*.[1]
In contrast, I use the term *gender labor* to describe the affective and bodily
efforts invested in *giving gender* to others or actively suspending self-focus
in the service of helping others achieve the varied forms of gender recognition they long for. Gender labor is the work of bolstering someone's gender
authenticity, but it is also the work of coproducing someone's gender irony,
transgression, or exceptionality.

The demand for gender labor is heightened where gender is most suspect,
most in need of witness, or becomes the sacred material of subcultural cele-
bration. The wave of transgender identification among dykes that occurred in
the late 1990s and early 2000s exemplifies a new gender formation made possible in part by collective efforts to nurture, witness, and celebrate those occupying an emergent and threatened gender category. In 2003, an article in the
lesbian magazine *Curve* described this mass emergence of FTM genders and
its relational effects for femme-identified lesbians and their "sense of self":

> Dykes are coming out in droves as transgendered, whether as "TG butches,"
> "bigendered," "FTMs," or everything in between. There is a lot of support for
> female born boys, but as the community is learning, partners of people in
> transition—particularly femme-identified lesbians—often get left in the dust
> when it comes to dealing with their own gender and sense of self.[2]

Drawing on tensions between an exceptionalized gender and one "left in the
dust," this chapter explores gender as a relation between people, one characterized not only by countless gestures that are interactively accomplished[3] and
performatively reiterated[4] but also by tedious acts of emotional, physical, and

sexual "support" that are undertaken to coproduce the gender coherence and/ or transgression of others.

Gender as Labor

My first aim here is to consider the relational, intimate, and sexual labor that has produced transgender subjectivity and to show how this labor is undertaken by people who fall both within and outside of the boundaries of transgenderism. Touching on the significance of trans relationality, Judith Halberstam contends in *A Queer Time and Place* that "before we dismiss [transgenderism] as faddish, we should know what kind of work it does, whom it describes, and whom it validates. . . . Transgender may indeed be a term of relationality; it describes not simply an identity, but a relation between people, within a community, or within intimate bonds."[5] Yet there has been very limited analysis of what could be called "transgender relationships," and that which has been written has described partners of trans people (who are not themselves trans-identified) in romantic terms, as people with "compassion and decency" who, in the case of partnership with FTMs, "find it within their hearts to acknowledge [transmen] as men and go on."[6]

Notably, Susan Stryker and Stephen Whittle's 720-page anthology, *The Transgender Studies Reader,* gives virtually no attention to the intimate relations of transgender world/home-making (e.g., the intimate labor of the home, the grocery store, and the bedroom) or the "wifely" and/or maternal care that often keeps genders, and masculinity in particular, in motion.[7] Here I place labor at the center of my analysis of femme–FTM relationships to focus attention not only on the emotional labors that constitute these relations (for example, compassion, nurturing, witnessing) but also on the physical and feminized labors that contribute to the production of queer (and normative) genders (for example, cooking, sexual services, nursing care, administering gender technology/hormones, dressing/chest-binding).

My second aim is to reveal the applications of linking "gender" and "labor" not only for queer analyses but also for understanding the collective work that produces masculinities and femininities in all of their various iterations. Indeed, examples of gender labor abound. Women friends, across the lines of race and class, rehearse for one another the self-effacing scripts associated with female validation ("I wish I had your body" or "no, you don't look fat, but I do"). Women of color come home from work and care for men of color, helping to ease their partners' presumably greater racial burden.[8] Femme dykes labor to treat butches and FTMs like "real" men; and butches and FTMs labor to treat femmes (and sometimes all women) like queens. That these efforts are often "labors of love" enacted for and by people who are denied gender validation within mainstream culture (women, men of color, queers) must not mask the ways in which gender is reproduced through routinized forms of care work. As I will show, these routine efforts—akin to the emotional labor enacted by service workers and described by Arlie Hochschild—may, and often do, result in the recurring misrecognition or diminishment of the laborer. As I demonstrate in the following discussion, all genders demand work, and therefore all people both give and require gender labor. However, some genders, principally those that are masculine and especially those that intersect with other forms of power (such as wealth and whiteness), make their demands less visible and more legitimate or deliver them with more coercive force. Gender labor, like other forms of caring, weighs down most heavily on feminine subjects, the people for whom "labors of love" are naturalized, expected, or forced.[9]

To the extent that gender is always a shortcoming or never-achieved ideal, I want to suggest that gender is always already bound up with the search for people and things that will offer relief, compensate for failure, enhance dignity, and create moments of realness. In this sense, gender labor is the act of giving gender to others in an attempt to fulfill these needs, thereby improving the recipient's capacity and potential to perform. Though these acts of giving, like care work in general, are performed by people across the spectrum of feminine and masculine genders, feminine subjects (straight women, feminine lesbians, transwomen, feminine gay men, faggy boys/bois, and so on) are held particularly responsible for the work of gendering. The "duties" that comprise gender labor—witnessing, nurturing, validating, fulfilling, authenticating, special knowing, and secret keeping—have long been relegated to the sphere of female work[10] and are often "diverted" to women of color by upper-class white women who have the means to opt out of compulsory caring.[11]

That both normative and transgressive genders are made possible by feminized labor has important implications for queer theory, in particular, which has often aligned the feminine with the nonqueer, or the homonormative.[12] Queer studies has embraced those utopic "ways of life" made most possible or necessary for masculine subjects—mobility, independence, extended identification with youth culture, grungy/alternative modes of consumption, risk taking—and disavowed those ways of life made most possible or necessary for feminine subjects—reproductivity, caretaking, shopping, homemaking, and safety making.[13] In contrast, to investigate gender labor is to reconnect these two seemingly distinct cultural and productive spheres; it is to see the ways that the construction of the former (the queer) has depended on the latter (the feminine)—even, and especially, for assistance in enhancing its capacity to reject the feminine on which it depends.

Femme Labor: Introducing the Study

This project began in 2004 as an interview-based study of FTMs' relationships with queer women, primarily women who identify as femme. In the course of these interviews, several FTMs spoke about having a hope or expectation that their partners would have sex, speak, dress, and think about gender and gender politics in ways that would bolster their masculinity. Conversely, femme interview participants described their relationships with FTMs as sites of frequent confusion, resentment, and hard work. It was during these interviews that I first began to think about gender labor, but I was dissatisfied with interviews as my only source for understanding these dynamics, and I expanded the project to include related forms of cultural production. Hence, the current project is based on transdisciplinary analysis of four sources: (1) a set of interviews I conducted in 2004 with thirteen FTMs and eight femmes living in Los Angeles, San Francisco, Seattle, or New York;[14] (2) four documentaries addressing FTM or genderqueer identities, spanning from 1994 to 2005 (*Shinjuku Boys*; *Mind If I Call You Sir?*; *Boy I Am*; and *The Aggressives*;—see bibliography); (3) two websites in which participants discuss trans/femme issues (transensualfemme.com and femme.com); and (4) FTM-related articles from two lesbian magazines (*On Our Backs* and *Curve*).[15]

My analysis focuses on two forms of gender labor that femme partners do to coproduce trans masculinity: the labor of being "the girl" and the labor of forgetting. These labors are in many ways particular to the temporal, regional, and subcultural context of trans/queer relationships in major cities of the United States in the mid-2000s; however, as I will illustrate, both also serve as examples of general mechanisms used to produce gender coherence for others.

The Labor of Being "the Girl"

In FTM identity narratives, trans masculinity has frequently been described as the experience of not being, or not wanting to be, a girl. As has been explored in other research on FTMs,[16] "not wanting to be a girl" speaks to an awareness, often beginning in childhood, of a gendered self and body that does not fit social, cultural, and familial expectations associated with girl-hood: "I didn't want to wear dresses," "I always felt more like a boy," "I hated my breasts," and so on. Yet beyond not wanting to be *a* girl, many FTM (and butch) identity narratives also describe the experience of not wanting to be *the* girl in a particular relational context, often during sex. In one study, for example, "Dick," a white FTM, explains why his transition led to a new sexual interest in men by stating, "what I figured out a lot later was that it wasn't about not wanting to be with a guy; it was about not wanting to be the girl."[17]

Similarly, avoidance of being the girl—and reference to women who, in contrast, embrace being the girl—is a recurring theme in the 2004 documentary *Mind If I Call You Sir? A Video Documentary on Latina Butches and Latino FTMs*. The film centers on butches and FTMs from the San Francisco area who are filmed discussing the contours of their masculinity while sitting around a table in an officelike setting. Scenes from this discussion are interspersed with more in-depth footage of individuals recounting stories of gender dysphoria, outsiderness, and/or transition and, in one case, an interview with a femme who is filmed preparing food in a kitchen while speaking about her partner's transition. During the discussion between butches and FTMs, Yosenio, a Latino FTM, tells the group that he is hesitant to "bottom" to his sexual partner because, as he states, "then I'll be a girl." Such narratives, which link "bottoming" with femininity, define girlhood, in part, by a comfort with sexual submission and lack of sexual control. Other scenes from the film illustrate that being a/the girl refers to more than sexual receptivity or submission (though sexual receptivity remains a central theme). In one scene, Diane, a Latina butch, describes her early awareness of her masculinity by telling the story of her difference from other Chicana political activists with whom she had worked. These women, Diane implies, were satisfied with their ancillary role in the Chicano movement:

> In my soul, I knew I was different. I wasn't like the rest of the Chicanas in the movement. . . . I was more man. I wanted to hang out with the men. I wanted to talk politics with the men. I didn't want to be in the kitchen. I didn't want to be stuffing envelopes. . . . So I was different.

Similarly, Yosenio, an FTM, explains his difference from women:

> I was always taught, women are less than. You don't want to be a woman . . . the poor lot in life of women. They struggle, and they struggle, and they struggle.

... And it's like, I don't want to be like that. But all the people that I gravitated to were women, all the people that I felt the closest to were women, and all the people that I always wanted to be around were women. And all the people who ultimately gave me the love to survive all the crap I went through as a child were women. And so it was a push me, pull you thing. I always want to be around you, but I don't ever want to be like you.

Although butches and FTMs are often theorized as stand-alone figures who are not reliant on femmes (or the feminine other) for public recognition, such accounts construct trans and butch masculinity by citing the existence of a satisfied feminine other, or a female subject who may be queer but is different from butches and FTMs in that she is happy to occupy the role of the girl. Diane describes her butch masculinity through an account of her disidentification not only with the costume of femininity but with the women she presumes were happy in the kitchen, happy stuffing envelopes, happy being barred from political talk. Yosenio describes disidentification not only with femininity but also with women's "struggle" and with being "less than." He says, in a kind of address to the women who nurtured his own escape from girlhood: "I always want to be around you, but I don't ever want to be like you." In Diane and Yosenio's narratives, butch and FTM subjectivities are not only those that reject feminine appearances or embodiment; they are also those that cannot tolerate the sexism directed at them.

The film highlights the ways in which the coherence of butch and FTM identity narratives *depends* on the existence of a feminine subject who experiences female embodiment, sexual submission, and sexism as more natural or trouble free than the butch/trans subject. My interest here is the way this reliance on the satisfied feminine other—whether as an abstraction ("somewhere out there, other women like being girls") or specified within a relationship ("my girlfriend loves being a girl")—has produced a demand for the labor of *becoming* this satisfied girl. Needless to say, many butches and FTMs do not have relationships with femmes (or feminine people, for that matter); however, the figure of the girl nonetheless remains an important element of the narrative of trans and butch difference. In cases in which FTMs do have femme partners, the interviews I conducted suggest that the latter are often compelled to embody this girl subjectivity or to work to enhance their own femininity and its apparent seamlessness to reinforce the masculinity of their partners. Keaton, a thirty-two-year-old white FTM, told me:

[I think some transguys] want their girlfriend or their partner, if they're dating a woman, to reemphasize their masculinity. These two FTMs [I know]
who are both dating women . . . apparently had both asked their girlfriends
to grow their hair out long since their transitions . . . And [my girlfriend] has
long hair, so they asked her if I did the same thing, and she's like, "no, and if
he did, I'd cut it all off."

Jimmy, a forty-year-old Asian American FTM, told me about a conflict that he
and his femme-identified partner had with one of their FTM friends. He said:

We had a friend who was . . . very warm and loving and wonderful in a lot
of ways but has this very clear sense of what he feels he needs to be as a man,
as an FTM person, and has really imposed his sense of the world on us as a
couple. . . . And I think he saw my wife as, "OK, you're the female, you need to
be the one who's doing clearly feminine tasks in support of your man." . . . He
really wanted to disregard her and put her in her place, and like snap at her or
whatever, and disrespect her.

Femmes also told similar stories about being compelled to occupy the
position of the girl so as to bolster trans masculinity. For example, Melinda,
a thirty-seven-year-old white femme, talked about her experience meeting
transmen online (through dating websites). She said:

I heard from three transguys in a row who all made comments about liking
my photographs, and specifically aspects of my appearance that were super
feminine. And they all said "I want to learn more about you" and followed up
. . . with some variation of "tell me why trans-people do it for you" and in one
case "tell me why trans-people are better for you, hotter for you than anybody
else on the planet." That was a very explicit solicitation for my femininity to
prop up their masculinity or validate it in some way, and it was really revolt-
ing, and at that point I decided, "no trans-people, no trans-men."

Similarly, another femme named Jennifer told me:

In my relationships with people who are trans-identified, there's been less
room for the politics around *my* gender. . . . They really wanted my identity
to be femme, and they really wanted the person they were with to help bolster
their own gender.

In femme–FTM relationships, being the girl produces scenes and intimate spaces in which FTMs become more clearly, or more easefully, "the boy"

or "the man." In the documentaries *Mind if I Call You Sir?* and *Boy I Am*, femmes are shown engaged in very material forms of care work, such as binding their partners' chests and cooking in the kitchen. In *Shinjuku Boys* and *The Aggressives*, femmes are shown in constant pursuit of intimacy—calling, clinging, asking questions, hoping for more—while butches and FTMs appear to forge their most intimate or long-term relationships with one another, if at all. In other cases, femmes work to facilitate their partners' ability to experience a lost boyhood or male adolescence, often through a synthesis of sexual exploration and maternal nurturing. A femme writing on a website called transensualfemme.com explains the femme/FTM "dynamic" by invoking the image of an erotic mommy figure who gently guides a young boy through his first sexual experiences:

> We are the pioneers. We are discovering what a femme trans-guy dynamic means. Thus far, for me it has mostly felt like a mothering role. In many ways, I'm acknowledging, encouraging, fulfilling and validating my partner's adolescent urges. I'm nurturing his maleness. I'm sexually initiating him, if you will. I feel older than him in many ways. I feel like the experienced one in bed. It is a discovery process . . . how much can he take? What does he want? Who is he? How does his body react now? How does his mind work? And it is also a discovery for me . . . Who am I with him? What can I expect from him? What do I want?

Curve magazine has described transensualfemme.com as a website for "partners of people in transition—particularly femme-identified lesbians—[who] often get left in the dust when it comes to dealing with their own gender and sense of self."[18] Yet most comments on transensualfemme.com suggest that the site provides an online community designed precisely for femmes to trade information about caring for FTM partners sexually, physically, and emotionally and to redefine themselves in relation to this work. Akin to the 1970s spate of self-help books designed to teach straight women how to probe the male psyche—how to catch him, understand him, care for him, and keep him—femmes avoid being left in the dust by becoming the "pioneers" of masculine territories.

Undoubtedly there are cases in which being the girl is a reflection of femmes' own sense of comfortable alignment with the conventions of femininity (with being in the kitchen, having long hair, and the like). Yet the above narratives also indicate that being the girl is a form of intimate labor that is undertaken to produce the masculinity of the other and to keep the social, emotional, and erotic structure of femme–FTM relationships intact. Femme labor not only involves embodying feminine contrast (if I'm the girl, then you are the boy) but also discovering, acknowledging, encouraging, fulfilling, validating, nurturing, and initiating masculine complexity. Like other forms of intimate and sexualized labor, femmes *give gender* to FTMs through efforts that augment masculine authenticity, offer moments of realness, and compensate for gendered shortcomings.

The Labor of Forgetting

Several of the FTMs interviewed for this project explained that new sexual relationships with femmes go through a kind of testing phase in which FTMs assess whether or not they can trust their new partner to interact with them, and their bodies, as male. In some cases, this involves developing trust that the femme partner has forgotten, or does not see, signs of femaleness. For example, several participants explained that they are most comfortable in relationships with women who can demonstrate that they have forgotten their partners' past femaleness and are not preoccupied with being in a "transgender relationship," even though their relationships require particular kinds of work and expectations related to trans identity. Some participants explained that they teach femme partners to learn a new trans vocabulary of the body, including ways of talking about sex, talking about the past, gender code switching when FTMs are not out to family or co-workers, and a new gendered division of labor (such as asking femmes to always buy the tampons and place them in the bathroom but never speak about them). Forgetting, in this case, is not the opposite of having knowledge but is a new kind of gendered knowing that includes a new vocabulary and a new set of gendered practices.[19] These relations of forgetting and knowing are marked by many of the elements Zelizer attributes to intimate labor: trust, privacy, secret knowledge, special access, and shared memories.[20]

For some FTMs, straight women and "high-femmes" play a central role in erasing femininity and offering masculine realness, primarily through their participation in heteronormative sex. Gaish, who is an *onnabe* in the Japanese documentary about FTM and genderqueer escorts, *Shinjuku Boys* (1995), describes sex with women clients this way:

> When it comes to doing it, it's not because it's fun . . . It's probably nice for her, but for me, to be honest, I just get worn out. The first time I do it with a

woman, it's a mental thing. If this girl is letting me do this, then I've fooled her. That's what I feel when I'm doing it. If she didn't see me in that way, she wouldn't do it. An ordinary girl. If she does it with me, and doesn't think anything of it, then I know she's thinking of me as the man and she's the girl. In other words, she has accepted me as a man, and I feel relieved.

When it is believed that a given woman has no sexual desire for femininity, her sexual receptivity becomes a valuable instrument for confirming that the FTM body is not a female body. Especially in the interaction between receptive femininity and stone masculinity, her sexual contribution is less about physical pleasure and more about the affective pleasure of being seen as male.

The corollary of the labor of forgetting femaleness is the labor of establishing trust that femmes see, know, and understand trans masculinity and can deploy and communicate this understanding through particular sex acts. Countless sex columns in queer magazines and websites now instruct readers on how to have sex with the trans or genderqueer body ("how to fuck a boi," "how to suck cock," "mommy/boy role-play," and the like). These advice columns often stress the importance of relating to trans masculinity as authentic, as well as the importance of ensuring that one's sex cannot be mistaken for lesbian feminist sex (circa 1970), which is typically represented as boring, unsexy, power-neutral, or passé. For example, in the magazine *On Our Backs: The Best of Lesbian Sex*, Rachel Venning instructs readers about "how to suck cock" by stating: "Get Real: treat the dildo like a real penis—focus on the things that feel good to bio men; stroke the vein along the bottom, tongue the slit, gently tickle the balls."[21] Femmes can learn how to affirm the gender identity of FTM partners not simply by forgetting or deemphasizing their partners' past femaleness but also by demonstrating knowledge of male physiology and desire. In some cases, interview participants shared stories of successful male recognition, such as R. J., a forty-two-year-old African American FTM:

My girlfriend tells me, "You're not a lesbian. . . . When I talk to you there's no woman there. . . . You're just male, you know. I don't relate to you like I've related to butch lesbians." She says, "I don't relate to you the same way. Nothing's the same." So I feel very lucky in that sense.

Yet, in other cases, femmes described the trans–femme erotic script as a site of negotiation, confusion, and hard work, one that is subject to an unspoken and often changing set of rules, particularly with respect to sex. Bridgette, one twenty-six-year-old white femme dating an FTM in Los Angeles, told me:

The question of breasts and what I'm allowed to do to them has always felt very confusing to me. . . . I can remember moments where every so often [one of my partners] would sort of be like, "hey, I have boobs too" and I would be like "oh, right, right, right," but I think there was this way that I had been given other messages . . . And also penetration to varying degrees was sort of confusing to me. I remember at some point [one of my butch partners] was like "you know how to fuck me the way a butch needs to be fucked." So I was like "What does that mean?" . . . And she couldn't tell me. She was like, "I don't know. You just do."

My review of femme websites indicated that femmes are keenly aware that not seeing femaleness and understanding maleness are central aspects of their role in the trans–femme erotic script. Among the women who post on transensualfemme.com and femme.com, successful femininity is often linked to a seemingly effortless or natural ability to see only her partner's maleness. As one woman states on femme.com:

No one ever "trained" me on how to understand their maleness. I just knew. I relate to my butch's female body as if it is male. In fact, thinking of or relating to a TG [transgender] butch as if he were female would be utterly confusing to me. I absolutely see TG butches as guys. It is difficult to express, yet it is extremely profound to me . . . very deep . . . deeper than words.

Many "transensual femmes" express their innate desire for trans masculinity in somewhat mystical terms that position this expression of desire outside of its social and political context. Such accounts obscure the ways in which transensual femininity, like other forms of gender labor, is scripted, routinized, and hierarchical (and learned through advice columns, SOFFA [Significant Others, Families, Friends and Allies] groups, and other authoritative sources); the more you can "automatically" see maleness and forget femaleness, often the more desirable and valuable you are as a transensual femme.

For some femmes who are in relationships with FTMs both before and after their transition, the labor of forgetting can also involve grief containment, or hiding one's internal mourning process, especially in communities in which grieving the loss of the wrongly gendered body is considered unsupportive or apolitical. For instance, a scene in *Mind If I Call You Sir?* focuses on Mariah, who speaks to the camera about the loss of her long-term partner Prado's pretransition self, Yvette:

A couple of weeks ago I had three really sad days out of nowhere. I had three days of mourning for Yvette. The voice difference is remarkable, and so sometimes I miss her voice. And that's actually how it happened. We were watching this old film [of Yvette]. Just hearing her voice and remembering this person, who's no longer here . . . I felt like I had this chance to recognize that somebody I loved was no longer alive. She's not in my life anymore. So I got sad about it. Oh, I got sad right now (Mariah then appears to cry on camera).

According to Jimmy, an Asian American FTM interviewed for this study, *Mind If I Call You Sir?* received criticism from FTM audiences in San Francisco who were uncomfortable with the scene in which Mariah is visibly sad about aspects of Prado's transition and in which she refers to Prado's past using female pronouns. In this example, Mariah's experience of loss was rendered inappropriate or unintelligible to some FTM viewers of the film, especially given the trans-celebratory context in which the film was shown. Yet silencing such forms of mourning—or containing them within the private and depoliticized sphere of support groups and individual therapy—not only reinforces the individualism embedded in many trans discourses, it also obscures the grief and loss necessitated by gender itself. Gender, as the embrace of some possibilities and the denial of others, arguably requires grief. In sum, the labor of forgetting not only entails learning to recognize maleness in the place of femaleness; it also involves the labor of grief management, containment, and internalization.

Conclusion

Focusing on gender labor draws attention to the collective work that produces and sustains gender. Though we already know that genders exist inside an interdependent gender system, little attention has been given to the laborious quality of reproducing other people's genders in daily life, and we remain without a clear mapping of the training, skills, duties, and specific efforts that various genders require. Here I have shown that, in many cases, FTM identities remain reliant on the labors of femininity that nurture and witness them, both within and outside of intimate sexual relations. It is not simply that femmes provide support to transmen (and butches); they also reproduce a trans/not-trans binary by training to be "the girl" in new and particular ways, many of which they are compelled to experience as easy and natural. In some cases, femmes learn to actively forget their partner's differently gendered past, to study up on male desire and male physiology, and to master a new set of sexual practices and erotic scripts. In sum, femme labor describes not only the emotional, physical, and sexual work of reproducing FTM subjectivity; it also refers to the work of adjusting one's own gendered self in relation to this process—such as the work of transitioning from "femme" to "transensual femme."

While I have focused on the gender labors femmes do to produce trans masculinity, a similar project could have explored the opposite relationship, as femininity requires very particular labors of masculinity to sustain it. However, I have attempted to show the ways in which many elements of gender labor—offering sexual validation, coconstructing realness, forgetting and grieving other possibilities, maternal nurturing, keeping one's complexity to oneself—mirror the practices of intimate labor generally assigned to women. This confluence reveals the ways in which gender itself takes form through feminized acts of service done for others, often at the expense of the laborer's own recognition, dignity, or assistance with gendered shortcomings. To the extent that these labors are performed within intimate spheres and through gestures of bodily, emotional, and sexual care, they are embedded in the historical and political-economic structures of women's work. Women do a disproportionate amount of the commercial care and sex work in the United States, but they are also held responsible—sometimes through legal and other structural channels—for relationship-based forms of caring[22] and relationship-based "sex work."[23] Though I have not undertaken a comparative study that could demonstrate the ways in which gender labor weighs down most heavily on feminine subjects, I have attempted to underscore the ways in which all genders may be bound up in intimate dependencies and feminized relations of nurture, giving, and collectivity.

Notes

Material in this chapter has been reproduced by permission of SAGE Publications Ltd., London, Los Angeles, New Delhi, Singapore, and Washington DC, from "Gender Labor: Transmen, Femmes, and Collective Work of Transgression," Jane Ward, in *Sexualities*, August, 2010 (Vol. 13, no. 2).

1. Butler, 1997; 2006.
2. Szymanski, 2003: 14.
3. West and Zimmerman, 1987.
4. Butler, 2006.
5. Halberstam, 2005: 49.
6. Devor, 1997: 445–446.
7. Stryker and Whittle, 2006.

8. Thanks to Raka Ray for offering this example and citing the PBS documentary *Clarence Thomas and Anita Hill: Public Hearings, Private Pain* as one instance.

9. Glenn, 2010.

10. Hochschild, 1983.

11. Chang, 1994; Romero, 1992; Wong, 1994.

12. In the 1990s, some trans activists and theorists described themselves as "gender outlaws" (Bornstein, 1994) and "gender warriors" (Feinberg, 1997) or rebels for whom genderqueerness came into being in spite of, rather than in productive relation to, the actions of more normatively gendered others. In these narratives, the invisibility of behind-the-scenes "gender supporters"—often women friends, partners, and caretakers—resonated with a broader tendency within queer studies to sidestep the intimate dependencies and feminized forms of care that sustain queer transgression. Though femme scholars responded with their own claims to gender dysphoria and queer marginality (Hollibough, 2002), even these critiques built on the theme of *self*-making, thereby drawing little attention to the ways in which queer forms of "undoing" and fluidity remain reliant on the normative genders and feminized forms of care work that queer politics rejects. Currently, much of queer studies continues to emphasize the project of defiant self-making. Queer subjects reproduce themselves through refusal of normative consumer and reproductive practices (Duggan, 2004), disidentificatory engagements with popular culture (Munoz, 1999), subcultural production and identification (Halberstam, 2005), and tragic interiorities (Love, 2007). Queer theorists explain that these actions and states of being are called into existence by the structural and cultural forces that forcefully align queer subjects with failure, loss, or death (Edelman, 2004), yet few describe how queerness takes form in and through the microsphere of relationality—particularly the feminized realms of caring and witnessing that literally nurture gender subjectivities into possibility and through the channels of loss and suffering.

13. See Halberstam, 2005: 1–2.

14. Interviews were typically two hours in length and covered topics including identity and transition; political and social affiliations; feelings about body, sex, and relationships; and connections between femme and transgender experiences and politics. Nine of the thirteen FTM interview participants were white, two were African American, and one was Latino, and one was Asian American; and they ranged in age from twenty-five to forty-two years old. The majority had begun taking testosterone; however, hormone therapy was more common among white participants than participants of color (none of the FTMs of color were taking testosterone at the time of the study). Five of the eight femme participants were white, two were Latina, and one was African American, and they ranged in age from twenty-three to forty. I used a snowball sample to identify interview participants by starting with my own social networks as a queer femme who was, during the study, in a long-term relationship with an FTM.

15. All interview participants for this research have been given pseudonyms to protect their confidentiality, and each signed a consent form agreeing to the recording, transcription, and publication of the interviews. Comments taken from public websites are cited by website only and without names or other identifying information, whereas subjects in nationally distributed documentaries have been identified by the names they use in the films.

16. Devor, 1997; Dozier, 2005.

17. Dozier, 2005: 312.

18. Szymanski, 2003: 14.

19. Halberstam, 2006.

20. Zelizer, 2007.

21. Venning, 2002.

22. Glenn, 2010.

23. Cacchioni, 2007.

Creating Intimate Boundaries
Culture and Social Relations

THE CHAPTERS IN THIS PART examine the intimate relations that workers—particularly nannies, elder care providers, and sex workers—maintain with their customers and employers. More specifically, these chapters illustrate the cultural and social dynamics of their relationships at work. None of these relations occur in a vacuum; they instead form in the contexts of particular cultural and social regimes. As Seemin Qayum and Raka Ray astutely illustrate in their chapter, the social experience of child care, for instance, would have profoundly different meanings in the cultural geography of Kolkota, where it would be embedded in its long history of a "culture of servitude" based in feudalism, and in the advanced capitalist space of New York City, where the ethos of liberalism translates to a norm of a modern but progressive contractual relationship between domestic workers and their employers. Building from Qayum and Ray, we assert in this part that the social meanings of the economic exchange of child care, elder care, and sex work form in the context of particular cultural and social regimes. The chapters in this part unravel these regimes so as to make sense of the social experience of intimate labor. Moreover, we illustrate how intimate laborers understand their social relations with employers and clients, make meaning of these relations, and accordingly construct intimate boundaries that would define economic transactions. In other words, workers perform what Viviana Zelizer defines as "relational work," creating social ties and relegating particular economic transactions as appropriate to that tie.[1]

The chapters in this part reject the notion that mixing intimate personal ties with economic transactions would contaminate and corrupt intimacy, while tainting the efficiency of commercial activities. For feminists who condemn the purchase of sex and for Marxists wary of capitalist alienation, such monetarization stands for the ultimate corrosion of society.[2] Such commentators often look at the reorganization of the family in late capitalism and lament the heightened commercialization of intimate life as reflected, for instance, in the decline of "family time" between parents and children.[3] Zelizer gives this view a history:

> Since the nineteenth century social analysts have repeatedly assumed that the social world organizes around competing, incompatible principles: Gemeinschaft and Gesellschaft, ascription and achievement, sentiment and rationality, solidarity and self-interest. Their mixing, goes the theory, contaminates both; invasion of the sentimental world by instrumental rationality desiccates that world, while introduction of sentiment into rational transactions produces inefficiency, favoritism, cronyism, and other forms of corruption.[4]

Dismissing this "hostile worlds view," the chapters in this part instead show how the commercialization of intimate activities is a more complex process that cannot be reduced to a simple exchange of money and intimacy.[5] The authors join with feminist economists who argue that the movement of money into the traditional private realm such as elder care is only one dimension in a complex relationship involving emotional exchanges of trust, affection, loyalty, and appreciation.[6] Likewise, Zelizer has repeatedly illustrated how economic transactions and intimate relations constantly mingle through "circuits of commerce" that bind and interpersonally tie individuals through transactions and transfers of goods and services.[7]

These chapters take to heart Zelizer's assertion that the social meanings of economic change shift according to their relational context; they thus question the notion that the commercialization of intimacy would represent a loss of moral fiber in society and the corrosion of identity and relations. Underlying the discussion of each of the chapters is the question of how the intersections of sentiment and rationality shape the work experience and process of intimate labor in care, domestic, and sex work. Do these intersections lead to the extraction of unpaid labor or a more complex range of relational dynamics? Qayam and Ray on domestic work and María de la Luz Ibarra on elder care work explore ways that the emotional ties between employers and employees blur the boundaries between work and family. Together these two chapters establish that the intersections of love and money do not simply result in the extraction of unpaid labor but result in the complex negotiations of employer and employee that could result in feelings of betrayal, abuse, or deep satisfaction. Likewise, the chapters on sex work by Rhacel Salazar Parreñas, Elizabeth Bernstein, and Kimberly Hoang explore the interpenetration of market forces and intimate life, illustrating how "the purchase of intimacy" does not lead to the blurring of the identity of sex workers as workers. But neither do they find their sentiments merely reduced to market demands.

This part begins with Qayum and Ray's ethnographically rich description of the relational dynamics between domestic workers and employers in late capitalism. They demonstrate how such relations travel across time and space. They ask whether employer desires for a "culture of servitude" based on a liberal capitalist notion of mutual benefit are possible. For domestic work to fit liberal capitalist tenets of mutual benefit, employers must situate employer–employee relations in what Qayum and Ray describe as a "rhetoric of love" based on friendship, affection, and loyalty. Employers negotiate the blurring of the public and private divide in domestic work with claims of friendship. Yet, as Qayum and Ray poignantly show, friendship does not erase servitude as the inherent basis of the relationship. As such, employee demands for equality are usually seen as a personal affront, thus limiting the rights of domestic workers even among the most well-intentioned employers.

Further complicating our discussion on the intersections of "love" and "money" or "friendship" and "labor" in employer–employee relations, de la Luz Ibarra introduces the concept of "deep alliance" to describe the cultural obligations and moral imperatives that define the feelings and attitudes of caregivers toward elderly wards. The personalism described and critiqued in the literature on domestic work as blurring the boundaries between work and family, Ibarra reminds us, comes not only from the sentiments of employers but also from the desires of elder caregivers to gain meaningful relationships in the workplace.[8] Elder care workers refuse to reduce their relationship with their wards to a contractual exchange void of social ties based on a common humanity.

Again questioning the assertion that intimacy and commerce would lead to moral contamination, Parreñas looks at the construction of morality among hostesses, meaning workers who provide flirtation to customers, in Tokyo's nightlife industry and describes their moral views on commercial sex. According to Parreñas, hostesses include moral conservatives (those who view paid sex as immoral), moral rationalists (those who morally accept paid sex), and lastly moral in-betweeners (those who morally reject the direct purchase of sex but accept its indirect purchase). The maintenance of a wide range of moral views among hostesses questions the assertion that the commercialization of intimacy would lead to moral degeneration. Illustrating the multiple kinds of relations that hostesses maintain with customers, Parreñas shows that the meaning of the commercial exchange of sex and money in hostess work changes not only according to each moral grouping of hostesses but also based on the process of the exchange, which hostesses determine depending on their social tie with the customer.

Also questioning the reduction of sex work to a commercial exchange void of social relations, Bernstein introduces the concept of "bounded authenticity," meaning the "sale and purchase of authentic emotional and physical connection" to describe an emergent paradigm of sex work in postindustrial societies. The rapid increase in the pace of life as well as the greater temporal demands of work have led to the need for not only physical but also emotional contact for an increasing number of professionals. Bernstein illustrates this cultural shift in the meaning of sex work, situating her discussion of the cultural construction of commercial sex in the structures that shape the exchange without reducing it to its structural determination. The need for bounded authenticity is best illustrated by the demand for the "girlfriend experience" by corporate professionals who negotiate the isolation that they are subjected to by work with the purchase of not just sex but intimacy. Bernstein is careful to point out that the interpenetration of intimacy and commerce in the selling of emotions by sex workers does not threaten the identity of the worker as it is reified by the attachment of a monetary fee.

Lastly, Kimberly Hoang builds on the generative work of Bernstein to examine the use of emotional labor by sex workers in Vietnam. Supporting Bernstein's assertion that emotions cannot be disentangled from sex work, Hoang traces the emotional labor attached to sex-for-money exchanges across three tiers of the city's sexual economy. Hoang questions the mainstream view that sex work is void of relational ties, adding to the work of Bernstein that even working-class sex workers who do not cultivate durable social relations with their clients, but only engage in fleeting sexual encounters, also do emotional labor. Her ethnographic work in Ho Chi Minh City illustrates that these workers do what she calls "repressive emotional labor," a job that requires them to hide their true feelings of disgust and discomfort toward their customers. Although geographical location within the city, the racial and ethnic background of the customer, and the fees the sex worker charges determine where the labor fits on the urban sexscape,[9] and while socioeconomic class may distinguish the degree and type of emotional work involved, *all* of her workers engaged in a form of relational work with clients. Her findings deepen the concept of intimate labor and challenge researchers to look for emotional as well as bodily and economic connection in other places.

Each of the chapters in this part illustrates the blurring of the division between public and private spheres in the commercialization of intimacy. At the same time, they establish that this blurring does not threaten the identity of the worker. Instead, workers are able to maintain their identities as workers in intimate encounters, intimate relationships, and intimate settings. Lastly, none of the chapters in this part reduces the relations that intimate laborers form at work to be "nothing but" an economic exchange.[10] Instead, the rich ethnography in all these chapters shows groups of workers struggling to negotiate their social relations with their customers and employers: Whether nannies or sex workers, these women refuse to disentangle their relations at work from the recognition of their mutual humanity, friendship, and social ties with both clients and employers.

Notes

1. Zelizer, 2005: 35.
2. Farley, 2004; Veblen, 1994.
3. Schor, 1992; Hochschild, 2003.
4. Zelizer, 2005: 289.
5. Zelizer, 2005: 20–26.
6. Folbre and Nelson, 2000.
7. Zelizer, 2000; 2005.
8. Romero, 1992.
9. Brennan, 2004.
10. Zelizer, 2005: 29–32.

Traveling Cultures of Servitude

Loyalty and Betrayal in New York and Kolkata

Seemin Qayum and Raka Ray

MUCH OF THE RECENT ATTENTION devoted to the institution of paid domestic work in the contemporary United States highlights the racial and ethnic divide between employer and employee—the former almost always white, privileged, and upper-middle class; and the latter, Latina, Caribbean, Asian, and to a much lesser extent African American (a historical decline that merits fuller scrutiny). Employers who are people of color rarely figure in the academic and popular literature on U.S. domestic servitude.[1]

While acknowledging the structuring force of class and gender, many scholars have invoked race, ethnicity, national origin, and immigration to explain the prevalence of paid female domestic labor and the gross distinctions of power, status, and autonomy in the employer-domestic worker nexus, as well as instances of deplorable working conditions and abuse.[2] As Mary Romero asserts in considering the history of the United States, "[W]e find the proliferation of master–servant relationships in which race, ethnicity, and gender replace class as immutable social structures dictating a person's place in the hierarchy," noting that for white domestics the occupation served as a bridge to upward mobility, whereas for women of color, domestic work rapidly became an "occupational ghetto."[3] Undeniably, existing race, citizenship, and gender inequalities explain which groups typically perform paid domestic work in any given historical moment, as well as their different trajectories.

Yet to argue that the inequalities that produce and are reproduced by the institution of domestic servitude are attributable primarily to racial hierarchies and citizenship status involves, we suggest, a certain misrecognition. Other scholars, such as Ruth Milkman and her colleagues, have given primacy to class and class inequalities in accounting for the "macrosociology" of paid domestic labor, while affirming the significance of race/ethnicity, gender, and citizenship in its "microsociology."[4] In fact, we suggest, the employer–domestic servant nexus is profoundly racialized to *substantiate* the inherent relation of domination/subordination.[5]

Even as the form of domestic servitude changes, moving from live-in to live-out work and becoming more contractual in capitalism,[6] what some scholars have deemed "feudal" or "premodern" elements—relations inflected by paternalism or, more correctly, maternalism, and other sorts of "extraeconomic" and intimate ties—remain or indeed may be part of the very fabric of this labor relation.[7] In both the past and the present, as we have shown in our study of Kolkata (Calcutta), India, discourses of family and fictive or false kin relationships have been employed to mediate servitude.[8] We have proposed that these are defining features of Kolkata's *culture of servitude* and the structure of feeling emanating from the lived experience of this particular labor form and relationship. Kolkata's culture of servitude can be summarized as stemming from three premises with origins in a feudal imaginary: (1) Servants are essential to a well-run and well-kept household; (2) Servants are "part of the family" and bound to it by ties of affection, loyalty, and dependence; and (3) Servants comprise a category with distinctive lifestyles, desires, and habits. These premises particularize and enact a culture of servitude that we have defined as one in which domination/subordination, dependency, and inequality are normalized and permeate both the public and domestic spheres. In our explication of the culture of servitude, domestic servitude inescapably joins the public and domestic spheres and makes domesticity a public phenomenon by its incorporation of structural inequalities and difference—fundamentally those of class, gender, and national origin, but also race/ethnicity, especially in the North. Cultures of servitude, of course, are neither timeless nor placeless; they arise in specific historical circumstances and in relation to other cultural and social forms.

In this chapter, we pursue this line of argument by placing Kolkata's culture of servitude in transnational context: Bengali employers and servants living in twenty-first-century New York. This entails an inquiry into the presence of a culture of servitude in New York, where we find the emergence of certain of the same elements that characterize Kolkata's culture of servitude, as well as significant divergences, which are discussed in the concluding section. We first examine the narrative of Ruchira, an upper-middle-class South Asian woman in New York, who employs another South Asian as her nanny. Both are women, immigrants, and people of color and come from the same culture of servitude; what divides them is class and power. The narrative moves back and forth between the relationship with the servant with whom Ruchira grew up in India and that with the nanny in New York, from the familiarities of an established culture of servitude to the complexities of an emerging one. Ruchira is married to a non-Bengali, a man of European descent, which is interesting, in the sense that comparisons and difference naturally arise in the course of daily life, but not unusual. We comment on Ruchira's narrative with evidence from other Bengali and mixed households in New York City.

We then turn to New Yorker Abigail Pogrebin's account of the relationship with her children's caregiver—one of the plethora of nanny tales spun out of that globalized, transnational city—which follows the classic pattern of white, upper-middle-class employer and immigrant nanny of color.[9] The juxtaposition of the two narratives allows us to speculate on the distinctive attributes and structure of feeling of domestic servitude as a labor relation in itself.

Situating Domestic Servitude in New York

> *The women's stories seemed to come from a backward country, or from a shameful time in the United States that many would sooner forget . . . Listening to domestic workers talk about their jobs can give a rude jolt to assumptions about social progress and the civility of the rich and upper middle class.*
>
> **New York Times** coverage of first National Domestic
> Workers' Congress, Manhattan, June 2008[10]

If in Kolkata it is a truism that everyone has a servant who is not himself or herself a servant[11]—in our fieldwork spanning several years in the city we came across only one couple who deliberately chose not to keep a servant—that has not been the case in New York in the postwar period, when keeping a servant has been the province of the wealthy. However, the situation seems to have changed significantly in the 1990s and into this century. The *New York Times* notes that "entire industries and neighborhoods would collapse without paid domestic help" in New York City.[12] Ruth Milkman and her colleagues have argued convincingly against modernization theorists who hypothesized that paid domestic work would inevitably decline and disappear with capitalist industrialization and modernization by demonstrating that income inequality and class polarization in the United States account for the geographic variation in the proportion of the female labor force employed as domestic workers, with increasing numbers in certain metropolitan areas such as the greater Los Angeles area.[13] In so doing they also provide an important corrective to the recent feminist scholarship noted previously that has tended to rely primarily on the dynamics of discrimination and exclusion based on race/ethnicity and national origin/immigration to explain the prevalence of female paid domestic labor.

The Bronx-based Domestic Workers United (DWU) estimates that there are about 200,000 domestic workers in New York City. However, the 1999 New York City Housing and Vacancy Survey gives a figure of 36,715 private household service workers. If we allow for the conceivably large numbers of undocumented and/or unregistered domestic workers in the city, we may come closer to the DWU figure. A recent study by the DWU indicates that most of the domestic workforce is made up of immigrant women of color—95 percent of the survey of over 500 domestic workers—but that the conditions for the growth in domestic work can be attributed to "increasing income disparity" or, as we maintain, following Milkman and colleagues, rising class inequality.[14]

Even if the expansion of paid domestic work in New York City and the country as a whole may never approach the dominance of domestic servitude as a social form in Kolkata and elsewhere in the South—or indeed as it once did in the United States in the nineteenth century through World War II—it is undeniable that new generations of employers and domestic workers are negotiating the intricacies of this labor relationship, giving rise to anxieties and tensions that are the focus of increased scholarly and popular attention.[15]

Ruchira's Story

Like most of the servant-employing middle and upper-middle class in Kolkata, Ruchira grew up with a family retainer, Chandra, whom Ruchira refers to as a "factotum," or a person employed to do all sorts of work. Chandra came from a peasant family in East Bengal and eventually made her way to Kolkata with a friend to find work.[16] Hired when Ruchira was just a baby, Chandra has now worked and lived with Ruchira's family for over forty years. The family retainer is an archetype of Kolkata's culture of servitude and, as such, carries the full weight of employer expectation and desire. It is a category based on long duration of service in one home and/or to one family, often over the course of decades, and is necessarily applied to a servant in retrospect. Ruchira echoes the descriptions we have heard of family retainers from Kolkata's employers. To her, Chandra was faithful, loyal, affectionate, dependent and dependable, and always there.

Ruchira's idea of a servant has been inevitably shaped by the experience of growing up with Chandra, whom she also calls her "second mother." Chandra is mentioned in Ruchira's mother's will, for Chandra "embraced" Ruchira's family and has "had no parallel life of her own." In evoking Chandra's "embrace" of the family, Ruchira's account tallies with the narratives of other employers, young and old, in Kolkata in which the relationship that family retainers have with employing families is privileged: "He adopted our family as his own"; or "They were not in an employment relationship; they were in a family relationship"; or "[They became] a part of you." And less overwhelmingly so on the side of servants: "We are happy here because they [the employers] maintain the house well and give everybody love"; or "When my mother died, I thought to myself, I will make these my own people."

The stake in what we call the *rhetoric of love* creates a world where structural inequalities and domination are perceived on an entirely different register such that relationships of servitude are defined—essentially by the employing classes—in terms of mutuality based on affection, dependency, and loyalty. The rhetoric of love encompasses employer claims of affection and familial relationships that bind servants and employers to each other. It is a complex discourse that both hides exploitation and makes it more bearable for some employers and, indeed, for some servants. The power of the rhetoric of love in that culture of servitude is such that, even having lived away from home and outside India for over twenty years, Ruchira continues to represent the relationship with Chandra as a family one. When Ruchira goes back to India, she goes back to her mother—and Chandra.

Yet as an adult, newly married, and living in New York City, Ruchira and her husband, Justin, "did not think it was philosophically correct to have servants or even weekly cleaners." In part the decision had to do with Justin's influence as someone who had not grown up with servants and could not conceive of others doing his dirty work but also with the deliberate adoption of a "modern and progressive" outlook that associates domestic servitude with the feudal past and unacceptable relations of domination and servility. In this sense, Ruchira did break with Kolkata's culture of servitude. Among her contemporaries back home, there has not been a rejection of domestic servitude per se. Rather, we have noted a desire for modern, more impersonal contractual relations instead of feudal family-retainer relations with their emblematic rhetoric of love and a concomitant move away from live-in servants who could be considered "part of the family" to part-time domestic workers who have homes of their own. But the institution of domestic servitude remains firmly in place.

People like Ruchira and Justin and their contemporaries in their thirties and forties in New York, who may or may not have grown up with servants, are increasingly acquiring paid domestic labor in a way that the previous generation in the city did not. For some, such as senior insurance company executive Shankar, recalling the early stages of his career twenty years ago, hiring a weekly cleaning woman was a "sign of progress on the success ladder" in corporate Manhattan. This was followed, on promotion and marriage to real estate broker Christine, with hiring a cook/housekeeper and a nanny, an automatic gesture on the birth of their first child: "There was no question about it; we didn't even discuss it; it was the thing to do." Shankar, having grown up with a household staff in Kolkata, had always expected to have the same once he joined the corporate sector, as his father did before him.

Ruchira and Justin's decision to give up their resistance to keeping a servant came not with the first pregnancy, as might have been expected from a couple where both partners had careers, but a move to South Asia where they ended up keeping servants. By the time Ruchira and Justin came back to New York City, Ruchira was pregnant, and they took advantage of the possibility of legally bringing back one domestic worker as a nanny. Ruchira wanted someone who shared the same culture, a common desire among South Asian employers in New York City. Other employers we interviewed in New York who are originally from India expressed a strong preference for hiring South Asian domestic workers. This is, in fact, a version of the strategy used by white employers that Julia Wrigley calls "choosing similarity." While Wrigley's employers seek European au pairs and nannies to impart certain kinds of cultural capital to their children, South Asian employers who choose similarity seek domestic workers who will cook familiar food and nannies who will impart specific manners, customs, and, above all, language to their children.[17]

Immigrant South Asian women report that it is easier to find jobs as domestic workers in the South Asian community when they first arrive in New York because of language, access, and cultural familiarity, especially because most have never worked as paid domestics before. Said Tahira, a domestic worker from Bangladesh, "If I stay with an American family, they won't know that I need to eat rice three times a day." Another important factor, according to domestic workers, is that South Asian employers tend not to ask for immigration papers, work permits, and legal status, whereas "Americans" almost always do. However, they have decidedly mixed opinions on whether they prefer working for South Asians over "white Americans" because, they claim, South Asian employers pay less, take advantage, and are more abusive.[18]

Justin suggested finding a South Asian nanny already living in New York, but Ruchira preferred asking their cook, Kanchan, to consider moving back with them, arguing that they knew Kanchan: Kanchan was tried and tested, had proven herself to be soft and gentle with children, read and wrote English, and was spotlessly clean like Chandra. Ruchira also justified the proposal as having the potential to improve Kanchan's life—she would be able to earn more money for her family, have the opportunity to live abroad, and do something new. Justin was opposed to taking her because she had two children of her own whom she would effectively abandon to the care of their father, and it was discomfiting to think that "she'll be taking care of mine." Implicit here is the moral dilemma that Kanchan would be taking love and care away from her own children and transferring it to Justin's, an emotional transference that has been referred to as the transnational "care drain."[19] We would submit, however, that this extraction of love and care from the Third World to benefit the First is a recent if extreme form of the ancient contradiction of some women being obliged to care for other's children in lieu of or in addition to their own, be they indentured servants or wet nurses—mothers separated from their children in the slaveholding or Jim Crow southern United States, between villages and cities in Bengal, or between boroughs in New York City.[20]

Kanchan has taken care of Ruchira's daughter since shortly after her birth. She has her own room, and, although she offered to sleep in the living room as a servant might typically do back home, Ruchira and Justin thought such practices were unacceptable. In contrast, another Indian employer in Manhattan told us that one of the reasons she preferred South Asian live-in nannies is that "they don't make a fuss about sleeping on the floor in my son's room." Ruchira and Justin set up things differently, they believe, from the way their friends and colleagues in New York (and for that matter, in South Asia) have done. They never asked Kanchan to look after the baby at night; they would get up themselves. They pay her a salary higher than the U.S. minimum wage; she works a forty-hour week, has two weeks' paid vacation, and is covered by medical insurance.[21] Kanchan also makes a trip every year to see her family, which usually coincides with Ruchira's visit home to Kolkata.

As Ruchira recounted the move back to New York, it became apparent that she was consumed by the story she wanted to tell. It was a story about friendship and betrayal and the articulation of the rhetoric of love, with its attributes of mutuality based on affection, dependency, and loyalty, in two different cultures of servitude. Although Kanchan was never described as "part of the family" in the Chandra family-retainer mold—after all, Ruchira and Justin consider themselves to be modern, enlightened employers, and they and Kanchan, all of whom are in their thirties and early forties, belong to a new generation that has presumably left such feudal trappings behind—another sort of intimate relationship was at hand. An affective bond between Ruchira and Kanchan had existed before they arrived in New York, and Ruchira believed that the understanding between them as women grew as Ruchira introduced Kanchan to the intricacies of modern institutions in the city and "empowered" Kanchan's newfound awareness of her choices and rights.

Then things began to change. As Kanchan began to learn the rules of the game for domestic employment in New York, she decided to ask not to work on weekends at all. For Ruchira this signaled the deterioration of the relationship with Kanchan: "This has become a big bone of contention. I am not going to pay extra for her to look after my daughter [on the weekend]. A movie costs ten dollars and the babysitting thirty dollars. And we raise her salary every year!" In the same vein, during Ruchira's second pregnancy, Kanchan made two other changes. First, she told Ruchira that she wanted to stop working on weekdays at 5:00 P.M. so that she could enroll in night classes to get her GED (General Educational Development) certificate. And second, she said that she would cook only two days a week and suggested that they hire a cleaning person. In other words, she was increasing her task specialization so that her work corresponded more specifically to that of a nanny, not a general domestic worker. Ruchira responded, "How can you expect to work *less* when we're going to have a second child?"

Ruchira then decided that she and Kanchan would sit down and have a serious talk to try to resolve matters. "I have learned how not to do things. It is too clichéd to say that you can't treat servants a certain way because they will then take advantage of you. But it is a question of parameters, and Justin doesn't understand, and she manipulates this." The management of the relationship thus falls to Ruchira, both because it is usually delegated to women as the "natural" housekeepers and because Ruchira believes the experience of growing up with servants made her more competent and capable to deal with such issues than Justin.

When Kanchan began to redefine her work conditions, she felt that she could not adequately express herself to Ruchira verbally, telling her: "I can't explain myself, so I'm going to put it in writing." Ruchira says, "She wrote me the most offensive e-mail saying that we had made her suffer for so many years. It was hurtful and accusatory, and one for the lawyers. I wrote back asking her why she had tolerated this for so many years—she was not indentured. We thought it was a mutually beneficial relationship." The use of e-mail enraged Ruchira in particular because she had taught Kanchan how to use the Internet to communicate with her children, who were, after all, so far away from her. Thus, it seemed to Ruchira that her attempts to educate and empower Kanchan were continually backfiring. Kanchan's singular recourse to the written word and to electronic communication as a means of distancing herself from the exigencies of an intimate and private relationship is indeed striking. Would conversations tête-à-tête have kept Kanchan within the confines of the rhetoric of love?[22]

Kanchan's insinuation of being somehow bound and subservient to them stunned Ruchira, even as she chafed against the demands for more freedom that Kanchan made. The "mutually beneficial relationship" was unraveling and revealing the possibility that it had actually been something quite different. Within the terms of the inherited culture of servitude, Ruchira's mother reached this conclusion: "You have spoiled her. You have taken her needs first over your own," an assessment with which Ruchira has come to agree. That the servant is essential is the primary premise of Kolkata's culture of servitude, but that essentiality is, in turn, predicated on the (dependent) labor that the servant performs for the employer, not on the ideology of mutual benefit often associated with more contractual relations.

We asked Ruchira why Kanchan was still with them given that tensions had escalated to such an extent. "I keep her because she is very loving with the children . . . She won't call me Didi anymore—I don't know why." Eventually, after Ruchira and Justin told Kanchan what they now needed and expected from her, she decided that this would be her last year with them. According to Ruchira,

Kanchan wanted to remake herself in the U.S. If anything stings, it is that I set out very consciously to empower her, and now that empowerment is biting me. My husband says that she is like a rebellious teenager. If I say something in anger, I have to remember that there is an inherent power relationship and that I can be nasty to her but she can't be nasty to me. It's not that I want her to be subservient, docile, or submissive, but she has manipulated us . . . It was especially bad when I was seven or eight months pregnant and it should have been easy sailing—I will never forgive her. Maybe she will be a better person, have a better life, and I contributed to that. But what I mind most is the betrayal of the friendship.

Ruchira's narrative makes clear that Kanchan is consistently distancing herself from the older culture of servitude by refusing to use familial terms with Ruchira, by placing limits around her workday, and by setting out arguments in favor of her rights. It is significant that she continues to be a good and loving child care worker. The betrayal that Ruchira speaks of does not then refer to the actual work performed by Kanchan but to her friendship. Perceptions of betrayal following attempts to empower, educate, or befriend domestic workers emerge in several narratives both in New York and Kolkata, particularly among liberal or progressive women employers. Let us turn now to Abigail Pogrebin's emblematic narrative of betrayal, which appeared in the popular weekly magazine *New York*.

Pogrebin's Story

> *Half of me wanted to implore her, "How can you do this?"*
> *The other half wanted to threaten her: "I'm not the fool you take me for."*
> **Abigail Pogrebin, "Nanny Scam"**

The faltering of a nanny's love and loyalty occasions much anxiety, as can be seen in Abigail Pogrebin's article "Nanny Scam," in which the following text invites us to identify with an employing mother: "What would you do if your trusted caregiver, someone you consider family, turned out to be stealing from you? Here is what one mother did."[23]

The words *trust* and *family* immediately invite a comparison to Ruchira's narrative. Abigail Pogrebin and her husband are one of many dual-career middle- or upper-middle-class couples with children in New York who turn to cheap and available child care provided by immigrant women. Maria, the nanny in the story, was thought to be perfect because she "cared lovingly and tirelessly" for the couple's children. We do not know whether, unlike Ruchira and Justin, they had hired domestic workers before they had children, but we do know that Maria was the fourth nanny—someone, unlike the previous three, who seemed to have Mary Poppins–like qualities. Yet—they discovered to their dismay—Maria had been stealing from them. How did Maria get the opportunity to steal? Apparently, Pogrebin was so trusting (and so unwilling to go to the bank herself) that she frequently sent Maria to the bank with her ATM card. Maria, Pogrebin discovered, had been withdrawing money for herself at the same time that she had withdrawn money for her employer.

Pogrebin's primary emotion appears to be the shocked realization that "maybe she's never been a friend in the first place" and that "the relationship was probably too imbalanced to be authentic."[24] She describes her relationship with Maria as laced with guilt because she was so aware of the "economic gap" between them. Thus, she compensated by buying Maria gifts, giving her bonuses, and not treating her as a subordinate. She and Maria shared lunch, "modeled bargain purchases from . . . Filene's basement for one another and on one occasion, even got our nails done side by side."[25] Given the racialized history of this occupation, the reader might be expected to be pleasantly surprised by the idea of the employer and nanny sitting side by side in a salon. Maria is, after all, embodying the latest iteration of a complexly racialized relationship that has developed over the past two centuries in the United States.

Pogrebin's dilemmas are echoed in the interviews with employers conducted during the DWU study. As one Manhattan woman employer agonized:

> I don't know what the solutions are because it is slavery . . . and it's horrible, and on one level I hated participating in it . . . She had dental problems, and I helped. She has been struggling with her rent, and I am throwing her an extra $100 per month. Her money problems are very different from mine. I have no idea [how to improve domestic work]. My brain isn't big enough for that. It's a horribly racist world. People take advantage, and it's a mess.

When Pogrebin and her husband realized that Maria had been stealing from them, a part of their world began to unravel. The story of Maria's theft opened the door to a torrent of "confessions" on the part of Pogrebin's friends about being similarly betrayed by their maids and nannies.[26] Pogrebin and her husband immediately dismissed Maria and then worried about how to break the news of Maria's sudden departure to their children, aged four and six. While the children cried at the news at first, Pogrebin was "surprised at how easily Maria drifted out of their lives; despite the intimacy, her disappearance wasn't a major upheaval . . . The strange thing though, was that *I* missed her."[27]

Pogrebin's narrative reveals immense hurt and a powerful sense of betrayal—"I lurched from incredulity to rage to heartache"[28]—but then the structural inequalities begin to assert themselves. Maria frequently called and left tearful messages on her former employer's answering machine, and Pogrebin's now angry reaction was to tape them in case they were needed as proof. She reported Maria to the local police and then, worried that Maria would not know how to protect herself, urged Maria to get a lawyer from Legal Aid. Finally, in an ultimate act of what can only be thought of as revenge, Pogrebin tracked down Maria's former references and told them what she had done, in effect making it next to impossible for Maria to find another job in the city. Yet Pogrebin ends her account on a note that resists the advice that "[a]n employee in your home will always on some level resent you," even as she knows she will never fully trust a nanny again.[29]

Reactions to this article were numerous and similarly passionate. Some letters to the editor scorned Pogrebin's naïveté, others excoriated her vengeful righteousness, some urged her to "get over" her liberal guilt, while yet others reminded her that she had crossed the line by asking her nanny to go the bank for her. The letters reveal, however, an awareness that this is a class relation of great power and that to deny it by putting a "liberal" face on it is disingenuous.[30]

Global Cultures of Servitude

These tales of betrayal, these loss-of-innocence narratives on the part of the employers in New York, do not stem from the same source and yet, taken together, perhaps hint at one of the enduring attributes of cultures of servitude. Certainly there are differences between the cultures of servitude in the two cities. All Kolkata households that can afford to do so, even those in the lower middle class, have at least one part-time domestic worker who daily comes to clean or wash dishes. Indeed, as various employer and servant narratives and the historiography have shown, keeping a servant as a sign of the attainment of middle-class status has been a constant in Kolkata since the late nineteenth century. In New York, even though a weekly cleaner may be commonplace, and having a daily or live-in housekeeper and/or nanny is becoming more so, keeping a servant has yet to become (once again?) a marker of the middle class, even if it is clearly a matter of status. In this sense, it may be more reasonable to say that, in New York, servants may not yet be considered essential or indispensable for a well-kept middle-class home, but they are certainly desirable and seen to be increasingly affordable.

In New York, the search is for an elusive horizontality; in Kolkata, the question of horizontality does not arise because the affective and emotional bonds with servants, old family retainers in particular, are expressed through familial discourses rooted in distinctions of power and status. Both Ruchira and Abigail Pogrebin tried to practice a liberal discourse of rights and women's empowerment with their servants, even though this attempt at horizontality ultimately ended in mutual unintelligibility. Once matters came to a head, these employers were left with the rage of betrayal and the regret of the loss of friendship—one-sided, it must be said, because there is little indication that Kanchan and Maria viewed their working relationships as anything other than that of employer and domestic worker, intrinsically unequal.

Although worlds apart, the cultures of servitude in New York and Kolkata nevertheless echo one another. Many aspects of the constitutive elements of Kolkata's culture of servitude—the essential servant, the servant as "part of the family," and the servant as distinctive in taste and personality—and their accompanying contradictions are found among employers and domestic workers, Bengali or not, in New York, as evidenced both by popular and scholarly writing and activist documents such as the DWU study. As in Kolkata, employers in New York struggle with relationships with servants, with the consequences of having domestic workers in the private space of the home; and servants grapple with the challenges of class and cultural distinction, of a relationship of domination, dependency, and inequality that is often channeled through the discourses of mutual benefit and friendship.

Ruchira was raised within Kolkata's culture of servitude infused with the rhetoric of love, where the servant was bound to the employer by ties of loyalty and dependency. Once in New York, like Abigail Pogrebin, Ruchira deliberately set about creating a new culture of servitude based on the assumption of workers' rights and empowerment. In this culture of servitude, different from Kolkata's, Kanchan had set hours, paid vacation, and a room of her own and lived as a contractual worker. Both Ruchira and Pogrebin believed that they were creating the space for an alternative culture of servitude based on a liberal capitalist notion of mutual benefit.

Yet the nature of the similarities between cultures of servitude in contemporary New York and Kolkata suggests that a classic capital–labor relationship cannot arise in paid domestic work because of the intimacy of the site of labor. Put another way, even if a perfect contract with perfect working conditions could be effected for domestic service, the power relations, hierarchies, and domination/dependency, which are as much idealist hallmarks of the home and family as love and loyalty, would not disappear. The arrangements that Kanchan was able to achieve in Ruchira and Justin's home in New York, although clearly imperfect as glimpsed through Ruchira's narrative, come perhaps the closest to an adequate setup yet were fraught with tension and conflict because of the structure of feeling of the home as a site of labor.

Both Ruchira and Pogrebin claimed friendship—which can arise only among equals—with their nannies, even as they were aware that they were not equals. The tenor of the employers' discussion of these friendships—teaching their maids about their rights, helping them make their way in the world, fretting about sexual affairs that they could be having—all suggest a relationship of maternalism, not friendship. And when that maternalism is thwarted, the friendship or loyalty seen to be betrayed, then comes the dismissal or the vengeance, or both in the case of Pogrebin. But why claim friendship at all in a market relationship? One argument for the claims of friendship could be that it makes a service relationship more palatable. But another, we suggest, goes to the heart of the contradiction of this work, done for a wage, within the privatized confines of a home. The home is not an emotionally neutral site—it is the site of love, trauma, and intimacy. The claims of friendship, then, are an "egalitarian" version of the rhetoric of love—to bind the worker to the family in a recognition precisely, as one elderly Kolkata employer eloquently told us, of preventing the market from "winning." Thus, claims of friendship not only make employers feel better about this unequal relationship but also trump the market calls for domestic workers to seek better lives and opportunities.

In these stories of friendship and betrayal, the assumption of rights and mutual benefit can be seen to dissolve in New York's culture of servitude. We may conclude, then, that these narratives suggest that the *site* in which domestic labor is performed and the labor relation itself entail a culture of servitude, in both the Global North and South, in which domination/subordination, dependency, and inequality are articulated and rearticulated.

Notes

Adapted from *Cultures of Servitude: Modernity, Domesticity, and Class in India,* by Raka Ray and Seemin Qayum. ©2009 by the Board of Trustees of the Leland Stanford Jr. University, all rights reserved.

1. Where employers of color do dominate is in the cases of abuse and exploitation involving foreign diplomats and international civil servants, often from Asian and African countries and living and working in New York or Washington, DC, who employ live-in migrant domestic workers under special visa arrangements. See Human Rights Watch, 2001; and Domestic Workers United, 2006.

2. Rollins, 1985; Romero, 1992; Wrigley, 1995; Hondagneu-Sotelo, 2001; and Colen, 1989.

3. Romero, 1992: 105, 57–58.

4. Milkman, Reese, and Roth, 1998.

5. As Judith Rollins concluded, "The presence of the 'inferior' domestic . . . supports the idea of unequal human worth: it suggests that there might be categories of people (the lower classes, people of color) who are inherently inferior to others (middle and upper classes, whites). And this idea provides ideological justification for a social system that institutionalizes inequality" (Rollins, 1985: 203).

6. See, among other studies, Katzman, 1978; and Romero, 1992.

7. See, for example, Hondagneu-Sotelo, 2001; Rollins, 1985; and Glenn, 1986.

8. See Ray and Qayum, 2009.

9. See Pogrebin, 2004.

10. Buckley and Correal, 2008; "Women's Work," 2008.

11. Cf. Rubbo and Taussig's division of Colombian society into servant-supplying and servant-employing households (Rubbo and Taussig, 1983: 12).

12. "Women's Work," 2008.

13. Milkman et al., 1998.

14. Domestic Workers United, 2006: 9–10.

15. See, for example, Flanagan, 2004; McLaughlin and Kraus, 2002; Lee, 2002; Rafkin, 1998; Ehrenreich, 2000; and numerous articles in the *New York Times* and *New York* magazine.

16. Migrants and refugees from East Bengal who settled in squatter camps and refugee settlements in and around Kolkata have historically been a source of domestic labor in the city.

17. See Wrigley, 1995: chapter 3.

18. Journalist Tracey Middlekauff recounts a not atypical saga of immigration and abusive working conditions in South Asian homes (Middlekauff, 2002). See also Bhattacharjee, 1992; and Samar Collective, 1994.

19. See Hochschild, 2002; and Parreñas, 2002. See also Nilita Vachani's film *When Mother Comes Home for Christmas*, 1996.

20. Mahasweta Devi's story, "The Breast-Giver," an excruciating tale of such "surplus extraction," tells of the ultimate betrayal of the wet nurse, Jashoda, who succumbs to breast cancer (Devi, 1997).

21. As such, the terms of the arrangement approximated the "creation of a businesslike environment" that Romero advocates for the necessary transformation of paid domestic work in the United States, except, of course, that Kanchan lives with Ruchira and her family (Romero, 1992: 165–192).

22. Cf. Alice Childress's use of conversational vignettes between an African American domestic worker and her friend—or, rather, monologue, because the reader is privy only to the former's side of the conversation—to convey everyday resistance and revindication in New York's culture of servitude of the 1950s in her satirical collection *Like One of the Family* (Childress, 1956).

23. Pogrebin, 2004; 18.

24. Ibid.

25. Ibid.: 20.

26. Cf. Hondagneu-Sotelo, 2002: 59–69. Also contrast the unrelieved earnestness of Pogrebin's account with Childress's send-up of employer fears about theft in "The Pocketbook Game" (Childress, 1956, 26–27).

27. Pogrebin, 2004: 20.

28. Ibid.

29. Ibid.: 23.

30. See "Letters," 2004: 5.

8 My Reward Is Not Money

Deep Alliances and End-of-Life Care
among Mexicana Workers and Their Wards

María de la Luz Ibarra

IN THE LAST THIRTY YEARS, processes of globalization have helped produce a new organization of social reproduction, wherein care is increasingly commodified and performed by migrant women in First World countries. Women from Latin America, the Philippines, the West Indies, Africa, and Eastern Europe are hired to look after children and private homes and increasingly for convalescent and elderly adults. While the practice of hiring less privileged women to clean and care is not new, the rate at which these jobs have proliferated after a period of precipitous decline in the occupation is "unprecedented in terms of the scope and speed."[1]

Increasingly important is the demand for private elder care within postindustrial societies.[2] This demand is not surprising considering, in part, the dramatic growth in the senior population. In the United States, for example, between 1950 and 2000, the population aged sixty-five to eighty-four grew by 188 percent; and the population over age eighty-five grew by 635 percent, so that today there are 35 million senior citizens.[3] In spite of the relatively "healthy" status of seniors in the United States, aging is inevitably related with varying degrees of disease and disability, so that individuals progressively require assistance with a range of activities. Consequently, there is a demand for many types of help within the formal and informal sector.

In this chapter, I provide two extended case studies on Mexican migrant women—Mexicanas—employed as private elder care providers in Santa Barbara, California, who have formed relationships of "deep alliance" with their wards.[4] Relationships of deep alliance imply that workers commit to stay and

care until the end and put their own lives at the service of another for a pro-
tracted and undetermined amount of time. These relationships are highly
personalistic and involve physical as well as emotional labor.

A classic argument in the domestic labor literature is that it is personalism
on the job—close personal relations between employer and employee—that allows employers to continually add tasks and exploit workers. The employee is
supposed to perform—out of loyalty, deference, or obligation—whatever tasks
are elaborated by the employer. In great part, personalism is the reason workers transformed domestic service from live-in to live-out work in the early
part of the twentieth century and the reason some workers have professional-
ized the occupation in the United States.[5] Notwithstanding these historical
changes, personalism continues to define the content of care work in private
homes,[6] and the tasks performed continue to go beyond what the wage allows.
Here, however, the delineation of paid care relationships highlights not only
the parameters of work as shaped by employers but also, from a worker's point
of view, from the cultural and moral imperatives that define the job.[7]

As I highlight workers' intentions and desires, I keep in mind the words
of Lulu Trujillo, who said, "My reward is not money." This sentiment was repeated in different ways by other workers, and I explore why, in addition to
money, women accept such difficult and emotionally costly labor. I argue that
caring for an elderly ward is about creating a more just world, of critiquing
through deeds the inequality of globalization that makes human intimacy so
difficult. For the Mexicanas in the case studies, moreover, religiously inspired
agency is also about gaining other rewards, including spiritual salvation.

My analysis is based on ethnographic fieldwork conducted between 1994
through 1996 and 2000 through 2001 in Santa Barbara, California. Over the
course of this time, I conducted anthropological fieldwork among sixty-five
Mexicanas employed as domestic workers in the city. These women form part
of a large and diverse group of Mexican immigrants in Southern California who left Mexico between 1980 and 2000. They came from both Mexico's
working and middle classes—groups hard hit by the country's economic cri-
ses during the 1980s and 1990s.[8]

In the discussion that follows, I first foreground the economic and social
context that helps create a demand for private elder care in the United States
and then focus on some of the general particularities of the private relationship itself, including the negotiation of power and meaning that takes place.
Thereafter I provide a brief description of Santa Barbara's care landscape and,
within it, the career trajectories that lead some Mexicanas into the informal

sector, where they labor as private care providers. Finally, I describe the development of deep alliances between two workers and their wards and the desires that care fulfills for these Mexicanas.

Globalization, Elder Care Choices, and the Negotiation of Meaning in Private Households

The demographic shift in the United States—alongside the economic shifts—has helped create a cultural context wherein seniors and their kin seek help from both the formal and informal market. Moreover, the type of "help" that has developed in the last thirty years has become broader. While nursing homes have never been the first choice of most families—at most 5 percent of the elderly population have been interned there at any point in time—nursing homes nonetheless were the dominant market model from the 1960s through the 1990s. Nursing homes have never been the first choice because here bodily care is prioritized and emotional needs ignored.[9] Morever, life in a nursing home has come to mean cruelty and dehumanization if not an outright synonym for elder abuse in academic studies and journalistic reporting.[10] Furthermore, moving away from home to a nursing facility puts people in "limbo": There is a loss of a familiar way of life,[11] and hope can dissipate quickly as the specter of death is a common, if not daily, occurrence.[12] Thus, the formal market has responded to a demand for more personalized options, with day care, assisted living facilities, private nursing, and cooperative "stay in place" care.

The growing availability of more personalized forms of care can be interpreted as an affirmation of aspects of life that people find meaningful. In the United States, aging individuals want to remain "independent"—that is, to be able to do for themselves all those things that represent adulthood for as long as possible.[13] They want to maintain a sense of self that embodies dignity and respect; and some aging individuals want to be around people and places that elicit a shared historical past or cultural community.[14] In some cases, likewise, they seek escape from what they consider to be controlling older children or judgmental relatives.[15]

The growing availability of more personalized care is not limited to the formal sector, of course. Families and individuals also hire migrant women to clean and care as private workers within the informal, unregulated sector in postindustrial societies.[16] While less has been written about paid private elder care arrangements than about child care or housecleaning, some general findings include the fact that some employers—typically the adult children of the elderly person—want to reproduce a "traditional" nuclear family experience and maintain the ideal of familialism;[17] some private informal care thus coexists alongside unpaid care by female kin of the elderly ward.[18] In other cases, the private care provider is one of several paid carers, and in still yet other cases, she labors alone.[19] Many workers have received no training as care providers, and they are often hired on the basis of gendered/racialized notions that they are culturally inclined toward care. In some Western European countries, the recognition that care providers need training has led to the creation of specialized programs for migrant women.[20] Some evidence also suggests that the proportion of men in the occupation is increasing, although care is predominantly performed by women, who earn relatively low wages and have few benefits.[21] Within the workplace itself, employees and employers engage in negotiation over work conditions, especially because tasks are often not specified but rather develop as part of a highly personalized relationship. Workers also negotiate the meanings of care that shape their conditions and that of their wards.[22]

It is this negotiation of meanings—"sets of culturally constructed and historically specific guides . . . of and for human feeling, intention, and action"[23]—in the context of a stratified, intimate work relationship that is of particular interest to me. What happens when the power-laden encounter between two individuals of different groups involves one who is living out the last stage of his or her life and who may be seriously ill or dying? What are workers' motivations and desires in this intimate encounter? Prior to addressing these questions, I will briefly describe the care landscape in Santa Barbara and the conditions under which ward and worker may eventually come together in paid, private arrangements.

Santa Barbara and the Evolving Landscape of Elder Care

In Santa Barbara, people who are sixty-five years of age or older represent 13.8 percent of the population and create an important demand for a range of care services in this affluent city.[24] In the formal sector, care facilities include assisted living homes, board-and-care homes, elder "day care" sites, nursing homes, and private nurses. In the informal sector, likewise, there is a range of day work and live-in care arrangements that pivots on a ward's physical and emotional capacities as well as his or her income.

At the time of the interviews, the majority of women in my study were employed as private care providers in the informal sector, but many had previously been employed in the formal sector, primarily as aides in nursing homes or for temporary employment agencies. In fact, for many the formal sector was seen as key for providing valuable training in the care of bodies. But the formal sector is also the site of great dissatisfaction, and thus eventually many women sought private, informal employment, in an attempt to have greater control and authority over conditions they found disturbing. A short description of the formal sector may help elucidate the appeal of the informal sector.

Careers in Care Work

Many women, prior to working as private care providers, begin their careers in the formal sector, principally as aides in nursing homes or for private contracting firms. Without exception, however, all Mexicanas cited dissatisfaction with the formal sector. Former nursing home aides spoke about what they considered improper care as the primary reason for quitting their jobs. Mexicanas, much like the workers described by other scholars,[25] spoke about the prevalence of "abuse." Mrs. Sarmiento, previously employed at a nursing home, described a sadistic nurse who would "punish" wards by leaving them to lie naked on the floor or by putting sugar in their eyes. Mrs. Sarmiento was so distraught that she complained to her supervisor, and when action was not quickly taken, she gained access into private files, called the wards' relatives and Protective Services for the Elderly. Shortly thereafter, in a surprise visit, an investigator came to the nursing home and saw firsthand the abuse described by Mrs. Sarmiento. The offending nurse was arrested, but she was not alone in her behavior. Later that year, in 2001, investigative reporting in the city, following a protest suicide by a nurse, revealed patient mistreatment at other nursing homes in the city. The U.S. Congress Committee on Government Reform later reported that all twenty-seven of the nursing homes in the city violated federal health and safety standards.[26]

Other forms of mistreatment were also addressed by Mexicanas. They spoke about class and race stratification, patient overload, and inflexible schedules. Elena described class and race segregation, affecting both patients and workers. In reference to patients, she described the social segregation of residents on Medicaid, who were placed in wards with higher patient-to-nurse ratios.[27] Here she routinely ran out of time and was unable to complete the necessary body work for patients, much less have time to talk with or console ailing individuals. In fact, workers repeatedly spoke with anger at not being able to "properly" care, to have to limit themselves to performing body work when in fact they could see that what was often needed was emotional care.

Workers also described their own inequality at the job site. Celia spoke about a hierarchical work structure where "white nurses with schooling" had voice and authority, whereas Mexicana nursing aides did not. She was most frustrated about not having a say in the overall treatment of a ward whose routines and preferences she felt were better known to her. In one example she said, "I knew that Mrs. Peters did not like to take the vitamins without food—she said it upset her stomach. But that person [the charge nurse] never listened. She told me to give it to her at 2 P.M., without any food. What difference could it possibly make to give poor Mrs. Peters her vitamins with her breakfast or dinner?!"

While the negative factors were disheartening, depressing, and often overwhelming for many workers, there was nonetheless agreement that nursing home employment had provided valuable knowledge about physical care. Workers spoke about the initial apprehension of performing what they considered very personal "service" such as toileting and about the fear of accidentally hurting an elderly patient as a result of inexperience. Over time, however, workers gained confidence as they learned many skills, including how to move incapacitated individuals and be attentive to physical changes in elderly wards—such as thinning skin—as well as to recognize the effects of various diseases, such as diabetes, on people's bodies.

In addition to working in nursing homes, some women began their paid care careers employed for temporary agencies, which referred them out to private homes. These women also described negative experiences, which included conflict with "American" nurses or supervisors, racism, or problems with temperamental wards. Problems with "American" nurses here stemmed from a variety of reasons, which included concern with how care is performed as well as control over that care. Mexicanas alleged that "American" aides were not as attentive to the needs of their wards as they should be or that they were too physically rough. Some also expressed fear that they would be blamed for "bruises" found on wards' bodies.

Workers also repeatedly described experiencing "racism" at the hands of their employers as well as their wards. Workers, for example, spoke about being assigned to less desirable night shifts. María said, "To me it was clear that, if you are Mexican, you have to accept whatever hours they give you." This she said after describing how for over a year she had unsuccessfully tried to get a shift change so as to spend more time with her teenage children and husband. Some wards likewise did not necessarily like to be attended to by Mexican workers. Sandra related an incident wherein an eighty-five-year-old man demanded that she leave his house and tell the agency that he wanted only English speakers in his home. She said, "For me that was the worst experience, because the language was just an excuse. We were able to speak to each other but he wanted an American . . . One feels like a zero."

Other serious problems associated with agency work included caring for individuals with emotional problems or dementia, without having proper training or support. Several workers described being physically attacked, including having their hair pulled, being spit on, and being stabbed with a dinner knife. Sandra spoke about one elderly charge who would immediately try to scratch her face as she approached her. "I got to the point where I was afraid to get near her. She did not want anyone to touch her—perhaps she had been hurt [by other care providers]. I could not do my job, and I could not help her." After two weeks of "trying," Sandra left the position.

For some women, moving into the informal sector is an attempt to better control their work environment so as to better care for people and themselves; it is in effect a critique of the medicalized nursing home model where only the physical care of the body matters. Women, by better controlling their work environment, also sought to escape what they saw as class and race stratification and a lack of control and input over the care of individual patients. In effect they sought greater authority and valorization of themselves. Moreover, women left the formal sector due to the lack of flexibility in the scheduling, which in turn deprived them of necessary contact with their own family members.

As they entered the informal market, some women learned to carefully screen whom they would care for and under what conditions, not unlike professional housecleaners described by Mary Romero.[28] Nonetheless, care in private homes is still a contested terrain of power. In previous work, I have described how workers come into conflict or alliance with their wards—or third-party employers, who are often the adult children of wards. Conflict is very common and results, in great part, from the personality of the ward and the types of demands she or he places on the workers. Sometimes, however, an alliance takes place. The formation of an alliance implies that a worker feels affection for her ward, and this affection translates into caring for and protecting her ward from harm or fear. That which primarily determines whether an alliance will develop is a ward's positive behavior toward the worker.[29] These alliances, in turn, may be further deepened for workers by the presence and role, or lack thereof, played by third-party employers—most often the adult children of wards. It is in these particular relationships of either disdain or empathy for the adult children of wards, and affection for wards themselves, that workers create "deep alliances" and commit to stay until the end—to care for the body, emotions, and even the soul of their elderly ward until his or her death.

Deep Alliance and End-of-Life Care

In the course of ethnographic fieldwork, I found women who engaged in the "serious" endgame of life and formed "deep alliances" with their wards. A deep alliance implies not only that the worker feels responsible to protect and care for her ward, but that a worker takes on the "other's project" as her own.[30] In this case, Mexicanas take on the project of death. Engagement with their ward's death, moreover, sometimes means that women engage religious feelings and beliefs that are part of their own project for spiritual sustenance, moral authority, and communion with the divine.

In the following two case studies, I delineate what leads Mexicanas to seek elder care work in private homes, the development of deep alliances, and the taking on of the project of death.

Norma Paredes

Norma Paredes is a native of Puebla and was forty-six years old when I met her in 2001. She had been in Santa Barbara for seven years, working to financially support her twin sons, who lived with her parents in Mexico. Her sons were conceived from an out-of-wedlock relationship with a married man, and he did not provide either emotional or financial support. Thus Paredes had considered her limited options in Mexico, as well as her parent's disappointment, and made a decision to go to Santa Barbara—where other family members lived—in search of work. Here she sought assistance from an estranged brother who grudgingly helped but clearly saw her as a burden and treated her as an "immoral woman," verbally belittling her. It was while living at his home, however, that she experienced a "beautiful" thing. One morning, three "Sisters" from the Jehovah's Witnesses knocked on the door to offer religious literature and conversation. This initial contact sparked an ongoing relationship, a religious conversion, and a live-in job caring for one of the church members. Eventually she would marry this seventy-one-year-old Mexican man. It was through him that she was able to regularize her legal status.

Because her husband required only what she considered normal demands for a husband—cooking and cleaning—Norma asked his permission to find a job so that she could continue to provide financial support to her children.

When he agreed, the Sisters suggested she seek a job in a nursing home, where she could do "the work of God." In spite of her lack of English proficiency, she was able to find a job and was employed here for two years. About this experience she said, "It was very difficult and at the same time very beautiful. I learned a lot about life, and what really matters through my work there. More than anything one learns that we are all the same—it doesn't matter if a person is rich or poor. Even someone who was important now needs help with the most basic of things."

But in spite of the intrinsic value of the work, she quit after two years. She noted the necessarily fast pace to the work, as she attended to thirteen people. She believed people were treated "worse than animals, because where I'm from, we give more time to our cows than these poor people receive." Many times she would come home feeling depressed because of the suffering that she saw and her inability to change it. Moreover, her employment did not allow for flexibility with her daily schedule, nor with her plans to visit her sons in Mexico during the summer. "I know that they had a need for me, and God wanted me to do this work; but when they did not give me permission to go see my children, I had to think about them, and about me." She thus quit her job in the home and went to Mexico to see her sons.

When she returned to Santa Barbara, the Sisters once again helped her, advising her to seek work from a caregiving agency. Here she received a referral to work for ninety-one-year-old Ben Johnson, who spoke Spanish and who seemed like a nice man. Moreover, she was able to negotiate work from 8 to 12 P.M. and then 2 to 6 P.M., so that she could go home to fix her husband his lunch and then come back in time to prepare dinner. She also negotiated for time to visit her sons in the summer.

From the very beginning, she felt a lot of "sadness" for Mr. Ben who, although he had two children in a nearby city, did not have regular visits from them. His children visited every two or three months and were very "detached" from their father's needs and condition. She said, "I don't think that they are bad people, but I think they created an illusion that he was the same person he was twenty years ago."

Because she considered Mr. Ben to be a good person, because he was appreciative and respectful, Norma quickly developed an alliance with him; and, not unlike other Mexicanas I have described elsewhere, Norma was exquisitely attuned to the details of his life and what she perceived to be the content of his character and person.[31] She described Mr. Ben as "very intelligent"—a former engineer who had traveled all over the world, working for many years in South America, and who therefore spoke Spanish very well. She dwelled on the peculiarities of his person and took pride in him. She also respected, in spite of her growing religiosity, that he was not a religious person.

When describing work during the first three years of her employment, Norma detailed the following routine: She helped Mr. Ben get up and get dressed; prepared his meals; cleaned the house and did the dishes; washed and ironed; did the grocery shopping; helped bathe Mr. Ben; accompanied him on walks, errands, and doctors' appointments; and generally provided him with company. During these three years, she went to Mexico once a year for one month and arranged to leave Mr. Ben in the care of two Sisters. "So when I left for Mexico, I felt comfortable. I knew that they would take care of him, like I would—with the same patience. They would also let me know how he was doing."

Three years into the relationship, her ward became "sick." He began to lose his eyesight, was lethargic, and increasingly fearful. She said,

> I could see that he was fearful because he always asked me, "When will you return?" I was the only person who saw him every day, and he was lonely, but he did not want to go to a nursing home. My conscience ate me up, but I could not be in two places at the same time. So I spoke to my husband, who told me: "Ask him what he wants." So I asked Mr. Ben, "How can I help? My husband and I are both willing." And that is when my husband and I began to sleep in his house. That's how it was . . . what he most wanted was to not be alone. Not to feel that he would die alone. From the moment I submitted to him, everything changed. I felt much more calm . . . I did not ask him to pay me for sleeping at his home; what I was paid was enough to send to my children.

The moment at which she "submitted" herself to him was the moment at which she developed a deep alliance, and she reorganized her life to care for him, knowing that this was a pivotal period at the end of life. "One only has one life, and I felt that he needed me, in order to live in the way that made him happy. Yes, it was a sacrifice, but it was through the Witnesses that I came to understand that it is only with acts of compassion that we can get closer to God. And more than anything he needed it, do you understand me?"

When I asked about Mr. Ben's death, she said, "He died two years ago, and I was the one who told his children when he became very ill—he stopped eating, he did not want to leave the bed. The waiting for his children to arrive were the most difficult hours because I worried that they would not get there in time and also because I knew he would die on me [cries]. Once they arrived, it was only a matter of a few days, and it was the last time that I could be with him. It was very sad . . . very . . . but I helped him end his life well, and I have the satisfaction that he was never alone."

After Mr. Ben's death she described a severe estrangement—she did not take part in the memorial services organized by his children, and she did not know them well enough to commiserate and share grief. Then one of the Sisters suggested she pray for Mr. Ben in their church. "More than anything that helped me. They treated him as if he were part of my family—they knew him, and they helped me say goodbye to him in a proper way. I had never spoken in front of so many people, but that day I gave him his goodbye so that his spirit could be closer to God."

Guadalupe Terrazas

In 1970, at the age of forty, Lupe arrived in Santa Barbara from Jalisco, Mexico, seeking work after her first husband died. She left her four children with her father and brothers and came to Santa Barbara because she did not believe she could financially provide for them with the jobs available to her in her hometown. She had old school friends who had married and had moved to Santa Barbara years before and who now offered her a job in a restaurant where they worked. It was while working here that she would eventually meet her "American" husband, a disabled Vietnam War veteran. Within two years she remarried, regularized her legal status, and brought her children to the United States. Then, over the next twenty years, she raised her children and cared for her disabled husband, while she was simultaneously employed in the restaurant and later at a nursing home. She saw her children grow, family members move into the city, and eventually her husband die in a car accident. In the period after his death, she turned more and more to the Catholic Church and to her own ideas about spirituality.

It was through the Church, in her late fifties, that she eventually received a referral to care for eighty-nine-year-old Constance. Guadalupe said,

> She was a person with a lot of money but only one son, who lived in London. He wanted to take her with him, but she wouldn't go. She said she had lived in Santa Barbara her whole life, and that is where she wanted to die. Because at the beginning she was still very active, I was the only one who came in [to provide care]. I would make her food, clean up her house, prepare her clothes—in other words, everything that she needed . . . And that was how we lived for

almost five years—I lived there in the house with her, and her son would visit about three times a year. He is a good man, but he lived too far . . . He said that the knowledge that I cared for his mother so well was a great relief to him. I knew that I could ask for more money, but I never did. The less you ask for, the more God will give you.

Over time, Constance's two best friends died, and that is when she began to lose her will to live—not right away, but slowly she began to withdraw:

I took care of her as if she were my mother. But her condition grew worse, and her son put me in charge of hiring other people on the weekends. The weekends were the days I visited with my family, and she could no longer be alone. I hired other people . . . Regularly, these were members of my family so that I could feel comfortable. I didn't want anyone to hit her or yell at her, which is very common. I couldn't just hire any person for my own peace of mind. I was always in contact on the phone for whatever thing that was needed; if we could fix it over the telephone we did, and if not I went there. It did not bother me.

In the third year of her employment, Constance fell and broke her hip. Lupe felt so guilt ridden (she had been cooking in the kitchen) that during her daily prayers she made a vow that, if Constance recovered, she would make a pilgrimage to the shrine of Virgin of Guadalupe in Mexico City. When Constance became stable, Lupe recruited her eldest daughter to care for Constance for four days, while she and two other church members went to central Mexico. Here Lupe went to the basilica, lit a candle, and prayed for Constance. Later she went to the Virgin's shrine and brought with her rosary beads and a small statue of St. Anthony that belonged to Constance. She held these objects close to the Virgin, symbolically bringing Constance into a transnational space of religious worship.

In the fifth year of her employment, Lupe knew that Constance's health was seriously deteriorating:

She would tell me, "I want death to come, I am ready." This is when I knew that it was time to prepare. I knew that I could do it because God does not give you more than you can bear, and I had already buried my mother and two husbands. . . . I never imposed my religion, she asked me for it. She liked to listen to the words of the Lord.

At the end, Constance was very clear about what she wanted, in spite of increasing mental and physical debility. She told Lupe, "'Call my son and tell him

I want to see him once again; tell him I won't die until he gets here.' And that's the way it was. I called, and he came—he stayed here until Constance died peacefully. She had a good death because her family members and son had said goodbye. Also she never suffered; we always attended to her in every way."

Unlike Norma, who had not been present at her ward's wake, Lupe was. Moreover, Constance's son had insisted that Lupe sit in the front pews with the family, as well as help pick out the clothes that Constance would be buried in. When I asked her if she would consider caring for another elderly person again, she said, "I don't know. The truth is that it hurts one a lot, when one loves. But also, like Jesus said, 'He who does not love, cannot come to know the Lord.' You know that love and compassion are the only things that open up the gates to heaven."

Conclusion

The classic argument about personalism and its effects on domestic workers allows us to analyze a deep alliance as a clear example of how personalism leads to the increased extraction of labor from workers. But this analysis is incomplete without addressing the intentions and desires that the work fulfills for Mexicanas who are the second half of a complex relationship.

I argue that, in part, caring for an elderly ward is about creating a more just world, of critiquing through deeds the speed up of life that makes human intimacy so difficult.[32] Deeds are thus a physical manifestation of how women define and pursue a moral life, in the face of an environment that runs against the moral grain and in the face of another's suffering. What Mexicanas intend is to fulfill the "needs" that they perceive people in the last stage of life require—to give not just physical but also emotional care. In private homes, some women thus provide—among many others things—empathy, companionship, affection, a sense of safety, and even the words and protection of their God. Moreover, in a deep alliance, workers intend to give their wards not only a good life but also a good death. And a good death means that the end is marked as significant, as a period in which what matters most is presence and time. Thus workers no longer function by the rationality of time around the wage. Instead, in the liminal space between living and dying, time has a different rhythm, dependent on the evolving and previously undefined needs of the ward. Of course this relationship is deeply costly to workers, both financially and emotionally. But in the end Mexicanas—like most people—would feel ashamed "to act in a way that goes against this core impulse to do the right thing"[33] when directly faced with human vulnerability and need.

For some workers, religiously inspired agency is also critical and helps to not only define need for their wards but also to establish a clear line of action. The principal points made about Christianity by Norma and Lupe is that it requires "love" and "selfless acts." And ultimately it is the practice of both that opens up the gates to the Kingdom of God.[34] Thus women are adamant that their love and compassion are not part of the wage. They give these things of their own volition—beyond the wage. Neither Norma nor Lupe asked for more money when work hours and responsibilities became longer: Their "reward" was the knowledge that they behaved in a correct way and that these actions would help to provide them with "salvation" after their own death.

In sum, the delineation of workers' intentions and desires helps us to better understand the personalistic relations that help define the content of private elder care work. What Mexicanas' words and deeds tell us is that in a relationship of deep alliance loyalty to one person is linked to broader moral imperatives, to issues of justice and responsibility in the face of dependency.

Notes

1. Hochschild, 2003: 3.
2. Ibarra, 2000; Lyon, 2006; Degiuli, 2007.
3. National Research Council Staff, 2002.
4. For a discussion of the validity of extended case studies see Burawoy, 1998. For discussions about the use of one subject case studies in anthropological writing see Bourgois, 1995; Farmer, 2004.
5. For a discussion of personalism in the traditional mistress–maid relationship see Coser, 1973. For a discussion of the transformation of domestic service from live-in to live out work in the United States, see Katzman, 1978. For a discussion of professionalization, see Romero, 1992.
6. Hondagneu-Sotelo, 2001. Hondagneu-Sotelo argues that, in the contemporary period, Latina domestics in Los Angeles, especially those who provide care work for children, want more personalistic relations while employers do not. Personalism, from the point of view of workers, is a bilateral relationship between individuals who see each other not solely in terms of their work role but as persons embedded in social relations and with joint aspirations.
7. Most anthropologists stress that, aside from the fundamental requisites for sustaining life, it is culture not nature that defines necessity. See Sahlins, 2004; and Lock, 1997. Culture, in turn, consists of ideas or beliefs of what is "right" and "wrong"—of what is, in other words, "moral." Kleinman argues that in order for people to live a moral life, their moral commitments must be "embodied" (Kleinman, 2006).
8. De La Rocha, 1994.

9. Foner, 1994.

10. For examples of academic studies on nursing homes, see Diamond, 1990; also see National Research Council, 2002; Tench (2007) describes care providers charged with death; Pear (2002) addresses unreported abuse in nursing homes.

11. Baker, 2007.

12. Gubrium, 1975.

13. Kauffman, 1986.

14. Meyerhoff, 1978.

15. O'Reilly, 2000; King, Warnes, and Williams, 2000.

16. Chin, 1998; Chang, 2000; Parreñas, 2001; Hondagneu-Sotelo, 2001.

17. Lyon, 2006.

18. Degiuli, 2007.

19. Ibarra, 2003.

20. Martinez-Buján, 2007.

21. Ibid.

22. Ibarra, 2003.

23. Ortner, 1999b. Ortner argues that, in the relationship between Nepalese mountain guides (Sherpas) and international mountaineers (Sahibs), power is a constant. Sherpas are dependent on Sahibs for their employment and thus their livelihood. However, Sherpa lives hold meaning and purpose beyond that which is defined by the dominant group. And while money obviously matters to the less powerful here, there are other things that matter as well. For the Sherpas, gaining respect and prestige is important.

24. U.S. Census Bureau, 2000b.

25. Diamond, 1990; Foner, 1994.

26. Investigative reporting in Santa Barbara by Joshua Molina and Scott Hadley reveals widespread abuse in nursing homes (Molina and Hadley, 2000).

27. Mor et al., 2004.

28. Romero, 1992.

29. Ibarra, 2002, 2003.

30. Ortner, 1999b.

31. Ibarra, 2003.

32. Intimacy is threatened by the pace of modern life, as argued by Harvey, 1990.

33. Kleinman, Das, and Lock, 1997: 3.

34. Deep alliances are not limited to religious individuals. However, in my non-representative snowball sample, the majority of those who formed deep alliances identified themselves as religious persons.

9 Cultures of Flirtation

Sex and the Moral Boundaries of Filipina Migrant Hostesses in Tokyo

Rhacel Salazar Parreñas

CLOUDING OUR VIEW of foreign hostesses in Japan is their one-dimensional portrayal as victims of forced prostitution. Fueling this myth are not only the labeling of hostesses as trafficked "victims" in the U.S. Department of State's *Trafficking in Persons Report* but also sensationalist media reports that loosely use the word *trafficking* to describe the conditions of employment for hostesses.[1] Contrary to these claims, forced prostitution is a far cry from the reality of hostesses, as most do not even engage in prostitution. Instead, most do no more than flirt with customers. Some brazenly use their sex and sexuality to arouse customers, sometimes admittedly engaging in prostitution. Most, however, do not and instead merely flirt using coy intimations of affection that entail no physical contact. In this chapter, I intend to counter the one-dimensional portrayal of hostesses as victims of forced prostitution and describe the culture of work, or more accurately the cultures of flirtation, at hostess clubs. I present a nuanced description of hostess work as a job that, in certain circumstances, entails coercion and forced labor but in most other cases is actually determined, controlled, and accordingly performed by the workers. Suggesting that hostesses have a certain degree of control over the labor process is the fact that they do not perform the work of flirtation uniformly.

Distinguishing the styles and degree of flirtation by hostesses are their moral views on sex work. Migrant Filipina hostesses belong in three moral groupings of conservatives, rationalists, and in-betweeners. The term *moral conservatives* refers to hostesses who restrict their sexual relations with customers and work toward gaining intimacy with customers while maintaining platonic relations. *Moral rationalists*, in contrast, are hostesses who willingly participate in the direct purchase of sex. They receive monetary rewards for the provision of sexual favors to customers. Lastly, the largest group of women falls under the category *moral in-betweeners*. They would *never* participate in the direct purchase of sex but scoff at moral conservatives who pursue hostess work. They use their sexuality to gain intimacy with customers but would, at most, if they ever did so, allow physical intimacy only with frequent customers who would pay them not directly but indirectly through gifts of cash and in-kind presents.

My discussion is based on participant observation I gathered in Tokyo while working as a hostess at a Philippine club, meaning a club that exclusively employs Filipino hostesses, for a period of three months and observations I made as a customer from regularly visiting ten other Philippine clubs for nine months in 2005. I also draw from fifty-six open-ended in-depth interviews I conducted with hostesses.[2] Migrant Filipinos have historically comprised the majority of foreign hostesses in Japan, making up nearly 60 percent of the foreign hostess population as recently as 2005.[3] The drastic decline in their numbers—from nearly 80,000 in 2004 to fewer than 10,000 in 2006—reflects the tightening of Japan's borders against the migration of foreign hostesses following their labeling as trafficked victims by the U.S. Department of State.[4]

My chapter begins with a description of hostess work and the moral groupings of these workers. Then, I acknowledge the structural constraints that hamper the ability of hostesses to control their labor. These include the migrant status of the worker, peer pressure, and the moral regime of the workplace. My discussion illustrates that, despite the vulnerabilities faced by migrant hostesses, forced prostitution is not the cultural norm in their workplace.

Hostess Work

Hostess work involves care work, sexual work (but without the provision of sex), entertainment work, and boundary work. Care work means having to pay attention to all of the needs of the customer: serving his drinks, lighting his cigarettes, and feeding him. At hostess clubs, care work is as personalized as it is routinized.[5] Care work begins with the demonstration of servitude by hostesses when welcoming customers into the bar. At the club where I worked, the *mama-san* (female manager) expected us to follow her style of greeting customers. The hostess assigned to the table would have to kneel and bow her head before proceeding to wipe the customer's hands clean with a moist *oshiburi* (washcloth). Then, the hostess would prepare the customer's drink and, as I soon learned after I started working there, while demonstrating a feminine and submissive demeanor.

As the *mama-san* repeatedly demonstrated to me, I would have to mix drinks with my head slightly tilted to one side, a smile plastered on my face, and my legs slightly crossed with one leg placed in front of the other. Then, before I took the first sip of my drink, I had to first thank the customer for his generosity and demonstrate my subservience by initiating a toast with the rim of my glass lower than his. As one experienced hostess told me, "You are below a customer. So your glass must all the time be below his." To further demonstrate my subservience, I also had to stay alert and attentive to the needs of the customer. I could not refuse requests by customers. If they asked me to sing, I must sing. If they asked me to dance, I must dance. If they asked for a kiss, I must blow a kiss if not wanting to give them an actual kiss.

In addition to care work, hostesses must also engage in entertainment work. Hostesses must entertain customers not only by singing and dancing on stage but also by providing lively conversation. They usually do so in the hybrid language of English-Tagalog-Japanese.[6] Lively conversation at the club is usually of a sexual nature. If not quite able to keep the customer's interests that way, my co-workers would then resort to singing and dancing.

At the club, a hostess performs sexual work by intimating a relationship of intimacy with the customer. She does this physically, by holding his hands, massaging him, holding his thigh, or allowing him to put his arm around her shoulder; or verbally, by vocalizing her physical attraction for him, whether real or not. I gradually grew accustomed to the suggestion of physical intimacy with customers. Not long after working at the club, I learned to share the attitude carried by most of my co-workers that "nothing will be lost from me" (*walang mawawala sa akin*) if I sometimes let a customer touch my thigh and put his arm around my shoulders. As one interviewee succinctly put it, "I will not get pregnant from a hug."

Perhaps I could carry a more relaxed attitude about the physical contact between customers and me because intimacy at a hostess club is usually nothing more than the insinuation of sex. Yet, hostesses have the job of reminding customers of this boundary. Explains Amanda, a former contract worker and now stay-at-home mother of three children:

> You entertain the customer at the [club], but really it is illegal for them to touch you on the breast or anywhere. You can fight the customer if they do that. That is the exception because that is a sign of disrespect. That is not part

of the rules but that just happens because Japanese men like to do that. So of course you have to learn how to protect yourself in a way that you do not hurt the feeling of the person you are resisting . . . The play there is if someone touches you, you have to know how to react. You have to flirt, for example, and say in a coy voice, "Oh stop it. I am ticklish there. No." You do that. You have to do it in a way that you do not hurt the feelings of the customers. You need to learn how to do that.

At the club, customers constantly extend sexual advances to hostesses, usually expecting hostesses not to concede to their advances but to coyly deflect them. Following this script, hostess work involves the boundary work of rejecting these advances and limiting intimacy. As Amanda explained, this work often involves the careful deflection of sexual advances in a way that avoids the blatant rejection of a customer so as not to threaten his patronage of the club.

To what extent can hostesses reject the advances of customers? In other words, what is the permissible extent of boundary work? The hostesses I interviewed often responded by saying, "*nasa kanya*," meaning "it depends on the person." In other words, not all hostess and customer relations are the same. Some hostesses allow more physical intimacy with customers than others; some choose to participate in the direct purchase of sex, and some do not; lastly, some decide to form romantic relations with one or more customers. Partially determining these different extents of intimacy are the morality of hostesses and the moral boundaries they maintain when it comes to the purchase of sex and sexuality. In the next section, I describe the three primary moral groupings of hostesses.

Moral Groupings of Hostesses: Conservatives, Rationalists, and In-Betweeners

The manipulation of sexuality is key to the job of a hostess, who must sexually excite customers either by seductive dance or song performances in scanty attire or by sexual banter in conversation and action at the table. In hostess clubs, styles of sexual titillation vary and include but are not limited to coy displays of innocent affection, overt but yet comedic demonstrations of desire such as blowing a kiss to the customer or jiggling one's breasts seductively, the engagement of blatant dirty talk, the use of witty conversation, and the display of subtle and sometimes not so subtle physical gestures of affection such as a hand around the shoulder or a hand on the thigh or a tap on the groin.

Distinguishing the ways that hostesses flirt with customers, in other words how far they go, are their moral boundaries.

As I mentioned earlier, there are three moral categories of hostesses among Filipinos in Japan: moral conservatives, rationalists, and in-betweeners. Members of each of these groups maintain different moral views about the intersections of sex and money. Despite their differences, the three moral groupings of hostesses are not mutually exclusive, as the morals of hostesses are not static but instead shift along with changes in their ideology and experience. Religious beliefs, economic needs, peer pressure, and work routines all shape the views and morals of hostesses. In the process of their migration, the construction of morals for hostesses does not necessarily constitute a teleological progression from a conservative intolerance against commercial sex that is espoused in a Catholic country such as the Philippines toward a greater tolerance as would be encouraged by the customs at a hostess club. Instead, some experienced hostesses could remain staunchly conservative, particularly born-again Christians. In contrast, others could become more tolerant as they become immune to the sexual overtures of customers. In this section, I provide a more thorough description of the moral groupings of hostesses.

Moral Conservatives

Minorities among hostesses, moral conservatives are those most likely to reject the direct purchase of sex as sinful and minimize their sexual banter with customers. Embarrassed about the stigma associated with their job, moral conservatives hide the nature of their work from family and friends in the Philippines, view their job as their last resort for employment, and consciously attempt to desexualize interactions with customers. They desexualize their interactions by constructing their customers as a "father figure," "big brother," or friend. Not completely rejecting hostess work, moral conservatives can do their jobs only if done with minimal reference to sex.

Moral conservatives tend to be first-time contract workers in Japan, some of whom had not expected that their job would entail close interactions with customers. It is rare to meet moral conservatives in Japan because they are those most likely to be sent back home to the Philippines prior to the end of their contract. Management is not likely to tolerate hostesses who are unable to adjust smoothly to the sexual undertones of club culture.[7]

Yet, moral conservatives also include long-term residents, particularly born-again Christians, who do this work only because of their minimal options in the labor market. Language difficulties, the lack of experience, or un-documented status block these women's entry into the formal labor market of Japan, thus limiting them to hostess or domestic work.[8] Rie, a born-again Christian whom I met in Tokyo, is a typical moral conservative who would rather not do hostess work but finds herself as an undocumented worker without other job options. She is able to do the work only because she views what is done with the job and not the job in itself as immoral. Responding to my question on whether doing hostess work is immoral or not, she stated:

> No, it is what you do that makes it bad. Inside me, I do not think that it is bad just as long as you know how to control yourself [with customers], and you know what you need to do, and you do not let the customers take advantage of you. There are some customers who offer you indecent proposals. They want to take you to a hotel. And they promise to get you all these things. But it is in you to handle this situation in whichever way you want.

Rie is currently looking for a job as a domestic worker in an expatriate house-hold, as foreign diplomats and corporate executives could sponsor her tempo-rary residency. Yet, after six months of failing to secure work in a private house-hold, she is resigned to doing hostess work. Her youth and lack of experience with child care seems to deter potential domestic employers from hiring her.

Moral Rationalists

In contrast to moral conservatives are moral rationalists, who reject the no-tion of commercial sex as immoral. I met plenty of moral rationalists, but only a few admitted to being one during our interview, perhaps because the stigma of prostitution deters hostesses from publicly admitting their involve-ment with commercial sex. Moral rationalists are hostesses who engage in commercial sex inside or outside the club. Commercial sex inside the club in-cludes fondling or performing a hand job discretely, because such acts would be cause for dismissal in most hostess clubs. Commercial sex outside the club would entail the direct purchase of various services including fellatio and sexual intercourse.

I encountered moral rationalists in informal settings in the community, during coffee after church services in the afternoon or after work in the early morning. Once a group of my friends surprised me when one of them began to describe her experience giving a hand job to a first-time customer at her club, vividly describing her disappointment over the size of his penis and complaining about her measly tip of 1000 yen (ten dollars) for her efforts. Others soon joined in and shared strategies for using sex to garner tips at work. In another instance, a friend who chose not to participate in my study complained to me about how a john she met at a nightclub refused to pay her after their encounter. These stories that I heard regularly suggest that some hostesses participate in commercial sex. Yet there seems to be a moral gauge in the community in which playing around with customers inside the club is more acceptable than engaging in commercial sex outside the club. I noticed that hostesses would freely admit to "crossing the line" with customers inside the club but not outside the club. The few who admitted to engaging in commercial sex outside the club describe paid sex as "easy money," value the financial gains of sex with customers, and see the use of their body for money as morally acceptable. Those who do are mostly long-time residents of Japan and describe themselves as having become "wise" from experience with customers who broke their hearts or fooled them with empty promises of marriage or money. They also include those in dire economic circumstances, including one first-time contract worker, Baby, who engages in commercial sex to cover the debt she incurred from labor recruiters prior to migration.

Moral In-Betweeners

The moral standards of in-betweeners encompass a wide range of principles concerning the intersections of money and sex. They will not hesitate to kiss frequent customers and use their sexuality to seduce customers, but they usually will not have sex with them for money. Unlike moral conservatives who would prefer only to sit across the table from customers, moral in-betweeners know that the use of their sexuality, whether jiggling their breasts in front of the customer or slyly touching his crotch, would likely generate more tips from him at the end of the evening. While members of this group openly use their sexuality to attract customers, they do not freely engage in sexual intimacy with customers inside or outside the club. Unlike moral rationalists, they would not allow customers to fondle them indiscriminately, including those whom they maintain sexual relations with outside of the club. Inside the club, they would usually do no more than place a hand on the thigh of the customer or kiss him with a closed lip on the cheek. Outside the club, they would never participate in one-night stands and "just charge for one sex act."

Hostesses who fall in the category of moral in-betweeners shun the direct purchase of sex but require some form of ongoing relationship with those whom they choose as potential sexual partners.[9] For them, social relations determine the extent and dynamic of their sexual activities with customers. Moral in-betweeners distinguish their customers as a boyfriend in the *club*, a boyfriend, or just a customer. They would label as a "boyfriend" those for whom they have a modicum of feelings and relegate as a "boyfriend in the *club*" or "just a customer" those whom they do not find attractive or desirable. A "boyfriend in the *club*" is a regular customer whom hostesses could call whenever business is slow. In contrast, a mere customer is an infrequent visitor to the club.

Moral in-betweeners do not engage in sexual intimacy with customers or boyfriends in the *club* and selectively do so with boyfriends.[10] As I noted, key to understanding the category of moral in-betweeners is the fact that they would never participate in the direct purchase of sex. In other words, they would never accept payment directly for any form of sexual act. They do, however, expect to receive financial compensation for maintaining sexual relations with customers, that is, those whom they have designated as "boyfriends," as they would engage in sex only with customers who could provide them with generous tips on a regular basis.

Interestingly, even though moral in-betweeners receive financial compensation from their sexual partners, they still distinguish themselves from those who fall in the category of moral rationalists, whom they would label as "prostitutes" or "hookers." Ela, a "retired" hostess who has been in Japan for more than twenty-five years, explains:

> We are formally not hookers. We are just using our head. If we are going to get together with a Japanese, we make sure that we get together with one who has money. Me, I also got a boyfriend. . . . I think people just misinterpret us to be hookers for the reason that Japanese men give us money. But I don't think we are hookers. What I mean is that our boyfriends are giving us money. Hookers are different. Hookers are those who stand around one area and get picked up by men. Isn't that what a hooker is?

Unlike moral conservatives, moral in-betweeners such as Ela accept the use of their sexuality at work, openly flirt and banter with customers, and engage in different degrees of intimacy with them. Moral in-betweeners do not think the use of sexuality is immoral but also do not think that the use of sex for money is universally acceptable. It depends on the circumstances, many told me. As I just pointed out, it also depends on their social relations with customers.

Constructing Moral Categories: Moral Regimes of Hostess Clubs, Peer Pressure, and Work Experience

I have just established that hostesses maintain different moral boundaries in regards to general customer–hostess relations and sex in particular. In this section, I address the question of whether the actions of hostesses conform to their moral standards. In other words, can hostesses do their work without violating their morals? Can hostesses perform the boundary work of protecting themselves from harassment? I address these questions so as to return to the claims of the human trafficking of Filipina hostesses in Japan by the U.S. Department of State, mentioned in the introduction.

Many hostesses insist that they carry a semblance of control over their relations with customers. As they repeatedly told me, the extent of intimacy between a customer and a hostess depends on the preference of a hostess. As they would say, "*nasa kanya*," meaning "it is up to the person." However, there is a limit to the control of hostesses. Various contextual forces shape the actions of hostesses at the club, sometimes resulting in the violation of their moral boundaries. It is when we take into account the moral regime of the club, the employment status of the hostess, and peer pressure that we see how the possibility of sex trafficking arises for them.

Moral Regimes

The provision of sexual flirtation is the premise of any hostess club, but the extent of flirtation that occurs in a club varies according to the club's moral regime of sex, which varies from one club to the next. By *moral regime of sex*, I refer to the prevailing notions of proper as well as improper use of sexual intimacy in the club. Moral regimes of sex shape the conditions of interaction between hostesses and customers. As May, a part-time worker since 1996, succinctly states, "Your situation really depends on the [club] that you enter." Philippine clubs in Tokyo fall under three moral regimes that mirror the moral groupings of hostesses. There are moral conservative, moral rationalist, and lastly moral in-betweener establishments. Clubs tend to have a reputation that accordingly determines their patronage. In other words, customers tend to seek clubs that maintain moral regimes that coincide or match their own morals.

In morally conservative clubs, physical contact between customers and hostesses, if it does occur, is limited to infrequent dances on the floor or hands held across the table. Usually, the customer and hostess sit across the table from one another and converse, perhaps sharing sexual jokes, but barely touching one another. The hostess usually "entertains" by singing and dancing with the customer or, if she has command of the Japanese language, through conversation. Morally conservative establishments are usually neighborhood snack bars frequented by older men who are sometimes accompanied by their wives. Customers either pay a per-hour table fee, reaching no more than 3,000 yen (US$30) per hour in these establishments, or instead buy a bottle of liquor that they keep in the house to consume every time they visit.

In sharp contrast to morally conservative establishments are moral rationalist businesses. In these places, management encourages hostesses to overtly use their sex and sexuality to secure the business of customers. These establishments vary in size from large clubs that employ more than ten hostesses who perform nightly variety shows of singing and dancing to small neighborhood bars that employ no more than three hostesses per night. In these establishments, management have been known to, but not always, demand that hostesses expose their breasts and wear skimpy and revealing attire during the variety show. In some cases, management encourages hostesses to allow customers to touch intimate parts of their body in the club or maintain sexual relations with customers outside the club. Moral rationalist businesses usually charge per-hour fees that are nominally higher than the entrance fees in morally conservative establishments. Rates in moral rationalist businesses that I visited or heard about from hostesses ranged from 5,000 yen ($50) per hour to 7,000 yen ($70) per ninety minutes. Hostesses do not necessarily earn more in a moral rationalist business than in other types of hostess establishments, but they are likely to garner more tips and gifts from customers in exchange for sex.

Most hostess clubs that employ Filipina migrants maintain morally in-between regimes of sex. In these clubs, sexual flirtation takes place between customers and hostesses but not those of the overt sexual kind such as the heavy petting and make-out sessions that one would encounter in a moral rationalist club. Instead, customers and hostesses usually touch only fleetingly, for instance a quick grope on the breast or a kiss on the lips are exchanged once or twice in one evening. In clubs with moral in-betweener regimes, hostesses overtly use their sexuality to seduce customers into becoming regular patrons. Seduction commonly takes place via entertainment through singing and dancing in sexually provocative but nonrevealing clothes. It also takes place via conversation in which customers and hostesses tease one another with sexual jokes.

The issue of sex trafficking arises when hostesses find themselves working in a club where the moral regime of sex does not match their own. For instance, a moral conservative working in a moral rationalist club is likely to confront serious moral violations at work. Possibly aggravating this situation would be employment status, particularly for contract workers, as they have limited recourse to quit their jobs. In the next section, I specifically describe how the employment status of hostesses limits their ability to control their labor.

Employment Status

Hostesses are aware that clubs have different moral regimes. As such, they accordingly try to find work only in clubs that would match their own moral beliefs on sex. Yet, hostesses are not always in a position to choose their club of employment and even worse are not able to quit their jobs. As I explain in this section, the employment status of the hostess, whether she is a contract worker or part-time worker, determines her ability to negotiate her work conditions. Part-time workers are basically in a better position to choose their club of employment than are contract workers because they are long-term residents of Japan. In contrast to contract workers, they have the flexibility to choose their place of employment.

Contract workers have little control over the type of club they will enter in Japan. Prior to their departure from the Philippines, labor recruiters have already assigned them to a club in Japan. They are contractually bound to work in their assigned club for at least three months. Aggravating their vulnerability is their minimal knowledge of their rights as migrant workers in Japan. For instance, not many know they can report contract violations to the Embassy of the Philippines, including management demands for them to work not only as a singer or dancer on stage but as a hostess at the club.[11]

Regardless of the protective stance taken by the government of the Philippines, contract workers usually cannot terminate their contracts without penalty. Talent managers in the Philippines who helped them secure a contract with a labor recruiter usually impose a $3,000 fine to hostesses who choose not to complete five contract terms to work in Japan within the next six years, while labor recruiters impose an equally significant fee to those who quit their jobs prior to the end of their three- or six-month contract. It is questionable whether such conditions of indenture would stand in the legal courts of the Philippines. For this reason, talent managers and labor recruiters often demand a blank check from contract workers prior to their departure and use this as a form of collateral to collect illegal penalty fees.

Most hostess clubs maintain a moral in-betweener regime. Still, contract workers and part-time workers could find themselves working in a moral rationalist business, which a part-time worker could more freely leave than a contract worker who must otherwise return to the Philippines if unwilling to work at the specific establishment to which she has been placed prior to migration. Aware of the different moral regimes in clubs, part-time workers try to work only in clubs that match their own moral beliefs on sex. Marietta, a permanent resident and hence part-time worker, is one woman who consciously measures the moral regime of every club she considers as a place of employment. As she explains:

> There are some [clubs] where you see the women doing things. You feel pressured to follow because everyone else is doing it. I am talking about having customers feel you up, do dirty dancing. They do not care that someone like their neighbor in the Philippines is going to see them do that.
> *Do you avoid those kinds of [club]?*
> I try to study the system. The first day I try to see if I can handle the place.

Like other part-time workers, Marietta would not work in a club with a moral regime that would go against her moral values.

Unlike part-time workers such as Marietta, hostesses with temporary work visas, that is, contract workers, cannot shop for places of employment that would suit their moral boundaries. It is also not convenient for them to quit their jobs and opt to return to the Philippines. If placed in a morally rationalist club, a moral conservative or in-betweener could without doubt find her morals compromised. It is in this situation that a hostess becomes vulnerable to trafficking, doing a job she wishes not to do and with limited recourse to quit. We see this in the case of Elizabeth, a former contract worker in Japan who eventually married one of her customers. She recalls,

> We were modern dancers . . . We would dance for one hour. Then it became ugly. We all started crying. We had to show our breasts. That was when I was a first timer . . . But that was not in our contract . . . At the end of the dance, we had to show our breasts. Before we leave the stage, we had to show our breasts. I am getting upset just remembering it.

Aggravating Elizabeth's situation had been her employment status. As a contract worker, Elizabeth thought she had no other recourse but to finish her six-month contract and bear the moral violations required of her to perform in the job. Because of the control of labor recruiters over their labor migration, many contract workers who experience moral violations at work tolerate it. However, not all passively accept their fate. Unlike Elizabeth, some insist on returning to the Philippines.

In considering the employment status of hostesses, we realize that contract workers are vulnerable to human trafficking. Yet, to be trapped in a situation of moral contestation does not automatically constitute trafficking. After all, they can quit, and I have found that some do. To a limited extent, hostesses also have the agency to shift their moral boundaries and adjust to the moral regime of their workplace. As I describe in the next section, a central factor that influences and transforms their morals is peer pressure, which is often imposed through the actions of co-workers. By recognizing the agency of hostesses to eventually adjust to what they would have once considered intolerable work conditions, I do not deny the existence of trafficking. Instead, I merely call attention to the fact that trafficking is not a universal occurrence in the case of foreign hostesses in Japan.

Peer Pressure

Moral regimes in clubs are not only imposed by management rules from above but are constructed by the actions that occur in the club.[12] The culture of hostess clubs shifts from one club to another according to the behavior of hostesses. Hence, the moral regimes of club are not static. The actions of those in the club, including customers, management, and workers, jointly determine, but not without conflict, the moral regimes that shape customer and hostess relations. Dominant cultural patterns emerge in hostess clubs, resulting in the pressure for hostesses to conform to the norm in each club.

Because everyday actions constitute the moral regimes of clubs, changes in action could engender a sudden shift in the culture of the hostess club. This occurred at the club where I did field work, which I quit after the arrival of three new hostesses drastically transformed the moral regime of the club from being a moral in-betweener club to a moral rationalist club. To my discomfort and that of six other co-workers, the actions of the three new hostesses fell under the regime of moral rationalists. The three new hires had no qualms about undressing on the dance floor to entertain customers. They also encouraged customers to touch their private parts in the view of others. These three new workers attracted customers who otherwise would not have patronized our club.[13]

Unhappy with the shift in moral culture at the club, my old co-workers quit one by one. They worried that the actions of the new hires would reconstitute the cultural expectations of customers who now would likely expect a greater level of physical intimacy from them. They also did not like the floor manager's repeated encouragement for us to engage in sex outside the club. It was not only my co-workers who stopped going to the club. Not all customers patronize hostess clubs to pursue sex. Some are likely to want no more than the thrills of flirtation. Not surprisingly, then, some did not appreciate the shift of culture at the club from a moral in-betweener to a moral rationalist establishment. They too began to stop patronizing our club.

Conflicts can surely arise when the culture of the club disagrees with the moral values of hostesses. Yet, in some cases, hostesses could possibly conform without difficulty to the cultural norms of a club. For instance, a moral in-betweener could learn to accept the values of moral rationalists, or a moral conservative could learn the values of moral in-betweeners. However, in many cases, a hostess is more likely to experience moral violations when working at a club with a regime that disagrees with her own. Part-time workers, such as the hostesses at my fieldwork site, could reject peer pressure and quit. Contract workers unfortunately have less flexibility to do so. One such hostess was Elizabeth, cited earlier. Aggravating her moral dilemma regarding the exposure of her breasts on stage had been the peer pressure she encountered from experienced hostesses to not make such a big deal of it. As she explains,

> [My co-workers and I] cried. We wanted to go back to the Philippines. We really did not know that we could complain. We were mostly first-timers, but there were some veterans telling us that it was no big deal. We just had to show our breasts. We first said no, and then the veterans spoke to us. They asked us if we were virgins, and if not, then it is no big deal to show our breasts. No one will be groping them. We just have to show them. We will eventually learn how to play along the longer we stay in Japan.

Notably, the construction of morals does not necessarily involve a teleological shift toward one's greater tolerance of commercial sex. Elizabeth, for instance, never adjusted to a moral rationalist regime, but she still took her risk and returned to Japan for a second labor contract prior to getting married to one of her customers.

Yet, unlike Elizabeth and my co-workers, others do learn to conform to the views of moral rationalists. Many hostesses who describe themselves as either "innocent" or a "country bumpkin" prior to migration claim to have eventually learned to accept the view of *"walang mawawala sa akin"* (nothing will be lost from me) when flirting openly with customers. These hostesses have learned to use their sexuality, including stripping in some cases, to maximize the material rewards of their labor. Experience, economic need, and peer pressure all have combined to expand their moral boundaries. However, Elizabeth and my co-workers remind us that not all do so. Some never quite adjust to the sexual norms in most hostess clubs.

Conclusion

Intimate relations between hostesses and customers are as dynamic as they are diverse. Not surprisingly, hostesses repeatedly describe intimate relations between hostesses and customers in the clubs as *nasa kanya* (meaning, "it is up to the person"). However, relations with customers depend not only on the moral standards of the hostess, which shift according to their experiences and ideologies, but they depend as well on the moral regime of sex in the workplace, the employment status of the hostess, and peer pressure. As we see in the case of Elizabeth, disagreements between the moral standards of hostesses and the moral regime of sex in the workplace could result in severe moral violations and potentially one's forced sexual labor.

Supporters of the U.S. antitrafficking campaign seem to think that the potential for moral violations arising for hostesses such as Elizabeth justifies the call for their rescue. However, the view of their experiences from below reveals that hostesses are not just victims in need of rescue, as they carry various degrees of control over their labor. After all, some could quit, while others could choose to expand their moral values and adjust to the moral regime of their workplace. Moreover, in the context of their limited labor market options as migrant workers, others prefer to remain hostesses despite the job's set of moral challenges. The risk of coerced labor haunts migrant hostesses, but the proposed solution of rescue recommended by the likes of U.S. government fails to meet their needs. Perhaps those who advocate for the welfare of migrant hostesses should consider ways they could have greater control of their labor.

Notes

An earlier version of this chapter appeared in "Hostess Work: Negotiating the Morals of Money and Sex," in *Economic Sociology and Work*, Vol. 19 of *Research in the Sociology of Work*, edited by Nina Bandelj. Bingley, UK: Emerald, 2008.

1. For example, a *New York Times* article insinuates the marking of forced prostitution when clubs require hostesses to "date customers" outside the club. As it states, "In Japan, the foreign women who are victims of trafficking end up working every-

where from Tokyo's red-light districts to rural areas unfamiliar to most foreigners . . . they serve as sex performers or hostesses at clubs outside of which they are expected to date customers." From my research, however, I know that the vulnerability incurred from dating customers outside the club does not result in forced prostitution.

2. My work experience opened the door to the world of Filipina hostesses. As I had worked at a hostess club, potential interviewees rightfully assumed that a good part of our interview would not be spent on explaining how hostess work is not prostitution. Instead we were able to focus on the nature of the work, its difficulties and challenges, and their conditions of migration.

3. Oishi, 2005.

4. U.S. Department of State, 2003; 2004; 2005.

5. Leidner, 1993.

6. To my surprise, many of our regular customers spoke a little bit of Tagalog. This is because many have frequented Philippine pubs for more than a decade, and some have married Filipino women.

7. Still, I managed to meet two first-time contract workers who fit this moral grouping. These two assert that they will try not to return to Japan for another contract.

8. Domestic workers are a minority in the Filipino community. They rarely work for Japanese households but instead cater to the expatriate community.

9. Without doubt, it is nearly unavoidable for hostesses to make a wrong choice for a potential partner and select one who wants no more than a one-night stand from them. For this reason, they try to secure as much money and gifts as possible for a set period of time prior to engaging in sexual intimacy.

10. Some have more than one boyfriend.

11. Reporting contract violations could enable hostesses to return to the Philippines, albeit not necessarily with pay.

12. Foucault, 1977.

13. Business had been slow prior to their arrival, and so our *mama-san* was only too happy to expand her clientele and condoned the actions of the women by not reprimanding them to stop.

10 Bounded Authenticity and the Commerce of Sex

Elizabeth Bernstein

IN THE BACK ROOM of a discreetly furnished apartment in a quiet San Francisco neighborhood, I am sitting on a brown leather sofa talking with Amanda, who has just said goodbye to the day's first customer. We drink tea as the early afternoon sunshine streams into the room, illuminating many overstuffed bookcases, an exercise bicycle, and Amanda herself—a slender woman in her late thirties with dark hair and serious eyes. Smiling slightly, she shrugs when I ask her how the session with her client went:

> Actually, I spent most of the time giving him a backrub, and we also spent a lot of time talking before we had sex. In the end, we went over [time] by about seven minutes ... You know it's really funny to me when people say that I'm selling my body. Of all the work I've done, this isn't abusive to my body. Most of my clients are computer industry workers—about half. Sometimes I ask myself: What about their bodies? These men spend forty hours a week hunched over a desk. They live alone, eat alone, drive to work alone. Other than seeing me, they don't seem to even have time for a social life.

Amanda goes on to explain that today's client was a marketing executive for a prominent Silicon Valley software company. This client is a "regular," someone she has seen before, who has often complained to her that he is overworked and too busy to meet women. I wonder aloud how it is that he nonetheless has the time to drive two and a half hours on his lunch break to come and see her. Amanda observes with bemusement that for the majority of her client pool—educated, professional men who have contacted her via an online ad—such paradoxes represent the norm.

This chapter is about the ways in which recent transformations in economic and cultural life have played themselves out at the most intimate of levels: the individual experience of bodily attributes and integrity and the meanings afforded to sexual expression. The lens through which I examine these transitions is sexual commerce, the exchange of sex for money in the globalized, late-capitalist marketplace. My contention is that experiences such as those of Amanda and her clients reflect and thus offer insight into broader trends at work within intimate life in the contemporary West.[1]

Once largely restricted to face-to-face interactions and the small-scale circulation of pornographic images, the scope of sexual commerce has grown to include a vast and ever-expanding range of commercially available products and experiences—live sex shows; all variety of sexually explicit texts, videos, and pictures, both in print and on-line; fetish clubs; sexual "emporiums" featuring lap and wall dancing; "drive-through" striptease venues; escort agencies; erotic massage; telephone and cyber-sex contacts; and sex tourism to developing countries and within global cities—what is purportedly a more than twenty-billion-dollar-a-year industry and a mainstay of both First and Third World economies.[2] By examining this growth and diversification of sexual commerce from the perspectives of the purveyors of sexual services and their consumers, my aim is to articulate a political economy of sexual practices and desires. By detailing the relationship between money and sex at the "micro" level of bodies and subjectivities, I seek to more broadly reveal the relationship between economy and desire.

My argument is that the global restructuring of capitalist production and investment that has taken place since the 1970s has had consequences that are more profound and more intimate than most economic sociologists ever choose to consider.[3] The desires that drive the rapidly expanding and diversifying international sex trade have emanated from corporate-fueled consumption, from an increase in tourism and business travel, and from the symbiotic relationship between information technologies and the privatization of commercial consumption.[4] At the same time, the rise in service occupations and temporary work, as well as an increase in labor migrations from developing to developed countries, has fueled the growth and diversification of sexual labor. For many sectors of the populations, these shifts have resulted in new configurations of familial life as well as in new erotic dispositions, ones that the market is well poised to satisfy.

Old and New Markets in Sexual Labor

To historically situate my claims about the "newness" of late capitalist configurations of eroticism and desire, it may be useful to briefly review some
of the scholarship that documents the shifts in the social organization and
meaning of prostitution that have taken place in the United States and Western Europe over the last few centuries. As social historians such as Judith
Walkowitz,[5] Ruth Rosen,[6] and Barbara Hobson[7] have pointed out, despite the
frequent equation of "prostitution" with the "oldest profession," what many
of us typically think of as prostitution has not existed for very long at all.
The rise of large-scale, commercialized prostitution in the West emerged only
with modern industrial capitalism and its attendant features in the late nineteenth century: urbanization, the expansion of wage labor, and the decline
of the extended-kin-based "traditional family." These structural transformations brought with them new cultural ideologies of gender and sexuality and
new symbolic boundaries between public and private life. Accentuated gender
differences produced a "double standard" in sexual relations, dichotomizing
women along class lines. While white, bourgeois, married women practiced
sexual restraint in the private sphere of the home, many working-class women
and women of color joined men in the public sphere as wage laborers and
sexually available prostitutes.[8] By the early twentieth century, numerous "vice
commissions" had been created to study—and thereby constitute—the social
problem of modern prostitution.

By contrast, what historians typically refer to as "premodern" forms of
sexual commerce were self-organized, occasional exchanges in which women
traded sexual favors during limited periods of hardship. Premodern prostitution was small in scale, frequently was premised on barter, and generally
took place within the participants' own homes and communities. Only with
the onset of modern industrial capitalism did large numbers of women find
themselves sequestered in a space that was physically and socially separate,
thereby affixing them with the permanently stigmatizing identity of "prostitute." During the Progressive Era in the United States, red-light districts
were officially shut down and the sex trade was criminalized, but this did not
fundamentally alter the meaning of modern prostitution, which marked the
female prostitute (but not her male customer) as a criminal outsider. Instead,
associations with the image of a dangerous and gritty underworld were dramatically exacerbated, and prostitutes now had to cope with the added stigma
of criminality.

The terms *modern* and *premodern* are of course heuristic devices, facilitating the comprehension of social realities that are in fact much messier than this simple categorization permits. Prototypically, "premodern" forms of sexual barter never disappeared entirely but exist to this day as the dominant mode of commercial sexual exchange in many impoverished communities throughout the world and in the sex-for-drugs barter economy of the inner city. The terms, nevertheless, capture something important in terms of large-scale social change. They highlight the ways in which new forms and meanings of sexual exchange emerge at particular historical junctures, coexisting with, and at times eclipsing, the forms that preceded them.

The globalized, late-capitalist era of the late twentieth and early twenty-first centuries has witnessed a similar transitional moment in paradigms of commercial sexual exchange (see Table 10.1). In postindustrial cities such as San Francisco, Amsterdam, and Stockholm, the boundaries of vice have been remapped in such a way so as to curtail the deviant underworld of modern prostitution, while the commercialization of sexual services overall has expanded.[9]

For example, in San Francisco, by the late 1990s the nine-square-block area of the city that had housed the city's primary street prostitution strolls for over seventy-five years was on its way to being incorporated into Union Square (the principle tourist district), as fashionable restaurants and high-priced apartment complexes had widened their spread. At the same time, advertisements for prostitution in the newspapers and through the new on-line services exploded, as did prostitution in eleven of the city's seventeen legal strip clubs. Many of the very same women and men who had been working on the streets now began to get cell phones and to take out ads or to look for work in indoor venues. Unlike streetwalking, the new markets in sexual commerce were not concentrated in a de facto urban red-light district but were dispersed throughout the city, housed in inconspicuous Victorians in quiet residential neighborhoods, or relocated to indoor businesses in the city's suburban periphery.[10] The explosion of commercial sexual services was met by an almost complete lack of concern by the police, despite their intense focus on visible streetwalking.

The transformation that was underway in San Francisco did not merely concern the fate of a few hundred street prostitutes and their customers but was about a more wide-sweeping reallocation of urban space, in which the inner city was reclaimed by the white middle classes, while those at the social margins were pushed to the city's literal periphery.[11] Although the neighborhood residents actively opposed flagrant and visible prostitution on their streets, it is important to note that, in contrast to "moral reform" movements

Table 10.1 Paradigmatic distinctions between modern-industrial prostitution and postindustrial sexual commerce.

	Modern-industrial prostitution	Postindustrial sexual commerce
What is being sold	Heterosexual intercourse or receptive oral sex	Diversified and specialized array of sexual products and services (images, performances, acts)
Where the exchange takes place	Red-light districts in urban tenderloins (brothels or streets); sequestration serves to maintain social divide between "public" and "private"	Dispersed throughout the city and surrounding suburbs (in private homes, hotels and commercial venues; over the telephone and on-line); no clear division between the sexual ideologies of "public" and "private" space
State interventions	Criminalized or regulated by state agents; where criminalized, gendered specification of "prostitution" as a crime	Interventions focus on street-based exchanges and/or illegal migrants
What is being bought	Quick sexual release (the emotionally void counterpart of private sphere romance and love)	Bounded authenticity (relational meaning resides in the market transaction)

of eras past, they did not issue a critique about the intermingling of sexuality and the market.[12] To the contrary, the young, white professionals who flooded the city during the 1990s to work in high-tech, multimedia, and other industries were at the forefront of a new economy in sexual services, both by creating a demand for them and in facilitating new conditions of production. The sex trade was not eliminated, but instead changed its predominant form: The subterranean world of street prostitution, along with its classic paraphernalia—the pimp; the police officer; the prostitute as "public," and therefore disreputable, woman—had begun to recede into the distance, while an array of spatially dispersed sexual services emerged to take its place.

The Subjective Contours of Market Intimacy

The economic transformations of recent decades have restructured not only the social geography of sex work but also the subjective meanings that guide the experience from within. While a fair amount has been written about the ways in which the new globalized economy has spawned a lucrative traffic in women and children from Asia, Africa, Latin America, and, more recently,

Eastern Europe,[13] I would like to point to a different level at which new global economic realities have been significant to the development of the sex trade in the West. They have contributed to a transformation in practices and meanings (what we might think of as the subjective contours of market intimacy) for participants on both sides of the commercial sex-work encounter.

In modern prostitution, what was typically sold and bought was an expedient and emotionally contained exchange of cash for sexual release.[14] To survive in the trade, prostitutes learned to develop strategies to distance themselves from their labor, to treat their commercial sexual activity as "work." In my interviews with streetwalkers, many strived to emphasize the difference between "career prostitutes" and "crack prostitutes," not only because crack prostitution involved sex for drugs rather than sex for money but also because most career prostitutes felt that crack prostitutes did not maintain a clear division between public and private selves.

For self-identified "career prostitutes," one important way that the public/private boundary is maintained is through a particular remapping of erotic bodily geography, in which one keeps certain sexual practices, aspects of the self, and segments of the body off limits. As the sociologist Susan Edwards has observed,

> The belief that, for women who supply the service, "anything goes," is widespread, as women who sell sex forfeit the right to say "No." . . . On the contrary, while sections of the public world may hold this view, the selling of sex by prostitute women is carefully circumscribed . . . Prostitute women care less about the genitals and breasts, and much more about the mouth, the lips, the kiss, and tenderness, for them the truest meaning and expression of intimacy.[15]

In addition to extreme vigilance about the use of condoms (as both a physical and a psychological barrier) and working "straight" (rather than drunk or high), most of the street-based sex workers whom I interviewed strenuously insisted that they would not engage their clients in a mouth-to-mouth kiss. In Oslo, one woman explained to me that her work had "nothing to do" with her sexuality because "the most intimate thing that I have is not what I am selling. I am simply selling the man his orgasm." Karolyn, a Swedish street prostitute, explained similarly,

> If you work like this, you need to have unseen borders you don't let people trespass. If you do, then you start to drink or use drugs, because you can't

bear to see yourself in the mirror afterwards. There are things that you allow, and there are things that you don't allow, things that you won't do for money. There has to be a private place inside of you. You can't be the same person when you go out to work.

And Ulla, who has worked on the streets of both Stockholm and Helsinki, described the necessity of "leaving my private me at home so that I can go to work."

By contrast, within an emergent *postindustrial* paradigm of sexual commerce, what is being bought and sold frequently incorporates a great deal more emotional, as well as physical, labor within the commercial context.[16] The term *sex work* has come into increasingly widespread usage since the 1980s, when it was first coined by prostitutes' rights activists to signal that the sale of sex for money need not imply a unique degradation of self.[17] Yet, ironically, it has been precisely during this period that the sexual labor that is exchanged within the transaction is less defined by the sexual acts themselves and more likely to implicate one's "private" erotic and emotional life.

With the relocation of sexual labor from the street to indoor venues such as private homes, rented apartments, and "gentlemen's clubs," the quality of sexual labor that is entailed is also transformed.[18] Sex workers increasingly emphasize the centrality of emotionally engaged conversation to their work, as well as a willingness to participate in a diversity of sexual activities (for example, bodily caresses, full body touching, receiving "pleasure," all of which can require a tremendous amount of emotional labor on the part of the sex worker) and to bestow mouth-to-mouth kisses. Compared to street-walkers, the labor of indoor, self-employed sex workers is likely to require a larger investment of time with each client (typically an hour, as opposed to fifteen minutes for streetwalkers), to take place within the confines of one's own home, and to remain outside the purview of the criminal justice system. Contemporary "intimacy providers" (as some in the industry have taken to calling themselves) charge by the hour rather than for specified acts, so their sexual labor is diffuse and expansive, rather than delimited and expedient.[19]

In contrast to the quick, impersonal "sexual release" associated with the street-level sex trade, much of the new variety of sexual labor resides in the provision of what I call "bounded authenticity"—the sale and purchase of authentic emotional and physical connection. The anthropologist Katharine Frank has similarly observed the premium placed on authenticity in contemporary strip clubs, arguing that clients' desire for the real and the authentic is palpable even amid the postmodern simulations of makeup, costumes, breast implants, and stage names (not to mention cash exchange). Based on ethnographic observations and interviews, Frank documents the numerous ways that clients seek to signal the authenticity of their commercial sexual transactions with strippers, including payments through gifts or cocktails (more personal than cash transactions), and the persistent interest in dancers' real lives and identities.[20] As both Frank's research and my own make clear, what is being bought and sold is something quite other than an ephemeral consumer indulgence, yet also distinct from premodern forms of sexual exchange that naturalize the provision of nonsexual forms of intimacy. In postindustrial sexual commerce, emotional authenticity is incorporated explicitly into the economic contract.

For many sex workers, the provision of bounded authenticity resides in fulfilling clients' fantasies of sensuous reciprocity through the self-conscious simulation of desire, pleasure, and erotic interest. For others, it may involve the emotional and physical labor of manufacturing *genuine* (if fleeting) libidinal and emotional ties, endowing their clients with a feeling of desirability, esteem, or even love:

> When I first started out, I enjoyed the sex. I'd go to work and "have sex." Now, I don't have that association that much. But my clients seem to think that being a nice guy means being a good lover. They do things to me that they should do with a girlfriend. Like they ask me what I'm into and apologize for coming too soon. So I need to play along. They have no idea that, for sex workers, the best client is the one that comes immediately.
>
> Amanda, thirty-nine, independent escort

> I have been told by certain clients that what I do is better than what the psychiatrists and psychologists do. I had one client who was very fat, kind of unkempt, and really, really ugly. Apparently, the week before he saw me, he had gone to see two escorts who had turned him down. They told him that not even for money would they fuck him. But I did, plus I made him feel really, really good. So he thanked me. And he said to me, "Don't ever let anyone try to tell you that what you're doing isn't important work. I was lonely, tired, and I needed someone to make me feel good, and that's what you did. What you provide is the most valuable service."
>
> Michael, thirty-seven, independent escort

> What I've noticed is that a lot of people really want to be witnessed when they come. They really want to feel that. You know, I totally get their desire, and I

want to be able to offer that. And so what I've learned how to do is to look at them deeply and very, very lovingly . . . For them, it feels great, like it's so personal, like girlfriend stuff. But I feel that I'm just offering them . . . love from the earth, coming up my feet and coming out to them. So they get love. I'm just channeling love.

Zoey, thirty, erotic masseuse

An apparent contrast to indoor sex workers' accounts of the premium that their clients placed on erotic authenticity was provided to me by the clients themselves. During our interviews, they repeatedly stressed to me that one of the chief virtues of commercial sexual exchange was the clear and bounded nature of the encounter. In prior historical epochs, this "bounded' quality may have provided men with an unproblematic and readily available sexual outlet to supplement the existence of a pure and asexual wife in the domestic sphere. What is unique to contemporary client narratives, however, is the explicitly stated preference for this type of bounded intimate engagement over other relational forms. Paid sex is neither a sad substitute for something that one would ideally choose to obtain in a nonmarket romantic relationship nor the inevitable outcome of a traditionalist Madonna/whore double standard.

Many of the clients I interviewed described a preference for a life constructed around living alone, intimacy through close friendships, and time-efficient, safely contained commercial sexual encounters. As such, they provide us with a concrete example of the profound reorganization of personal life that has occurred in postindustrial urban centers and nationwide during the last thirty or so years. Demographic transformations such as a decline in marriage rates, a doubling in the divorce rate, and a 60 percent increase in the number of single-person households have had subjective and erotic consequences that few sociologists have paused to consider.[21]

In a 1982 article, Harold Holzman and Sharon Pines argued that it was the fantasy of a mutually desired, special, or even romantic sexual encounter that clients were purchasing in the prostitution transaction—something notably distinct both from a purely mechanical sex act and from an unbounded, private-sphere romantic entanglement. They observed that the clients in their study emphasized the warmth and friendliness of the sex workers as characteristics that were at least as important to them as the particulars of physical appearance.[22]

The clients whom I interviewed were also likely to express variants of the statement, "if her treatment is cold or perfunctory, I'm not interested." They

"I want more than anonymous sex. I want anonymous intimacy."

were consistently critical of sex workers who are "clockwatchers," "too rushed and pushy," who "don't want to hug and kiss," or who "ask for a tip mid sex act." As a recent cartoon in the *New Yorker* (Figure 10.1) humorously sought to represent, for clients, successful commercial transactions are in fact ones in which the market basis of the exchange serves a crucial delimiting function that facilitates—*rather than inhibits*—the fantasy of authentic interpersonal connection.

One of the most sought-after features in the prostitution encounter has thus become the "girlfriend experience," or GFE. Among both clients and providers, the GFE has often been described in the following way (and here I quote from the explanation of one sex worker who specializes in this service):

> A typical non-GFE session with an escort includes one or more of the basic acts required for the customer to reach a climax at least one time, and little else. A GFE-type session, on the other hand, might proceed much more like a nonpaid encounter between two lovers. This may include a lengthy period of foreplay in which the customer and the escort touch, rub, fondle, massage, and perhaps even kiss passionately. A GFE session might also include activities where the customer works as hard to stimulate the escort as she works to stimulate him. Finally, a GFE session usually has a period of cuddling and closeness at the end of the session, rather than each partner jumping up and hurrying out as soon as the customer is finished.

Ads for escorts in print media and on-line now feature this in their advertisements, and there are entire web pages where people who specialize in this "service" can advertise.

Note, however, that the GFE is not, from the client's perspective, a sad substitute for a real girlfriend. The attachment of a monetary fee to the transaction provides a crucial boundary for both client and sex worker. The bounded quality of the exchange is illustrated by the consequences that ensue when boundaries are violated. Amanda, one of the few sex workers I've spoken to who admitted to occasionally looking for dating partners among her client pool, said that she had given up the practices of offering her preferred clients "freebies" or "bargain rates" because it inevitably met with negative results:

> They pretend to be flattered, but they never come back! If you offer them anything but sex for money, they flee. There was one client I had who was so sexy, a yoga teacher, really fun . . . Since good sex is a rare thing, I told him I'd see him for $20 (my normal rate is $250). Another guy, he was so sexy, I told him, "come for free." Both of them freaked out and never returned. The men want an emotional connection, but they don't want any obligations. They don't believe they can have no-strings-attached sex, which is why they pay. They'd rather pay than get it for free.

Christopher, a male sex worker who had also once tried to redefine his relationship with a client, recounted something similar: "I called a trick once because I wanted to have sex with him again . . . we agreed in advance that it was just going to be sex for sex's sake, not for pay, and that was the last time I ever heard from him!"

The notion of bounded authenticity that I'm striving to articulate here has been misinterpreted by some critics of prostitution, who continue to regard the commercial sexual encounter from within a paradigm of romantic love that is premised on monogamous domesticity and intertwined life trajectories. Thus, Carole Pateman[23] asks why, if not for the sake of pure domination, would "15 to 25 percent of the customers of Birmingham prostitutes demand what is known in the trade as 'hand relief,'" something that could presumably be self-administered. Yet, as one client insisted, after explaining to me that he studied and worked all the time, and consequently didn't have time to pursue a traditional relationship, "It's more real and human than would be satisfying oneself alone." This client reveals an underlying erotic paradigm that is premised on the discrete sexual encounter and thus compatible with the rhythms of his individually oriented daily life. Increasingly, this is also true for other men like him, with similar white, middle-class, sociodemographic profiles.

Transformations in Economy, Kinship, and Sexuality

Finally, I'd like to consider some of the broader social implications of the shift in commercial sexual markets that I have been describing (see Table 10.2). Notably, I do not intend to suggest an absolutist, teleological model of history. What's crucial to recognize about the aspects of social life that are summarized under the heading "postindustrial" in the final column is that they do not supplant the features of the prior historical epochs but take their place (however comfortably or uncomfortably) alongside. As with the series of economic, familial, and sexual transformations ushered in by modernity, the shift to a "postmodern" sexual ethic has been gradual and highly uneven. Nearly a quarter of Americans still live in nuclear families, and more than half continue to work in "nonflexible" jobs.[24] In the most recent national survey of sexual attitudes and behaviors in the United States, nearly 15 percent of those surveyed stated that they believed sex should be for procreation only.[25] Despite the evident frailty of marriage and long-term relationships in late-capitalist society, romantic love of the modernist variety remains a crucial repository of meaning for significant numbers of individuals. At present, there is a fierce political struggle being waged in the United States between the "old" and "new" regimes of intimacy, which has crystallized most visibly around the issues of gay marriage and abortion (both of which signal a distance from the "procreative" normative orientation toward sex).

Nor do I intend to suggest that the defining features of what I have termed the "postindustrial" paradigm of sexual commerce have emerged without

Table 10.2 Paradigms of economy, kinship, and sexual ethics in three historical periods.

	Early modern capitalism	*Modern-industrial capitalism*	*Late capitalism*
Economy	Domestic production	Wage labor	Services, finance, and information; flexible accumulation
Kinship	Extended kin networks	Nuclear	Recombinant families/isolable individuals
Sexual ethic	Procreative	Amative/companionate	Bounded authenticity

important historical precedents. The tradition of the European courtesan (prized as much for conversation and culture as for her erotic capacities) and the "patronage prostitution" of Japanese geishas and Indian *devadasis* are but two well-known instances of emotionally expansive yet explicitly transactional erotic arrangements.[26] Although it is my contention that contemporary commercial sexual transactions are characterized by some decidedly new features—both in terms of their formal organization and in terms of the explicitly *bounded* and *commoditized* (as opposed to naturalized) quality of the intimacy that is transacted—sex workers have clearly traded in capacities other than sex throughout much of history. The widespread range of such cases suggests that the "Taylorized sex" featured within the paradigm of modern-industrial prostitution may constitute an exception, rather than the rule.[27]

Although sociologists and historians of sexuality have amply described the "modernization" of sex, they have barely begun to theorize its "postmodernization" in the contemporary period. Theorists such as Manuel Castells,[28] Steven Seidman,[29] and Zygmunt Bauman[30] do begin to point us in this direction. When Castells speaks of the "normalization" of sex, when Seidman refers to "unbounded eros," and when Bauman describes "the postmodern erotic revolution," they are most certainly evoking something similar. As Bauman writes, "sex free of reproductive consequences and stubborn, lingering love attachments can be securely enclosed in the frame of an episode, as it will engrave no deep grooves on the constantly re-groomed face being thus insured against limiting the freedom of further experimentation."[31] In a sweeping journey through global sexual politics, emergent sexual subcultures, and different varieties of globalized sex commerce, Dennis Altman has perhaps gone furthest, declaring it his aim to "connect two of the dominant preoccupations of current social science and popular debate," globalization and the preoccupation with sex.[32] Altman excepted, most of the existing efforts to link sexuality and globalization are implicitly premised on a naturalism that I seek to avoid. In these analyses, "sex" is something that exists beneath the social layers of human existence, by which it can either be constrained or freed. Although I diverge from Foucault[33] in granting primacy to material conditions, with him I suggest that there is no "true" form of sex that lurks beneath its socially paradigmatic expressions.

Meanwhile, social historians such as Kristin Luker[34] and John D'Emilio[35] have linked the "relational" model of sexuality (also referred to as "amative" or "companionate") to the rise of modern romance and the nuclear family under capitalism, contrasting it with the prototypically procreative orientation of preindustrial society. Thus, Kristin Luker[36] has deciphered contemporary abortion debates in the United States in terms of a contest between procreative and relational worldviews, linking women's ideological positions on the question of abortion to disparate sets of material interests. In similar fashion, John D'Emilio[37] has explained the ways in which the peculiarly modern notion of gay identity could emerge only within a sexual ethic premised on intimate relationship because both were products of the individualizing freedom from domestic production and extended kin networks that were provided by a system of wage labor.

Following D'Emilio's analysis of the emergence of a relational sexual ethic during the rise of industrial capitalism, I propose that the proliferation of forms of service work, the globalized information economy, and "postmodern" families peopled by isolable individuals have produced another profound transformation in the erotic sphere. Both the traditional "procreative" and the modern "companionate" models of sexuality are increasingly being supplemented by a sexual ethic that is premised on bounded authenticity. Instead of being predicated on marital or even durable relationships, this sexual ethic derives its primary meaning from the depth of physical sensation and from emotionally bounded erotic exchange. Whereas domestic-sphere, relational sexuality derived its meaning precisely from its ideological opposition to the marketplace, bounded authenticity bears no antagonism to the sphere of public commerce. It is available for sale and purchase just as readily as any other form of commercially packaged leisure activity. When sex workers advertise themselves as "girlfriends for hire" and describe the ways in which they offer not merely eroticism but also authentic intimate connection for sale in the marketplace, when overworked high-tech professionals discuss their pursuit of emotional authenticity within the context of paid sexual transactions, and when municipal politicians strategize about the best means to eliminate the eyesore of street prostitution while encouraging the development of corporate "gentleman's clubs," we can witness the unfolding of precisely this transformation.

Conclusion

What is the significance of the transformations that I have described for sex workers and clients, as well as for other inhabitants of postindustrial cities? This chapter has sought to complicate the view that the commodification of sexuality is transparently equatable with emotionally diminished erotic experience. Such an argument does not do justice to the ways in which the spheres of public and private, intimacy and commerce, have interpenetrated one another and thereby been mutually transformed, making the late-capitalist consumer marketplace one potential arena for securing authentic yet bounded forms of interpersonal connection.

Venturing into modernity, and postmodernity, may be seen as the ambivalent privilege of individuals from specific classes, racial-ethnic backgrounds, regions, and nations. It should thus come as no surprise to find that more men than women, more middle-class professionals than working-class people, more of the young than the old, and more whites than blacks have been among the first social groups to fully partake in the sexual ethos that I have termed "bounded authenticity."[38] A thorough assessment of the meanings of the incursion of the market into intimate life can therefore be a difficult and contradictory task—particularly for women. What Arlie Hochschild has termed "women's uneasy love affair with capitalism"[39] is made all the more acute when we consider that many of the flourishing sectors of the late-capitalist service economy—such as child care, domestic labor, and sex work—are commercialized refinements of services that women have historically provided for free. As service industry workers, women now conduct this labor within the context of market-generated (as opposed to status-based) social hierarchies. As consumers, women as well as men are gradually gaining access to the particular conveniences, pleasures—and emotional confinement—of commercially mediated interpersonal relations.[40] The emergence and success of new sexual markets provide evidence that female, as well as male, sexuality is currently being reconstructed as a series of isolable techniques for the provision of meaning and pleasure, as opposed to an expression of enduring connection with a particular individual. For increasing numbers of women as well as men, passion, emotional authenticity, and connection have not disappeared but have been packed ever more tightly into market commodities.

Notes

This article is adapted from Elizabeth Bernstein, *Temporarily Yours: Intimacy, Authenticity, and the Commerce of Sex* (Chicago: University of Chicago Press). Reprinted with permission. © 2007 by The University of Chicago. All rights reserved.

1. Ethnographic fieldwork and face-to-face interviews were conducted with a diverse array of sex workers (both female and male), clients, police officers, and municipal officials in San Francisco, Stockholm, and Amsterdam between 1994 and 2001. The names and identifying features of all individuals that I quote here have been changed to protect their anonymity.

2. Weitzer, 2000; Kempadoo and Doezema, 1998; Lopez, 2000.

3. Of the multitude of recent works on "global economic transformations," two massive edited collections (Held and McGrew, 2000; Lechner and Boli, 2000) are indicative of this omission. While they include sections on the implications for politics, culture, and identity, only one essay, notably titled "The Gender Dimension" (Steans, 2000) makes any mention of the body or sexuality. Harvey's 1990 landmark treatment of the transition from Fordism to flexible accumulation and Sassen's 1998 analysis of the emergence of significance of global cities also lack sustained discussions of the sexual domain.

4. By the "international sex trade," I am not referring to a coordinated social or economic network but to a highly diversified set of dispersed transactions and actors.

5. Walkowitz, 1980.

6. Rosen, 1982.

7. Hobson, 1987.

8. Despite the fact that male prostitution was also prevalent in urban centers during this period, male prostitutes were typically subsumed under the new and more socially salient banner of "homosexuals" in sociological, medicopsychological, and political discourses (Weeks, 1997).

9. By "postindustrial cities," I am referring to cities with local economies weighted heavily toward tourism, business and personal services, and high technology (Smith, 1996; Milkman and Dwyer, 2003; Swedish Institute, 2001).

10. My colleague Elizabeth Wood, who similarly observed the suburbanization of sexual commerce in one midsized New England city, has referred to this pattern as the "strip-mall" phenomenon.

11. Smith, 1996; Pred, 2000; Solnit and Schwartzenberg, 2000.

12. For an analysis of evangelical women's "moral reform" movements in the nineteenth century, see Hobson, 1987. Although contemporary Christian Right and

radical feminist critiques of prostitution (as exemplified by groups such as the Coalition against Trafficking in Women) object to the intermingling of sexuality and the market in private as well as in public, articulating a critique of prostitution that is strikingly similar to earlier moral reform movements, the neighborhood residents in San Francisco did not espouse this view.

13. Demleitner, 2001; Ehrenreich and Hochschild, 2002; Bales, 1999.

14. Laura Agustín has described a transition from "preindustrial" to "industrial" forms of sex work for migrants from Latin America who come to Europe to work in brothels: "[D]isplaying himself [sic] nude in a window in Amsterdam for fourteen hours a day, or standing next to a road in the Casa de Campo in Madrid . . . are forms of prostitution which might be described as 'industrial,' compared with types at home that perhaps involve dancing and drinking with clients in a more leisurely manner and having sex with two or three in one night" (Agustín, 2000).

15. Edwards, 1993: 98.

16. The phrase *emotional labor* derives from the work of sociologist Arlie Hochschild (1983: 7). She defines the term as that which is required "to induce or suppress feeling in order to sustain the outward countenance that produces the proper state of mind in others . . . This kind of labor calls for a coordination of mind and feeling, and it sometimes draws on a source of self that we honor as deep and integral to our individuality."

17. Leigh, 1997.

18. As Katherine Liepe-Levinson observes, the number of strip clubs (or "gentleman's clubs") in major U.S. cities roughly doubled between 1987 and 1992 (Liepe-Levinson, 2002).

19. For similar observations, see Lever and Dolnick (2000).

20. See also Bernstein, "The Meaning of the Purchase," for a fuller discussion of the significance of authenticity to prostitutes' clients; Frank, 2002.

21. By 1988, nearly a third of American households consisted of a single individual. In Western European countries, single-person households have been the most rapidly growing household type since the 1960s, with from 25 percent (in the United Kingdom) to 36 percent (in Sweden) of the population living alone. In the United States, the percentage of unmarried adults rose from 28 to 37 percent between 1970 and 1988. And according to the most recent U.S. census data, by 2000, fewer than a quarter of Americans were living in nuclear families (U.S. Census Bureau, 1989; 1992; 2000a; Sorrentino, 1990; Kellogg and Mintz, 1993).

22. Holzman and Pines, 1982.

23. Pateman, 1988.

24. Manuel Castells defines "nonflexible" employment as full-time, year-round, salaried work with three or more years in the same company (Castells, 2001).

25. On the distribution of "procreational," "relational," and "recreational" normative orientations toward sexuality in the United States, see Laumann et al., 1994.

26. Griffin, 2001; Dalby, 1985; Downer, 2001; Ramberg, 2006. Historians have also noted that commodities other than sex were on offer in the luxury bordellos of eighteenth-century Paris as well as in nineteenth-century China, where clients would come to dine, to socialize, or to share confidences with the madam (Norberg, 1998; Hershatter, 1997).

27. The term *Taylorized sex* derives from the work of Alain Corbin, 1990.

28. Castells, 1996.

29. Seidman, 1991.

30. Bauman, 1998.

31. Ibid.: 27.

32. Altman, 2001:1.

33. Foucault, 1980.

34. Luker, 1984.

35. D'Emilio, 1993.

36. Luker, 1984.

37. D'Emilio, 1993.

38. See Laumann et al. (1994: 518–529) for a detailed statistical breakdown of the correlation between normative sexual orientation and membership in master status groups in the United States.

39. Hochschild, 1997: 229.

40. Although the bounded authenticity that women seek in their erotic lives is not necessarily provided by the direct purchase of commercial sexual services, there is nonetheless a growing market in sexually evocative romance novels, sex toys, "women-friendly" pornographic texts and performances, and sex classes and sexual advice manuals for female consumers (Snitow, 1983; Loe, 1998; Juffer, 1998; Hardy, 2001).

11 Economies of Emotion, Familiarity, Fantasy, and Desire

Emotional Labor in
Ho Chi Minh City's Sex Industry

Kimberly Kay Hoang

A RICH BODY OF LITERATURE has emerged in recent decades documenting the global sex industry, including studies done in the Caribbean, the Dominican Republic, Thailand, Indonesia, Malaysia, and the Philippines.[1] In particular, over the past ten years, scholars have paid attention to the growth of global sex tourism, marked by the convergence between prostitution and international tourism, between the global and local, and the production and consumption of sexual services.[2] In the new global economy, sex work is constituted by highly diversified demographic groups of consumers and providers of sex, and it is frequently linked to the specific transnational flow of men from industrialized nations to less developed nations, where purchasing sexual services is possible because it is seemingly more affordable in places where men can remain anonymous.

In this chapter, I examine the contemporary global sex industry in Ho Chi Minh City (HCMC), formerly known as Saigon, a city that entered the global economy through dramatic market-oriented socioeconomic changes implemented in Vietnam over the past twenty years. I analyze and compare the relationships between sex workers and their clients in three different sectors of HCMC's contemporary sex industry and trace the patterning of emotional labor in these relationships. With respect to male clients, I found that some men were willing to pay higher prices for emotional intimacy that goes beyond sex. On the worker's side, I found that the classed sector of service determines the type of emotional labor required of them with the higher-paid sex workers doing a greater extent of expressive emotional labor.

My analysis highlights the varied dynamics of emotional labor and desire in the practices and interactions between sex workers and clients across three sectors of sex work: the low-end, mid-tier, and high-end sectors. Although there are variations within each sector of the different "types" of workers and clients, I present typical relations between men and women in each of the sectors.[3] The women in the low-end sector cater mainly to local Vietnamese clients. They are among the lowest paid; they have short and quick interactions with their clients; and they engage in forms of repressive emotional labor.[4] Sex workers in the mid-tier sector cater to white men in the backpacker's district. In the mid-tier sectors, the women use their emotions as a form of currency, to induce feelings of sympathy and love through a series of lies designed to sustain and advance their standard of living. In contrast with women in the low-end and mid-tier sectors, the women in high-end sector cater to *Viet Kieu* (overseas Vietnamese) men and are the highest paid. Women in high-end sector capitalize on their desirability and their feigned emotions of care, designed to live a five-star lifestyle year round. Although all of the women in my study disguised their work in various forms, the most explicit sex-for-money exchanges occurred in the low-end sector, while the clients and workers in high-end sector often mingle economic activity with intimacy.

Elizabeth Bernstein is the only scholar, to my knowledge, who has attempted to compare sex workers in different sectors of a particular sexual economy, in her case in San Francisco.[5] Bernstein's research documents the emotional labor performed by middle-class and high-class sex workers through what she calls *bounded authenticity*. In contrast, she argues that the lowest-paid street-level women in her study are involved in relations that are characterized as quick impersonal acts of "sexual release" that do not involve emotional labor. I extend Bernstein's work through my examination of three sectors of sex work in HCMC. Contrary to Bernstein, I found that low-end sex workers involved in direct sex-for-money exchanges were most often engaged in a form of repressive emotional labor as they suppress emotions of disgust that they feel toward their client's bodies and age. In contrast, I found that sex workers in both mid-level and high-end sectors of HCMC were engaged in a form of expressive emotional labor, helping men to display masculinity in some of HCMC's most public spaces.

Ho Chi Minh City

After the fall of Saigon in 1975, Vietnam effectively closed its doors to the foreign world. Under the postwar socialist state, between 1975 and 1986, pimping was controlled, and prostitution was reduced, but even in the absence of a market economy, men persisted in producing a market demand for women's bodies. Moreover, rehabilitation programs and socialist prohibitions did not completely eliminate prostitution; many women returned to prostitution catering to local Vietnamese men in poverty-stricken postwar Vietnam.[6]

Following nearly a decade of lagging productivity and rapid inflation, the Vietnamese government introduced an extensive renovation policy called *Doi Moi* in 1986, which moved Vietnam from a socialist economy to a market economy.[7] This market reform, heightened most recently when Vietnam joined the World Trade Organization in 2006, thrust Vietnam into a global system, opening its doors to foreign trade and investment following similar moves by other socialist countries.[8] Over the past twenty years, scholars have documented the widespread social implications of Vietnam's movement from a complete socialist welfare system to a partial free-market economy for Vietnamese society with respect to family structures, gendered relations, and the return of Vietnamese transmigrants from abroad.[9] However, little attention has been paid to the rise of sex work in this globalizing country.

I carried out seven months of fieldwork in three intervals between June 2006 and August 2007, spending the summers of 2006 and 2007 and the winter of 2006 in HCMC. During this time I conducted participant observation in local bars, cafes, sex workers' homes, malls, and restaurants and on the streets. My research is limited to women over the age of eighteen who work as independent agents in local bars and clubs because I wanted to focus on adult sex workers who chose to enter into sex work rather than those who are trafficked or forced to work.[10] I began my research by spending time in local bars and on the streets trying to meet and develop rapport with various sex workers and clients before asking the women to participate in my project. I also befriended two local motorbike taxi drivers who took me to various pockets of the industry that catered to local Vietnamese men and helped me find different ways to approach women in the low-end sector.

Low-End Sector: "I Have to Finish Him Off in Twenty Minutes"

Sex workers who cater to local men often operate out of places disguised as barbershops, in small cafes, and in parks. These places are located far away from District One, the central business area of HCMC, where wealthy locals and foreigners spend most of their time and money. One summer afternoon, Khoa, a motorbike taxi driver, drove me to a back alley in the district of Tan Binh, located about forty-five minutes away from the city center, where there were over twenty-five barbershops lined up in a row.[11] All of the shops looked exactly the same, each roughly four feet wide and five feet long with two or three sex workers seated inside. Without Khoa, I would have never guessed that these places offered sexual services because they looked like other legitimate, often dilapidated barbershops scattered around the city.

We stopped at one shop with a large mirror inside and two leather barber seats. Toward the back of the room was a floral curtain hanging with a black leather bed behind it that looked like it could fit only one small adult. The place was dilapidated, without any sink or bathroom. The walls were painted bright blue and covered with posters of different male hairstyles. The women often pay roughly forty U.S. dollars a month to rent these spaces. I met Thuy, Yen, and Thu, three women who were cousins in their mid-thirties. Unlike sex workers in other sectors, none of these women wore makeup or fancy clothes. These women resembled local housewives. As objects of desire for poorer local men, these women have the kinds of bodies that local clients felt comfortable and familiar with. I made several visits to this shop, which, like all the shops on this street, operated mainly during the mornings and late afternoons and was closed by five or six o'clock in the evening. This time structure enabled the women to conceal their work from their families, and it allowed them to be there when their children arrived home from school. These women engaged in a form of *survival sex*, making at best three U.S. dollars per client.[12] All of the services happen in the shop on the black leather bed behind the floral curtain. I learned about the clients in this sector mostly through Khoa, the motorbike taxi driver, who drove many clients to this particular shop. The vast majority of the men who participated in this sector either were unemployed or unskilled laborers who made on average fifty U.S. dollars per month.

Thuy, Yen, and Thu are all single mothers whose husbands left them for younger women. After their desertions, each of them entered sex work so that she could support her children. On average they serve a total of three clients daily, making at most about eighty U.S. dollars each per month, which, according to Thuy, is nearly forty U.S. dollars more than they would make as maids or workers in restaurants. On arrival, the clients come in and sit down in the barber chairs where the women begin with a head and neck massage. If the clients are new, these women generally wait for the clients to ask them for "extra" services, which implies that they know about the availability of sex. Some men, in fact, do come in just for haircuts, but few go away with just that. Regular clients often arrive at the shop to request specific sexual services. All of the barbershops along this road and in other outlying districts of the city operate in a similar way.

A typical client–worker interaction takes about twenty minutes unless the women are having a difficult time "finishing off" their clients, in which case, another worker comes in to assist; the client pays the same price of three U.S. dollars. I sat for three hours in the shop one afternoon chatting with the women before Phong, a client in his mid-forties, arrived, dressed in gray slacks and a short-sleeved button-down T-shirt. When he came into the shop, he sat down on one of the two leather seats, but there were no verbal exchanges between him and the women working there or me. Thuy gave me a plastic chair and motioned for me to sit outside on the front porch because the shop had become crowded inside with one extra person. I watched as Thuy massaged the man's neck for about five minutes, and then she asked him, "Are you ready?" Without saying anything back to her, he went to lie down on the bed while Thuy pulled the floral curtain across the wall to cover them up. While Thuy was with the client, Yen and Thu joined me outside, and I asked them, "Is he a regular?" Yen responded, "Yeah, he usually comes once a week and always asks for Thuy.[13] Every time he comes here we get nervous because he is a difficult client." I asked her, "What do you mean by difficult?" She said, "He's an older man, and for some reason Thuy has a difficult time with him so we have to go in there and help her. I just hate it because he squeezes us really hard. Sometimes it hurts so much, but we can't say or do anything because he is paying us." On the arrival of another man in his mid-seventies, Thu informed him that they were busy and offered to get him a coffee while he waited. Twenty minutes later Thuy and her client walked out. Without saying anything to her or to the rest of us, he got on his motorbike and drove off. Yen then invited the older man into the shop. She asked him, "What can I do for you?" He said, "My wife is sick, and she can't do anything for me." The two of them went behind the curtain while Thuy, Yen, and I sat outside. I asked Thuy, "Did you two talk to each other?" She looked at me and said [in Vietnamese],

> No, there is nothing to say. They come in here and get what they need, and then they leave. What would we talk about? It's not like they care or even respect us. Sometimes when the three of us sit and talk, we just cry to each other because men like that guy whom I just served can be very difficult. They are rough with us, and they want to make sure that they get what they paid for. If we can't "finish them off" they don't pay us, so sometimes all three of us have to take turns to try to make them "go."

At that point Thu and the seventy-year-old man walked out. He paid her, thanked her, and said goodbye to all of us. Thu said to us, "He is a nice man. He is calm and patient." This type of interaction often involves a direct sex-for-money exchange without much bargaining or emotional effort. Compared to the women in the mid-tier and high-end sectors, these women do not work to develop intimate relationships with their clients. The women in this sector engage in what Hochschild defines as a form of *"emotional control or suppression in which the cognitive focus is on an undesired feeling that is initially present."*[14] These women suppress their feelings of disgust toward many of their clients. The clients come in and get serviced, and within twenty minutes they leave the shop. The women in this sector spend the majority of their time between work and home and do not explore the possibilities of working in a higher-paying sector.

Male clients in this sector were often the most difficult for me to engage in conversation with because of the temporal nature of client–worker interactions. Therefore, Khoa, the motorbike taxi driver I became acquainted with, often engaged in conversations with local men, asking questions for me while I sat and listened. I met Thuc, a local truck driver in his mid-thirties, while sitting in a small café in the Tan Binh district with Khoa. Trying to start a conversation, Khoa asked Thuc, "Do you stop in this café often?" Thuc responded, "Yeah, I come here on my way out of [HCMC]." Khoa then asked him, "So how are the women here?" Thuc said,

> These women are all village women; they are fresh and clean, but you can't talk to them. I come in and release, and then I leave. I mean they are only 50,000 dong (three dollars); what do you expect? They aren't the high-class women who go with white men. They are just poor women from the village who cannot find other kinds of work to do.

The women in this sector sell more of their physical labor than their emotional labor because their clients are not looking to purchase more than just sex. Client–worker interactions are swift sexual encounters where clients can engage in sexual relations with women with whom they are comfortable. Although clients do not expect these women to engage in forms of *expressive* emotional labor, the women in this sector engage in deep acting to *suppress* their feelings of disdain toward their clients.

Mid-Tier Sector: "She's a Strong and Honest Person"

Like nearby Bangkok's Khao San Road or Kuala Lumpur's Petaling Street, HCMC has a thriving "backpacker" area on Pham Ngu Lao Street in central

District One. These areas cater to international tourists at all socioeconomic levels but are popular for budget hotels and travel services. There are numerous souvenir shops, mini hotels, tourist agencies, restaurants and cafes with foreign foods, and, of course, loud bars that cater especially to white men. The streets in this area are also full of Vietnamese street vendors, street children, and a culture that heavily caters to English-speaking clients. I conducted participant observation in seven bars of a similar type located in this area. The mid-level experience is exemplified by interactions I observed in Azul, a small bar about four feet wide and thirteen feet long, with a marble countertop bar along the wall with six high stools for clients to sit and drink. Toward the back of the bar was a leather L-shaped couch. Outside on the front porch, there were two tables with chairs where the owner usually sat and socialized with customers. The sex workers who work in this bar disguise themselves as paid bartenders. While they are a key attraction for customers entering the bar, they receive no wages from the bar owner. The sex workers use the bar as a space to meet foreign clients, and they work with no intermediaries to set prices for them. Bar owners stipulate that each time a worker leaves the bar with a client, she must pay the bar a fee of seven U.S. dollars. These workers charge their clients anywhere between thirty and one hundred U.S. dollars, with price differentials based on the demand for individual women and the men's ability to bargain. Bars in the backpackers' district have a high turnover rate, not only because the women often move around from one bar to another with hope of meeting new clients but also because these bars shut down and reopen on a regular basis. All of the women whom I met in this area were in their late twenties, and the vast majority of them were single mothers.

I met Hanh in June 2006 and continued to establish ties with her through August 2007, after which she migrated to the United States with her American husband William. When I first met Hanh in Azul, she struck me as one of the most sophisticated women working in the bar. At five feet four inches, she often wore clothes that accentuated the curves on her body. Her makeup was light and natural, and she wore a bracelet, a necklace, and two rings all filled with diamonds. On the surface, Hanh had a whole lot of money, and the women in the bar all looked at her jewelry with great envy.

The first night that I saw Hanh in the bar, I initiated a conversation with her. She quickly revealed that she was previously married to a Vietnamese man named Thanh, with whom she had three children. Her ex-husband, their three children, and her extended kin all live about one hour from the city center. Her friend, Trang, had introduced her to Co Thuy, the owner of Azul, a few months before, and she started working as a bartender. Initially, Co Thuy told Hanh that she would make an income only through tips from foreign clients. During her first month there, she made approximately seventy-five U.S. dollars. Then, soon after, she learned that she could make much more if she was willing to "go home with a client." She said to me, "Co Thuy never pressured me to go with any of these men. But she told me that I would make much more money this way. Then I started working, and I was making about seventy dollars per client."

After about two months of working there, Hanh told me the story of how she met a man from Connecticut named William in the bar. Initially, William showed an interest in her and was a high-paying client (120 U.S. dollars per night). Over the course of two weeks, they developed an intimate relationship with each other, sharing life stories, and spending time with each other during the day around the city. William left Vietnam and returned to the United States in August 2006 and communicated with Hanh through Internet chatting systems and e-mail. During that time, he sent her five hundred dollars each month to help cover her living expenses and pay for English classes. Five months later (January 2007), William returned to Vietnam, Hanh divorced her local husband, and the two got married. Soon after, Hanh gave birth to a baby girl named Jessica, and they all moved out of their hotel room into a three-bedroom apartment in the Phu My Hung district—a new suburb with luxury condominiums and villas catering to the new rich. Hanh and William paid $1,200 U.S. dollars a month for their apartment, which was twelve times more than the average cost of rent in HCMC. It was in one of the newest and most expensive apartment complexes, which is located in a district that has undergone massive renovation. William and Hanh agreed that he would stay in Vietnam until she received permission to migrate abroad.

I asked Hanh why she continued to work in the sex industry when she clearly had what most women in this sector strive for: a foreign husband, money, and the opportunity to migrate abroad. She said [in Vietnamese]:

The girls in here tell me that I am greedy. I work here for two reasons. The first is that I need to send money home to my ex-husband and our kids. I still love my [first] husband. I have to pretend to love William, and I have to take good care of him because he has done so much to help my family already. It's not that I don't love William. It is just a different kind of love; the kind of love where you grow to love the person because they have done so much for you. Second, there is no guarantee that William will be my ticket out of Vietnam. The embassy does a lot of investigations on fake marriages, and they could easily deem my marriage as a fake one because I am a divorcee, so I need to have backup plans.

Even though Hanh has grown to "love" William, her emotions have shifted from evoking emotions of love and care and engaging in a form of deep acting around William. However, over time, as William engaged in acts of reciprocity by helping her take care of her family, the boundaries between emotional labor and authentic emotions of love have become blurred. Hanh continues to work in the sex industry even though she has secured herself a foreign husband because her socioeconomic position is still precarious and she needs to ensure that she will have a constant cash flow to remit to her family.

On one evening in August 2006 Matthew, an Australian man in his mid-fifties, walked in and sat down at Azul. Matthew was dressed in green cargo shorts, a white tank top, and flip-flop sandals. He had a long red beard and was sweating from the heat outside, and so Hanh walked over with a wet towel and a comb. She began wiping down the sweat on his face and combing his beard, something she frequently did for men to demonstrate her care for them. The two sat and made small talk with each other with Hanh's limited English skills. They exchanged typical questions, including, "Where are you from?" "How long are you here for?" "How old are you?" After a few drinks, Hanh, nudged him and asked, "Where you go tonight?" He smiled and asked, "Why, are you coming with me?" After which she said, "OK, you pay me 100 dollars?" He laughed and said, "Too much . . . I pay you sixty." They smiled silently at each other for several minutes before she said, "OK, eighty." They got up and left. Soon after, Matthew went back to Australia and maintained ties with Hanh through e-mails, which I helped her translate. Like many of the women in this sector, Hanh developed multiple scenarios of crisis, including stories of her having heart problems, the desire to open her own clothing shop, debts she owed to the Mafia, and an alleged ailing child. Matthew sent her nearly $2,000 over the course of one month to help her with these crisis situations. Women like Hanh are able to capitalize on the location of the country as poor and Third World in the global order to create an imaginative fantasy, making their clients feel like heroic saviors to their poverty.

After about two and a half months of spending time with Hanh at the bar, in cafes, and shopping centers, she began to open up to me with details about her life with William. One afternoon in August 2007, she invited me over to her apartment, where I met William and their daughter Jessica. During my conversation with William about his life in Vietnam, he said to me,

> You know people always have bad images of white men marrying Vietnamese women. But I fell in love with Hanh from the first day that I met her in Azul. . . . She is not like women in the U.S. who are demanding to be your equal. She knows how to care for me. She is affectionate, and she makes me feel loved. Even though we have a maid who cooks and cleans, she makes sure that the maid knows how to prepare dishes that I like to eat.

I asked him, "How did you decide that you were going to marry her as opposed to someone in the United States?" to which he replied,

> I was a bus driver in the U.S. for twenty years, and it was hard for me to find a lover, you know. No one wants to marry a bus driver. Think about it. After my father died, I inherited a lot of money, and so I decided that I would take a world tour. My last stop was Vietnam. I fell in love with the country and with Hanh. I don't speak Vietnamese, and she doesn't speak English very well, but we understand each other. I feel good taking care of her too. When I saw how Hanh's parents were living and how her children were living I gave them fifty thousand dollars [in total over six months] to rebuild the home. We send them 200 dollars a month for food and stuff too. Hanh, you know, she is a strong woman who is very loving.

Men who met women like Hanh saw compelling reasons why she entered sex work. Hanh and William engaged in a form of reciprocal care, as both parties shared personal stories, emotions of love (whether true or false), and care with each other. William expressed to me the desire to "care for" an honest and strong woman like Hanh as well as a desire to save her from a lifetime of work as a bar girl because, unlike women in the West, Hanh made William not only feel loved but needed and in fact important as he funded the renovation of her old home. In contrast to the sex workers described earlier, who cater to local Vietnamese men, Hanh's ability to speak English, navigate foreign spaces, and induce feelings of love and sympathy in her clients enabled her to convince multiple men like William to regularly support her. The stories of men and women like Hanh and William demonstrate how women enact forms of expressive emotional labor as a strategy to obtain multiple remittances, advance their standard of living, and migrate abroad.

High-End Sector: "She's Desired by Other Men, but She's with Me"

Women in the high-end sector of the sex industry in Vietnam do not charge a direct price for their services. In this sector, economic and intimate relations are complexly interconnected in such a way that the men and women often carefully highlight the emotional dimensions of their relations while talking less explicitly with each other about the transfers of money.[15] High-end sex workers engage more in "relational work" and disguise the fact that they are working as an attempt to generate more money and expensive gifts.[16] Although the women in the high-end sector sometimes receive between one and two hundred dollars per night with a client, most women garner much more than that by requesting expensive gifts. High-end women have the economic, social, and emotional capital to confidently carry a conversation and ignite the interest of men whom they meet in high-end bars. They spend a significant amount of money each night in local beauty salons and bars, conveying to their clients the image of a wealthy club-goer. However, unlike local women spending time with friends in a club, these women know they are working women. They capitalize on both their beauty and their ability to commodify their emotions. The clients who engage in relations with high-end workers are paying for more than just sex; they are paying for beautiful and desirable women who spend more time talking with them in restaurants and cafes than engaging in the performance of sex. I illustrate the dynamics of the high-end sector through two distinct stories of a high-end sex worker and a high-paying client of Vietnam's sex work industry.

At the hotel where I was staying in June 2007, I met Thanh, an overseas Vietnamese man who was working as a computer technician in Paris prior to returning to Vietnam for a family visit. One evening, Thanh agreed to let me follow him on one of his outings into HCMC's nightlife. As we walked into Whisper, a bar located in the center of District One, Thanh said to me [in English], "They [the women here] are all working; you just have to put out the right price." When I asked him to clarify, he said, "It's all about the kind of drink that you buy. I think it is standard to buy a bottle of Remy [a cognac that costs about one hundred dollars a bottle] and then invite women to come drink." After about an hour of talking Thanh said to me, "They [sex workers] aren't coming to the table because you are here with me." He told me to leave the table and not to come back until there were women at his table. I left for roughly twenty minutes, and two women appeared at his table. He motioned for me to come back and said to me, "I told them that you are my sister because they didn't want to be at the table with you here." Chau and Hoai, the women who came after I had left the table, both wore short black dresses and high heels. Chau was twenty-three, and Hoai was twenty-four years old. Both women told me that they had spent several hours getting their hair and makeup done in a local salon. When Thanh introduced me to the two women, we exchanged smiles but had limited conversation because of the loud music at the bar. Thanh took a liking to Hoai, and they began to dance seductively with each other. At the end of the night Thanh and Hoai exchanged numbers, and over the course of two weeks the two spent time with each other on dates in cafes, restaurants, and bars. The day before he left to return to France, I invited Thanh out to coffee, where I informally interviewed him. One of the first things Thanh said to me captures the commodification of women's beauty but also the men's willingness, if only temporarily, to spend large sums of money on high-end sex workers [in English]:

> I'm only here for two weeks, and it's nice to have someone beautiful to be with here, you know. It's implied, you know, that as a Vietnamese guy that I buy her jewelry, clothes, and give her money to spend while we are together. White guys are cheap. They think about every penny that they spend, whereas Vietnamese people, we are just more open. I'm a good guy, you know, I give her money and buy her things. You know I take care of her. It's OK for me to blow a lot of money in two weeks. It's my vacation.

When I asked Thanh how much money he thought he had spent on Hoai during the two weeks they spent with each other, he told me, "I don't know. I bought her a lot of things, and I probably gave her two hundred dollars here and there . . . probably six or seven hundred dollars on the low end." In talking about his understanding of the wide range of sex workers in Vietnam as well as the convertibility of his foreign currency, Thanh explained to me [in English],

> These girls are expensive because they are young, pretty, and other guys want them. You know they are smart, and they speak English. They know how to talk to a man. . . . I knew if I didn't give her enough money she would move on to another guy. I don't want to go for those ugly girls that you see with old white guys. That is just dirty! In Vietnam everything is so cheap. . . . One hundred dollars goes so far here that I can live like a king for two weeks and then go back to my wife and my work in France.

As transnational migrants, *Viet Kieu* men like Thanh come to Vietnam to consume more than just sex. These men are purchasing the services of high-end sex workers who are young, beautiful, relatively well off, and desired by other men, and who, most importantly, make them feel desired. The women also enable men to capitalize on the high convertibility of their Western dollars, thereby working to create fantasies of luxury imbued in a five-star lifestyle. Sex workers in the high-end sector commodify their emotions to induce feelings of desire and a sense of power for their clients by helping these men display masculinity in public places.[17] This cultural logic of desire is embedded not only in Thanh's ability to pay a high price but also in Hoai's ability to expend emotions as she spent time accompanying Thanh in cafes, restaurants, and bars.[18] In the high-end sector, gifts become obligatory mediums of exchange. By compensating women with expensive gifts, sex workers and clients both distinguish themselves from men and women in the mid-tier and low-end sectors who engage in more explicit sex-for-money exchanges.[19]

The ability, and occasional difficulties, in providing what Hochschild calls "deep acting" is experienced by many of the sex workers in this sector. One was Kim-Ly, whom I first met in August 2006 at Whisper through a mutual female friend. As with many women I met and whom I suspected worked in the sex industry, I waited until I had developed enough rapport with Kim-Ly before asking her direct and explicit questions about her work. Similar to some women in the high-end sector of HCMC's sex industry, Kim-Ly comes from a relatively well-to-do family. Her parents own a makeup shop in District One selling a variety of Japanese and Korean makeup lines. At the time that I met Kim-Ly, she was dating two *Viet Kieu* men from the United States; one was from San Jose, California, and the other from Pittsburgh, Pennsylvania. As with many of the workers in the high-end sector, Kim-Ly told me that these men were her boyfriends, not her clients. Even though she spoke English and could easily tap into a market that caters to white men she said to me [in Vietnamese], "I only want to be with *Viet Kieu* men because I think that women who go with white men [backpackers] are cheap. And rich local Vietnamese men always know if you are working girl. It is a small city." At the age of twenty-one, Kim-Ly spent most of her weekend nights in high-end bars.

One evening in June 2007, Kim-Ly and I went to Whisper, and I watched as several men approached her. She smiled back but turned down several offers from men who were interested in her. That night I learned that one distinct pattern among high-end sex workers, compared to women in other sectors, was that these women frequently turned down clients whom they found unsuitable, as Kim-Ly did on this evening. The strategy of turning down men was frequently done to convey to her clients, particularly overseas Vietnamese men, that she was, in fact, a woman with choices. Moreover, it conveyed to her clients that she chose them over other men who desired her. She said to me [in English]:

> With *Viet Kieu* men you have to make them think that you are not a working woman. You have to know how to talk to them. If you know how to talk to them, you know when to get money from them. You don't just go in there and say, "OK, I sleep with you, and you pay me." If you want more money you have to be patient, and you have to know how to talk to them.

When I asked her to clarify what she meant, she said [in Vietnamese],

> You know girls who are shy, they will ask a man right away for money. But they are stupid. Like me, I will say, "Honey, you should save your money. Let's eat at a cheaper place." Then they will think that you are thinking about them, and then they will just give you money. You don't even have to ask for it. You understand? The thing is that *Viet Kieus* are more generous with [their money]. You have to show them that you care about them by doing little things, and they normally just give you nice gifts like these [pointing to the set of white-gold bracelets on her wrists].

In situations like this, women like Kim-Ly engage in a form of emotional labor and a form of care work. Kim-Ly's pretended concern over her clients' money enabled her to make her clients feel cared for, so that when she asked for something they were more willing to be more generous.

When I asked Kim-Ly how she comes to determine which men she eventually sleeps with, given that she does not reveal up front that she is a sex worker to the men she meets, she explained,

> I don't sleep with them right away. You know I spend time talking with them in cafes and eating. I don't sleep with them until they give me a gift or money. You have to make them work; otherwise they won't respect you. If I think that they are cheap, I just stop answering their phone calls and hanging out with them.

This highlights the temporal dimension of relations in the high-end sector. The women spend days, sometimes weeks, with these men creating fantasies of accessible luxury while waiting for payment in the form of gifts or money before they are willing to sleep with their clients. The women like Kim-Ly operate as local wealthy club-goers working in HCMC's most expensive bars and clubs, where they spend between ten and one hundred dollars per night on drinks alone. Unlike sex workers who cater to local and overseas men, high-end women work as independents without ever explicitly revealing their identities as sex workers. By framing their forms of compensation through gifts, both men and women protect their public image. This is effective because transmigrant *Viet Kieu* men like Thanh want beautiful women with whom they can spend time in cafes, restaurants, and bars and who make them feel desirable.

Conclusion

Client–worker relationships differ in many ways across the three sectors of HCMC's sex industry with respect to location of work, the types of clients, emotional labor, care work, temporal arrangements, economic and intimate intertwinements, how women procure clients, and by the type of relationship sex workers have with their clients. Women who enter into the low-end sector engage in a form of survival sex in unpleasant places to escape poverty, while women in the high-end sector come from relatively well-to-do families and have the economic, social, and cultural capital to navigate into and around some of the most expensive parts of HCMC. As producers of sex, women capitalize on and engage in forms of expressive and repressive emotional labor. Mid-tier sex workers make white backpackers feel empowered and needed in their financial ability to care for a poor Third World woman; high-end sex workers make *Viet Kieu* men feel desired and loved by a trophy woman; while low-end clients engage in relations with women who come from their similar class backgrounds. As one examines the nature of client–worker relations from the bottom of the market to the very top of the market, there is more sex and suppression of emotion in the lowest-paid sector, while very little sex and more expressive forms of emotional labor are required of the highest-paid women. Female sex workers who are able to commodify their expressive emotions and engage in a form of relational work with their male clients are able to sell themselves to clients at a higher price, while the lowest-paid women engage in direct sex-for money exchanges with clients where they often suppress their feelings of disgust.

The patterning of emotional labor in these relationships illuminates the broader structural conditions that shape the range of choices experienced by both men and women. By examining the cultural side of emotional labor, this chapter illustrates the various ways sex workers manage their relations with local Vietnamese men, white backpackers, and *Viet Kieu* men in different ways, thereby illuminating the hierarchical complexity of HCMC's sex industry. The significance of this work not only lies in what it tells us of sex work in HCMC but also provides comparative insight into the commodification of repressive and expressive forms of emotional labor, which vary with respect to both men and women's socioeconomic class positionings.

Notes

Reproduced by permission of SAGE Publications Ltd., London, Los Angeles, New Delhi, Singapore, and Washington DC, from "Economies of Emotion, Familiarity, Fantasy and Desire: Emotional Labor in Ho Chi Minh City's Sex Industry," by Kimberly Kay Hoang, in *Sexualities*, August, 2010 (Vol. 13, no. 2).

I am indebted to Barrie Thorne, Hung Cam Thai, Raka Ray, Irene Bloemraad, Michael Burawoy, Peter Zinoman, and Paul Spickard for their comments, feedback, and penetrating questions on multiple versions of this paper. I would like to thank Suowei Xiao, Julia Chuang, and Leslie Wang for helping me think through the empirical data and theoretical framework. I am also grateful to Rhacel Salazar Parreñas and Eileen Boris, who organized the "Intimate Labors" conference at UC Santa Barbara, where the first draft of this chapter was developed. Lastly, I would like to thank Jessica Cobb for her unfailing encouragement and for helping me think through many of the ideas developed in this chapter.

1. Bales, 2002; Denise Brennan, 2004; Lim, 1998; O'Callaghan, 1968.

2. Brennan, 2001; Kempadoo, 1999; Opperman, 1998; Wonders and Michalowski, 2001.

3. I was unable to penetrate the sector that caters to rich local Vietnamese men. The clients participating in each sector were purchasing different kinds of labor (emotional and physical).

4. For a discussion of repressive and expressive forms of emotional labor see Xiao, 2009.

5. Bernstein, 2007.

6. Barry, 1995.

7. Turley and Selden, 1993.

8. Hoogvelt, 1997; Sassen, 2000.

9. For family, Luong, 2003; for gendered relations, Barry, 1996; for transmigrants, Thai, 2008.

10. For debate on prostitution versus sex work, see Bernstein, 1999.

11. The names of the various districts within Ho Chi Minh City were not changed; however, I have changed the names of shops, streets, and people to protect the subjects in my study.

12. *Survival sex* was a term that Dr. Becky Ross used in her comments on this chapter. Due to the low cost for services, the women in the low-end sector rarely use condoms or birth control.

13. All conversations I had with women in the low-end sectors were in Vietnamese.

14. Hochschild, 2003: 95.

15. Zelizer, 2005.

16. Ibid.

17. Allison, 1994.

18. For a discussion of the cultural logics of desire, see Constable, 2003.

19. On gifts as a medium of exchange, see Peiss, 1986.

III

Organizing Intimate Labor
Politics and Mobilization

INTIMATE LABOR POSES CHALLENGES for worker organizing and empowerment. In this regard, the "hostile worlds" analysis is particularly detrimental because it not only rejects the notion that good care can take place for money, rationalizing poor compensation, but, in obscuring the status of worker, it throws roadblocks against labor rights and unionization. The chapters in this part interrogate the efficacy of models developed through social movement, community-based, or service sector organizing for intimate labor. In the process, they show that the mobilization of domestic, care, and sex workers illuminates the possibilities for reaching low-paid, immigrant, and women of color workforces that straddle formal and informal economies and involve active communication or engagement between workers and clients.

Looked at in sectoral terms, intimate labor often resembles service jobs, like wait work and retailing, for the involvement of a third party other than the employer and employee: the consumer.[1] There are distinctions, however, among kinds of intimate labor. Receivers of health, child, and elder care are not actually customers, despite the embrace of the name "consumer" among many senior and disability rights activists. Rather than being marked by an ability to pay, those with inabilities, including meager finances and impaired or not yet developed capacities, often distinguish such recipients from shoppers of other goods and services. Moreover, fourth and fifth parties are central to the transaction: family members who hire and supervise the worker and the state (represented by administrators, social workers, and other government officials), which determines eligibility, cuts the check, and oversees care either directly or through private entities, both non- and for-profit agencies, as Eileen Boris and Jennifer Klein show for home care and Ellen Reese illuminates in the case of family child care. Even among sex and body workers, as with Miliann Kang's manicurists and Becki Ross's prostitutes, exchanges are not interchangeable, as clients have their own needs, and each interaction holds the promise of contingency, unpredictability, and something new.

Unions, worker centers, and other advocates seek to change the terms of intimate labor. Organizers have faced a persistent difficulty in trying to convince providers that they are employees. But obstacles have emerged, and not just because intimacy can engender emotional ties that lead to working off the books at additional tasks and thus possibly falling into self-exploitation. Much intimate labor occurs in decentralized public as well as private spaces that obscure its presence. Such spaces include the realm of the illicit, like massage parlors, hostess clubs, and public alleys, but also institutional or commercial settings, like hospitals and hotels, where bodily exchange occurs. Homes especially represent a hidden locale for employment, both for paid substitutes for mother work and household chores and for a range of intimate services, including health maintenance and sex. Moreover, much of this work has stood apart from labor law, which in the United States has placed the home and intimacy outside collective bargaining or defined such workers as independent contractors.

The conflation of intimate labor with love or family obligation has justified lower wages. But how does this misrecognition function to devalue domestic, care, and sex work and thus provide an ideological basis that reduces the overall wage packet of women and families? To begin to understand such processes, we need to turn to the ways that intimate labors, even when they appear private—in the home, between the sheets, or in the voluntary nonprofit sector of the economy—depend on public financing, legal definitions, and regulation or, in the case of sex work, even criminalization. Boris and Klein historicize the emergence of home care as a distinct occupation born of political and social struggle over its defining characteristics. Long associated with public assistance or welfare, home attendants became the preferred vehicle for long-term care in response to demands of organized seniors and the disability rights movement. The rise of home care occurred amid neoliberal structuring of the welfare state that sought devolution of responsibility away from the federal government to states and cities and from government to the market and families, whose employed wives and mothers no longer could perform such intimate labors at home. In this context, unions had to gain, through politics, tools to win recognition and obtain worker and consumer rights.

As Boris and Klein discuss, not until the mid-1970s did private household employees come under the Fair Labor Standards Act—and, even then, those who lived in remained ineligible for overtime. That domestics gained legal recognition as workers had everything to do with their participation in the civil rights movement and its decades-old struggle for dignity, respect, higher wages, and better working conditions.[2] Through the case study of Dorothy Bolden and the Atlanta-based National Domestic Workers Union of America (NDWU), Premilla Nadasen illuminates the innovative strategies necessary for improving intimate labor. Against a scholarship on servants that emphasizes the "hidden transcripts" of the weak—such as borrowing clothing, spoiling dinners, and quitting without notice—Nadasen stresses the use of public stages. Buses, parks, and neighborhood streets turned into contact zones where workers interacted away from the prying eyes of employers. Participation in Maids Honor Day, Nadasen recognizes, reinforced attention to worker behavior rather than employer conduct but nonetheless signified the value of household labor and offered poor black women a venue for the display of pride. In seeking to professionalize the occupation as well as protect its workforce, the NDWU promoted labor standards, pushed legislation, and trained individuals to negotiate with as well as care for the homes of employers. Shifting attention away from unionization to mutual aid and self-help traditions within the black community, Nadasen recovers a model for social change now being deployed by groups like Domestic Workers United.

Just as the dependency of the mistress on the maid could generate worker power, while personal closeness could tighten the bonds of exploitation, so intimacy has proved to impede as well as promote organizing among the workforce of Korean, Vietnamese, and other Asian manicurists in New York and California. Through close observation, Kang captures the ways that intimacy in body work benefits the owners of nail salons through worker attention to the needs of customers over their own safety. Shared ethnic origins between employers and employees, the "labor maternalism" of employers, and employee aspiration toward entrepreneurship further inhibit organizing. Certainly class and ethnic dynamics pervade the relationship of customer to worker as well, even among those who support labor rights. Nonetheless, attachment creates openings for a coalition of community organizations, ethnic associations, and other advocates to fight for healthier conditions, advance worker rights, and regulate manufacturers of toxic cosmetics. The expectation that the manicurist will engage in conversation with the customer allows for education about mutual exposure to noxious solvents and other chemicals. Despite conflicting class interests, then, coalition politics have emerged around health and safety issues. However, Kang finds that worker power derives more from customer fear of loss of the service than from concern for "healthy" workplace practices.

In contrast, home-based child care workers built on previous efforts of professional and advocacy groups to ally with parents to improve the accessibility and quality of the service. Like domestic workers, they mobilized in a framework set by state policy and law. But they were able to draw on discourses of "virtue" and "care" that appealed to notions of the public good, much as have health and home care unions. As Reese carefully documents, state funding of child care initially increased with welfare reform, with new moneys going for more slots rather than higher wages. Fiscal constraints subsequently generated a gap between need and availability, bringing grassroots and community advocates into coalition with unions to enhance subsidized services. By comparing their victory in Wisconsin with the more limited results in California, Reese highlights the significance of electoral politics—of who rules—for the success of organizing workers who depend on public funding, not only for payment but also for the creation of the very group of clients with whom they develop intimate relations.

Becki Ross's ethnography of the political economy of Vancouver's West End puts the consequences of state persecution of sexual labors in spatial perspective: how closing down, even if temporarily, the Penthouse Cabaret, known as "a union shop for hookers," in the mid-1970s pushed the trade into the street, removing visible solicitation to the abandoned industrial edges of the city. The destination spot that the West End became in the 1970s generated a form of gay gentrification that, in alliance with politicians, moralists, and economic interests, banned the public labor of sex; the remaking of neighborhood space, enactment of various prohibitive ordinances, and legal rulings expressed the dominance of the powerful, negating the rights of assembly and free speech of prostitutes. But, like working-class historians who find resistance along with repression, Ross also introduces prostitute activists, their organizations, and allies, who fight the good fight but find little feminist support for their struggle against both violence and criminalization.

Notes

1. Cobble, 2001.
2. Boris and Nadasen, 2008.

12

Making Home Care

Law and Social Policy in the U.S. Welfare State

Eileen Boris and Jennifer Klein

IN 1975, THE U.S. DEPARTMENT OF LABOR removed home care workers from the Fair Labor Standards Act (FLSA). The year before Congress had extended the wage and hour law to private household workers through amendments that sought "to raise the status and dignity" of domestic service. In the process, it exempted from minimum wage and overtime provisions those persons, such as teenage babysitters and elder companions, who presumably did not support themselves through such work or regarded it as a vocation. Consequently, the secretary of labor, who was empowered to promulgate regulations regarding the amendment, excluded "persons employed in domestic service employment to provide companionship services for individuals who (because of age or infirmity) are unable to care for themselves," even if they worked for a private agency hired by families for this purpose and therefore previously had come under the law.[1] A quarter century later, in 2007, the Supreme Court unanimously affirmed this action in *Long Island Home Care v. Coke* as a legitimate use of administrative rulemaking.[2]

What accounts for the Court's refusal to view the companion exemption as a violation of congressional intent and hence an improper deployment of executive power? How did the intimate labor of personal assistance, which enables others to perform basic activities of daily life in their own homes, lose recognition as protected work? Some scholars point to the stigma of the labor and the exploitation of this predominantly African American, Latina, and immigrant female workforce and thereby emphasize the cultural ways that linking such women with dirty tasks maintains dominant power relations. They underscore the legacies of slavery, segregation, racism, and discrimination associated with paid household labor.[3] We take such insights as foundational but insufficient to unravel the standing of home care in law and social policy. Instead, we turn to the development of home care as an occupation and focus on the actual political and social struggle over its defining characteristics.

Home care originated as a distinct job amid the crisis of the Great Depression. After World War II, clashes between social work and medical professionals, government and public employees, providers and receivers, state and federal governments, and competing state agencies then shaped how it became incorporated into welfare and health policy. The contestation over what was welfare and what was care, over independence, dependence, and employment for the deserving and undeserving shrouded the realities of the job. We seek to restore this history to explain the low pay and substandard conditions that have kept those who perform such intimate labors poor.

The conflation of home care with domestic labor, we thus argue, is historical and not merely some categorical equivalency. Not only has home health care as work been defined against and through domestic service, but home care laborers, their hospital and nursing home counterparts, and household employees often have been the same people, who have moved in and out of public assistance as well.[4] Labor law reflected and subsequently reinforced this identification. The extension of women's work for the family into the market had created an arena easily cordoned off as impossible to regulate. New Deal measures refused to recognize the home as a workplace, partially an outcome of the Southern Dixiecrat hold over Congress that eliminated from major legislation occupations where African Americans predominated, setting exclusions that immigrant workers in the same jobs also faced. Private-duty nurses, homemakers, and other in-home care workers became classified as domestic servants, thereby outside coverage of old age insurance, unemployment benefits, collective bargaining, minimum wages, maximum hours, and other labor laws. Nor did employees of nonprofits come under the labor law, omitting most nurses and health aides until the 1960s and 1970s.[5]

The reclassification of home care workers under the FLSA in the mid-1970s occurred just as the demand for long-term care began to explode, with well-organized senior citizens and a dynamic disability rights movement calling for community- and home-based alternatives to institutionalization in the face of nursing home scandals. These changes happened amid neoliberal structuring of the welfare state that sought devolution of responsibility away from the federal to local governments and from government to the market and families. Many families were incapable of taking up the slack. With the increase of women's labor market participation, smaller households, longer life spans, and geographic dispersal, the question of who would perform these labors of care became central to the remaking of the welfare state.

Here we untangle layers of job definition that the 1975 rule ignored and the subsequent Supreme Court decision did not view as within its purview. First we look at the attempt to distinguish home care from domestic service and the triumph of a medical model of home care that reinforced this connection. The association with domestic service, even if only a partial identification, should have led to coverage of agency employees because the 1974 amendment extended the FLSA to household labor in private homes. But it did not, and that requires explanation. Thus we discuss the outsourcing of home care from the state to nonprofit agencies, an attempt to provide maximum service without increased funding and to slough off the state's responsibility as an employer to avoid unionization. In this context, we consider the fight against the 1975 Department of Labor (DOL) ruling. The Service Employees International Union (SEIU), which brought the suit on behalf of Evelyn Coke, sought to use the state to facilitate organizing. The SEIU had gained some legislative victories, most notably in California, that turned the counties into the employer for collective bargaining purposes. Yet, even where workers became organized, as in New York and Illinois, unions were stymied. When states faced budget shortfalls, employing agencies, in turn, fell back on their legal exemption from the FLSA. When the SEIU failed to lift the exemption rule by administrative means during the Clinton years, it turned to the courts, which after two decades of conservative remaking proved unsympathetic. After *Coke*, mainly legislative options remained for dropping the companion designation.

Social Workers Create a New Job

Urban settlement houses, charities, family welfare agencies, and social work professionals initiated homemaker services in the early twentieth century for "a very limited task: the replacement of the sick mother in the household."[6] The New Deal created homemaker or housekeeper services programs "primarily as a method of employing needy women," as the U.S. Children's Bureau admitted.[7] These public works projects sent a "substitute mother" into the home to cook, clean, and comfort when a mother was ill or incapacitated. Soon, the programs served as an alternative to the notorious street-corner "slave" markets for unemployed domestic workers by sending homemakers to care for children, chronically ill adults, and elderly persons. At a time when domestics and laundry workers barely earned a cash wage, the homemakers worked thirty hours a week and gained the prevailing relief rate for the "unskilled."[8]

The New Deal legacy persisted through the rest of the century. Although tied to the medical sector, home care would be organized by the states through welfare departments and private family agencies. That is, third parties employed home care workers from the start. Second, policy experts and welfare administrators saw female public assistance recipients as a ready supply of labor for home care. And, third, confusion existed over the name of this job, which combined aspects of nursing with domestic service. Although institutionally home care would be located in agencies focused on children, increasingly homemaker services made a priority of support for aged persons. This shift in clientele, to those who needed someone first thing in the morning but not all day, encouraged the use of part-time workers, further casualizing the labor.[9]

After World War II, welfare professionals and the Children's Bureau sought to create and define a new occupation—a job that took place in the home but performed the public work of the welfare state.[10] It would be a good job for women who had spent years doing family labor. In 1947, the *Social Work Year Book* described homemaker service as "supervised placement by a casework agency of a woman, chosen for her skills and her ability to get along with people, in a home where her services are requested and needed to maintain and preserve the home as a unit."[11] The social agency context separated this work from other forms of household labor. Still, its advocates could not escape the equation with domestic service. The 1949 entry for *homemaker* in the federal *Dictionary of Occupational Titles* accepted the caseworkers' definition, adding the care of elderly family members to enumerated tasks. The *Dictionary*, however, undermined the distinction cultivated by social workers by listing *homemaker* as a subsection of "Housekeeper, Working (dom. serv.)."[12] Such classification—along with the home location and tasks performed—cemented the association with domestic service.

The specter of servile labor haunted the job. Some families called social welfare agencies "looking for a domestic."[13] Agencies had to remind their African American workforce "that they are staff members and not maids" in the face of aged clients demanding window washing and spring cleaning.[14] Unlike domestic work, homemaking included emotional labor with "the client," such as to "preserve fully his capacity for self-maintenance." The homemaker was to "maintain a sympathetic, warm, and objective attitude."[15] Most had to undergo examination for physical and moral fitness—a carryover from fears that servants carried syphilis and lacked proper values.[16]

In numerous consultations, the Bureau insisted on greater compensation for homemakers than that for domestics to attract and retrain the "right" kind of woman.[17] New York's Welfare Council took the lead in devising wage rates based on practical nursing and domestic service, the very occupations from which it sought to distance homemakers. For bureaucratic ease in determining work assignments, it promoted time off rather than time and a half as compensation for labor that overflowed a standard workweek. Because many had been on public assistance, advocates intended this to be a breadwinner occupation that would end their "dependency." Such concerns underscored the creation of a standard, as opposed to a temporary or casual, job. The Council urged making homemakers staff members and paying them the same kinds of benefits as other employees.[18]

During the 1950s, agencies attempted to adhere to these standards. Half placed all their homemakers on salary, but those with twenty-four-hour duty were paid for working only ten to sixteen hours. Paid vacation and sick leave after a year's work were common. In short, social workers forged a job mostly within the boundaries of standard employment and drew on state and federal aid to the aged, children, and totally disabled for financing.[19] By the early 1960s, forty-four states, the District of Columbia, and Puerto Rico had over 300 agencies with publicly supported homemaker service programs.[20]

The Competing Medical Model

Beginning in the 1930s, registered nurses (RNs) limited the repertoire of tasks and undermined the homemaker's status as a care provider. Maintaining labor control through training schools, professional associations, and state boards, they drew a distinct line where "simple home care" ended and nursing care began. They approved of homemakers "making bed for patient, helping patient with daily personal care, giving bed pan and care of it, filling of hot water bottle, preparing and serving meals for patient, and helping patient to take simple medicine." Instructions went to the patient, who assumed responsibility, rather than to the homemaker. Excluded were "installation of nasal or eye drops . . . helping the patient apply a brace, hypodermic injection of insulin, and administration of enemata and douches"—all procedures that social workers thought possible but RNs rejected as belonging to the practical nurse.[21] Seeking to protect nurses from deskilling, nursing authorities restricted the tasks that home aides might perform, reinforcing their classification as unskilled.

Despite traveling to patients, visiting nurses actually delegated most home care to those below them on the medical hierarchy. After hospital discharge, the first RN visit to homebound patients could be the last.[22] Across the nation, in the late 1950s, the U.S. Public Health Service found that three-fourths of families with ill or disabled persons in all types of home care programs received no professional nursing. With "a family member, the homemaker, or some other person assisting in the home" undertaking daily care, the job of home attendant remained conflated with that of unpaid family or friend.[23]

Meanwhile, home care offered a possible solution to a number of postwar dilemmas. Voluntary and public hospitals alike sought to lessen both serious overcrowding and the cost of chronically ill, often impoverished, patients— without abandoning them. Hospitals with budget shortfalls attempted to concentrate resources in areas of maximum income. They wanted to attract medical school affiliations by offering more exciting research challenges than those presented by older, chronic diseases. Moreover, faced with disabled veterans who needed help in resuming the role of breadwinners, physicians and hospital administrators argued that it was possible for "the handicapped and crippled" to have "more normal lives and take their proper place as productive members of society" by returning home.[24] In 1948, at a third the cost of ward care, New York City municipal hospitals began "the Home Care Program," advertised as "an actual extension of the hospital into the home—with a provision in the home of every service required by the patient."[25]

This evolving medical model promoted "teamwork" among physicians, nurses, therapists, medical social workers, and vocational rehabilitation counselors.[26] Although the home visits of aides were far more regular than those of presumed team workers, their labor went unrecognized. Like other forms of domestic or care work, the hospital-based programs treated this labor as informal, voluntary, and open ended. "Available" neighbors, hospital administrators thought, would take up the slack.[27] Whereas social welfare administrators repeatedly stressed the "professional" character and training of public homemakers, the medical social worker hired "any individual she deemed to be suitable to perform housekeeping duties," including relatives and friends. Hospitals viewed themselves as providing "housekeeping aid"—a limited program of five to ten hours a week, even if the actual tasks performed were the same as those done by homemakers.[28] Around the country, hospitals adopted the term *housekeep-*

ing or *housekeeper service.* Lost was the social worker hope that health officials would see the "trained housekeeping aide" as an auxiliary worker performing valued labors of care.[29] No longer the substitute mother, never the nurse, for medical professionals this worker was not much more than a maid.

The differentiation in occupational titles, however, also reflected a proliferation of sponsoring programs and funding sources. Beginning with welfare reform in 1962 through the War on Poverty and Great Society of the 1960s, new programs—such as Medicare, Medicaid, the Older Americans Act, social services grants, and job training—directed more money and workers into the field. Because each policy had a different goal, this expansion heightened the confusion over what the provider of home care actually did.

From Civil Service to Contracted Service

Amid this clash of definitions, home care moved from a civil service occupation to a contracted service in the 1970s, with some workers reclassified as independent contractors rather than employees of anyone. In California and New York, which absorbed a disproportionate share of federal money and had created the most developed services, local and state governments sought to distance themselves from responsibility for the labor conditions of workers who carried out state programs.[30] When it came to home care, privatization further entrenched a low-wage and racialized workforce that could perform the social intervention of the state in the most intimate matters of health and welfare.

Since the end of WWII, New York City had located homemaker service in the social assistance division of the Department of Welfare (DOW).[31] Holding staff positions, homemakers regarded their jobs as permanent civil service positions; the division experienced very little turnover during the 1950s. In 1963, there were 263 full-time workers, covered by a collective bargaining contract with the American Federation of State, County, and Municipal Employees (AFSCME). Private social welfare agencies were smaller, with more part-time workers. The Catholic Charities of the Archdiocese of New York, for example, had seventy-six full-time and 107 part-time employees. Some of the private providers, however, offered the best personnel packages in the country, paying for major medical insurance, pensions, and life insurance. DOW homemakers still earned just above minimum wage.[32]

In the late 1960s, the political assault on the War on Poverty would reshape home care yet again. As federal funds dried up, cities, counties, and states sought to adapt to new budget constraints, encouraging casualization.

California turned to an "independent provider" delivery system. To meet fiscal and political imperatives, the state also shifted costs to Medicaid and satisfied disability rights demands to hire and control their own attendants, which muddied the employment relationship. New York City made clients into employers, who were to recruit, supervise, and fire the worker. The client received a grant, disbursed as a two-party check made out to both the client and home attendant. Social services merely maintained a home attendant roster with a list of persons whom individuals could hire. Wherever possible, the family of the client was to oversee the care, thus saving the program additional money by doing away with the need for a supervisory caseworker.

By the early 1970s, New York City had devised three programs—the municipal employee homemaker, the independent contractor housekeeper, and the home attendant employed by a vendor agency. Home Attendant Service, redefined as a medicalized program, became the major arena for home care during the 1970s after the city obtained federal approval for Medicaid coverage in 1973. Because Medicaid had no spending caps and paid 50 percent of the cost, the city began to transfer more and more of its elderly caseload to Home Attendant Service. To maintain federal cost sharing, the city went to great lengths to insist that a home attendant was very different from a housekeeper—and to keep her off the city books—a fiction workers themselves sought to puncture. As Elizabeth Johnson, a Brooklyn home care worker, explained, "They say they have separate departments, . . . that they are different jobs, but that is not true because I am a home attendant and I do a housekeeper's job too. I have to bathe, wash, and take care of this woman, plus I have to take her to the doctor, make sure her medication is properly taken . . . plus cook, clean, and take care of her house too."[33]

The city had a political reason for moving toward the independent contractor model: unionization of the welfare department. In the public work of the welfare state, labor issues became bound up with social policy.[34] In the mid-1960s, with intensified workloads and deteriorating pay, social worker militancy erupted with a wave of organizing and strikes not seen since the Great Depression. When the city refused to bargain over working conditions, such as a cap on caseloads and improved training opportunities, 8,000 welfare employees went on strike in January 1965.[35] Among those walking out were homemakers. After four weeks, the union won substantial wage increases, full city payment of health insurance, caps on caseloads, and new hiring.[36] During the next two years, department workers continued to protest impasses in negotiations. Union militancy and pressure also seeped through the porous boundaries between public and private welfare. Because private agencies also relied on public funding, unions turned to the city and, using the threat of a strike, demanded intervention. They took work done in homes, run by a private agency, and recast it as public.[37] They used the welfare state location of home care as an arena of struggle to transform the conditions and status of the work.

Finally, the state found a way to utilize collective bargaining and programmatic changes to curb militancy. In 1969, the city reached an agreement with three unions to reduce social service personnel. Employees from caseworkers to homemakers received immediate wage raises, but job eliminations decreased promotion opportunities. A major reorganization of social services turned into a vehicle to strip workers of recent gains.[38] Referring to the 1969 contract as "slow death" and "taming of Welfare staff," one militant caucus emphasized that case aides, homemakers, and home aides, workers in "predominantly Black and Hispanic titles," were being treated as "second-class citizens."[39] After 1970 the city stepped up its contracting out of home care to new home health agencies, old settlement houses, and War on Poverty neighborhood centers refurbished as community development corporations. It shed direct responsibility for all but a few homemakers who still tended to children.[40] What looks like privatization actually was a strategic move by city government to expand service by renaming, or redefining, it and thereby shifting costs to a new federal funding source.

The Elder Companion Rule

That home care belonged to the policy realms of welfare, poverty, health, and aging, not labor standards, further explains the 1975 rule. New Jersey Democratic Senator Harrison Williams, a champion of worker rights and cosponsor of the 1974 amendments, was well aware of the need for home aides. In 1971 he unsuccessfully sought to extend Medicare payments for nonmedical household assistance. Yet in stressing the plight of "frail individuals" and monetary savings from shorter hospital stays, he had ignored the aide, who entered his 1971 bill as a means for the betterment of others rather than as a subject in her own right. During debate over the FLSA amendment three years later, Williams made no mention of the emerging home care industry. While he sought to end the persistent treatment of domestic workers as "slaves," he analogized the elder companion to the babysitter: "a babysitter is there . . . to watch the youngsters" and that "'companion,' as we mean it, is in the same role—to be there and to watch an older person." Thus he distorted the labor of home care.[41]

Further obscuring public understanding in the early 1970s was Nixon's new Senior Companion Program. This initiative offered opportunities for those over age sixty to assist the "homebound."[42] Community-based antipoverty groups long had sought out neighborhood women to tend to their neighbors. Some social welfare agencies also sponsored elder companion programs to supplement formal homemaker or home health aide services. In undertaking tasks associated with the home care worker, but under the rubric of volunteering, such efforts blurred the distinction between friendship and work and further devalued the skill involved.[43] Such programs fed into the perception that a home care worker was an elder companion.

The Senate Committee on Labor and Public Welfare in 1974 explicitly refused "to include within the terms 'domestic service' such activities as babysitting and acting as a companion."[44] Two decades later, the Private Care Association, Inc., known at the time as the National Association of Companion Sitters and Referral Services—essentially a nurse registry—claimed to be "one of the principal proponents" of this exclusion, arguing that FLSA coverage "would adversely impact the care recipient."[45] Other organized interests—like the National Restaurant Association—and antilabor senators raised the cost to their workforce as a reason to keep home care out of the law. Sympathizing with one of his store managers, Allen Nixon of the Southern States Industrial Council complained, "They [his manager and his wife] cannot get the parents in a nursing home. They cannot afford it. If the minimum wage is applied to domestics, such as this case, you have a real problem."[46]

Whether from notions of the elder companion as a volunteer or plain ignorance about the maintenance of impaired individuals, lawmakers ignored the actual work of home care, which involved a range of household tasks that allowed the family or individual to function in a domestic environment. Congress classified household chores as "making lunch or throwing a diaper into the washing machine" as "incidental" rather than integral to the labor.[47] The resulting legislative language opened the way for the DOL administrative rule that in narrowing coverage contradicted the aim of Congress to expand the FLSA. The rule change occurred at precisely the time that old age, social welfare, and health funding was fanning the growth of a home care industry.[48]

The final rules excluded previously covered home care workers employed by a hospital, private welfare or health care agency, or the government. Only a few years before, the DOL's wage and hour administrator had determined that an employer of home aides and live-in companions could not claim an exemption from the FLSA as a "retail" business.[49] In October 1974, initial rules included companions in the definition of *domestic service* and placed "companionship services for the aged or infirm" outside the casual limitation. These rules also excluded from the definition of *companion* "trained personnel, such as a registered or practical nurse" and suggested that those who spent more than 20 percent of their time in housework not directly related to care of elderly or infirm persons were domestics, not companions. In promulgating final rules the next February, the DOL decided that exemptions could extend to third-party employers because the statutory language applied to " 'any employee' engaged 'in' the enumerated services." While it referred to public comments from distraught mothers who would have to pay full-time babysitters minimum wage, it offered no explanation for changing the status of home attendants, now renamed "companions."[50] A shifting political economy made this change fortuitous.

Challenging the Rule

For nearly twenty years, the elder companion exemption stood as a roadblock toward improving worker compensation. Meanwhile, state initiatives and federal funds decisively shaped home care as a viable alternative to institutionalization, encouraging aging, disability, and health stakeholders to seek its expansion—with a focus on the concerns of the receivers rather than the providers of care. Though unions began organizing home care workers in the mid-1970s, it took more than a decade for these campaigns to gain enough traction to address the misclassification of the workforce. In coalition with some home care agencies and with senior and disability activists, the SEIU slowly won policy innovations from state governments. In Chicago and New York, union locals obtained enhanced reimbursement rates from state legislatures, which in turn led to improved worker pay through more robust collective bargaining contracts. In California during the 1990s, the union spearheaded creation of the county-level public authority as an employer for collective bargaining purposes for "independent providers."[51]

With the election of Bill Clinton, the SEIU turned to the companionship exemption. The Department of Labor proposed new regulations late in 1993 that would have placed the home care worker in the same relation to the wage and hour law as any other household laborer: covered when employed by a third party but not when hired by the family for whom she worked. Some disability advocates, like the United Cerebral Palsy Associations, and provider associations, like the American Network of Community Options and Resources, protested that such a rule burdened people with developmental disabilities.[52] Due to "confusion about the impact and effect," the DOL withdrew the proposal.[53] Six years later, it again attempted to realign the companionship rule in light of the subsequent growth of the home health industry. It offered a new definition of companionship as intimate and sustained fellowship between provider and receiver of care that would eliminate most home aides from this designation.[54] But the timing of its proposal—issued the day before the inauguration of George W. Bush—was inauspicious. The Bush administration soon withdrew the rule change, claiming a more extensive negative economic impact than originally suggested.[55]

Assumptions about home and care pervaded public comments during both attempts to revise the rule. Agencies stressed the crucial role of the exemption in allowing people "to remain in their own homes." The proposed rules, some asserted in 2001, would inhibit compliance with the Supreme Court's *Olmstead* decision, which prohibited "unnecessary institutionalization" under the Americans with Disabilities Act.[56] Objectors easily invoked the specter of greater cost. Oregon's Senior and Disabled Services Division warned, "'Care providers will be regarded as employees of the State and therefore be eligible for State pensions, health insurance, and other employee benefits."[57] Opponents of rule change cited *McCune v. Oregon Senior Services Division* (1990), in which the Ninth Circuit declared: "These critical services reach more elderly or infirm individuals than they otherwise would precisely because the care-providers are exempt from the FLSA." The working assumption was that "nothing should be implemented that would in *any way* limit the number of companions available"; raising their wages would have that impact.[58]

Labor and immigration groups defended the rule change. Among these were the SEIU-led Quality Homecare Coalition of Los Angeles, which included senior and disability activists, and a coalition of progressive legal centers led by the National Employment Law Project. They stressed the breadwinner status of the home care workforce, full of women seeking to move "from welfare to work." Health policy experts warned that doing otherwise would "perpetuate poverty-level jobs, offering to its most vulnerable citizens care that is hurried, care that is delayed, and increasingly, care that is foregone."[59]

Stymied in the executive branch, the SEIU went to court. It found a plaintiff in seventy-three-year-old Jamaican immigrant Evelyn Coke, a resident of Queens, New York, who spent twenty years cooking for, cleaning up after, and bathing clients on Long Island, sometimes working twenty-four-hour shifts but rarely paid for overtime. Companionship, rather than housework and personal care, was "incidental" to her work.[60] Briefs before the Supreme Court in early 2007 repeated previous arguments. Those who asked the Court to affirm the rule, like New York City, rationalized the exemption on the basis of expense and justified the power of the agency to carry out the legislative act.[61] In contrast, civil, women's, and immigrant rights groups stressed the purpose of the 1974 amendments to correct prior discrimination against household workers and revalue domestic labor. Though the American Association of Retired Persons and the American Association of People with Disabilities came out for Coke, others pitted workers against consumers.[62] During oral testimony, Associate Justice Stephen Breyer worried whether "millions of people" would be able to afford home care if they had to abide by the nation's wage and hour law.[63] In foregrounding the concerns of receivers of domestic and personal services, Justice Breyer erased the presence of the providers.[64] His subsequent decision for a unanimous Court went against Coke and the rest of the 1.4 million home care workers.[65]

The Court opened the door to a political solution: Congress could legislate, or the DOL could promulgate new rules. Either road would require a new administration in Washington. Disability rights advocate Senator Tom Harkin (D-Iowa) joined Congresswoman Lynn Woolsey (D-California) to introduce the Fair Home Health Care Act in the fall of 2007. They would counter the Supreme Court by limiting the definition of *casual* to those who worked fewer than twenty hours a week; otherwise, home care workers would come under the FLSA.[66] Subsequent hearings emphasized questions of dignity and justice. "Under the Fair Labor Standards Act, I would get time and half pay for my overtime hours for performing the same tasks for Mrs. G. *if she was in a nursing home facility*," testified Manuela Butler, a sixty-five-year old home care worker unable to afford retirement and faced with becoming a public charge in her old age from a lifetime of inadequate wages. "But because my work helps her stay in her home, I am deprived of overtime pay. That's just wrong and unfair."[67] In January 2010, six months after Coke's death, the *New York Times* still urged passage of "the Evelyn Coke Fair Pay for Caregivers Act."[68]

Conclusion: The Home as Workplace

Home care continues to exist in a clouded netherworld between public and private, employment and family care. One of the fastest growing occupations of the twenty-first century, it is also among those low-waged jobs characterized

by the National Employment Law Project as subject to "wage theft."[69] By definition, the work occurs in the privacy of client homes, a space socially constructed as better than institutionalized venues for care. As work for women,
and especially women of color, home care lacked the status and standards of
formal employment. It was the dense network of state contracts to private agencies that obscured both the public nature of the service and the employment
status of the workforce. So did confusion over the actual labor process: Was
the worker engaged in mere housework, personal care with intimate touching,
or companionship with lifting, ambulation, and other physical tasks? Such
struggles over definition underscore the complexity of both domestic and care
work—and their continuing entanglement under a political economy that ex-
pects intimate labor on the cheap.

Notes

The authors would like to thank the following funders: the National Endowment
for the Humanities; the Faculty Senate, UCSB; ISBER, UCSB; the Hull Chair; the UC
Labor and Employment Research Fund (Boris); the Rockefeller Foundation Bellagio
Residency (Boris and Klein); Morse Fellowship Yale University (Klein).

1. Molly Biklen, 2003; *Federal Register*, 2001, 1975.
2. U.S. Supreme Court, 2007.
3. Smith, 2000; Palmer, 1989.
4. U.S. Department of Health, Education, and Welfare (HEW), 1977: 21.
5. Poole, 2006; Palmer, 1989.
6. Fraenkel, 1942: 68.
7. Morlock, 1964: 4.
8. Fraenkel, 1942: 93–94.
9. Boris and Klein, forthcoming.
10. U.S. Children's Bureau, 1943: 1–2, 5.
11. Brodsky, 1958: 11.
12. U.S. Department of Labor, 1949: 677, 59.
13. Maud Morlock to Wado C. Wright, July 5, 1947, Box 414, 4-11-6, RG102, CF
1949–52, USCB Records; Jewish Family Service, 1950.
14. U.S. Children's Bureau, 1947; Elinor McCabe to Maud Morlock, May 16, 1951,
Box 412, file "August 1952," RG102 CF 1949-52, USCB Records.
15. Jewish Family Service, 1950: 2–3.
16. U.S. Children's Bureau, 1948.
17. "Recommendations for Personnel Practices for Homemakers."
18. Rose E. Drapkin to Maud Morlock, September 30, 1946, Box 120, file "5-1948,"
RG102 CF 1945–48, USCB Records.

19. Stewart, Pennell, and Smith, 1958: 12, 19–23, 39.

20. Morlock, 1964: 11.

21. Fraenkel, 1942: 100–101.

22. Thompson, 1951: 233–234.

23. U.S. Division of Public Health Methods, 1958: 63–64.

24. Stevens, 1989: 11; Opdycke, 1999: 81–90; Edward M. Bernecker, Commissioner of Hospitals, to Mayor William O'Dwyer, April 26, 1948, NYAM Health and Hospital Planning Council, box 106, folder 2: home medical care, 1948-1952, NYAM Archives.

25. City of New York Department of Hospitals (DOH), 1948: 8, 51; DOH, 1950: 19; DOH, 1951: 16. Russell Sage Foundation, "Extension of Medical Care and Social Service into the Home for a Selected Group of Indigent Patients at Queens General Hospital," May 19, 1948, RG 102, CF 1949-52, box 119, folder: visiting housekeeper aide, USCB Records.

26. Hospital Council of Greater New York, 1956: 106.

27. Ibid.: 109, 111–112.

28. Ibid.: 379, 23, 39; Maud Morlock to Mrs. Minna Field, Montefiore Hospital, Feb. 11, 1949 and Minna Field to Maud Morlock, Feb. 28, 1949, RG 102, CF 1949-52, box 414, USCB Records.

29. Maud Morlock, Memorandum: Telephone Conversation with Mr. John P. Sanderson, Hospital Permit Bureau, Municipal Center, Washington D.C., June 2, 1948, RG 102, CF 1949-52, box 119, folder: visiting housekeeper aide, USCB Records.

30. Layzer, 1981.

31. Stewart et al., 1958: 9.

32. "Welfare's Homemakers Honored," 1959; "A Decade of Service," 1961; Shick, 1989: 48; Medical Care Administration Branch, 1964: 212, 206, 208; Stewart et al., 1958: 8, 98.

33. U.S. House Select Committee on Aging, 1978: 27.

34. Stetson, 1966; 1967.

35. Freeman, 2000: 201–205.

36. Ibid.: 205–206; Perlmutter, 1965: 19.

37. Carroll, 1967; "Officials of a Welfare Agency Discuss Union with Ginsberg," 1967; "Homemakers Groups to Recognize Union," 1967.

38. Perlmutter, 1969; Walkowitz, 1999: 268–274.

39. Social Service Employees Union (SSEU) Members for a Militant Caucus, "Let's Fight Back," *Militant Voice*, May 2, 1969; "Black Caucus & Community Action," *Militant Voice*, June 2, 1969, both in SSEU Records.

40. Community Council of Greater New York, 1977; Shick, 1989: 69–70; New York State Office of the Comptroller, 1978: 11; New York State Department of Social Services, 1977.

41. Williams, 1971: 963; Palmer, 1995.

42. Shapiro, 1994.

43. For example, see Goldberg, 1967.

44. Biklen, 2003.

45. This discussion relies on letters and other materials obtained by the SEIU through the Freedom of Information Act, referred to as FIA Materials, in the authors' possession. To Richard M. Brennan from Russell A. Hollrah, November 6, 1995; notes on meeting, with Russell A. Hollrah, and others, November 6, 1995.

46. U.S. House Committee on Education and Labor, 1973: 138–140.

47. U.S. Senate Committee on Labor and Public Welfare, 1976.

48. Section 13 (b) (21); testimony of Susan K. Kinoy, in U.S. Committee on Ways and Means, 1979: 656.

49. U.S. Department of Labor, 1972.

50. *Federal Register*, 1974, 1975.

51. Boris and Klein, 2007.

52. "Proposed Rules, Department of Labor, Wage and Hour Division, 29 CFR Part 552," September 8, 1995, ANCOR to Maria Echaveste, February 21, 1994; UCPA to Echaveste, February 28, 1994, SEIU Files in authors' possession.

53. *Federal Register*, 2001: 5485.

54. Ibid.: 5484.

55. *Federal Register*, 2002: 16668.

56. For example, Suellen R. Galbraith, ANCOR, to Kerr, March 19, 2001, and attachments, 1; Meltzer, Kippe, Goldstein, and Schlissel to T. Michael Kerr, March 20, 2001; Robert M. Gettings, National Association of State Directors of Developmental Disabilities Services to Kerr, March 20, 2001, 2, SEIU Files in authors' possession.

57. Forrest Roberts, "Comments on Proposed Changes to 28 CFR§552.109," November 6, 1995, 2; Susan Dietsche to Brennan, November 2, 1995, SEIU Files in authors' possession.

58. Forrest Roberts to Echaveste, February 28, 1994, 2, 3; see also Rick E. Temple to Echaveste, February 28, 1994, SEIU Files in authors' possession.

59. Lilibeth Navarro, Armentress Ramsey, and Evan LeVang, Quality Homecare Coalition, Los Angeles to Administrator, March 20, 2001; Catherine Ruckelshaus, National Employment Law Project, et al. to Thomas M. Markey, March 20, 2001, esp. 5; Helen Miller, SEIU 880, to Administrator, March 20, 2001; Marta Sotomayor and Edgar E. Rivas, National Hispanic Council on Aging, July 20, 2001; Steven L. Dawson to Administrator, March 20, 2001, 4, SEIU Files in authors' possession.

60. Greenhouse, 2007; Draft Brief by Plaintiff, *Coke v. Long Island Care at Home*, for motion of summary judgment, in authors' possession.

61. New York City Law Department, Office of the Corporation Counsel, 2007.

62. AARP, 2006; Urban Justice Center, 2007.

63. U.S. Supreme Court, 2007: 27.

64. Toosi, 2007.

65. U.S. Supreme Court, 2007.

66. "Home Care Bill Would Undo DOL's 'Casual Basis' Interpretation," 2007.

67. U.S. House Committee on Education and Labor, 2007: 1–2.

68. *New York Times*, 2010.

69. McGeehan, 2007; Bernhardt, McGrath, and DeFilippis, 2007.

13 Power, Intimacy, and Contestation

Dorothy Bolden and Domestic Worker
Organizing in Atlanta in the 1960s

Premilla Nadasen

IN THE STEAMY SUMMER OF 1968, shortly after the assassination of Martin Luther King Jr. and in the wake of urban upheavals in Baltimore, Chicago, Washington, D.C., and a hundred other cities around the country, domestic workers in Atlanta met to talk about reforming the occupation of domestic service. Inspired by the civil rights movement, emboldened by other poor people mobilizing for change, they ushered in what domestic leader Dorothy Bolden called a "new birth"—or, as she put it, "a voice to be raised for domestic workers."[1]

That summer these domestics formed the National Domestic Workers Union of America (NDWUA)—a misnomer on two counts because the organization was neither national nor a union. They were not the first domestics to organize, nor the first people to try to reform domestic service, but they did succeed in reaching thousands of Atlanta women—both employers and employees—whom they educated about the rights and responsibilities of this kind of work.[2] Their agitation, along with that of dozens of other groups around the country, helped bring domestic work under protection of the Fair Labor Standards Act (FLSA) in 1974 and reshaped the character of the job. Most importantly, they transformed domestic workers' self-perceptions and enhanced their dignity and sense of self-worth.

Dorothy Bolden was one of the founders of the NDWUA and served as president for most of its history. She was born in Atlanta in 1920 and started domestic work at the age of nine. After a split-day session at school, which ended at noon, she went to the home of a Jewish family, for whom she babysat, washed diapers, and did light cleaning. She earned $1.50 a week. When she was a teenager, she dropped out of high school and began working for another family from 8:00 A.M. until after the dinner dishes were washed. For a twelve-hour day of cleaning she brought home $3.00 a week.[3] After traveling to Illinois, North Carolina, New York, Virginia, and Alabama, Bolden eventually returned to Atlanta. She spent nearly her entire life as a domestic worker. In the early 1960s she became involved in a campaign for safe and decent schools in her Atlanta neighborhood. A few years later she began organizing domestic workers and was part of a nationwide movement to raise wages and increase respectability. In the mid-1970s she reflected on shifts in the occupation:

> In the past seven years there's been a great deal of change. These women used to be embarrassed about saying they were maids. You had to take such hardships that you didn't want nobody to know you were. Now it's different. You can't tell a maid from a secretary anymore. In the past, if a black woman was a maid you could tell by the way she dressed. Now they don't carry the shopping bags as much, they go neater, and they look more lively and intelligent.[4]

This chapter surveys household worker organizing in Atlanta, Georgia, in the 1960s and 1970s. I examine the alternative mobilization strategies employed by domestic workers, their use of public space, and the way they redrew the boundaries of hierarchy and deference that defined employer–employee relations. Their politics were rooted in the interlocking systems of oppression—race, class, gender, and culture—that they experienced every day as poor black women. They formulated a political program that addressed the most egregious aspects of domestic work, including low pay and lack of respect. Domestic workers were agents of change, but they operated within the circumscribed boundaries of the occupation, which determined the kinds of tactics they had at their disposal. They didn't engage in protests and marches; instead they challenged the scripts of proper behavior, worked to standardize the occupation, and trained domestic workers to negotiate on their own behalf. Through these efforts, they eroded some of the racial and class power that employers wielded and won greater dignity for domestic workers.

Organizing Domestic Workers

Domestic work is notoriously hard to organize. It is an atomized occupation, with tens of thousands of employees—30,000 in Atlanta in the 1960s—and even more employers. Because many domestics worked for more than one family, there may have been close to 100,000 employers. The traditional shop-floor model of union organizing with elected representatives serving as bargaining agents was simply not an option for these workers. They were unable to shut down their workplaces with a sit-down strike as workers in large-scale industry sometimes did. They did not wield the same kind of collective power as unionized workers because replacing a single disgruntled employee was far simpler than replacing a thousand. Moreover, domestic workers had a degree of ambivalence and anxiety about unions. As Dorothy Bolden explained: "A lot of the maids were afraid to join. They were skeptical because they knew what unions had done in the past, and at first 'union' was part of the name. I don't think we realized how much 'union' frightens people."[5] Their very marginalization, however, proved to be an opportunity to formulate innovative strategies.[6] Out of necessity and with an arsenal of creativity and imagination, domestic workers in Atlanta developed alternative labor organizing strategies. These household service workers, poor women of color, engaged in innovative organizing, in part because they realized the futility of employing traditional labor strategies.

Domestic service was an isolating occupation in which the ostensibly private space of the home became a workplace.[7] For much of U.S. history, domestic servants—usually young immigrant women in the South and West and African American women in the South—lived full time with their employers and were in many cases cut off from family and friends. As historian Elizabeth Clark-Lewis has demonstrated, at the beginning of the twentieth century, African American women, who worked as domestics even after they were married with children, transformed household work into a live-out occupation.[8] But, even as live-out employees, they worked extended days in isolated settings apart from other workers, sweeping, dusting, scrubbing floors, washing windows, doing laundry, preparing food, and caring for children. During working hours they had almost no contact with anyone other than their employers. For organizers, a persistent dilemma was how to build support. Domestic workers couldn't post signs in washrooms as union organizers did. They couldn't conspire with their co-workers on the production line, and they couldn't leaflet outside the factory gates. So, public spaces—and public transportation in particular—became a central site of organizing for the NDWUA. Atlanta was a segregated city. And, in the early morning hours, domestic workers in predominantly black neighborhoods such as Vine City boarded the buses to head for the suburban white enclaves to begin their workday. NDWUA organizers handed out fliers at bus stops and initiated conversations with other domestic workers while riding the bus to work.[9] City buses became mobile meeting grounds. These "freedom buses"—as I call them—were perhaps the equivalent of the rural freedom schools of the 1960s that were centers of political education and sites of organizing. They were venues where poor women could share grievances and concerns, trade stories of abuse, exchange information about wages and workload, and learn about their rights.

Domestic workers also encountered a deeply personal employer–employee relationship.[10] They labored in the most intimate spaces of the home and found themselves enmeshed into the daily lives of families. Their workspace was a private site of leisure and personal caretaking of others. The boundary between being a worker with specific responsibilities and acting as a personal attendant was a fuzzy one, even for household cleaners who theoretically were not caretakers. The confusion extended beyond assigned tasks and blurred the distinction between status as an employee and as a resident of the household. This fostered a work environment where employees' character, not only their ability to complete specified chores, became a measure of one's job performance. Domestic workers were often, especially in the 1960s, hired and fired because of particular personality traits rather than their occupational skills.[11] The intimate nature of the job and the paramount importance of character led employers to sometimes refer to a domestic worker as "one of the family." This claim has been used to extract additional work and to encourage employees to take leftovers and hand-me-downs rather than payment. Domestic workers were often expected to ensure that family members were taken care of and household tasks completed, even if doing so meant longer hours and no additional pay, because people—especially women—routinely engage in caretaking out of love or responsibility without compensation.

Yet, the personal relationship that made this job so capricious and unpredictable could also be a source of power for domestic workers. Families became dependent on individual workers because of the emotional ties and bonds of trust that had been forged and because their personality seemed well suited for the job. Some children saw caretakers as "second mothers," and some employers relied on housekeepers to ensure the smooth functioning of the home. One employer referred to her maid as a "security blanket, always there to help me."[12] Domestic workers—in many cases considered essential to the management of the household—used this power of loyalty to win demands from their employers. "Maids was very valuable to a household," explained Bolden.[13] The reliance of the family on specific domestic workers enabled employees to use this leverage to their advantage. Bolden explained: "I always understood that the employer was a human being too. You have to learn how to sit down and relax and talk to her."[14] So, many women in NDWUA negotiated higher salaries and better working conditions precisely because employers could not imagine life without "their maid." Bolden used this dependence on household employees to demand reforms that would benefit domestic workers, including a better public transportation system—a campaign that NDWUA had been working on for several years. At a public meeting about bus routes she declared: "We work as butlers and maids out in your fine areas and you have good bus services for us to get back downtown . . . But, if you want us to keep taking care of your babies and cleaning your houses, you're going to have to give us better service back to where we live, because we are important, too."[15]

The nature of the work also shaped how workers negotiated. Because each employer—in the vast majority of cases—had only one employee, and because employees were isolated from one another, they engaged in one-on-one bargaining. According to Bolden, "[NDWUA] can't negotiate with private employers, private homes. You have to teach each maid how to negotiate. And this is the most important thing—communicating. I would tell them it was up to them to communicate. If I wanted a raise from you I wouldn't come in and hit you over your head and demand a raise—I would set out and talk to you and let you know how the living costs have gone up."[16] A lone domestic worker could not be represented by others and had to act as her own bargaining agent. So, rather than relying on a union hierarchy to speak for them, domestic workers were individually empowered. This method of negotiating is instructive as a model for labor organizers. Rather than placing their fate with union leaders whom they may or may not have voted for, NDWUA's approach put the power in the hands of individual workers who could decide for themselves their priorities and under what circumstances they would work.

Even though individuals negotiated by themselves, collective demands and mobilization were central to the movement. Domestic workers in Atlanta shared grievances and came up with common solutions that strengthened their bargaining positions. NDWUA sought to standardize the occupation so maids across the city would earn a minimum wage. Bound by few regulations, employers had little accountability and enormous autonomy to structure the occupation as they saw fit—including hours, wages, and responsibilities. The association wanted to change those power relations. It fought to set wages at $13.50 a day plus car fare if an employee worked four days a week or more for the same family and $15.00 a day plus car fare if she worked for a family one day a week. It further sought two weeks of paid vacation and one week of paid sick leave. The association ran an employment placement service and offered counseling to both employers and employees to ease impasses and help develop agreements that were both fair and just. To push for long-term change, the women lobbied for legislation that would assure all domestic workers the protections of the FLSA. The FLSA, passed in 1935, guaranteed minimum wage and overtime pay for most American workers. But the law excluded domestic and agriculture workers from its protections because of compromises made by New Deal politicians to entice white Southern Democrats—who wanted to maintain control over the largely black, regional labor force—to support New Deal legislation. The NDWUA's campaign for FLSA protection included writing to representatives, meeting with reformers and lobbyists, and speaking at public hearings. The collective efforts gave domestic workers confidence to assert themselves, honed negotiating strategies, and offered ideas about what to ask employers for. They served as an important resource when "sitting down to talk" proved unfruitful. Moreover, these campaigns aimed for structural reform and standardization that would benefit all domestic workers.

Along with other domestic worker rights groups, NDWUA saw educating the public as critical. It designed informational brochures and pamphlets and held programs to educate employers and others about the rights and responsibilities of domestic workers. A short booklet published by the organization in 1977 outlined domestic workers' rights to Social Security, overtime pay, and unemployment benefits. It also listed chores that domestic workers wouldn't do, including climbing ladders, washing windows out of reach, scrubbing floors on knees, and cleaning walls out of reach. At the same time, NDWUA listed a number of "Rules for Maids": "Must be dependable. Must be trustworthy. Must have a clean body. Must have neat appearance. Must watch language."[17] Its vision was one of mutual responsibility, rights, and respect.

Dignity and Domestic Service

A core goal of the NDWUA was to increase the stature and dignity of domestic work. Given the racism of U.S. society, domestic work was racialized as well as gendered. Despite the immense knowledge necessary to care for small children and to maintain a household, most people judged domestic work as unskilled labor. This perception, in conjunction with menial pay, limited rights, and poor working conditions, contributed to the occupation's low status. Moreover, domestic work was tied to the historical legacy of slavery. Even in regions of the country where slavery was not widespread, servants were overwhelmingly immigrant women and women of color Thus, only women with few other options usually turned to domestic service. In 1940, 60 percent of employed black women identified themselves as domestic workers. Although this declined to a little under 18 percent in 1970, as greater employment opportunities opened up for African American women, they were still a disproportionate share of the private household workforce.[18] In many cases, employers constructed their domestic workers as racially different, rendering them invisible and justifying low pay and poor working conditions.

In addition, household employees engaged in what traditionally has been considered "women's work." So, domestic work is also degraded because of its association with unpaid labor in the household.[19] Historian Phyllis Palmer, in her important study, examines how household work created boundaries among women of different class and race backgrounds—defining some women as clean and pure and other women as dirty and tainted.[20] Domesticity is central to the perceptions and status of both middle-class women employers and poor women domestic workers.

Despite the occupation's low public standing, most domestic workers didn't have a negative view of household work.[21] They didn't see it as an inherently degrading occupation but took pride in the work they did. Dorothy Bolden felt the same way and explained that, although she had lots of jobs, "I always went back to domestic. I love children, I really love children."[22] Her sentiments paralleled that of many other women in the NDWUA, which never organized explicitly to move their members out of domestic service but rather sought to improve conditions within the occupation. Women in the NDWUA sought to reorder household arrangements and redefine the boundaries that shaped domestic work. They questioned the assumptions that domestic workers should take hand-me-downs, show deference, and do any and everything asked of them. They wanted to professionalize and raise the status of their work. Scripts of deference, inflected by both the race and class of the women doing the work, became the site of contestation. In combination with improved wages, hours, and benefits, they sought individual empowerment and both public and private displays of respect.

One strategy employed to recognize the contributions of domestic workers and thus raise their status was Maids' Honor Day, initiated in 1970. One day each year the NDWUA would honor an outstanding maid in a posh and public ceremony. Employers nominated domestic workers; the employers explained in letters why their maid should be named Maid of the Year. The NDWUA saw Maids' Honor Day as a way to bring respect and dignity to the occupation. According to the NDWUA, "The purpose of this event is to rec-ognize and honor outstanding women in the field of domestic labor, for their courage and stability, and the remarkable ability of being able to take care of two households at one time. This event is held once a year to bring pride and dignity to the working place of women."[23] The women gathered each May for a banquet at which they participated in a formal ceremony with distinguished speakers, citations and awards, and a benediction.

In some ways, Maids' Honor Day reinforced the power of employers to define the terms of employment, to determine what distinguished a "good" from a "bad" worker. One employer referred to her worker as "the epitome of quiet, gentle strength."[24] Another employer nominated "Sophie" because, even though she had her own family, she worked for thirty years for her em-ployers acting as "pediatrician, psychologist, advisor, counselor, confidant, companion and contributor to spoiling our son."[25] In another case, a domestic worker "swooped in like Mary Poppins" and saved the family from being bro-ken apart, while accepting a "very low salary." This same woman "sustained third-degree burns of her forearm when she risked her life to put out a kitchen fire which endangered my baby."[26] Clearly, these employers lauded the values of deference, loyalty, and self-sacrifice (even to the point of a maid putting her own life in jeopardy)—the very aspects of the occupation that domestic worker rights activists found intolerable. Rather than scrutinizing the behav-ior of employers, Maids' Honor Day redirected attention to how well employ-ees conducted themselves and whether or not they fulfilled the expectations of their bosses. Nevertheless, for poor black women who scrubbed floors and picked up daily after others, to enjoy a lavish dinner, participate in a formal ceremony, and dress up in their finest attire provided a rare opportunity to publicly take pride in who they were. Even workers who did not win the honor of Maid of the Year undoubtedly garnered some much-needed satisfaction and recognition from hearing the praises of their employers.

Another central goal of the NDWUA was to professionalize the occu-pation. Updating the advancement project of earlier black women activists like Nannie Helen Burroughs, the NDWUA started training programs for domestic workers so they could acquire "specialized and technical training to provide better services in the field of Household Management."[27] Train-ees engaged in comparison price shopping, cooking lessons, driver education, child care, elder care, and first aid. They learned how to dress, answer the telephone, and set the table. On completion of the course, they participated in a ceremony, received a certificate, and, according to Bolden, became "professional women." Such training, they believed, would lead to higher wages. Training functioned as a form of recognition—that household work was not unskilled labor but that it required both a level of knowledge and a measure of instruction.[28]

In 1971, the NDWUA entered into a contract with the Georgia State Department of Family and Children Services to begin a homemaker skills training program to train women on welfare how to keep house and care for their children. This program placed domestic workers in a position of leadership and expertise to train and instruct other, poorer, women in housekeeping. The welfare recipients who joined the program underwent six weeks of intensive training in "home management, child care, health, budgeting and resource development," which would then enable them to be employed as "homeworkers" for other poor families.[29] It became a program of the poor helping the poor. Framed as an antipoverty initiative, the goal was to rid the home of "filth, disorder, disease, injury, child neglect, improper diet" and make it "a more satisfying place" for these families.[30] This was a double-edged sword: On the one hand, as a program run by the NWDUA, it elevated the skills of domestic workers, but it also denigrated the housekeeping of women on welfare—two groups of women that were not entirely distinct.

The NDWUA's reform strategies did not "stop the wheels of production," so to speak. Because of their limited resources and dependence on their employers, these women eschewed confrontational politics. They rarely marched in the street; they didn't go on strike or organize boycotts. Neither did they campaign to place African American women in alternative employment. Most members of the NDWUA embraced their occupation rather than attempting to escape it. It was an occupation they valued and wanted others to value as well. Instead, they used alternative strategies to undermine the degradation of the occupation. They established uniform standards and collective demands to empower individual domestic workers in their dealings with their employers. Their campaigns for Maids' Honor Day and professionalization did not seek to eliminate the distinction between themselves and their employers. Their goal was to minimize the power differential with their employers and increase the stature of domestic service. A graduate of one of the NDWUA's training programs testified that when her employer insisted that she scrub the floor on her hands and knees, she responded: "I have completed my training as a household technician and know that I don't have to scrub floors down on all fours anymore."[31] The training programs and Maids' Honor Day helped reinforce solidarity and identity among domestic workers and erase some of the shame publicly associated with domestic service.[32]

Conclusion

Dorothy Bolden and the NDWUA formulated a politics of resistance that spoke to their specific needs and constraints as black domestic workers. They operated within the interlocking systems of oppression that black feminists have theorized.[33] Thus race, gender, and class were instrumental in their political evolution. Their lived experiences as poor black women made class and political economy central to how they conceptualized their struggle and their freedom.[34]

The NDWUA hoped to reframe the class relations that defined domestic work. They challenged the hierarchy, the power, and the racial and class differences that others had attached to the labor. That reframing meant putting employers and employees on a more equal footing and erasing the vestiges of racial servitude that were so closely tied to domestic service in this historical moment. As historian Dorothy Sue Cobble explained: "Dismantling the 'mammy' stereotype with its expectations of self-sacrifice and deference required an assault against multiple ideologies of domination."[35] Similarly, sociologist Judith Rollins argued that the social and psychological components of domestic service work perpetuate notions of inequality.[36] The NDWUA's programs to honor a Maid of the Year and to professionalize the occupation challenged the scripts of proper behavior and modeled alternative modes of interaction, which transformed the demeanor of household workers and raised the status of the occupation.

In their efforts to reform domestic service, the NDWUA didn't organize sit-ins or blockade buildings. By 1960s standards, these women were tame. As middle-aged women with children to support, they simply couldn't risk losing their jobs. "I didn't want anybody to protest. We women didn't believe in it, especially in this field. Because if thirty thousand women get without a job, and that's how many maids there are in Atlanta, where else have we got to go to?" Bolden recalled. "So we couldn't go out demonstrating, and we weren't ram-rodding anything down anybody's throat. Just if we weren't getting paid, we just walk off the job."[37] This reluctance to protest is consistent with the research of scholars such as Robin Kelley and James Scott, who have suggested that the poor and disenfranchised must find alternative resistance strategies.[38]

In contrast to the Kelley/Scott thesis that examines the "hidden transcript" behind ostensible on-stage accommodation, however, it was precisely to the public stage that domestic workers directed their energies.

Prior to the 1960s, domestic worker resistance had been elusive and masked. With the formation of the NDWUA, it took on a public institutionalized life. The NDWUA made home the site of contestation.[39] The domestic sphere became the battleground and their individual relationship with their employers the most important fight. "The personal is political" rang as true for them—if not more so—as for other feminists of this period. In this struggle they wanted to improve working conditions, not transform them. The NDWUA fought to reconfigure the ideological construction of the good maid and the good employer, as well as to carve out spaces of autonomy for domestic workers.[40] They wanted to win greater public respect for an occupation that they felt was valuable and rewarding. Their struggle had limitations but also transformative potential, for it taught poor black women how to speak for themselves and represent themselves, an accomplishment we should not underestimate when the fate of the vast majority of domestic workers continues to be exploitation, invisibility, and dehumanization.

Notes

1. NDWA, brochure, box 1, Dorothy Bolden Thompson Collection.

2. The historical literature on domestic service work is extensive. See, for example: Boris and Nadasen, 2008; Katzman, 1978; Palmer, 1989; Glenn, 1986; Romero, 1992; Van Raaphorst, 1988; Rollins, 1985; Cobble, 2004; Hunter, 1977; Rio, 2005; Dill, 1994; Coble, 2006; Smith, 2000. For sources on the NDWUA, see Beck, 2001; and Christiansen, 1999. There is also a voluminous literature on the contemporary situation. See, for example: Parreñas, 2001; Hondagneu-Sotelo, 2001; Chang, 2000; Das Gupta, 2007; Repak, 1995; Milkman, 2006; Tait, 2005; Nadasen, 2009.

3. See Yancy, 1986.

4. Seifer, 1976: 167.

5. Ibid.: 162–163.

6. Julie Yates Rivchin similarly argues that the exclusions of some workers from the NLRA has fostered new kinds of labor organizing that emphasizes grassroots participation and a community orientation that ultimately has strengthened the labor movement (Rivchin, 2004: 397).

7. Boris, 1994.

8. Clark-Lewis, 1996.

9. Yancy, 1986.

10. See Rollins, 1985.

11. Anderson, 2000.

12. Elizabeth Runyan to NDWUA, 25 May 1976, NDWUA Papers, box 1628, folder 90.

13. Lerner, 1972: 237.

14. Ibid.

15. Dorothy Bolden, quoted in *Atlanta Daily World*, March 23, 1975, NDWUA Papers, box 1623, folder 182.

16. Lerner, 1972: 237.

17. NDWA, booklet, "National Domestic Workers of American, Inc. (1977?), NDWUA Papers.

18. *Statistical Abstracts of the United States*, 1975: 364.

19. Strasser, 2000.

20. Palmer, 1989.

21. Dill, 1994.

22. Lerner, 1972: 235

23. NDWUA Brochure, 18, NDWUA Papers.

24. "Maids' Honor Day Nomination" NDWUA Papers, box 1627, folder 87.

25. "Maids' Honor Day Nomination" NDWUA Papers, box 1627, folder 87.

26. "Maids' Honor Day Nomination" NDWUA Papers, box 1627, folder 86.

27. NDWUA, "Proposal to Implement a Training Program for Household Management Technicians in Metro-Atlanta." June 26, 1974, NDWUA Papers, box 1625, folder 52.

28. NDWA, "A Manpower Development, Training and Placement Program" 1975, NDWUA Papers, box 1625, folder 53.

29. NDWA, "Homemaking Skills Training Program" 1971, NDWUA Papers, box 1625, folder 50.

30. NDWUA, Proposal for Homemaking Skills Training Program, NDWUA Papers, box 1625, folder 52.

31. NDWUA, "Proposal to Implement a Training Program for Household Management Technicians in Metro-Atlanta," 4, June 26, 1974, NDWUA Papers, box 1625, folder 52.

32. Alan Wolfe (1992) argues that boundaries and distinctions are not always bad but that they can function to enhance group solidarity.

33. For example, see King, 1988; Higginbotham, 1992; Zinn and Dill, 1996; Collins, 2000; Guy-Sheftall, 1995.

34. Helen Neville and Jennifer Hamer explain the need for black feminists to take into account class and capitalism, crafting what they call a revolutionary black feminism. They argue that black women's experiences cannot be interpreted without looking at political economy (Neville and Hamer, 2001).

35. Cobble, 1999.
36. Rollins, 1985.
37. Seifer, 1976: 161.
38. See Kelley, 1996; Lee, 2006.
39. For more on this see Lee, 2006.
40. Scott, 1985.

14 Manicuring Intimacies

Inequalities and Resistance
in Nail Salon Work

Miliann Kang

HALF A DOZEN PROTESTORS stand in front of a Manhattan nail salon carrying crumpled cardboard sign boards, saying: "Hey Nail Plaza! Women workers should have the right to breaks"; "Sweatshops are not glamorous"; "No gloves, no masks, no pedicure!" Representing several different organizations, including the Chinese Staff and Workers Association and the National Mobilization against Sweatshops, they have gathered in support of a dismissed worker, Do Yea (Susan) Kim, who has filed a lawsuit accusing the salon of not giving breaks or paying overtime. Two well-heeled, elderly white women come out of the salon, huddling together with nervous smiles. One of the protesters yells, "Don't support this salon—they don't respect worker's rights." One of the customers yells back, "That's not true. She takes good care of us. She's very nice." The protestor retorts, "She's nice to you, not to her workers! All you care about are your nails, you don't know what's going on in there!" The customer calls back—"Yes we do!"—and then hustles away. Later, another woman, a former customer at this salon, stops by the picket and comments, "I'm actually really surprised to see so many people still going in there. This is the Upper West Side, we have a reputation of being very liberal, big Hillary supporters. We're known for supporting the underdog—unions, teachers . . . I guess people are attached to their manicurist so they're willing to break the picket."[1]

What are the attachments among nail salon customers, manicurists, and nail salon owners, and how can these ties inhibit or support organizing to improve the working conditions in these sites? In the scene described above, the intimacy involved in the exchange of a manicure translates into customers' loyalty toward a particular owner and salon and overrides concerns with labor rights. People who arguably would not cross a picket in other circumstances are willing to do so to be cared for by a favorite manicurist in a familiar and comfortable setting. This example highlights how intimacy often blurs, conceals, and justifies inequalities in the workplace and poses a barrier to organizing. At the same time, these same attachments, by making it difficult to replace the service provider, can increase the value of this work and provide an impetus for mobilization in the nail industry. The lens of intimate labor helps us both recognize the many important organizing efforts to upgrade nail salon work and also identify and address potential challenges and barriers.

According to Viviana Zelizer, "Intimacy takes many forms. So does its purchase."[2] The dynamics of nail salon work illuminate the connected nature of intimacy and economics and how these dynamics shape efforts to raise the value of this work. Intimacy in body service work, such as that provided in nail salons, is fleeting and asymmetrical and, in most cases, overwhelmingly benefits the customers and owners while serving as an obstacle to various organizing approaches. Nonetheless, because intimacy can raise the value of the service, particularly by making it difficult to replace the provider, it can serve as a possible leveraging point toward collective action. The ways that the dynamics of intimate labor can both support and undermine social change appear in the arenas of (1) occupational and public health; (2) labor rights; and (3) regulation of manufacturers. These areas are not mutually exclusive, and many organizations engage in more than one of them; however, I treat them as analytically distinct. In each area, I identify the main issues, describe organizing efforts, and analyze how the characteristics of intimate labor are significant in shaping the process and outcomes of these efforts.

Research Methods

The data collection for this project involved fourteen months of intensive fieldwork and open-ended interviews with nail salon customers, owners, workers, community leaders, and industry representatives. I conducted the initial research in 1997 and 1998, adding new and follow-up interviews and participant observation from 2001 through 2003. During the summers of 2007 and 2009, I interviewed members of labor rights, public health, and community organizations regarding organizing and regulatory efforts to upgrade work in the nail industry.

The research design included ethnography at six sites: (1) Uptown Nails and Exclusive Nails, located in predominantly white, middle- and upper-class neighborhoods; (2) Downtown Nails and Artistic Nails, in predominantly black (African American and Caribbean) working- and lower-middle class neighborhoods; (3) Crosstown Nails and Convenient Nails, in racially and socioeconomically mixed neighborhoods. In addition, the research included in-depth, semistructured interviews ($N = 87$) with thirteen Korean nail salon owners, fifteen Korean nail salon workers, twenty-three black customers, twenty-six white customers, and, as mentioned above, ten key informants working on nail salon industry issues. In addition, I conducted dozens of in-formal interviews with owners, workers, and customers in various public settings, including organizational meetings, restaurants, and public transit.

Background of Asian Immigrant Women's Work in Nail Salons

Manicures, once mostly performed by women in the privacy of their own bathrooms, are now increasingly bought and sold. Nail salon growth began in the 1980s and took off exponentially in the 1990s. According to trade industry sources, the number of nail salons in the United States grew from 32,674 in 1993 to 53,615 in 2003, a 67 percent increase in a decade.[3] In the high-concentration areas of New York and California, Asian immigrants own and operate roughly 70 percent of these salons. Most states do not collect information on the ethnic breakdown of license holders, so these figures are difficult to ascertain. Nonetheless, industry sources estimate that Koreans own 80 percent of nail salons in New York and New Jersey,[4] and Vietnamese comprise 80 percent of the nail technicians in California and 25 percent nationwide.[5] Chinese have also made significance inroads into the niche.

The New York City nail salon niche, and its domination by Koreans, is part of a broader pattern of new Asian immigrants of various ethnicities establishing nail salons throughout the United States. The juxtaposition of a highly skilled and highly paid advanced service sector against the low-skilled and low-wage ethnic labor market in "global cities"[6] creates the conditions for the emergence and proliferation of Asian immigrant–owned nail salons in multiple sites. Lack of fluency in the English language, inability to transfer credentials earned in other countries, and discrimination in the mainstream labor market based on race, gender, and immigration status contribute to Asian immigrants clustering in this ethnic-dominated niche. This employment and self-employment has allowed many Asian immigrants, especially women, to earn a basic livelihood, but not without costs. In recent years, various Asian American, immigrant rights, public health, and environmental organizations have mobilized to upgrade work in the nail salon industry.

Organizing around Occupational and Public Health Concerns

Paula Abdul's 2005 testimony before the California Senate Business and Professions Committee and other high-profile cases have focused public attention on consumer concerns regarding the spread of fungus and disease in nail salons.[7] With far less publicity, Asian American community groups have raised occupational health and safety concerns from the perspective of nail salon workers. Through public education and participatory action research, these organizations have sought to increase awareness and foster safer practices for both nail salon customers and workers.

Constant handling of polishes, solvents, glues, and acrylics can expose workers to potentially carcinogenic, allergenic, and/or reproductively harmful substances such as dibutyl phthalate, formaldehyde, toluene, acetone, benzene, methylene chloride, glycol ether, and the banned but still used methylmethacrylate (MMA). As a result, nail salon workers experience numerous occupational health-related symptoms, including skin problems, eye irritations, allergies, neck or back discomfort, and asthma.[8] Julia Liou of Asian Health Services in the Bay Area and cofounder of the California Healthy Nail Salon Collaborative, noted a possible connection to pregnancy difficulties and cancer: "It's been suspected that there is an increased incidence of breast cancer and statistics show that cervical cancer is higher among Vietnamese women. Again, it's hard to say what the cause is, but in California, 59 to 80 percent of the nail salons are Vietnamese. Most of these women are of reproductive age." The fears of one nail salon worker summed up many: "I worry most about my health here—because I don't know how bad it is, sometimes I just feel dizzy—there's nothing you can do." These factors make for a complex health profile among workers, as well as a complex profile with regard to organizing to upgrade nail salon work. The nature of the work itself, especially the processes of intimacy that shape it, further complicates organizing strategies and mobilization for change.

Various organizing efforts have sought to address occupational and public health issues in the salons through educational outreach and participatory research with salon owners and workers and partnerships between federal, state, and local government; community organizations; and the local business community. Examples of these efforts include the National Healthy Nail Salon Alliance, Asian Communities for Reproductive Justice's Participatory Research, Organizing and Leadership Initiative for Safety and Health (POLISH) project; the Nail Salon Project in Houston; the National Asian Pacific American

Women's Forum (national office and Yale Chapter); the Toxic Use Reduction Institute at the University of Massachusetts at Lowell; and Women's Voices for the Earth. These efforts concentrate on identifying and publicizing best practices in nail salons for the protection of both workers and consumers, and they have significantly raised awareness in communities across the country. However, even when clearly understood by nail technicians, best practices are sometimes difficult to follow when they involve possibly upsetting customers or owners. Thus, there is often a wide gap between what manicurists know they should do and what they actually are able to do.

Intimacy complicates public and occupational health practices at the level of implementation. For example, the Asian Law Caucus and the University of California, San Francisco, Community Occupational Health Project offer guidelines for protecting nail salon workers against infection. These include wearing gloves, frequent hand washing, and disinfecting of tools. They recommend precise steps for what to do if a client bleeds.[9] While these procedures are certainly reasonable and desirable, implementing them in the workplace is another matter. As one experienced nail salon worker in Manhattan, thirty-seven-year-old Julie Suh, recounted:

> When you use gloves, customers feel bad, so I don't use them . . . The owner doesn't like it when you wear a mask with regular customers . . . because she wants you to talk to them . . . In black and Hispanic neighborhoods people wear more masks because they do a lot of tips, but where I work it's mainly manicures. It would be strange if no one is wearing a mask or gloves and you're the only one wearing them . . . (*What is the hardest part of the job for you?*) I'm afraid I'm going to make the people bleed . . . If you make them bleed, the customer gets really upset. You just have to apologize a lot and take care of them . . . You can't put on gloves for that little amount of blood. To save time, you have to touch it, then just throw it away. I never heard of anyone contracting a disease, but I worry about it. I have a family so that's what I worry most about.

Manicurists like Julie must respond to customers' needs, both physical and emotional, even if this means subordinating proper hygienic protocols as well as their own health concerns. Because customers expect a certain level of conversation, physical contact, and emotional attentiveness, workers at times must make a priority of customers' comfort and feelings about safety and health procedures. In addition, because owners often pressure them to work quickly, manicurists are hard pressed to follow time-consuming disinfecting and cleaning protocols. Thus, occupational safety and health issues are closely connected to labor rights in the salons.

Intimacy and Labor Organizing in Nail Salons

How do the dynamics of intimate labor affect labor organizing and advocacy? The protest at Nail Plaza highlights commonly experienced labor rights issues. Like Do Yea Kim, many workers complain of irregular meal and break times; unhealthy work conditions, including exposure to toxic chemicals; low wages; and lack of overtime pay. Here I describe labor rights issues and organizing campaigns in the salons and examine how intimate ties between coethnic owners and workers complicate organizing. I also address how racialized perceptions of Asian immigrant women as passive and easily exploitable serve to normalize their substandard working conditions. These issues are further complicated in that some workers are classified as independent contractors, which shifts responsibility for wages and breaks away from the owners.[10]

Workers interviewed for this study verify that many nail salons follow lax protocols regarding legally mandated breaks and wages. With regard to lack of regular breaks, one manicurist in Queens commented, "I don't know any salons that give you an hour break at a set time everyday. Sometimes we have to eat in ten minutes, depending on whether it's busy or slow. Sometimes it's so busy, the boss won't even tell you can take a break, so you just have to keep working." As for wages, Kyung Shin, a twenty-seven-year-old manicurist in Manhattan, stated, "I'm still learning, and I don't have a license, so I get paid $40 a day. But those more experienced earn $100 in salary; tips are extra." On the days she works, Kyung is in the salon for roughly ten hours, from 9:30 A.M. to 7:30 P.M., thus earning significantly less than minimum wage. However, she accepts this as a temporary situation, in which she trades off training for low wages until she becomes more skilled and can earn higher wages and tips.

While different organizations have attempted to draw attention to workers' rights in the nail salons, labor organizing and advocacy in the industry are just at the beginning stages. Several organizations have represented nail salon workers in back-wage cases. The Asian American Legal Defense and Education Fund (AALDEF) and YKASEC–Empowering the Korean American Community collaborated in support of a former nail salon worker from Flushing, Queens, and won a back-wage settlement of $17,500 in January 2006.[11] That July, the U.S. Department of Labor won $222,036 in back wages and interest for 152 workers at six New York City salons under a single owner for violations of the federal Fair Labor Standards Act (FLSA).[12] In New York City, the Committee against Anti-Asian Violence started its Women's Worker's Project in 1995, focusing on health issues among low-wage immigrant women workers "in the new 'service sweatshop' economy," including nail salons, laundries, child care, and housekeeping.[13]

The months of protesting at Nail Plaza coalesced on September 16, 2007, in the kickoff of the Justice Will Be Served Nail Salon Workers Network. Sponsored by the National Mobilization Against Sweatshops (NMASS), Chinese Staff and Workers Association (CSWA), and 318 Restaurant Worker's Union, the campaign called for: "(1) Justice for the Nail Plaza workers; (2) City-funding for a study and treatment program for nail salon workers; and (3) Government regulations to protect workers in the nail salon industry." This was the first time a nail worker had stood up, one campaign organizer observed, adding, "Only by challenging the sweatshop practices of owners is change going to happen. All the pressure is going to come from workers, as they are the ones whose lives are at stake."

If effective labor rights organizing in the nail industry rests on workers standing up to confront owners, the complex dynamics of worker–owner relations among coethnics becomes a central concern. Here, too, the framework of intimate labor offers insights. The strength of social networks in immigrant communities can make workers hesitant to challenge unfair labor practices, as their ties with the owner are not simply that of worker and boss but involve other forms of intimacy: the ties of friendship, church, hometown, and neighborhood. Many workers depend on owners for rides to work as well as for sponsoring their work visas. Finally, the dream that they will one day become owners themselves often undermines solidarity with other workers. Thus, while coethnic employment can add to the comfort and attractiveness of nail salon work, it also subjects workers to a higher degree of social control, inhibiting resistance.

Portes and Manning use the term *labor paternalism* to refer to the system of obligations based on kinship and community networks and the enmeshment of ethnic labor relations in these networks.[14] Coethnic workers trade off low wages, long working hours, and, in some instances, derogatory treatment in return for jobs, training, support in adjusting to their new country, and potential assistance in establishing their own businesses. Nail salon work reveals a parallel form of "labor maternalism" emerging between coethnic women owners and workers. On the one hand, women's social networks can enable them to work, especially in cases when these women have not been previously employed, and possibly gain training and resources to start their own businesses. At the same time, because workers may have few employment options, are not fluent in English, and lack understanding of U.S. labor laws, they are easily exploitable. Some of the owners are very strict, and the workers feel constant pressure to work hard and are uncomfortable talking among themselves or reading a book even when there are no customers. Sarah Lee, a Korean manicurist in Brooklyn, complained: "When it's slow, I have to find something to do so I look like I'm working hard. When there are a lot of customers waiting, I try to work faster so the customers don't leave. But then she doesn't pay us any more when business is better." Thus, workers' sense of obligation is often one sided, as close ties do not necessarily translate into better treatment and pay by owners. Workers' expectations that they will receive support in starting their own businesses are often unreciprocated by owners, especially given increasing competition.

Esther Lee, a long-term manicurist in Manhattan, described how workers' interests are often treated as secondary to those of owners within ethnic community business associations, regarding not only labor issues but also toxic exposures. When asked about participation in any ethnic business associations, she guffawed: "They do not care about people like me—they are just trying to help the owners make more money. The one time they helped workers was when the new law [requiring licensure] came out . . . Even then, I think they really cared more about how to keep owners from losing workers and losing business, rather than really trying to help the workers."[15] Owners, she claimed, may be more invested in keeping toxic exposure issues under the radar than in improving working conditions. Rather than joining with workers and customers to publicize and mobilize around these issues, owners may in fact counter such efforts.

Similarly, Michelle Wong, copresident of the Yale Chapter of the National Asian Pacific American Women's Forum, discovered a complex set of relationships around exposures. "Both employers and workers are trying to maximize the number of customers daily, and in some cases, this might mean using acetone nail polish remover, which works much more quickly than acetone-free products," she observed. But "owners were slightly hesitant (to allow us to conduct a workshop in their salon), and thus we did not get the chance to work with them." Wong understood that owners have various constraints on their supporting better working conditions, such as the cost and availability of less toxic products. Thus, efforts to address labor rights issues must also factor in the role of cosmetics manufacturers. While confronting the reality of different class interests between owners and workers, labor rights issues, especially concerning toxic exposures, cannot be solved solely at the level of salon practices but also must take into account corporate responsibility in the production of toxic cosmetic products.

Intimate Labor and Regulation of Manufacturers

Efforts to pressure cosmetics manufacturers to produce safer products mainly have focused on a strategy of creating coalitions of owners, workers, and customers around issues of toxic exposure. While intimacy can foster shared investment in these issues, it can also blur the potentially conflicting interests of different parties. In examining efforts to make manufacturers take greater responsibility for toxic exposures, the lens of intimate labor brings attention to the interests of the least powerful members within coalitions, particularly workers, and how their concerns can be overlooked or toned down so as not to alienate other members.

"It's like a modern-day DDT story—it's analogous to the exposure that farmworkers have experienced," declared Liou of Asian Health Services. Liou cofounded the California Healthy Nail Salon Collaborative, a coalition of twenty-five organizations that focuses on policy, research, outreach, and education in the nail salon industry and involves participation from nail salon owners and workers from Los Angeles and the Bay Area; prominent Asian American community organizations; public health–related organizations; environmental action groups; labor rights groups; unions; and government agencies. While taking a multipronged approach, the collaborative focuses on "holding the manufacturers accountable." As opposed to the European Union, which has regulated cosmetic manufacturers, in the United States, Liou pointed out, "They regulate themselves—they have their own Cosmetic Industrial Review Panel, they are not EPA regulated . . . They argue that the carcinogenic material is minimal, but they're looking at just one product. There's no study of accumulated exposure to *many* products over time, and they certainly don't look at it from the workers' perspective of long-term, chronic exposures, six to seven days a week, eight, nine, ten hours a day."

While the collaborative highlights workers as the most vulnerable population with regard to toxic exposure in the salons, at the same time, its members advocate a strategy of building alliances through shared interests. Liou elaborated: "(W)e don't want to scare people. There has been a lot of negative publicity around the salons, and they don't want to scare customers away. This is their livelihood, so we approach it as, 'Safe practices are better for your business. It's good for everyone.' Our approach is to target the manufacturers and bring owners and worker together." This goal of bringing owners and workers together is important and laudable; however, it may not be feasible or even appropriate in all situations. Owners' and workers' interests are not always the same, or even compatible, as discussed earlier with regard to labor rights issues. Thus, there is a fine line between working to build coalitions and inadvertently silencing concerns of certain members, especially workers.

Only an organizing strategy of building coalitions around shared interests seems best able to end toxic exposure, improve working conditions, and sustain individual firms. Alexandra Gorman Scranton, director of Science and Research for Women's Voices for the Earth, a nonprofit environmental health advocacy group and one of the founding organizations of the Campaign for Safe Cosmetics, has insisted: "In order to engage nail salon workers and owners, we found it is best not to use language which appears to put the blame on them (for using products containing toxic chemicals.) We also found a resistance to language which implied that visiting a nail salon was dangerous for a consumer. We found that successful language focused on the chemicals themselves and the manufacturers' responsibility for ensuring their products were safe to use."[16] On the one hand, this strategy can build on the intimacy of nail salon work, which, unlike other kinds of small businesses, fosters sustained interactions in which the kind of language and communication that Gorman advocates can potentially develop. A customer is more likely to participate in an informed conversation about a variety of issues with a manicurist with whom she sits down for half an hour every week than with a dry cleaning clerk to whom she drops off her dirty laundry or a grocer from whom she buys her fruits and vegetables.

On the other hand, intimacy can inhibit the willingness to raise uncomfortable issues in salon interactions, especially when customers are already averse to thinking about toxic cosmetic products. Joy Onasch, Community Program Manager at the Toxics Use Reduction Institute (TURI), University of Massachusetts, Lowell, finds "a combination of lack of interest and lack of information and a false sense of security." Customers do not want to acknowledge dangers, let alone participate in actions to address them. First, a general ignorance or even denial regarding the lack of government regulation of the cosmetics industry prevails in the United States (even at academic conferences where I have presented, many are surprised to learn this). Second, the ethos of the beauty service industry relies on creating a relaxing, carefree experience for customers, thus making it difficult to publicize, let alone protest against, potential health threats.

Mobilizing Intimacy: Prospects and Pitfalls

The months of protesting at Nail Plaza on behalf of Do Yea Kim, described at the beginning of this chapter, coalesced in an important victory. The Asian American Legal Defense and Education Fund filed a lawsuit on Kim's behalf, charging lack of overtime pay and wrongful termination, and a federal court awarded her $182,000 for back pay, overtime, and damages in October 2007.[17] While this case is encouraging, the challenges of ongoing organizing to upgrade nail salon work remain formidable. It cannot be assumed that the intimacy involved in nail salon work, or any work, translates into mutual investment by all parties—owners, workers, and customers, let alone cosmetic manufacturers—in improving the various conditions involved in this work. In fact, the opposite is more often true.

Other scholars have argued that the emotional ties between workers and employers, as well as between workers and customers, largely mask unequal power relations and exploitative conditions in various industries, ranging from sex work to nursing to domestic service.[18] For better or worse, I find these patterns replicated in the nail industry. In certain cases, intimacy can be mobilized for the benefit of organizing but not because intimate ties are valued in and of themselves or because they engender greater concern for workers. Instead, intimate ties can increase the value of the work performed because they make the worker difficult to replace. Just as childcare and elderly care workers form close bonds with their charges, so do nail salon workers fulfill important emotional and physical needs in relationships that are difficult and time consuming to reestablish. Customers who show some concern for the health and safety of their manicurists often do so not out of a commitment to fairness but because they do not want the inconvenience of having to locate another service provider who meets their needs.

For example, Emily Goldberg, a customer in Manhattan, has a close relationship with her manicurist, Hannah Kim, whom she has visited for over ten years. Emily shared that "I like Hannah because she knows what I like and she does what I say, like not cutting the top of the cuticle, just the sides. She's very clean—she indulges me . . . Like when I ask for a new paper towel and she says she just changed it, I say, 'Change it again!' and she just does it . . . I read in the papers about some of the problems they've had, so I don't take a chance." Emily and Hannah have worked out a partnership in which they are able to achieve the high level of health and safety practices that Emily desires as a customer. However, this partnership does not necessarily translate into greater concern or protection of Hannah's health as a worker. When I ask Emily if she was aware of any occupational health issues related to the manicurists, she gives a response that I found typical among customers in this study: "I have to admit, I never thought about it." However, she does comment later, "Of course I don't want her to get sick—who would do my nails!"

Thus, the intimacy of this work can foster greater attention to healthy practices and willingness to communicate about them but mostly for the benefit of the customers and owners rather than the workers. At the same time, the difficulty of reestablishing the intimate ties necessary to carry out this work can generate concern for the worker, if only as a means to an end rather than as a priority in and of itself. In the case of nail salon work, intimacy often serves to polarize rather than galvanize different actors, as it raises the stakes of interaction and magnifies conflicting interests and power relations. The pervasive belief that intimacy should not be commercialized further undermines attempts to raise the value and improve the conditions of intimate labor. As economists Paula England and Nancy Folbre assert, "The principle that money cannot buy love may have the unintended and perverse consequence of perpetuating low pay for face-to-face service work."[19] An understanding of intimate labor thus illuminates obstacles to implementing safe practices in nail salons. It is difficult for nail salon workers to negotiate safe practices with owners and customers, especially when these negotiations involve sensitive and sometimes thorny emotional and embodied service interactions. Owners and customers, whether intentionally or inadvertently, can undermine efforts by manicurists to protect their own and their customers' health with the result that manicurists may simply sidestep these procedures and the discomfort associated with them.

In analyzing racialized reproductive labor, sociologist Evelyn Nakano Glenn cautions that "forging a political agenda that addresses the universal needs of women is highly problematic not just because women's priorities differ but because gains for some groups might result in a corresponding loss of advantage and privilege for others . . . This does not mean that we give up on the goal of concerted struggle. It means that we give up trying falsely to harmonize women's interests."[20] Just as Nakano Glenn demonstrates that raising wages for reproductive labor performed mostly by women of color threatens the ability of relatively more privileged women to afford these services, so does raising the price of manicures performed by Asian immigrant women undermine the ability of certain customers to purchase them. The physical intimacy of the service exchange heightens concerns with cleanliness and other public health issues that can override political commitments in support of fair and just working conditions. In addition, upgrading the conditions of nail salon work can also cut into the profits that Asian immigrant small business owners generate through the low wages of their workers.

At the same time, these higher stakes can provide opportunities for addressing concerns that participants in most service exchanges would not regard as worth the time and effort. Similar to the negotiations involved between domestic workers and employers, where the welfare of a child or the care of a home are involved, certain concerns need to be raised and addressed, however uncomfortable. Likewise, when the stakes involve spread of infectious diseases, exposure to toxic chemicals, and the general health and comfort of the body, the unavoidable intimacy of these exchanges can translate into heightened concerns regarding the various issues that arise across the manicuring table.

While intimacy heightens the investment of customers in certain services, like manicures, it does not necessarily increase concern for, or commitment to, the service providers. At the same time, intimacy makes it harder to separate the service from the provider. By making the service itself more precious to customers, the dynamics of intimate labor can also foster greater valuation of the service worker and potentially leverage organizing efforts. Thus, greater understanding of the dynamics of intimate labor can serve as a crucial link in supporting organizing efforts not only in the nail industry but also across a range of service occupations.

Notes

Miliann Kang, *The Managed Hand: Race, Gender, and the Body in Beauty Service Work.* (Berkeley: University of California Press, 2010). Reprinted with permission.

1. Field notes from participant observation at Nail Plaza protest on August 11, 2007, at Amsterdam Avenue and 67th Street in Manhattan.

2. Zelizer, 2005: 308.

3. Dickson, 2005. In 2006–2007, industry figures estimated 58,330 nail salons and 347,898 nail technicians in a $6.16 billion industry (*Nails Magazine* 2008: 62).

4. Greenhouse, 2007a.

5. Hill, 1997: 100.

6. Sassen, 2001.

7. According to Abdul, an unsanitary manicure caused yearlong complications that necessitated hospitalization: "Being a professional dancer, I'm no stranger to pain, but this time the pain was so excruciating that even my hair touching my thumb caused me to scream" (Associated Press, 2005).

8. The survey of 100 workers, conducted by the New York Committee for Occupational Safety and Health and a Korean workers' group, Empowering the Korean American Community, is cited in Greenhouse, 2007a.

9. Asian Law Caucus, 2005, 8–9.

10. Bernhardt et al., 2007.

11. Asian American Legal Defense and Education Fund (AALDEF), 2006.

12. U.S. Department of Labor, 2006.

13. CAAAV Organizing Asian Communities, 2010.

14. Portes and Manning, 1986.

15. The "new law" she is referring to regards licensing manicurists in New York State, which did not require licenses until 1994; see New York State, Division of Licensing Services, 1994. The Korean Nail Salon Association of New York was able to lobby successfully for a grandfather clause so that women who could prove that they had been working in a salon for at least a year did not have to go to nail school for a license.

16. See Gorman and O'Connor, 2007.

17. AALDEF, 2007; Gonnerman, 2007. Despite this legal victory, Kim has not been able to collect back wages as the salon owners declared bankruptcy (Lee, 2009).

18. Choy, 2003; Glenn, 1986; Parreñas, 2001; Hochschild, 2003; Hondagneu-Sotelo, 2001; Kempadoo and Doezema, 1998.

19. England and Folbre, 1999.

20. Glenn, 1992.

15 But Who Will Care for the Children?

Organizing Child Care Providers
in the Wake of Welfare Reform

Ellen Reese

THIS CHAPTER EXAMINES THE RISE of unionization campaigns among home-based child care providers and their efforts to improve the U.S. child care system in the wake of welfare reform. These campaigns show the changing face of organized labor as they involved thousands of low and moderate-income women, many of whom are African American and Latina, as well as the children and parents they serve. Drawing on feminist theory and social movement studies, I argue that state policies had contradictory impacts on the efforts to unionize these intimate laborers. On the one hand, the expansion of subsidized child care that accompanied the implementation of federal welfare reforms and a history of activism facilitated this new wave of care worker organizing. The emphasis of putting poor mothers to work within welfare reform created setbacks in terms of poor mothers' rights to care for their own children at home, but it increased opportunities to expand and improve subsidized child care programs. The expansion of subsidized child care, and tough new work requirements, increased both the numbers of low-income working mothers who needed these services and the numbers of home-based child care providers. In response to problems in the administration of welfare reform and subsidized child care, both of these groups, mainly women of color, became more organized and brought new grassroots energy into state and local campaigns to improve state-funded child care programs.[1] But they came up against the challenge of existing labor laws. As independent contractors or businesswomen, they lacked the right to collective bargaining and could establish this right only through the adoption of new state policies.[2]

Problems plaguing the child care system helped to make providers and their clients ripe for mobilization, while the intimate nature of home-based child care work facilitated their collaboration. Historical background on, and a national overview of, the rising activism among U.S. child care providers illuminates these problems and collaborations. Case studies of campaigns in Wisconsin and California illustrate the importance of political power—who rules—for determining the outcome of unionization. Whereas California's Republican Governor Arnold Schwarzenegger repeatedly vetoed legislation authorizing the right to collective bargaining, Wisconsin's Democratic Governor James Doyle established it through an executive order.

These case studies also illustrate how child care providers' struggles were motivated not simply by interests in improving their labor rights but also by an "ethic of care."[3] As other scholars have noted, child care providers and their advocates strategically deployed a "vocabulary of skill" as well as a "vocabulary of virtue." They emphasized their training and skills to justify better wages and benefits. They also expressed their concern for their clients' welfare and fought for policies to improve the quality and accessibility of subsidized child care for low-income families.[4] Toward those ends, providers built "community-labor" alliances by organizing families dependent on their services and collaborating with other child care advocates. I argue that the intimate nature of home-based child care facilitated efforts by providers to mobilize clients in the fight to improve the system of subsidized child care. These campaigns thus provided new grassroots energy and resources for the labor movement as well as for the improvement of the U.S. child care system. In my conclusion, I reflect on the implications of this story for organizing intimate labor.

Subsidized Child Care: A Mountain of Grievances

Although the 1996 welfare reform act largely cut back and restricted government assistance to low-income families, it expanded publicly subsidized child care to ease transition from welfare to work.[5] By 2002, thirty-three states were spending more in state and federal funds on child care than on cash assistance for poor families.[6] Even so, subsidized child care programs were insufficient to meet the need for them, which was growing as maternal employment increased and real wages stagnated and declined for most Americans.[7] National studies found that only about one-third of parents who left welfare for work received child care subsidies, while at most 15 percent of those eligible for federal child care subsidies received them. Poor outreach, cumbersome application procedures, high copayments, and shortages in child care spaces (particularly for infant care and night care) contributed to these low figures.[8]

To make matters worse, when fiscal conditions declined after 2001, at least half of the states began to rollback subsidized child care.[9] States instituted cutbacks by lowering real income limits for eligibility, creating waiting lists, increasing copayments, or reducing reimbursement rates for providers or funds to improve the quality of child care. By 2008, about one-third of states reported waiting lists for child care assistance, affecting hundreds of thousands of children.[10]

State policies also failed to address the staffing crisis that the low compensation of workers exacerbated. A national study of the salaries of preschool teachers and child care workers found that their average annual incomes remained just above poverty levels in 2006. Child care workers earned an average of $18,820 annually.[11] Average turnover among child care centers is about 41 percent per year. A study of ninety-two child care centers found that 76 percent of all child care workers had left their jobs within a four-year period.[12] Expansions in child care funding did little to raise child care workers' salaries because few of these funds were used to improve workers' training and wages. Instead, as child care services for low-income families increased, "voucher payments limited by market rate reimbursement policies increased as a proportion of public funding, and the lion's share of the public resources flowed increasingly to the least-trained and worst-paid sectors of the industry."[13] Most welfare recipients, like most parents, relied on informal, license-exempt child care workers or licensed family-based providers who were paid the least.[14]

State policies contributed to these low salaries; more than half of states set payment rates for providers of subsidized child care below the seventy-fifth percentile of private costs. As fiscal conditions worsened, about one-third of states lowered or froze their payment rates between 2001 and 2008.[15] Bureaucratic delays and problems in the approval and payment of child care subsidies and lost paperwork further exacerbated providers' financial difficulties.[16] Those caring for welfare recipients' children risked foregoing their pay or receiving it very late, causing many providers to refuse to serve this population and others to go out of business.

Providers' and clients' joint frustrations with the subsidized child care system made both groups ripe for mobilization. The intimate nature of home-based child care work facilitated their collaboration in child care organizing campaigns. Home-based child care providers often provided clients with flexible scheduling not offered at larger centers. Because they worked at home, these providers would allow parents to drop off their children at early hours in the morning or to pick them up late at night, and they renegotiated child care schedules to accommodate parents' shifting work schedules. Providers also gained parents' trust and friendship through the intimate care that they provided to their children and personal conversations with them. Providers and their clients often lived in the same neighborhood and were linked through personal referrals and relationships, including those between their children, which also helped to strengthen clients' feelings of personal loyalty to providers. The children under providers' care also frequently developed feelings of adoration and respect for them and personally benefited from state-subsidized child care. All of these factors, in addition to parents' own grievances with the child care system, helped providers to solicit the support of clients to improve the subsidized child care system and gain collective bargaining rights. Providers presented unionization as a way to strengthen their capacity to improve the quality and accessibility of child care services.[17]

The Rise of Child Care Providers' Unionization Campaigns

Efforts to organize child care providers began in earnest in the 1970s with the "worthy wage" movement. Child care teachers in various cities began to raise consciousness about their need for higher wages and better working conditions. They framed their demands in terms of economic justice and women's liberation and as part of a broader movement for a better child care system. After gaining support for higher wages within their professional associations, they later raised public consciousness about the issue through community and labor organizing. The Worthy Wage Campaign, a multiyear public awareness drive, started in 1991 and quickly spread across the country. This campaign involved a variety of actions, including walkouts by providers, marches, demonstrations, and public forums.[18]

After 1995, with the growth of the child care industry, the movement became increasingly visible. The child care staffing crisis and the new activism among child care providers and their clients helped to increase support from unions and other allies. So did new research on the importance of children's early years and continuity of care for brain development and on the impact of higher wages on worker turnover. State and local governments in the 1980s and 1990s funded various prekindergarten programs; they also developed small-scale and temporary initiatives to compensate child care workers' training, which aimed to enhance workers' retention and professional development.[19]

Some activists in the Worthy Wage Campaign formed unions. As early as the 1960s, the American Federation of State, County, and Municipal Employees (AFSCME) organized child care workers in New York City. Center workers in Massachusetts, Michigan, and Wisconsin joined the United Auto Workers (UAW) in the 1970s. In the 1980s and 1990s, the Service Employees International Union (SEIU), the American Federation of Teachers (AFT), the International Brotherhood of Teamsters, and the Painters' Union began organizing child care providers in centers and Head Start programs. These early unionization campaigns were fairly small in scale and mainly done "in response to requests by center employees to join a union."[20] As of 2004, only 3 percent of the total child care workforce belonged to a union or were under a union contract.[21]

Until the late 1990s, unions had little interest in organizing family-based child care workers. As small business owners and independent contractors, these providers lacked the legal right to collectively bargain and so organized in the 1980s and 1990s through independent associations, such as Direct Action for Rights and Equality (DARE) in Rhode Island.[22] Other challenges further discouraged unions from investing many resources into organizing child care workers. Job turnover was extremely high, and the work was highly decentralized—job sites usually employed only a few people. Many child care workers also saw themselves as professionals and did not identify readily with unions. Nevertheless, low pay, payment problems, long hours, the lack of health insurance, and concerns about improving the quality and accessibility of child care generated a ripe climate for organizing. Formal and informal social networks created through professional associations and training classes facilitated organization.[23]

Renewed concern with organizing child care workers, including home-based providers, emerged from a convergence of interests: Unions sought to gain new members in an expanding industry, and advocates sought greater influence over child care policies. From the perspective of unions, home-based child care workers represented a growing sector of the low-wage labor force, one that could not be outsourced away. By 2007, there were approximately 1.8 million home-based providers, 99 percent of whom were women, who cared for about 42 percent of all children receiving such services in the United States. All but 650,000 of these providers were relatives. Some of these providers ran regulated home-based centers, while others were friends, family, or neighbors exempt from licensure.[24]

Early successes in organizing child care, including home-based providers, in the 1990s by the SEIU, AFSCME, and advocate groups like DARE, encouraged unions to organize more child care workers. National conferences
of child care advocates in 1996 and 1998 generated new organizing strategies. The Center for the Child Care Workforce also approached several unions
about the formation of a national child care union. The SEIU's success in organizing home-based health care workers also helped to demonstrate that
home-based child care providers could be organized.[25] Eventually, both the
SEIU and AFSCME began large-scale efforts.

These unions developed a model for organizing home-based providers
based on home health care campaigns, which gained national attention in
1999 with the SEIU's massive victory in Los Angeles. Home-based child care
providers were very similar to providers of home-based health care in many
ways. In both cases, the labor involved in providing these services, often associated with women of color and conflated with domestic labor, was highly
devalued. The home-based location of this intimate labor rendered the social
contributions of these workers even more invisible to the public. We long
have presumed that the skills involved in caring for others come naturally to
women, rather than through training and experience. Like home-based health
care workers, home-based providers sought greater public recognition of their
skills and training. In public testimonies, they emphasized how they were not
"babysitters" or "playmates" for children but serious workers with knowledge
about child development. Moreover, as with home health care providers, the
state paid home-based child care providers with subsidies, providing a rationale for treating the state as the employer for collective bargaining purposes
and as a political target for campaigns to improve these services. Like home
health care workers, home-based child care providers had to first gain the legal
right to collective bargaining through new state legislation or gubernatorial
executive orders before unionization was possible. They otherwise lacked these
rights as independent contractors or the owners of small businesses.

Finally, both industries involved personal services whose clients could
be mobilized in support of organizing campaigns. Care workers employed
in both home-based health and child care provided a service that was intimate in nature, creating close bonds between clients and workers that could
be used to forge community–labor coalitions. Both services were also grossly
underfunded, creating joint interests among clients and workers to improve
state payments. Because improving compensation has been shown to reduce

worker turnover in these industries, many clients were supportive of providers' demands for higher wages. As they did in home-based health care campaigns, unions organizing providers drew on social movement and community organizing tactics and strategies developed by earlier efforts to organize these workers outside of unions. Such strategies included the formation of client–worker alliances to pressure states to recognize workers' rights to bargain collectively and to maintain and improve funding for these services.[26]

By 2007, campaigns to unionize home-based providers had occurred or were underway in at least fourteen states.[27] The SEIU and AFSCME took the lead, but the AFT, UAW, Communications Workers of America (CWA), and Association of Community Organizations for Reform Now (ACORN) were involved as well. The SEIU and AFSCME resolved a fierce and bitter turf war by agreeing in 2006 to divide the organizing between them in seventeen states and within Minnesota. They also created a joint union, the United Child Care Union, in California and Pennsylvania. AFSCME further formed partnerships to organize child care providers with the UAW in Michigan and CWA in New Jersey.[28] The AFT, whose educational foundation merged with the Center for the Child Care Workforce in 2002, developed a national Child Care Workforce Alliance, an "associate membership program" for child care providers to join together to improve their working conditions and unite "worthy wage" activists both inside and outside labor unions.[29]

Between 2005 and 2007, twelve states—Illinois, Iowa, Kansas, Maine, Maryland, Michigan, New Jersey, New York, Oregon, Pennsylvania, Washington, and Wisconsin—gave unions legal authorization to represent child care workers and to negotiate with state officials. Child care providers' unions also obtained local authorization to represent them in three Minnesota counties and two counties in Ohio.[30] These efforts brought new vitality to state and local campaigns to improve child care services because, in organizing child care providers, unions also organized families receiving child care subsidies. Campaigns in Wisconsin and California illustrate both the promises and challenges of this dual organizing.

Child Care Providers' Campaigns in Wisconsin

Wisconsin provides an example of a successful unionization drive that built on prior organization of providers in the wake of welfare reform. This campaign underscores how an "ethic of care"—as well as concern for labor rights—shaped provider campaigns. The adoption of welfare reform, Wisconsin Works or W-2, tripled Wisconsin's investment in subsidized child care and succeeded in eliminating the state's waiting list for care.[31] Yet complaints from parents and providers about the inefficiency of the child care system mounted, such as those concerning delays in approving the service that caused teen parents to miss school and employed adults to have siblings care for younger children.[32] Once approved, participants had to renew their eligibility every three months, a cumbersome task for many working mothers.[33] The expansion of subsidized child care services and rising complaints about their design and delivery enlarged the potential base of support for child care organizing campaigns.

Delays and breakdowns in child care approvals and payments caused considerable hardship among welfare recipients, but they also negatively affected child care providers. The problems became so severe in Milwaukee that Annette Wilburn, vice president of the Metropolitan Child Care Association and a member of the Milwaukee County Child Care Task Force, formed a new group to represent providers' concerns: Providers Taking Action, consisting of seventy-five home-based child care providers. Day Care Advocates of Milwaukee, representing about forty child care centers, also criticized the new system.[34] Providers Taking Action managed to gain support from sympathetic county supervisors, who helped to prod county employees to fix individual payment problems and pay providers more quickly. This pressure led to improvements in providers' payments.[35]

Home-based providers in Wisconsin did not simply mobilize around their own financial concerns. They used a "language of virtue" and displayed an "ethic of care" for their clients' and potential clients' well-being. As providers sought to maintain or increase state investments in subsidized child care, they highlighted the virtuous contributions they made to working parents, welfare-to-work participants, and their children.[36] They promoted various policy changes to expand low-income families' access to subsidized child care and gained a significant victory when Governor Tommy Thompson finally agreed to significantly reduce the copayments required of teen parents to a maximum of $5 per week.[37]

Child care providers and other advocates also urged state officials to lower the copayments for adult recipients and to raise the income ceilings for eligibility.[38] Rallying at the capitol, they demanded that the state use unspent child care funds to reduce parents' copayments. Providers held "day care dolls," a visual reminder of their service to children.[39] Madison Mayor Sue Bauman claimed that high copayments caused too many child care centers to close.[40]

In response to public pressure, Governor Thompson approved legislation to reduce the maximum copayments from 16 to 12 percent of families' gross income, and he lowered the income ceilings for eligibility.[41]

Worsening fiscal conditions after 2001, along with increased use of subsidized child care, stretched child care program budgets thin. Through administrative fiat, the state attempted to cut the rates given to providers. State politicians proposed various other ways to reduce spending, such as increasing parents' copayments, creating a waiting list for subsidized child care, and limiting eligibility to even lower incomes. The state AFL-CIO, child and welfare groups, and faith-based advocates all opposed such proposals.

More than 500 providers met at a local child care center in Milwaukee to discuss the problems that the rate reduction would cause.[42] A staff person from 9 to 5 explained, "There was very real pressure on them [legislature] from a number of groups who were advocating for families to be able to access the childcare . . . [Funding] is going to be maintained and that was a huge victory."[43]

Providers, parents, and advocates celebrated in 2005 when Governor James Doyle, elected with union support, prevented deeper cutbacks to subsidized child care by vetoing a proposed increase in copayments that would have cost families as much as $500 more per year and restoring $8 million for child care improvement projects.[44]

The expansion of subsidized child care facilitated unionization by AFSCME in 2006. The union took advantage of the prior organization of providers through professional associations and advocacy groups.[45] Both urban and rural providers joined AFSCME's statewide union, Child Care Providers Together. The union was racially and ethnically diverse, including black, white, Latina, and Asian as well as Spanish- and Hmong-speaking members.

In October, 2006, Governor Doyle issued an executive order permitting all subsidized and unsubsidized family child care providers and subsidized "family, friend, and neighbor" providers to form a union and to negotiate with the state. The governor's executive order lists various bargainable issues, including "quality standards, training and certification requirements, reimbursement and payment procedures, health and safety conditions, and 'any other matters and regulations that would improve recruitment and retention . . . , encourage certified providers to become licensed and improve the quality of the programs they offer'. . ." AFSCME was certified to represent the providers after registering union authorization cards from a majority of the 7,000 certified and licensed providers covered in the order.[46]

The new union became a vehicle for continuing the fight against child care cutbacks. As one provider put it, "Once again they're trying to stretch [the budget] on the backs of child care workers. It's just not the answer."[47] Facing budget deficits, policy makers adopted higher copayments in 2006.[48] In 2007, state officials froze reimbursement rates to 2006 levels, stopped filling vacant positions, and began to reimburse providers based on attendance rather than enrollment. They again considered the creation of a wait list, raised income ceilings for eligibility, and lowered reimbursement rates. Milwaukee-area legislators opposed the cutbacks, as did advocates of working women and children.[49] Hundreds of child care providers attended a series of legislative budget hearings where they urged full funding for the program.[50] Despite other child care cutbacks, legislators fully funded child care subsidies in 2007, another important victory for the new union.[51]

In short, child care providers and their allies, who emphasized the importance of their work to children, working parents, and welfare recipients, made a number of important advances in Wisconsin. They formed a new union and gained the legal right to negotiate with state officials over policies affecting working conditions. They also managed to expand eligibility for subsidized child care through lower fees and higher income ceilings for eligibility, and they averted a number of cutbacks in subsidized child care.

Child Care Providers' Campaigns in California

California too witnessed an expansion and restructuring of subsidized child care with welfare reform that generated new opportunities for unionization. As in Wisconsin, providers organized, first outside unions and then within them, to expand and improve low-income families' access to subsidized child care as well as for providers' rights to collective bargaining. Yet, whereas Wisconsin's governor authorized providers' collective bargaining rights, those rights were blocked through gubernatorial veto in California. The California campaign illustrates the challenges that existing labor laws created for providers' unionization but also shows how providers could improve child care policies through mobilization even without union recognition.

By 2000, there were about 47,000 child care providers in California, with 11,000 located in Los Angeles County. ACORN's campaign grew from efforts to organize welfare mothers, many of whom had difficulty with finding child care. The county frequently paid their providers late or failed to pay for all hours worked. In response, many providers refused to take care of children from families on welfare, creating an obstacle for maternal employment.[52] As they organized to improve the administration of subsidized child care, welfare mothers brought their providers to meetings and actions. In 2000, ACORN brought together mothers and providers to protest the county's pay structure: $2.93 per hour per child for licensed-exempt (in-home) providers and under $4 per hour per child for the licensed. Many caring for the children of relatives or friends attended to only one child and so earned less than the minimum wage.

In the welfare rights tradition, ACORN encouraged direct action. To protest low wages, a group of about twenty welfare mothers, child care providers, and lawyers called on the state labor commissioner to investigate violation of the minimum wage law. Wielding giant stuffed dogs, they expressed outrage that child care providers were paid far less than the county's dog catchers. This was seen as devaluing not only providers' work and skill but also the worth of their clients. As one mother said, highlighting the importance of subsidized child care to the success of welfare reform, "When we have to leave our children in the hands of under-paid and resentful providers, we as parents have a much harder time staying focused on our work. How can the state place such a low priority on the well-being of our children?"[53] At the time of the protest, the state had a $12 billion surplus, which ACORN members argued should be used to increase the wages for child care providers.[54] Although the labor commissioner agreed to look into the matter, there was no official change in county pay scales.

Within a year, ACORN's Child Care Providers for Action grew into a 300-member organization of mostly Latina and African American women. To maximize Spanish-speaking members' participation, Providers for Action hired a bilingual organizer, used simultaneous translation equipment for meetings, and translated all flyers into Spanish. Members carefully elected a balanced number of African Americans and Latinas to leadership positions.[55] Membership meetings drew about eighty people, while a Child Care Providers' Health and Safety Fair attracted several hundred.[56]

Providers for Action initially held the county's resource and referral agencies accountable for their irregular payments to providers but then focused on lobbying public officials. It negotiated agreements to create a grievance system and to process providers' complaints in a timely fashion.[57] The most resistance came from an agency called Equipoise. Only after providers and allies stormed its offices did officials agree to adopt the new grievance procedures, which made it possible for providers to obtain back pay.[58] In 2001 and 2002, the group asked legislators for living wages and health insurance for workers and increased subsidies to cover more families. Along with more than 200 other ACORN members, the group traveled to the state capital to demonstrate and lobby. Highlighting the social worth of their work in raising the next generation, providers testified how they deserved better wages and benefits because they were serious and skilled workers, not "babysitters," whose services kept parents, including welfare recipients, employed.[59]

Like counterparts in Wisconsin and elsewhere, organized providers in California embraced an "ethic of care" for low-income families. They mobilized to expand funding and coverage for subsidized child care and actively opposed proposed cutbacks. Total state and federal child care funding increased more than threefold in California between 1996 and 2005, from $926 million to $3.3 billion.[60] Nevertheless, the growing demand for subsidized child care required additional moneys. As a result, by 2003, an estimated 260,000 California families were on waiting lists for subsidized child care. In nine counties, 71 percent of families had waited for over one year, and about half of these waited for at least four years for subsidized care.[61] Because priority went to current and former welfare recipients, the most serious child care shortages were among low-income families.

Beginning in 2001, as fiscal conditions worsened, expansions in subsidized child care slowed, and the state proposed various new restrictions. These included time limits on child care subsidies for former welfare mothers, increased parent fees, cuts in providers' rates, lower child age limits, and lower income ceilings for eligibility.[62] Child care providers, along with low-income parents and other children's advocates, mobilized against these impending cutbacks and for increased funding for subsidized care. In 2001, Providers for Action initiated a postcard campaign, collecting signatures from Los Angeles parents using their services.[63] In 2002, providers signed petitions against the plan and, in a meeting with the state welfare director, claimed that the proposed fees were unrealistic and would force families out of the child care system.[64] The coalition of providers, parents, and advocates testified that cutbacks would force parents back onto welfare and put child care centers out of business.[65] In 2004, about 1,000 people marched, organized by the Say Yes to Children Network, in opposition to proposed cutbacks in social services in Los Angeles. Providers, children enrolled in their centers, parents, unions, and other children's advocates voiced opposition to "a budget balanced on the backs of our children."[66]

By 2004, Providers for Action claimed 1,200 members in Los Angeles and had attracted the interest of the SEIU. Seeking to launch a statewide effort to organize child care providers, the SEIU offered a large sum to ACORN to transfer their campaign to the union. ACORN staff agreed, believing that the union had more resources. Providers for Action members ratified this decision, which ACORN announced at its national convention.[67]

The SEIU then engaged in a statewide "organizing blitz." As many as forty organizers collected union cards in Los Angeles and across the state.[68] The SEIU then assigned a local staff to organize regional meetings, distribute newsletters, and develop members' leadership skills. According to an agreement with AFSCME, the SEIU then represented child care providers in thirteen counties, including Los Angeles, while AFSCME represented providers in the rest of the state's counties, and the two unions agreed to pool resources for common campaigns.[69] Nevertheless, tensions between the two unions inhibited collaboration until 2007, when they engaged in a joint Child Care Lobby Day.[70]

The SEIU and AFSCME pushed for a bill that would give them the legal right to form a union and engage in collective bargaining, At lobby days, clients held signs that emphasized the bonds between children, parents, and providers: "I love my child care provider," "Keep California working," "I can't work without child care," and "Stand up for kids and support our child care providers." In visits with legislators, providers explained how the right to collective bargaining would help improve the quality of the service. But Governor Schwarzenegger, hostile to labor, repeatedly vetoed legislation authorizing home-based providers' rights. The union also failed to gain state legislators' support for subsidizing health insurance. In 2008, Child Care Providers United offered a basic health and dental insurance plan to its "associate members," but the group was unable to obtain a plan with comprehensive coverage because it lacked collective bargaining rights.[71] The unions were more successful in protecting subsidized child care.[72] In response to public pressure, the governor restored child care funding and avoided proposed cutbacks.[73]

In 2006, children's advocates and child care providers' unions promoted a ballot initiative, Proposition 82, to create a statewide universal preschool program for all four-year-old children. Through a well-funded campaign, business groups managed to defeat the proposition despite early polls showing broad support for it. But the legislature authorized $50 million to expand preschool programs for children living in the areas of the lowest-performing schools and another $50 million to improve preschool facilities.[74] This program paled in comparison to preschool initiatives in other states, such as Georgia, which spent $245 million for preschool for four-year-olds for a population about the quarter of the size of California's.[75] Nevertheless, this expansion helped to relieve the demand for child care for thousands of low-income families.

AFSCME and the SEIU made uneven investments in organizing child care providers, making it difficult to maintain support from members and leaders. While the SEIU in 2005 assigned half a dozen organizers to the Los Angeles campaign, by 2008 it had only two organizers for the entire state.[76] The union was hesitant to do more when Governor Schwarzenegger repeatedly vetoed bills authorizing their right to represent home-based providers. Yet, even without collective bargaining rights, organized providers and their clients had helped to safeguard the state's subsidized child care system from various proposed cutbacks and to gain support for additional public funds for child care services.

Conclusion

Campaigns to unionize home-based child care providers illustrate both the challenges and the opportunities faced by intimate laborers providing publicly funded social services within the United States. First, welfare state restructuring has increased the reliance on private contractors to deliver all sorts of publicly funded social services, including the delivery of welfare-to-work classes, the administration of Temporary Aid to Needy Families, and home-based child care and health care. This trend creates an extra challenge for organizing care workers because independent contractors are outside existing labor laws, and their right to collective bargaining must be established through the adoption of new state policies. The public oversight and funding of these services nevertheless helps to establish the state as an "employer of record" as well as a target for political mobilization to expand services.[77] However, as we have seen, the state is not always forthcoming in authorizing collective bargaining rights, even when service providers and their clients are highly mobilized in support of them. "Who rules" constrains the political opportunities for unionizing care workers in important ways. So does the level of existing funding for social services, which shapes the size of the potential base of support among providers and their clients with whom they have established relationships, the hallmark of intimate labor.

Campaigns to unionize home-based child care services lent new resources and political muscle behind community-based and grassroots efforts to organize providers and to improve subsidized child care. Providers highlighted their training and skill as well as their contributions to society to justify better wages and benefits. They also mobilized on the basis of an "ethic of care" for low-income families, fighting to expand and improve the quality of publicly funded child care services. This helped to gain clients' active support for their unionization campaign, as did their personal ties to their clients.[78]

The payoffs of unionization appear to be substantial for both the providers and the clients of subsidized child care. By 2008, child care unions negotiated statewide contracts in five states: Illinois, Iowa, Michigan, Oregon, and Washington.[79] These contracts included significant gains for child care providers, including "substantial increases in reimbursement rates, more efficient payment procedures, a process for resolving grievances, greater access to training, and a stronger voice in rulemaking. And in the cases of Illinois and Washington, the unions won state financing for some [home-based] providers." Contract negotiations also led to rate increases for child care centers receiving state subsidies.[80] Unions, even those without state recognition, helped to increase pressure on public officials to make and keep child care more accessible to working families.[81] Thus, both child care providers and working families gained from providers' organizing campaigns.

Clients' interests in improving the quality and accessibility of services provided them, and their feelings of personal loyalty to service providers, have been similarly mobilized in support of the unionization of other types of intimate care workers, even those employed in the private sector, such as medical personnel. Client support for intimate care workers' unionization is probably most easily forged when unions actively support policies and practices that benefit clients and when service providers' conflicts of interest with clients are minimized. Conflicts of interest between service providers and clients are more difficult to overcome when service providers act as "gatekeepers" and make eligibility decisions, or when they deliver state-mandated rather than voluntary services, such as welfare-to-work classes. Otherwise, the intimate nature of personal service work provides a powerful bond between clients and workers that can be mobilized in support of unionization, as home-based child care campaigns have shown.

Notes

This chapter is based on a chapter from my book manuscript in progress, *They Say Cutback, We Say Fight Back! Welfare Reform Activism in an Era of Retrenchment.*

1. Whitebook, 2002.
2. Boris and Klein, 2008.

3. McDonald and Merrill, 2002; Cobble, Chapter 18 in this volume. The term *ethic of care* was coined by Carol Gilligan in 1982 and revived by Joan Tronto in her 1993 book, *Moral Boundaries: A Political Argument for an Ethic of Care* (Personal communication with Dorothy Sue Cobble, July 1, 2004).

4. McDonald and Merrill, 2002.

5. There are four major sources of child care funds: (1) child care block grant funds, (2) discretionary child care block grant funding, (3) TANF funds, and (4) state child care funds (Parrott and Mezey, 2003).

6. Marcucci, 2002.

7. Whitebook, 2002.

8. Giannarelli and Barsimantov, 2000; Savner, Strawn, and Greenberg, 2002.

9. Parrott and Mezey. "New child care resources are needed to prevent the loss of child care assistance for hundreds of thousands of children in working families."

10. Schulman and Blank, 2008.

11. National Women's Law Center, 2008.

12. Whitebook, Howes, and Phillips, 1990; Whitebook, Sakai, Gerber, and Howes, 2001, cited in Brooks, 2003.

13. Whitebook, 2002.

14. Official labor statistics show that, in 2000, of the 2.3 million workers paid to care for a child age five years or younger in the United States, 28 percent were family-based providers, while 35 percent were paid relatives (Center for Child Care Workforce and Human Services Policy Center, 2002).

15. Schulman and Blank, 2008.

16. Brooks, 2005.

17. See also Boris and Klein, 2008.

18. The movement was largely coordinated by the Child Care Employment Project, which later became a Washington, DC–based research and lobbying organization called the Center for the Child Care Workforce.

19. Whitebook, 2002.

20. Keystone Research Center, 2006.

21. Chalfie, Blank, and Entmacher, 2007.

22. Whitebook, 2002.

23. Brooks, 2003; 2005.

24. About 298,000 nonrelatives worked in the child's home (Chalfie et al., 2007).

25. The SEIU began to organize home-based providers in 1996. ACORN (a community organization) also began in the late 1990s (Whitebook. 2002; Keystone Research Center, 2006; Brooks, 2003, 2005; Boris and Klein, 2008).

26. Keystone Research Center, 2006; Boris and Klein, 2007, 2008.

27. Chalfie et al., 2007.

28. Keystone Research Center, 2006; Chalfie et al., 2007.

29. Whitebook, 2002.

30. Chalfie et al., 2007; AFSCME Works Online, 2007; SEIU Kids First Maryland, 2007; Smith, 2007; American Federation of Teachers, 2007.

31. Stewart, 1997.

32. Huston 1997, 1998b, 2000; Dembski, 2002.

33. Bleidorn, 1998.

34. Huston, 1998a.

35. Those improvements were later undercut by reductions in county staff and employee turnover (Providers Taking Action leader, telephone interview with author, July 2007).

36. Union Labor News, August 2000.

37. "Poor Teens to Get Free Day Care," 1998; Interview, Ad Hoc W-2 Coalition, Milwaukee, WI, September 2000; "Governor Says Teen-Age Mothers Will Pay Less for Day Care," 1998.

38. Huston, 1998a; Callender, 1998.

39. Callender, 1998.

40. Schneider and Callender, 1998.

41. Milfred, 1999; "Legislative Changes May Make Child Care Subsidies More Available," 2000.

42. Abdul-Alim, 2003.

43. 9 to 5 member. 2001. Personal Interview with author in Milwaukee, June 20.

44. Groves, 2005.

45. Providers Taking Action leader, telephone interview with author, July 2007.

46. Chalfie et al., 2007: 19; Early Childhood Focus, 2006.

47. Davidoff, 2007a.

48. Sensenbrenner, 2006.

49. Walters, 2007.

50. Davidoff, 2007b.

51. Ibid.

52. Field notes, Los Angeles, August 31, 2000.

53. Cited in Los Angeles ACORN [Press Release]. May 18, 2000, author's personal files.

54. Field notes, Los Angeles, May 18, 2000.

55. Field notes, Los Angeles, October 15, 2001, and March 17, 2001.

56. Field notes, March 17, 2001; Los Angeles ACORN. [Newsletter], October 2001.

57. The county contracted first with ten agencies but later with twelve.

58. ACORN-Los Angeles. [Flyer]. July 9, 2001, author's personal files.

59. California ACORN [Newsletter]. May 29, 2001, author's personal files.

60. Graves, 2005.

61. Ibid.

62. Ibid.

63. Field notes, Los Angeles, March 17, 2001.

64. Brown, 2002a, 2002b.

65. Personal communication with member of Child Development Policy Advisory Committee, Pasadena, CA, April 7, 2002.

66. Field notes, Los Angeles, March 25, 2004.

67. Field notes, Los Angeles, June 27, 2004.

68. SEIU staff, interview with author, Los Angeles, April 9, 2005.

69. SEIU staff, phone interview with author, April 19, 2006.

70. AFSCME staff, telephone interview with author, May 23, 2006; personal communication with SEIU organizer, 2005.

71. Field notes, Los Angeles leadership meeting of Child Care Providers United, June 21, 2008.

72. Bluth, 2004.

73. De Sa, 2002; Marcucci, 2001; Nugent, 2006.

74. Lowest-performing schools were those performing in the bottom 30 percent in terms of the statewide Academic Performance Index (Geissinger, 2006).

75. "Opposition to prop. 82 duplicitous," 2006.

76. SEIU staff, telephone interview with author, April 24, 2006; SEIU staff, telephone interview with author, February 3, 2007.

77. Boris and Klein, 2008.

78. Cobble, Chapter 18 in this volume.

79. "Historic Election Will Improve Quality of Child Care for Thousands of Pennsylvania Working Families," 2008.

80. Chalfie et al., 2007.

81. This is revealed in the case studies above. Also see Brooks, 2003, 2005.

16 Sex and (Evacuation from) the City

The Moral and Legal Regulation of
Sex Workers in Vancouver's West End,
1975–1985

Becki Ross

SEX WORK INVOLVES TOUCH and bodily exchange—other indicators of intimacy, from partial to full exposure of "private" parts to emotional concern, often exist in the negotiated play between provider and consumer. Such acts occur behind closed doors as well as on streets, in alleyways, parks, and cars. As a varied practice, there is hardly one form of sex work, and thus political struggles over the past century across North America and beyond reflect specific locations and embattled interests. To explore what happens when intimate, sexualized labor impinges on space designated as "public," this chapter explores the debate about outdoor sex work in Vancouver's West End neighborhood during a pivotal decade, 1975 to 1985. Following the police closures of downtown nightclubs on prostitution-related charges in 1975, in-house sex workers took to the streets of the West End, where they were met by residents and business owners who instigated a full, frontal assault on "sexual perversion."[1] Lobbyists, as well as politicians, journalists, urban planners, police, and vigilantes, strove round-the-clock to formulate an "antihooker" consensus centered on the sex worker as *object* of inquiry and management. In the face of unrelenting hooker bashing, the Alliance for the Safety of Prostitutes (ASP) formed to raise awareness of the whore stigma and to combat politicolegal maneuvers enacted to expel them and other street-level sex workers from their moorings in the West End.

My analysis of interview-based and archival data reveals how the West End became not only desexualized and sanitized but whitened and made safe for (a certain kind of queer) capitalism and residential occupation, with lethal consequences for outdoor sex workers in the city. The work of Phil Hubbard on the "geography of prostitution" inspires me to uncover how the West End became imbued with complex spatialities of power, desire, and disgust.[2] This class-bound, gendered, and racialized contestation over space was also a struggle over the meaning of public and private and ultimately about the power of intimate work to unsettle commonsense perceptions of labor, leisure, love, and community.

Pushed Out: West End Troubles Engineered by CROWE

In 1975, after decades of soliciting clients indoors at hotels and nightclubs downtown such as the Penthouse Cabaret and the Zanzibar, a heterogeneous, racially diverse community of sex workers—some of whom were queer—was forcibly pushed by the police department's vice squad onto the streets of Vancouver's West End.[3] Here, in the face of a mounting antiprostitution backlash, approximately 250 sex workers who took pride in their pimp-free community began to solicit clients.[4] While women—including African Canadians and Aboriginals—made up the majority, a minority of male hustlers and male-to-female transsexuals also sold sexual services on and around Davie Street—the first tranny stroll in the city. Portrayed sensationally as she-males in fetish pornography, ridiculed in tabloids, pathologized in medical texts, and condemned as "mutilated, masquerading males" in Janice Raymond's vitriolic tract, *The Transsexual Empire*, trans sex workers capitalized on customers' desire for what Jamie Lee Hamilton calls "the full-package deal"—both tittie and clittie (*clittie* being the feminine term for cock).[5]

In response to the increasingly visible street sex trade outside the boundary of the city's historic East End track, a community organization, Concerned Residents of the West End, or CROWE, emerged as a juggernaut for disaffected citizens. Established in 1980, CROWE assumed a well-organized, well-funded leadership role in coordinating a vigorous crusade, including vigilante action, against the West End's prostitutes. CROWE's members—predominantly white, middle-class residents and business owners—launched a crackdown on "sex deviance" with the most exercised throwing eggs, tomatoes, and beer bottles at community meetings and during public altercations. Led by a charismatic gay man, Gordon Price, and sporting a large gay male membership, CROWE strove to set the agenda, define the terms of debate, and influence the levers of legal and political decision making. Over the course of six years, the organization became the envy of antivice lobbyists across Canada. Indeed, CROWE's ability to frame and tactically manage the conflict was later emulated by similar organizations from Victoria to Edmonton and from Toronto to Halifax. Not unique to the Canadian context, contentious "urban renewals" were engineered in the 1960s, 1970s, and 1980s in New York, Pittsburgh, Detroit, San Francisco, and Birmingham, among other cities.[6]

Members of CROWE, in concert with Vancouver's mayor, city councilors, provincial premier and attorney general, federal members of Parliament (MPs), the chief of police, and journalists—from all points along the political spectrum— were in agreement: Street solicitation represented a "blight on urban life."[7] While lobbying to stiffen antiprostitution laws in the criminal code, Pat Carney— the Conservative MP for Vancouver Centre—referred to the West End as a "sexual zoo."[8] In formal correspondence through briefs, letters, and articles to different levels of government and the media, CROWE emphasized that street prostitutes in the West End "commandeered its streets," accelerated "the process of decay," and made the area "vulnerable to criminal invasion."[9]

In 1983, Mayor Mike Harcourt channeled the fear of a "takeover by hookers" into support for stepped-up federal criminal sanctions against prostitution.[10] British Columbia's Attorney General Brian Smith described his abolitionist mandate in the West End as a "war on hookers."[11] Vancouver's city politicians, provincial legislators, residents' groups, business owners, realtors, and police force formed a powerful network with a single-minded mandate to criminalize prostitution and purge prostitutes from the West End. Especially after 1980, when Vancouver was designated the host for the international fair, Expo 1986, CROWE championed the interests of multiple stakeholders feverishly intent on transforming the port town into a "world-class city" through a slate of cleanup initiatives.

In the early 1980s, in spite of the heavy capitalist investment in the neighborhood, the discursive reformulation of the West End as a uniquely "residential" space void of commercial activity became central to CROWE's coordinated "not in my backyard" (NIMBY) campaign. CROWE's leader, Gordon Price, disingenuously called for greater police enforcement of laws against prostitution, insisting that "street soliciting is incompatible in a residential area."[12] Ironically, the West End made manifest key elements of American urban planner Jane Jacobs's vision for high-density dwelling mixed with diverse, street-level workplaces, commerce, and cultural sites, all enabling the hustle and bustle of intertwined social and economic relationships.[13] Moreover, there were signs aplenty that the West End had begun to cater to a "pink market" of gay consumers, both locals and tourists alike.[14] In spite of these contradictions, night after night, from corner to corner, members of Shame the Johns (CROWE's militant arm) engaged in aggressive monitoring of on-street sex workers—a form of extrastate spatial surveillance, or "subpolicing," to quote an ex-member—all the while enacting a systematic governance of self.[15] As the boundaries between social groups hardened, the clashes became especially charged for female and trans prostitutes of color who endured the predominantly male residents' sexist and racist belligerence.

Not content to stop at calls for pumped-up policing, CROWE doggedly lobbied the Vancouver City Council for more concrete intervention. In August 1981, councillors voted unanimously to reconfigure the physical space of the West End to thwart the occupational and geographic mobility of street prostitutes.[16] Faithful to its own blueprint—the West End Traffic Plan—the Engineering Department oversaw the construction of cement traffic diverters, traffic islands, signage for new turn controls, traffic circles (or roundabouts), alleyway lighting, and one cul-de-sac. The automobile (including the taxicab), reimagined as a conduit of vice, became a target of moral and material regulation.

Alongside community-based abolitionists and urban planners, print and broadcast journalists fuelled what John Lowman terms a "discourse of disposal"[17] to justify the purge of throwaways. News articles that dramatized and sensationalized the conflict flooded the *Vancouver Sun* and *Province* with headlines such as "Prostitution Swells in the West End,"[18] "Hookers: Lazy Crooks or Victims?"[19] and "Can New Bylaw Hook the Hookers?"[20] And yet far from the negative image of all prostitutes as unstable and transient, most West End sex workers lived and worked in the neighborhood.

However, on arrest for "communicating" in the late 1970s and early 1980s, some were forbidden by police from returning to their homes. Jamie Lee Hamilton, an Aboriginal transsexual sex worker and part-time entertainer at BJ's Lounge, a gay bar, was arrested for soliciting clients outside of a West End liquor store in the late 1970s. She recalled: "I was charged and put in jail. It was Halloween, and I remember the police were throwing firecrackers at me as they booked me. They made me strip in front of them, they strip-searched me, and they threw me in the male section of the jail."[21]

Humiliated and violated, once released Hamilton was given an "area restriction," which forced her to move out of the West End. Clearly only certain expressions of sexual commerce—discreet, indoors, and taxable—were legitimated and accommodated, while others were rendered illegitimate, "out of place." In effect, some residents were accorded the rightful status to work and inhabit the West End as "honest citizens," to quote Mayor Mike Harcourt, while others were cast as a menacing nuisance to be roughed up, belittled, and expunged.[22] While middle-class gay men had achieved a measure of respectability, political and social capital, and residential entitlement in the West End, prostitutes (and their clients) were subjected to evermore intrusive tactics of "spatial governmentality," to cite Lisa Sanchez, in ways that amounted not only to removal but also to a denial of the prostitute's legal subjectivity and cultural existence.[23]

Legal Rulings and Their Pernicious Effects

In April 1982, in response to relentless pressure from CROWE, the Vancouver City Council passed a "street activities" bylaw that imposed fines of $350 to $2,000 on those convicted of purchasing, attempting to purchase, selling, or attempting to sell sexual services on Vancouver streets. Dubbed the "antihooker" bylaw in the mainstream press, it was widely applauded as an ingenious, municipal solution to controlling a crime defined under the federal criminal code. The bylaw, much like the one adopted by the City Council of Calgary, Alberta, in 1981, specified "the noise made and uncivil behavior of the persons seeking to sell and purchase sexual services."[24] Further, it maintained that sexual commerce on streets (and sidewalks) owned by the city of Vancouver "seriously interfered not only with the rights of others to use the streets but also with the rights of persons to peacefully occupy property adjacent to such streets."[25] In the first six months, a reported $28,000 in fines was collected from accused persons who pled guilty to prostitution-related charges; by contrast, sex for wages occurred inside the city's massage parlors with almost no police intervention.[26]

Challenged by sex workers and their lawyers as an unconstitutional breach of freedom of expression and assembly enshrined in the Canadian Charter of Rights and Freedoms, the bylaw was upheld by B.C. provincial court judge David Moffett in September 1982. Moffett wrote: "The buying and selling of a prostitute's services on the streets of Vancouver has been prohibited by an elected body in our democratic society for the sole purpose of remedying a nuisance." He insisted that placing limits on Charter rights was not only reasonable, but "demonstrably justified in a free and democratic society."[27] Here Moffett affirmed what Appeal Court judges in Calgary, Alberta, identified several months earlier as, "the need to protect citizens who use the streets from the irritation and embarrassment of being unwilling participants in the

[sex] market."[28] Under this adversarial formulation, the rights-based claims of sex workers were rendered undemocratic, hence unworthy of defense, if not altogether unintelligible. However, in 1983, the Supreme Court of Canada struck down the bylaw in Calgary (and by extension, the sister bylaw in Vancouver) as an invasion of the exclusive federal power to pass criminal law.

Exasperated by the legal limbo, Vancouver's CROWE, politicians, and police stepped up the pressure on provincial and federal governments to fill in the gap left by multiparty foot dragging. In response, using the commission as a century-old technology of colonial rule,[29] federal parliamentarians struck the Special Committee on Pornography and Prostitution in early 1984 to research, hear submissions, and make recommendations, with the goal of resolving jurisdictional skirmishes.[30] As the committee traversed the country, Chief Justice of the British Columbia Supreme Court Allan McEachern executed a preemptive, unprecedented strike: In July 1984, in response to an application for a legal injunction from the province's attorney general, he banned "blatant, aggressive, disorderly prostitutes" from the West End to preserve the "peaceful integrity of the community."[31] More than a decade before the Prostitution-Free Zone Ordinance was passed in Portland, Oregon, in 1995,[32] McEachern described the situation in the West End as an "urban tragedy," chastising those who "defiled our city" by "taking over the streets and sidewalks for the purpose of prostitution."[33] To Stacey, a former sex worker, the injunction decimated her West End community: "When they moved us, they broke us. They totally disenfranchised all of us."[34]

Mindful of McEachern's ruling, and in defiance of progressive recommendations made by the Liberal-appointed Special Committee in early 1985, the new right-wing Conservative majority in Parliament passed Bill C-49 of the criminal code in November 1985. Closed to the possibility of prostitution in licensed brothels and other unregulated spaces, Bill C-49 tightened the screws to prohibit "all communicating in a public place for the purpose of prostitution."[35] No longer was it necessary for soliciting to be "pressing and persistent" (defined in 1978 by the Canadian Supreme Court in *Hutt v. Regina*); the broad new law eliminated the need to prove that the act of solicitation had taken place on more than one occasion. Moreover, under this new legal framework the definition of "public" was enlarged to include the interior of a motor vehicle. The maximum fine set for the offence was $2,000 and six months in jail. Vehemently opposed by sex workers and allies twenty-five years ago, the draconian anticommunication law remains in place, unchanged, in 2010.

Sex Workers and Allies Mobilize

At a one-day conference on prostitution sponsored by CROWE at the West End Community Centre in October 1981, politicians, a psychiatrist, police inspectors, and social planners addressed the "prostitution problem." CROWE organizers said they would consider "serious requests" from prostitutes to address the gathering but only on CROWE's terms.[36] The Alliance for the Safety of Prostitutes (ASP) attempted to speak. Emboldened by the news of activism catalyzed by COYOTE (Call Off Your Old Tired Ethics) in San Francisco,[37] the Alliance had formed earlier that year to resist police incursions and nightly "Shame the Johns" patrols. At this forum and several others, ASP leaders were not only muzzled but subjected to nasty verbal abuse.

On April 20, 1983, members of ASP marched on Broadway Street to a demonstration in front of Vancouver's City Hall. Handing out leaflets to passersby, the marchers chanted "Hookers unite, fight for your rights."[38] In her speech following this first-ever public protest by sex workers and allies in the city, ASP member Michelle stressed the importance of providing a service to men who "find it hard to release their innermost feelings."[39] The message on Michelle's sign, "Harcourt is Our Pimp" was a brilliant mockery of the mayor's hypocritical collection of fines for the state's coffers on the backs of sex workers engaged in "illegal" trade.

In June 1984, ASP demonstrated again, this time in the city's West End. Striving to articulate an empowering reverse discourse, sex workers and allies orchestrated public action; community meetings; a monthly newsletter, the *Whorganizer*; and "Bad Trick Sheets" to warn workers across the city of entrapment, beatings, and robberies. Also, in their nuanced brief to the federal government's Special Committee on Pornography and Prostitution in January 1984, ASP recommended, first and foremost, decriminalization to "reduce the abuse heaped on women who work in the sex trade" and to "allow women autonomy over their working and living conditions."[40] In addition, they insisted on the reentry of prostitutes into bars and nightclubs (like the Penthouse), together with the right to "collectively apply for a license to operate a bawdy house with a specific capacity, much like seating capacities in restaurants."[41]

Reflecting on the ups and downs of her thirty-six-year career in the sex industry, Jamie Lee Hamilton calls the West End days "The Golden Age of Prostitution." In an interview with me, she stressed the camaraderie among West End workers in the early 1980s: "We ate together, we lived together, took breaks together. We looked after one another. We built a community—an outdoor brothel."[42] She added that within her close-knit culture, she and co-workers supplied clients with myriad services ranging from sex surrogacy, fantasy, and companionship to emotional support, instruction, and sex therapy. While activists in ASP worked in solidarity for social justice with sex workers like Hamilton, most feminists dissociated themselves from prostitutes or disregarded them altogether. Some were outwardly hostile toward women who, they argued, participated in their own victimization and exploitation by men.[43] Marie Arrington, cofounder of ASP, recounted that her organization was "suddenly ostracized by the feminist community because Sally de Quadros, ASP's co-founder, was a whore."[44] Vocal feminists across North America prioritized campaigns and firebombings against the "scourge" of commercial pornography throughout the late 1970s and early 1980s, leaving sex workers without access to the organized support, resources, and skilled leadership of second-wave women's liberation, including feminists in the legal profession and the labor movement.[45]

While some gay activists grappled with the complexities of street-level sexual commerce, other gay men openly demeaned prostitutes as vulgar, lower-class, and deviant—the very pejoratives hurled at "queers" a mere decade earlier.[46] In fact, for some gay men, political alignment and resource sharing with "normal" residents of the West End may have had the desired effect of weakening the stigma attached to homosexuality. I also suspect that female and transsexual prostitutes' brazen, hypervisible femininity triggered misogyny in some gay men eager to celebrate a macho, butch masculinity—the San Franciscan "Castro clone" archetype far removed from the stain of effeminacy.[47]

Notwithstanding the shortsighted abandonment that continues to blunt the potency of coalition-based organizing today, a small number of feminist, gay, and labor activists echoed sex workers' condemnation of a police-led crackdown.[48] In 1983, city alderwoman Libby Davies called for enforcement of existing laws to combat noise, street fighting, and traffic violations, not the introduction of new laws that would inevitably mean more punishment of prostitutes. Interviewed for a feature story in the *Vancouver Sun*, Davies argued: "Throwing prostitutes in jail is not going to help the prostitutes."[49] In the same story, Joanie Miller of Vancouver Rape Relief is quoted as saying, "We women must have the freedom to set standards for our own sexual encounters [which] includes the right to charge money."[50] Marie Arrington warned that changes to the criminal code "would give the police more license to beat up prostitutes."[51] To protest the increased violence spawned by Judge McEachern's injunction, ASP members took refuge in a West End Anglican church for four days and nights in July 1984.[52] ASP spokeswoman Sally de Quadros noted that the cathedral was chosen because churches were known to have operated as sanctuaries for oppressed people in the past.[53]

The Germinated Seeds of a New Homo-Norm

Ultimately, the legally mandated (and unappealed) purge of sex workers from the streets of the West End resulted in the rupture of prostitutes' relationships and community formation. The banished became exiled from their intricate, intimate emotional networks of kin and care, the bricks and mortar of home, and the economic and social stability of work on the Davie Street strolls.[54] Bullied by CROWE's vigorous defense of "neighborhood standards" and the "social fabric of the community," sex workers were reclassified as trespassers with no legal, civic, or moral purchase on the definition of either "standards" or "community," reminiscent of restrictions that confined prostitutes to the margins of medieval European cities.[55] Intrinsic to CROWE's narrative of redemption was the possibility of rescuing a city space and, by extension the Canadian nation, from the contaminating grip of deviance.

In ways that parallel Zoë Newman's critique of the remaking of "Toronto the Good" in the 1970s, Vancouver's West End clean-up was about consolidating bourgeois whiteness through coercive boundary control and the assertion of respectability.[56] That white, upwardly mobile gay men wrestled control from "uppity hookers" is a distinct variation on stories about commodified relations of space fundamental to what Henri Lefebvre terms the "logic of capital accumulation."[57] By the mid-1980s, the seeds of a new cultural phenomenon—white, middle-class, homonormative community formation— had been planted and taken root.[58] In the West End, unlike many other city districts in the West, a new gay moralism was rooted less in the defense of heterosexual family values or a "healthy, wholesome suburb"[59] than in an emergent, privatizing, and gay-inflected rhetoric of domesticity, decency, and consumption. Conventional notions of intimacy supplanted the care work and sex work that previously had defined this space.

The Age-Old Trade Perpetually Imperiled

Three decades ago, Vancouver's West End was an imagined community built on gendered, class-bound, and racialized inclusions and exclusions. To adapt the insight of Dorothy E. Smith, a line of fault or disjuncture emerged between the everyday lives of street-level sex workers and the extralocal, institutional relations and discourses of ruling that produced "hookers on Davie Street" as heinous public trash.[60] Forged through violent political struggle and legal re-makings in the early 1980s, the West End became a site of collision. The mass eviction of on-street prostitutes from a city space initially founded on the bru-tal dispossession of Musqueam, Burrard, and Squamish First Nations struck a doubly bitter, neocolonial blow to Aboriginal women in the industry, includ-ing Jamie Lee, Raigen, Michelle, and Gina. For young gay hustlers, evacuation from the West End's "gay utopia" signaled a similarly painful irony.

Central to the "victory" celebrated by CROWE and its antihooker lobby was an intricate weave of commonsense assumptions about prostitution and property. As Nicholas Blomley puts it, the enactment of a right to property—both private and public—"erases and effaces in ways that are both symbolic and ineluctably corporeal."[61] Indeed, West End sex workers became construed as loose impediments to be removed "in order to honor," said Chief Justice McEachern, the "rights of others to freely use the streets,"[62] which included buying and selling property (and goods) unencumbered by what CROWE warned were the "depressed values" of a "de facto red light district."[63] In the city's popular, racist imaginary, the historic Chinatown stroll on the east side—*the* red light district—remained the "logical" and "natural" repository of sexual iniquity and racial otherness. Sex workers of color, in particular, had long been associated with, and consigned to, segregated zones of the city com-monly equated with disorder, crime, filth, and degeneracy.[64]

Through real and symbolic processes of spatial differentiation and "cleansing,"[65] street-level prostitutes in the West End were deemed anathema to what David Ley described in 1980 as Vancouver's postindustrial, neolib-eral "accent on individual gratification, physical health, pleasant exercise, and quality of life."[66] Rather, white bourgeois subjects, led by respect-hungry gay men, grabbed the reigns of a "revanchist" or "revenging" neighborhood under siege.[67] Regardless of the fact that 80 percent of West End residents rented (rather than owned) their homes, CROWE and elite allies engineered an emo-tionally charged campaign for the right of "ordinary citizens" to "safe and secure" residential occupancy and belonging.

In *Imperial Leather,* Anne McClintock argues that "abject peoples are those whom industrial imperialism rejects but cannot do without ... the abject re-turns to haunt modernity as its constitutive, inner repudiation: the rejected from which one does not part."[68] In Vancouver from 1975 to 1984, sexual civility was contingent on the repeated avowal of sex workers' uncivil, carnal disobedience and the repeated disavowal of sex workers' substantive citizenship. The manifold penalties meted out to female sex workers sounded a cautionary note to all women who pushed against the idealized, patriarchal norm of heterosexual marriage, monogamy, and motherhood. In addition, the involvement of young men and transsexuals in the West End ramped up what I term the "deviance quotient" in the eyes of antivice crusaders. The whore stigma appeared remarkably elastic: It was stretched to snare and punish all "deviants"—male, female, trans, and queer, both white and nonwhite—who dared to make claims on illicit street-based commerce. Discredited and dehumanized, attributed an "undesired differentness," to quote Erving Goffman, streetwalkers were re-marked as moral and physical contagion.[69] To extend the wisdom of Judith Butler, CROWE and allies shortsightedly repudiated the vulnerability of "unfamiliar" Others in their midst on the cusp of devastating loss wrought in the neighborhood (and beyond) by HIV/AIDS from the mid-1980s forward.[70]

After the provincial Supreme Court's cavalier injunction of 1984 and the punitive stance taken toward solicitation in the federal Canadian criminal code in 1985, West End sex workers were forcibly relocated to an isolated, poorly lit industrial zone in Vancouver's East End, where they began to go "missing" in ever greater numbers.[71] The few still alive recall the horrible aftershocks, including the barriers to reestablishing safety plans—exchanging stories of bad dates, copying down license plate numbers, taking "coffee and smoke breaks" together at cafes, and sharing affordable rental apartments—that had once been fundamental, mutually beneficial elements of life in the West End.

Mass Murder Foreshadowed

In short, the explosive urban contest in the West End—its interventions and displacements—endangered the lives of outdoor sex workers and haunts the industry today. The series of legal rulings described above, which formalized withdrawal of legal protections for sex workers, worked to sanction extralegal forms of discipline and spaces for violence.[72] Twenty-five years later, the history of a vibrant, mixed community of sex workers who lived, loved, labored, played, and cared for one another in the West End has been eradicated from popular memory and from the enclave's physical spaces (save the concrete remnants of the traffic plan). A now sanitized, gentrifying landscape is imbued with the potent ideology of forgetting.[73] What remains is the chilling fact that more than sixty-five survival sex workers from the city's downtown Eastside, two-thirds Aboriginal, have been murdered since 1978.[74] The carnage, which would have constituted a national emergency were the slaughtered white, upper-crust university students, occasioned much public hand-wringing, particularly during and after the ten-month trial of convicted serial killer, Robert (Willie) Pickton in 2002, but little comfort or justice for sex workers, their families, or supporters.[75]

Current debate rages on in the federal Canadian House of Commons about the efficacy of prostitution-related laws in the criminal code. In August 2007, lawyers for the Downtown Eastside Sex Workers United Against Violence, a group of mostly Aboriginal women, filed a statement of claim with the B.C. Supreme Court alleging that Canada's prostitution laws put them at grave risk of injury, kidnapping, and death.[76] A constitutional challenge underway in both British Columbia and the province of Ontario explicates how the threat of violence is inextricable from and symptomatic of the illegality and stigma attached to the sex trade. Harm reduction and sustainable support services for people working in the sex industry have been ignored, underfunded, or flagrantly slashed in neoliberal fashion. For four decades, activist sex workers have identified prostitution as a legitimate work relation and prostitutes as workers deserving of occupational control and the same rights, respect, and protections extended to other citizens in Canada and beyond.[77]

In 2007, the B.C. Coalition of Experiential Communities began organizing a cooperative akin to cooperatives of farmers, bakers, and artisans a century ago, with the intention of establishing above-ground brothels to service locals and visitors in open defiance of nineteenth-century bawdy house laws.[78] Coalition member Susan Davis explained that her group sought an exemption similar to the one granted to Insite, the safe injection site for heroin use in Vancouver. However, in early 2008, the Canadian federal Conservative government flatly rejected all recommendations to decriminalize prostitution, stating, "We are not in the business of legalizing brothels, and we have no intention of changing any of the laws relating to prostitution in this country."[79] In the end, there is much to learn from our not so distant past about mistakes made, vulnerabilities exploited, the failures of progressive social movements, the intransigence of abolitionist ideology, and the fighting spirit of unrepentant sex worker activists and allies, past and present.

Notes

This chapter is drawn from a larger project funded by the Social Sciences and Humanities Research Council of Canada. I am grateful to Eileen Boris and Rhacel Salazar Parreñas for envisioning this anthology, as well as to anonymous reviewers. I would like to thank research assistants Jamie Lee Hamilton, Rachael Sullivan, Casson Brown, Cecily Nicholson, and Mandy McRae, as well as interview participants. Our project's website is: www.westendsexworkhistory.com. Reproduced by permission of SAGE Publications Ltd., London, Los Angeles, New Delhi, Singapore, and Washington DC, from "The Expulsion of Sex Workers from Vancouver's West End, 1975–1985: A Cautionary Tale," by Becki Ross, in *Sexualities*, August, 2010 (Vol. 13, no. 2).

1. See Salmi, 2000: 17.
2. See Hubbard, 1999: 4.
3. See Ross, 2009: 79-80.
4. For a brave portrait of sex workers in the West End, see the documentary film *Hookers on Davie* by Holly Dale and Janis Cole, for Spectrum Films.
5. See Raymond, 1994: xxiv, 30–31. Interview with Jamie Lee Hamilton.
6. See Freeman, 2006; Thomas, 1997; Hartman, 2002; Crowley, 2005; and Hubbard, 1999.
7. "To Book a Hooker," 1983: B1.
8. Cited in Menyasz, 1982.
9. CROWE, "A Submission to the Standing Committee on Justice and Legal Affairs from the Concerned Residents of the West End." Mayoral Fonds, 66-G-1, File 2 (March 8, 1982): 3.
10. Cited in Barrett, 1983; and "Harcourt Warns MPs on Hookers," 1983.
11. Cited in Herald Staff, 1983; and Mackie, 1984.
12. Cited in Bohn, 1982.
13. See Jacobs, 1961: 154–164.
14. Fairclough, 1985.
15. Foucault, 1991; interview with Gerry Stafford.
16. See City Manager's Reports, "Traffic Plan." City Council Minutes, 30 October. Microform, Series 31, September–November, 1981.
17. See Lowman, 2000: 1003–1004.
18. See Goad, 1983.
19. Bohn, 1983.
20. McMartin, 1984.
21. Susan Stryker writes that transgender women in San Francisco's Tenderloin were similarly vulnerable to sexual assault, rape, and murder when arrested and thrown into the men's jail. See Stryker, 2008: 67.
22. "Fast Action Urged on Hooker Problem," 1982: A10.
23. Sanchez, 2004: 864–865.

24. Moffett, 1982.

25. Ibid.

26. "Hooker Ruling Appealed," 1982.

27. Moffett, 1982, 9.

28. "Supreme Court Ruling," 1983.

29. Stoler, 2002: 87–89.

30. Special Committee on Pornography and Prostitution, 1985.

31. McEachern, 1985: 110.

32. Sanchez, 2004: 864.

33. Ibid.; McEachern, 1985: 110; and Thompson, 1984.

34. Interview with Stacey.

35. See Brock, 1998: 151–153.

36. "Hookers Invited to Speak," 1981.

37. See Jenness, 1990.

38. "Hookers Parade over Proposals to Change Laws," 1983.

39. Ibid.

40. Alliance for the Safety of Prostitutes (ASP). "Prostitution." Submitted to the "Fraser Commission," January 1984. Service and Office Retail Workers Union of Canada Papers, Legal 1984, Box 1, File 13, 20.

41. Ibid., 20.

42. Interview with Jamie Lee Hamilton.

43. *Not a Love Story: A Film about Pornography,* 1981.

44. Arrington, 1987: 105.

45. See Barry, 1979; and Dworkin, 1981.

46. Kinsman, 1996.

47. Serano, 2007: 14.

48. See Gilmore, 2009.

49. Boei, 1983.

50. Ibid.

51. Ibid.

52. Cox and Schaefer, 1984

53. Ibid.

54. Thompson, 1984; and Ousten, 1984.

55. Roberts, 1992.

56. Newman, 2002: 128.

57. Lefebrve, 1991: 56–57.

58. Warner, 1999.

59. Hubbard, 1999: 218.

60. Smith, 1987: 49.

61. Blomley, 2004: xxi.

62. McEachern, 1985: 110.

63. CROWE, "NDP Split on Issue of Street Soliciting," Mayoral Fonds, 66-G-1, File 1. (December 8, 1982a): 3.

64. See Razack, 2002a: 144.

65. Hubbard, 1999: 163.

66. Ley, 1980: 243.

67. Smith, 1998: 8–14. In 1984, Terry Glavin reported that CROWE admitted to having reached faulty, unsubstantiated conclusions blaming prostitutes for a $14-million decline in West End property values. See Glavin, 1984.

68. McClintock, 1995: 72.

69. Goffman, 1963. In 2004, "the steps" in front of the of the Second Cup Café in Toronto's gay village were bricked in by the store's managers to rid the space of "unwanted degenerates"—the homeless, drug dealers, street youth, and sex workers. See Alison Burgess, 2008.

70. See Butler, 2004: 38–42.

71. Jiwani and Young, 2006.

72. Sanchez, 1997: 575.

73. Pratt, 2005.

74. Pivot Legal Society, 2004, 2006; and Amnesty International, 2004.

75. De Vries, 2003; and Culbert, Hall, and Neal, 2007.

76. Lev, 2007.

77. See Benoit and Millar, 2001; Gall, 2006; *Tales of the Night Fairies*, 2002; and Kempadoo, Sanghera, and Pattanaik, 2005.

78. Levitz, 2007.

79. Cited in Greenaway, 2008.

IV

Conclusion
Thinking Ahead

17 Caring Everywhere
Viviana Zelizer

HERE IS HOW AN AUSTRIAN WOMAN reports her response to being paid by Caritas, a Roman Catholic Charity, for taking care of her mother-in-law:

> You can only say that I simply felt as if I had been promoted. Society also saw it totally differently then. Suddenly it was, "Aha, you're doing a job." Although I didn't do anything differently from before, it was suddenly seen as self-evident. But if you then say that you're working for Caritas, people say to you, "Wow, you're working now" . . . As soon as you're in employment and can say to the doctor that you have your own health insurance, it appears you are a better type of person. From the point of view of society, this type of employment is very good for women.[1]

This woman, who had earlier cared for her father-in-law outside the Caritas payment system, is one of the respondents interviewed in a remarkable cross-national study of "cash for care" schemes conducted by British researcher Clare Ungerson, Sue Yeandle, and four research teams in five European Union countries: Austria, France, Italy, the Netherlands, and the United Kingdom.[2]

Why is this woman, like so many of us, surprised by the unexpected effects of paid kin care? Because, sadly, the prevalent commercialized view of the labor market has sharply truncated people's view of what counts as genuine work that deserves serious compensation. In the process, we have neglected the economic significance of nonmarket, nonfirm work. This neglect is particularly consequential when it comes to intimate labor.

As we will soon see, developing clear ideas about the actual operation of intimate labor will enhance our collective understanding of both intimacy and labor. It will also help sweep away erroneous notions about their intersection and thus provide valuable guidance for social criticism and public policy. I hope that this chapter will stimulate discussion on these crucial issues. Let us start by clarifying what we mean by *intimacy* and *labor*.

We can think of relations as intimate to the extent that *interactions within them depend on particularized knowledge received, and attention provided by, at least one person—knowledge and attention that are not widely available to third parties.* The knowledge involved includes such elements as shared secrets, interpersonal rituals, bodily information, awareness of personal vulnerability, and shared memory of embarrassing situations. The attention involved includes such elements as terms of endearment, bodily services, private languages, emotional support, and correction of embarrassing defects.

Intimate social relations thus defined depend on various degrees of trust. Positively, trust means that the parties willingly share such knowledge and attention in the face of risky situations and their possible outcomes. Negatively, trust gives one person knowledge of, or attention to, the other, which if made widely available would damage the second person's social standing.

This broad definition of intimacy covers a range of personal relations, including parent–child, godparent–godchild, siblings, close friendships, and sexually tinged ties. It also extends to the varying degrees and types of intimacy involved in the relations of psychiatrist–patient, lawyer–client, priest–parishioner, servant–employer, prostitute–customer, spy–object of espionage, bodyguard–tycoon, child care worker–parent, boss–secretary, janitor–tenant, personal trainer–trainee, and hairdresser–customer. In all these social relationships, at least one person is committing trust, and at least one person has access to information or attention that, if made widely available, would damage the other.

Intimate relations, then, come in many varieties. They vary in kind and degree: The amount and quality of information available to spouses certainly differs from that of child care worker and parent, or priest and parishioner. The extent of trust likewise varies accordingly. Because we are dealing with a continuum, exactly where we set the limit between intimate and impersonal relations remains arbitrary. But it is important to see that in some respects even the janitor who knows what a household discards day after day gains access to information with some of the same properties as the information flowing in more obviously intimate relations. In this chapter, I will therefore adopt a relatively expansive definition of intimacy.

We also need a relatively expansive definition of *labor*: not only paid market employment, but any effort that creates transferable use value, including the use value that economists commonly call "human capital."[3] Thus housework, child care, advice giving, and school attendance all count as labor to the extent that they do in fact augment the use values of their performers and/or recipients.

Intimacy and labor intersect in the main subject matter of this volume: intimate labor. Within intimate labor, we should distinguish four different sites for personal care: unpaid care in intimate settings, unpaid care in economic organizations, paid care in intimate settings, and paid care in economic organizations such as hospitals, day care centers, and doctors' offices. These four sites differ significantly in the character and organization of intimate labor. I will stress widespread confusions that have arisen in thinking about differences among these four sites.

What do we mean by *care*? Caring relationships, in my view, feature sustained and/or intense personal attention that enhances the welfare of its recipients. Care thus counts as labor even if it provides pleasure to its givers and recipients. We might set the minimum for "sustained and/or intensive personal attention" at a manicure in a nail salon or a brief telephone counseling session on a mental health hotline. The maximum might then take the form of lifetime mother–daughter bonds or the devotion of a long-term personal servant.

This definition of *care* excludes two other areas of interpersonal relations: first, relatively impersonal provision of welfare-enhancing benefits; and, second, intimacy that does not enhance well-being. Relatively impersonal forms of welfare enhancement include such attentions as a pharmacist's advice on the best over-the-counter cough remedy and a government's provision of unemployment compensation.

As for the second exclusion, we too often mistakenly equate intimacy with care. We thus ignore those intimate relationships where the parties remain indifferent to each other or even inflict damage on one another. Abusive sexual relations, for example, are certainly intimate but not caring. Such relationships supply risky information to at least one party and thus entail trust of a sort, yet do not include caring attention. Intimacy and care do often complement each other, but they have no necessary connection.

Intimate labor is both puzzling and fascinating because so many people imagine that, if a relation is intimate, it cannot, and should not, involve labor. Where does this assumption come from? It draws from two powerful fallacies: We can call them "separate spheres" and "hostile worlds." Separate spheres notions claim that the world divides into separate spheres of sentiment and of rationality; hostile worlds beliefs say that contact between those separate worlds corrupts in both directions. Their mixing, goes the argument, introduces contaminating self-interested calculation into the world of sentiment, but it also introduces nonrational action into a world in which efficiency should reign.

These pervasive assumptions blind us to the prevalence of, and variation among, intimate labors. More specifically, they prevent us from understanding and explaining crucial differences among four very different sites of intimate labor: unpaid intimate care in intimate settings, unpaid intimate care in economic organizations, paid care in economic organizations, and paid care in intimate settings. Because we have ample documentation for paid care in economic organizations, let me concentrate on the other three: unpaid care in intimate settings, unpaid care in economic organizations, and paid care in intimate settings. A separate spheres perspective identifies the first—unpaid care in intimate settings—as natural. It sees the other two as anomalous, peripheral phenomena, instead of recognizing their crucial significance.

Unpaid Care in Intimate Settings

Let us first consider unpaid care in intimate settings. As I said at length in my 2005 book *The Purchase of Intimacy*, intimate relations regularly coexist with economic transactions without being corrupted. Of course, not all intimate interactions consist of labor, yet a significant share of them does. For example, couples buy engagement rings, parents pay nannies or child care workers to attend to their children, adoptive parents pay lawyers and agencies money to obtain babies, divorced spouses pay or receive alimony and child support payments, and parents give their children allowances, subsidize their college educations, help them with their first mortgage, and offer them substantial bequests in their wills. Friends and relatives send gifts of money as wedding presents, and friends loan each other money. Immigrants dispatch hard-earned money as remittances to kinfolk back home.

Indeed, people who maintain intimate relations with each other regularly pool money, make joint purchases, invest shared funds, organize inheritances, and negotiate divisions of household work. No loving household would last long without regular inputs of economic effort.

When it comes to unpaid intimate labor, consider the obvious examples of food preparation, child care, and health care. Even in a day of takeout and fast food, unpaid domestic preparation of food still counts as one of the major forms of labor in capitalist countries, not to mention the rest of the world. Child care likewise continues to absorb enormous amounts of value-enhancing effort across the world. Despite the advances of scientific medicine, further-more, health care remains a major form of unpaid intimate labor.

In the case of health care, Geneviève Cresson's close study of French households underlines the extent to which household members—especially adult women—work to sustain each other's health.[4] Far from serving as ad-juncts to professional health care specialists, the women in the forty house-holds Cresson interviewed clearly provided the bulk of all health care their family members received. Furthermore, they made the decisions as to which specialists to consult and when. None of them received direct compensation for their health services. Indeed, most of them underestimated the frequency and extent of those services; even those who maintained health care diaries at Cresson's request tended to omit the daily tasks they simply folded mentally into food preparation and child care.

Even when medical professionals provide instructions or medicine, fam-ily members regularly take part in supplying care. They assure hygiene, fetch drugs and other medical supplies, and learn medical technologies such as in-jections and monitoring of vital signs. Household members also manage sick persons' schedules and their transportation, as well as the special diets and other comforts appropriate for their condition. In Los Angeles, for instance, Cecilia Menjívar studied the health practices of Guatemalan immigrant women.[5] The women relied heavily on their interpersonal networks to secure medical care for themselves and their family members. Through a variety of informal ties, the women gained knowledge and access to both American medicine and unofficial means of healing, such as herbs, rituals, and medi-cines regulated in the United States but available without prescription in the home country.

As a consequence, mothers involved themselves daily in the delivery of health care at home. Menjívar reports of Aida, one of the Guatemalan women she interviewed:

> Like almost all the women in this study, Aida feels fully responsible for her family's health needs . . . She is always mindful of her family's health and is industrious in putting together whatever treatments she can find. There was a reminder to herself on the refrigerator door: *Darle las vitaminas a la beiby.*

Ponerle las pastillas en la lonchera a Luis. (Give the vitamins to the baby. Put the pills in Luis's lunchbox.)[6]

Indeed, over recent decades, the development of health management orga-nizations and the aging of the American population have combined to place a growing burden of health care on households. In Canada, Pat and Hugh Arm-strong's 2005 study of changes in the health care system found that a shift to day surgery, shorter patient hospital stays, and deinstitutionalization resulted in a significant increase in women's unpaid domestic care work, including the management of such "complex care technologies . . . as catheters, intravenous tubes and oxygen masks [that] are sent home with the patients."[7] They also note that the women who do the work seldom define it as care, leading to an underestimation of the hours women spend doing this work.[8]

In the legal arena, courts regularly treat care provided by one family member to another as ineligible for monetary compensation, even in cases of inheritance and divorce. When they do award compensation to household members, including nannies, maids, and dependent kin, furthermore, courts generally distinguish between services naturally provided by intimates to each other, which remain uncompensated, and services going sufficiently be-yond natural obligation to deserve compensation at something like market rates. Separate spheres doctrines thus persist in the law.

Nevertheless, American courts sometimes actually recognize that domes-tic health care merits financial compensation. In 1985, the Supreme Court of Minnesota took on Alice Ann Beecham's claim to a portion of her mother-in-law's $166,000 estate. The mother-in-law, Sara Edith Beecham, had cut Alice from her will in favor of her four grandchildren. Two years after marrying Edith's son, Alice had taken the elderly, sick woman into her home. For the last six and a half years of Edith's life, Alice cared for her full time, not only cook-ing and cleaning but performing delicate nursing tasks. The court ruled that despite their family relation, Alice was entitled to a portion of the estate.[9]

When Alice had first contested the will, the trial court had ruled in her favor, finding an implied contract to pay for her personal services. The court noted that Edith had shown no reciprocity for Alice's strenuous care, except for an occasional five- or ten-dollar "tip" for transportation expenses. An ap-peals court reversed that decision on the grounds that Alice's services, because they involved a family member in the absence of an oral or written contract, had to be gratuitous.

The Supreme Court, however, reinstated the initial decision to award Alice compensation, supporting the trial court's finding of an implied contract. Alice's "around-the-clock care" of Edith, the Minnesota Supreme Court concluded, went "beyond services usually and ordinarily gratuitously rendered to family members." Based on experts' estimates of Alice's home care services' commercial value, the court set compensation at $32,000, toward the lower end of the estimated range. As we analysts of care should, in this instance the courts recognized the great economic value of unpaid care in intimate settings.

Unpaid Care in Economic Organizations[10]

While separate spheres assumptions conceal everyday unpaid intimate labors, they also prevent us from observing and explaining unpaid intimate care in economic organizations, which separate spheres doctrines treat as anomalous. Although, on the average, relations within economic organizations involve less intimacy—less access and trust—than relations within intimate settings such as households, forms of intimacy such as close friendships and confidential relations do appear in economic organizations. Indeed, they commonly include provision of personal care: sustained and/or intensive attention that enhances personal well-being.

In theory, intimacy is not supposed to matter in formal organizations. Indeed, organizational analysts and managers tend to think of such care as inefficient noise or, worse, as a threat to organizational efficiency and productivity. Concerns about what we can call "intimization" lead to the construction of what legal scholar Vicki Schultz calls the "sanitized workplace."[11]

Such close students of the subject as Schultz detect a substantial increase in workplace regulation of intimate relations, going well beyond sexual harassment legal requirements. These range from "no-fraternization policies" prohibiting romantic involvement between supervisors and employees, even when consensual; to "date-and-tell" policies, where employees involved in such relationships must disclose their romance to management and be subject to monitoring, reprimand, or transfer; as well as "cupid" or "love" contracts for employees about to embark on a romantic relationship.

In a light-hearted report on couples waiting in a New York City marriage bureau, for example, the *New York Times* interviewed a man and woman who had just lost their jobs in a box-making factory, saying that "they were so in love that they were fired for being unproductive," thus confirming managers' wariness about intimacy in the workplace.[12]

And it's not just fear of sexual liaisons: the prestigious Conference Board recommends a "personal relations policy" that includes a wide range of relatively intimate relations, such as close after-hour friendships, noting that:

> "old boy" buddies—and now "old girls," too—get more job perks than "lovers." That's why a policy should address potential conflicts with marital, extended-family, and close-friendship relationships as well as romantic ones.[13]

In a parallel move, since the 1980s employers (especially in the public sector) have been increasingly imposing no-spouse and antinepotism rules. What is more, legal attempts to challenge nepotism rules that prohibit couples from sharing a workplace have generally failed.

Yet, despite these determined efforts to ban workplace intimacy, actual observation suggests the constant presence of care among co-workers. Of course, because of separate spheres thinking, we have only scattered evidence of workplace intimate labors. We know little, for instance, of exactly how co-workers cover for each other's defects or absences, what sort of mentoring old-timers provide newcomers, how workers console each other for managers' injustices, what sorts of favors they exchange on the job, and how they support each other by such practices as taking up collections and pooling leaves.[14]

We get some early glimmers of such caring practices from Susan Porter Benson's study of department store saleswomen in the first decades of the twentieth century:

> In one department, women contributed to the support of Aggie, a particularly destitute co-worker; they paid her insurance and sick-benefit premiums, bought extra food for her lunch, and helped her to stretch her meager clothing budget. But their actions went beyond self-help within the department to confront management on Aggie's behalf. When a manager halted their yearly collection to send Aggie on vacation and made them return the money, they ostentatiously collected it again outside the employees' entrance. They knew, however, that the only real solution to Aggie's problems was a higher salary, and their most impressive victory was in backing up her successful quest for a raise.[15]

Despite giving more attention to resistance than to mutual aid, Randy Hodson has advanced our knowledge of co-workers caring by combing and cataloguing more than a hundred ethnographies of workplace interaction. The ethnographies report such caring practices as gift giving in a chemical factory and mutual covering among sleeping car porters.[16] "Coworkers," concludes Hodson:

> help provide meaning in work through the sharing of work life experiences and through friendships. Coworkers can also provide a basis for group solidarity and mutual support in the face of denials of dignity at work.[17]

Hodson identifies caring friendship and mutual aid as major compensations for physical hardship, tedious work routines, tyrannical managers, and even low wages. Without caring, we can infer, many workplaces, far from operating more efficiently, would actually collapse. Hodson reports a striking study of Washington, D.C., firefighters. A firefighter recalled:

> It's hard to describe the closeness that you felt with the guys in the fire house. I don't think my wife has ever really understood it. I just used to love to come to work—especially on those long Saturdays when we'd have a big roast or a ham or something and sit around and talk or play cards. . . . Firemen then were a great bunch and a rough bunch. . . . They played hard and rough. But when the bells hit, nobody would do any more good for you than a fireman. It's a group of men with a unique brotherhood feeling—they'll never let you down.[18]

Over a wide range of workplaces, then, mutual caring turns out to be a crucial element of job satisfaction and solidarity.

We even have scattered evidence that intimacy enhances organizational performance. Since the 1930s, of course, industrial sociologists have stressed the positive impact of workplace solidarity on productivity. But that older literature generally neglected caring practices in favor of practices fostering group identification. More recently, a number of studies report the prevalence and even the management promotion of job recruitment by current employees of friends and kin. Mutual recruitment often benefits the hiring organization by enhancing employee productivity.[19] So far as we can tell, mutual hiring tends to integrate new hires more firmly into workplace networks and to give them greater access to caring attention.

More generally, a surprising variety of studies document the positive effects of workplace caring relationships on economic productivity. Consider these vignettes:

- Economist K. K. Fung provides a strong theoretical rationale for concluding that horizontal favor exchanges enhance organizational efficiency.[20]

- Business school professor Francis Flynn finds evidence that workers who exchanged favors were significantly more productive than their fellows.[21]
- A large 2001 Gallup poll identifies a strong connection across firms between the proportion of workers who had best friends in the workplace, on one side, and firm profitability, productivity, safety, and customer loyalty, on the other.[22]
- In 2007, a survey of senior executives and workers in the country's thousand largest firms found widespread agreement that workers with co-workers who were "buddies" both on and off the job were more productive and committed contributors to firm performance.[23]
- A substantial literature on family firms indicates not only that, on the average, they create more worker-friendly environments than their nonfamily competitors but that they also enjoy greater organizational effectiveness.[24]

Conservatively, then, we can conclude that workplace caring deserves much greater and more systematic attention from students of care. More daringly, we can conclude that unpaid care within economic organizations should be a new frontier for analyses of care's enhancement of human welfare.[25]

Paid Care in Intimate Settings

As we have seen, unpaid care in intimate settings strike most people as so natural as to be almost invisible. Unpaid care in economic organizations remains equally invisible, despite its near universality, but for the opposite reason: because it doesn't fit the prevailing frame. Paid care in intimate settings, however, has raised a hue and cry because it defines a moral and political battleground: on one side, whether paid personal attention merits compensation comparable to that received in economic organizations; on the other side, whether payment for care generally degrades its quality.

If separate spheres reasoning were not so widespread and powerful, either position would seem illogical. To the extent that paid care does enhance its recipients' welfare, beneficiaries and third parties should compensate it generously. One might think, furthermore, that care would be easy to gauge in monetary terms: Simply compute the benefit gained by the recipient and third parties. But the separate spheres notion that personal care occurs naturally as a free good blocks systematic reasoning and justifies gross inequities.

Indeed, the first American study focusing on the relative pay of care work documents a significant "wage penalty" for face-to-face service providers such as teachers, counselors, health care aides, and child care workers.[26] Although both men and women involved in care work pay this penalty, women do so more often because they are more likely to be involved in care work.[27]

The problem is not simply that people dumbly accept false beliefs. People who give and receive personal care in intimate settings are actually negotiating definitions of their social relations in a rapidly changing world. Everywhere and always intimates create forms of economic interchange that simultaneously accomplish shared tasks, reproduce their relations, and distinguish those relations from others with which they might become confused: Are you my mother, my sister, my daughter, my nurse, my maid, or my best friend? Each has its own distinctive array of economic interchanges. In each case, people draw on available cultural models, and they use power and persuasion to negotiate unequal social relations. Paid care in intimate settings raises the fundamental questions: Who are we, and what do we owe each other?

Negotiation over appropriate interpersonal relations certainly goes on within households, but it also occurs over a much larger scale. In recent years, local, regional, and national governments have responded to changing household circumstances by intervening increasingly in compensation for care given within households. The United States has lagged behind other Western countries in public policies governing payment for household care.

In the United Kingdom, for instance, we find a legally established category of young carers (children under eighteen) who receive government subsidies for providing care to a household member. The 1995 Carer's Act acknowledged children's caring work, by adding children under eighteen to the category of private informal carers entitled to social services. Under specified conditions, local councils have the authority to make direct payments to the sixteen- and seventeen-year-olds who are providing care. Thus British social policy compensates qualified child carers by awarding them direct access to social services as well as the possibility of monetary payments.[28]

In France, as Florence Weber has shown, the doctrine of "undue enrichment" provides another sort of compensation for household-based care.[29] To the extent that they exceed ordinary filial duty, unpaid contributions of a child to the care of elderly parents during the parents' lifetime established the child's rightful claims for compensation from the parents' estate. In the Minnesota case we discussed earlier, such a principle would have made clear from the start that the dutiful but unpaid daughter-in-law deserved a share of her mother-in-law's estate.

We can return to Clare Ungerson and her collaborators for a systematic comparison of national policies.[30] Ungerson's group studied paid care in five European countries. They made two valuable distinctions: first, between systems in which the government regulates the working conditions closely and those in which they intervene primarily by means of payment; and second, whether relatives can or cannot receive payment for the care they provide. For example, the highly regulated Dutch and Austrian systems qualify as "fully commodified," including payments to relatives. The evidence they collect suggests not only that such systems deliver care effectively but that caregivers and recipients express great satisfaction with the arrangement.

The Dutch scheme, for instance, compensated a daughter for the care she gave to her parents, elderly stroke victims, five mornings a week. The mother reported:

Things are excellent the way they are now. And I am happy if she receives some money. I and my husband receive help and that is the main thing for us. I don't know how we would manage otherwise. And he will not have anyone else. He doesn't want a nurse, which is why our daughter does it.[31]

Thus, public policy can not only facilitate superior delivery of care but help redefine relations within kin groups. Not for a moment am I saying that all such schemes work fairly or well, that the more paid care the better, or that kin are always the best providers. On the contrary, we must return to the main point: that parties to care, including government agencies, for better of worse, are negotiating matches among the quality of care delivered, the social relations among the parties, and the compensation that caregivers receive.

I have deliberately avoided discussing paid care in economic organizations on the ground that we already know more about the varieties of care provided by medical professionals and other licensed caregivers than we do about caring elsewhere. Even there we can gain a clearer understanding through recognition that, in the delivery of care, professionals and their clients are likewise negotiating definitions of their social relations and forms of compensation to represent those definitions. In the cases of unpaid care within intimate settings, unpaid care within economic organizations, and paid care within intimate settings, we have plenty more to learn about how people create viable relations and for that matter how and why things go wrong in the delicate mingling of intimacy and labor. Our exploration has just begun.

Notes

I have adapted a few paragraphs from Zelizer, 2005.

1. Ungerson, 2004.
2. See also Ungerson and Yeandle, 2007.
3. See Tilly and Tilly, 1998.
4. Cresson, 1995.
5. Menjívar, 2002.
6. Ibid.: 452–453.
7. Armstrong and Armstrong, 2005: 185.
8. See also Bittman et al., 2004: 73–74.
9. *In re Estate of Beecham*, 1985.
10. This section draws from Zelizer, 2009.
11. Schultz, 2003.
12. Fernandez, 2007.
13. Lever, Zellman, and Hirschfeld, 2006: 39.
14. See Marks, 1994; McGuire, 2007.
15. Benson, 1986: 247.
16. Hodson, 2001: 201.
17. Ibid.: 200.
18. Ibid.: 223.
19. Castilla, 2005; Férnandez, Castilla, and Moore, 2000; Grieco, 1987.
20. Fung, 1991.
21. Flynn, 2003.
22. Ellingwood, 2001.
23. "Birds of a Feather," 2007.
24. For example, Anderson and Reeb, 2003; "Family, Inc.," 2003.
25. See also Williams, Giuffre, and Dellinger, 1999; Pettinger, 2005.
26. England et al., 2002.
27. See also Budig and England, 2001; Correll, Benard, and Paik, 2007.
28. Olsen, 2000. See "Carers (Recognition and Services) Act 1995"; also personal communication, Chris Dearden, February 9, 2006.
29. Weber, 2003.
30. Ungerson, 2004.
31. Ibid.: 197.

18 More Intimate Unions

Dorothy Sue Cobble

THE OLD MYTH THAT WOMEN are unorganizable has largely been demolished. The stories of successful labor organizing among women generated by decades of feminist scholars have had an impact.[1] But there are still myths and outmoded paradigms that hamper our ability to think clearly and productively about the labor organizing of intimate workers. I call this outmoded paradigm the "factory paradigm" of labor organizing. It is a hangover in part from the glorious but by now long-gone heyday of mass production organizing and industrial unionism. It also owes much of its staying power to the economistic and "factory proletarian" biases that still shape present-day theories of worker consciousness and collective action.

This chapter asks how our analysis of collective mobilization would change if we moved beyond the factory paradigm and took the experiences of intimate labor and of intimate workers as prototypic rather than exceptional. To help answer that question, I draw on the rich history of labor organizing among intimate workers as well as the now considerable body of feminist scholarship that challenges theories of identity and agency premised on narrow and singular notions of human motivation and desire.[2]

Worker resistance and activism takes many forms, but in this chapter I will focus on the efforts of intimate workers to create unions and other workplace-based institutions.[3] Such institutions include unions affiliated with the two major U.S. labor federations, the AFL-CIO and, since July 2005, the Change to Win Federation; unaffiliated or independent unions representing workers; as well as worker associations and centers that may not, as do most unions, seek a collective bargaining relationship with an employer to advance and secure their goals.

Creating a model of labor organizing that incorporates the realities of intimate work and intimate workers, of whom the majority are female and people of color, is necessary if our theories of collective mobilization are to reflect the twenty-first century economy. It is also crucial to making possible "more intimate unions," another central concern of this chapter. The phrase *more intimate unions* has multiple meanings. It signals a focus on how *more* unions of intimate workers can be organized as well as on how a more *intimate* labor movement can be encouraged. Such a movement would be one in which intimacy is no longer feared and in which attention to the interpersonal in all realms of life, including the union movement itself, is recognized as essential for advancing freedom, human dignity, and social justice. Having more intimate unions in both senses, I will argue, has the potential for revitalizing the labor movement as a whole and for benefiting those who serve and those who are served.

In the spirit of this anthology, I rely on "intimate workers" as a category of analysis. In my usage, it is a broad category that refers to those who do care work, sex work, household labor, as well as any other job that involves servicing others. I will use it interchangeably with the term *personal service workers.*[4] At times, I also refer to "interactive" or "frontline" service workers, both terms that foreground a significant structural element shared by many intimate workers: that is, their interaction with clients, patients, or customers— that third party so aptly termed by saleswomen as "our friend the enemy" in Susan Porter Benson's classic history of department store workers, managers, and customers.[5]

I welcome the concept of "intimate labor" because it crosses occupational boundaries and focuses on what workers in a range of service jobs have in common. It also helps us capture the complexity and multidimensionality of personal service work. The service occupations I have studied, be they waitresses, flight attendants, clerical or household workers, confound easy categorization. None can be captured by a *single* distinguishing characteristic. Neither do they fit easily into *one* of the now popular categories of "care work" or "sex work."[6] Many of these jobs may involve care work and "emotional labor"; yet many may not.[7] At the same time, many *also* fall into what could be called the sexual service sector, a term I first encountered in Baxandall, Gordon, and Reverby's 1976 women's history documentary collection, *America's Working Women.*[8] Jobs in the "sexual service sector" involve the selling of one's sexual self. Prostitutes, strippers, and other "sex workers" are part of this sector, but so too are many workers in the retail, hospitality, and entertainment sectors not commonly thought of as doing "sex work." Indeed, with the increasing sexualization of work and the heightened emphasis on appearance as well as aesthetic and erotic titillation, few jobs are wholly without a sexual dimension.

Intimate labor is also a useful term because it does not presuppose a particular affective state on the part of the service provider. Intimate exchanges may vary in their degree of caring and closeness, being, as C. Wright Mills once noted, both "more impersonal and more intimate."[9] The relationship of the worker to her work is left unspecified: The worker may be engaged in "deep" and potentially "self-alienating" forms of emotional labor or simply "surface" ritualistic performance.[10] Service encounters then may be exploitative as well as mutually beneficial. There is room for multiple and shifting possibilities.

The Factory Paradigm of Labor Organizing

What are some of the deeply embedded—and I might add untested—assumptions that are part of the "factory paradigm" of labor organizing? At its core, it is a theory that presumes that workers who most closely resemble the archetypal male proletariat toiling away on the mass production assembly line are the most likely to organize. There are many derivatives of this ideal that misshape our theories of who will organize and for what ends.

First, it is a model that privileges a "market or waged work" identity and assumes it correlates more closely with collective action than other identities and self-conceptions. Despite the longstanding feminist insight that work must be conceptualized broadly to encompass productive and reproductive labor and span the household and market realms, some theorists of labor organizing still worry that women wage earners whose identity rests primarily or even secondarily on the work of social reproduction don't yet have a fully developed consciousness as "workers" and hence will be less likely to turn to collective action.

Chandra Mohanty, for example, in *Feminism without Borders*, writes of her desire that the women workers she is studying discard their family identities and adopt a "worker consciousness" based on their paid work; it is only then, she suggests, that they will move toward "solidarity" and collective resistance.[11] Other scholars worry that care workers may not be ready to unionize or assert their rights because they offer "unpaid" or voluntary care as an add-on to their paid job, thus resisting the valuation of their work in market terms and lacking sufficient autonomy from those they serve. What is the underlying teleology that is being expressed here? What does a fully realized "worker consciousness" look like? Does it require the shedding of other less desirable identities, such as those tied to household, family, and community and the development of an autonomous market-based self? And is such a narrow and self-interested "worker identity" a necessary precondition for collective mobilization?

History suggests otherwise. Women's ties with family, household, and community as well as with those they serve—or put another way, their sense of themselves as mothers, daughters, sisters, lovers, partners, good caretakers, or providers—have sparked successful workplace-based organizing as much as deterred it. For many women, as scholars of African American and working-class women's consciousness have shown, identity as a mother or a housewife was inseparable from identity as a deserving wage-earning woman.[12] Whether we call it "womanist," or "female consciousness," or "feminist," the organizing of working-class women on behalf of themselves *and* those dependent on them has been a powerful, if not dominant, force for change.[13] Macdonald and Merrill find a similar confluence of identities spurring today's labor organizing among child and family care providers. These workers are seeking collective power to secure their own independence and dignity; they are also organizing to advance their beliefs in an "ethic of care" and to gain recognition, culturally and economically, for their work as "good providers."[14]

A second lingering inheritance from the "factory paradigm" is the idea that factory jobs are easier to organize than other jobs. If the first notion privileges a market and individuated consciousness more associated with men, this second assumption privileges the kind of working-class jobs traditionally held by men. The imagined factory on which much organizing theory is based is the mass-production factory system peopled by men: It is located outside the home and is most commonly a large, bureaucratic enterprise with full-time, highly routinized waged employees. It is this workplace, the story goes, with its large concentration of homogeneous alienated workers, that will lead most readily to collective mobilization. The popularity of George Ritzer's 1993 study, *The McDonaldization of Society*, for example, was based in part on its assumption that as service jobs "McDonaldized," or came to resemble the Taylorized mass production workplace of old, and as service workers "proletarianized"—a concept based on perceived transformations in factory labor and its long inevitable march toward routinization and deskilling, a new wave of worker resistance would ensue.[15]

But intimate workers are often found in work settings that differ dramatically from those common to the mass-production enterprise. Intimate work tends to take place in smaller, less bureaucratic settings; "tightly constrained" or rationalized work systems make up a small fraction of all service environments.[16] The employment relationship, where it exists, may be personal and informal, and the line between employee and employer is often blurred and easily crossed. And, unlike workers in goods production, a third party—the customer, client, patient, passenger—complicates and transforms the old employer–employee dyad. The quality of the server's relationship to that third party may be more important to his or her overall well-being, materially and psychologically, than the relationship to the boss or "employer."

In addition, intimate workers are often geographically dispersed, scattered among many worksites rather than concentrated in a single large enterprise. They may work in the "privacy" of the home, be it their own or that of someone else; or they may ply their trade in the hidden and ephemeral "public" spaces carved out for sexual exchange. Many are part-time or "nonstandard" workers; few have long-term permanent relations with a single employer. It is these characteristics of the intimate workplace—smaller, dispersed, more personal and privatized—and of the intimate worker—casualized and lacking a classic adversarial class consciousness—that many see as impediments to unionism.[17]

But one of the surprising truths about the history of organizing in the United States is that the majority of workers who joined unions did not fit the mass production stereotype. All too often we conflate unionism with mass production unionism, which in the United States reached its peak in the mid-twentieth century. But prior to that, millions of nonfactory workers unionized. Certainly, the waitresses I studied—a service trade in which one-quarter of all workers were organized by the mid-fifties—were unusual in their proclivity for collective organization, but they were not alone. Neither was their approach to labor organizing, what I've called "occupational unionism," atypical. Occupational unionism with its emphasis on the trade or occupational community and its control over hiring, training, and job performance was the dominant form of labor organization before the advent of mass production unionism. And when mass production organization surged in the 1930s and 1940s, so too did organization among those outside of manufacturing: in hospitality, communication, maritime, transportation, and other sectors.[18] The largest U.S. union in the post–World War II era was not the United Auto Workers but the Teamsters, a union of workers, many of whom were independent contractors or owner-operators, who spent most of their day alone in their trucks hurtling through space.[19]

Nonfactory unionism continued to flourish in the 1960s and 1970s with the organizing of public sector workers, the majority of whom were in interactive service jobs such as teaching, social work, and health care. Union density in the U.S. private sector is now a quarter of what it was in the 1950s, down to 7 percent in 2008. Public sector unionism, however, rose to 37 percent by the early 1980s and is still at that level.[20]

In short, the organizing that is taking place today among intimate workers is not such a break from the past as we imagine. It is actually part of a long history of successful nonfactory organizing. It is these workers—as much as those among the fabled industrial proletariat—who turned to collective organization and built powerful and long-lasting workplace institutions. It is their story that is continuing today.

The Declining Factory Advantage

Part of that story, and an inspiring part, is how intimate workers organized despite the legal and cultural obstacles they faced.[21] Many of these barriers existed because the state assumed the factory as its paradigmatic work setting and the industrial blue-collar male head-of-household as its model worker. Historically, only "industrial market work" was deemed "real work," and hence those who diverged from that ideal often lacked "employee" status and the legal rights and protections that flowed from that status. Initially, for example, broad swaths of nonfactory workers fell outside the parameters of the 1935 National Labor Relations Act (NLRA) guaranteeing workers the right to form unions; they also were frequently exempted from the network of state and federal legislation regulating wages, hours, and other working conditions. Of course, it was no accident that the excluded jobs were ones predominantly held by African Americans and people of color: Racism has operated historically to deny those with darker skins the privileges of economic as well as political citizenship.[22] Yet the particular "nonfactory-like" characteristics of intimate labor reinforced this racism.

At times, the courts agreed with employers who claimed, as did hotel owners, that any job resembling household labor should be exempt from labor legislation because of its nonindustrial character.[23] At other times, the location of work in the private noncommercial realm of the home prompted its exclusion. The home was seen, in Vivien Hart's apt phrase, as a "rights-free enclave."[24] In part because of these intersecting, overlapping prejudices, the majority of domestic workers, for example, were not covered by federal fair labor standard legislation until 1974.

Today, many intimate workers still lack basic labor rights and protections because they are in the underground cash economy or are defined as "self-employed" or "independent contractors," as is often the case for domestic cleaners, exotic dancers, and family care providers. The lack of legal recognition thus remains a formidable barrier to labor organizing for personal service workers.

At the same time, the legal terrain in the United States is shifting, lessening the once stark distinctions between unprotected nonfactory workers and others. Today, personal service workers are not alone in their lack of legal protections: Some one-third of *all* private sector workers are outside of NLRA protection.[25] And of equal significance, a consensus is rapidly emerging that most successful labor organizing at present happens outside the framework of U.S. labor law. In other words, the legal protections for organizing under U.S. labor law have eroded to such a degree that even those who "enjoy" such coverage find it of little help.[26] This is not to say that it is now easy for personal service workers to organize; it is only to say that the playing field has been leveled to some degree, making it as hard to organize those who supposedly have legal protections and those who don't.

The playing field is also being leveled in other ways with the rise of global manufacturing and outsourcing. In terms of the global spatial politics of labor organizing, intimate workers have advantages over many other groups of workers. Personal service jobs are simply not as vulnerable to relocation as goods-production work.[27] Of course some interactive service work can be outsourced, as is the case with call center employees; and intimate workers are vulnerable to consumer whimsy, too: Sex tourists can move around the globe as the supply of sex workers fluctuates or the idea of the perfect sex partner changes. But, in general, capital mobility has proceeded more rapidly in goods-production. In a majority of the union campaigns among U.S. manufacturing workers in the 1990s, employers relied on plant closings, real and threatened, to thwart worker's collective representation.[28]

The strong bond many interactive service workers have with a third party is another advantage for them in labor organizing. Historically and into the present, workers from every industry and occupation have relied on allies to help them in their efforts to extract their just due for their labor. Sympathy strikes, boycotts, influencing public opinion, and political action are all key weapons in the arsenal of labor activists. Intimate workers, however, have had an ace up their sleeve: They serve the public every day and hence have the opportunity for numerous personal encounters. Not only can they reach out for support to the general public, they can also mobilize their networks of customers, clients, or service recipients. The restaurant owners I studied were invariably surprised when their customers sided with the restaurant "help" during strikes. The striking waitresses, who earlier had hollered out complicated and highly specific breakfast orders to the cooks even before their hungry early-morning customers found their seats, were not.[29]

The Rise of Intimate Unions since the 1980s

The final nail in the coffin of the factory paradigm of labor organizing may turn out to be the upsurge of workplace organizing among intimate workers since the 1980s. Not only are interactive service workers initiating and winning union campaigns more frequently than any other group of worker, they are doing so in record numbers.

Seventeen percent of nurses are affiliated with one of the many unions vying to represent them, making them among the more organized groups in the United States, and much of this growth has occurred since the 1980s. Sizeable numbers of nurses and other health care professionals now belong to the healthcare divisions of the American Federation of State, County and Municipal Employees (AFSCME), the American Federation of Teachers (AFT), and the Service Employees International Union (SEIU).[30]

Nurses also have demanded more unionlike representation from their professional nurse associations. Although the American Nurses Association (ANA), the national professional organization representing nurses and nurse supervisors, dropped its opposition to collective bargaining in the late 1940s, few of its affiliated state nurse associations seriously pursued the union route. In the 1990s, however, as the registered nursing shortage reached crisis proportion and the conditions of staff nurses worsened, dissatisfaction flared over the ANA's commitment to representing the divergent interests of direct-care nurses and nurse managers. In 1995, the California Nurses Association (CNA) broke its ties with the ANA over the issue and dedicated itself to unionizing direct-care nurses. By 2007, their membership had grown fourfold, reaching 75,000. In 2009, CNA joined with two other nurse associations to form the 150,000-member National Nurses United (NNU). The new organization, now the largest national union representing direct-care nurses, seeks to organize all direct-care RNs and serve as a national voice for nurses' rights and health care reform.[31]

The 1990s also witnessed a phenomenal rise in the unionization of home care workers who assist the elderly and disabled in their homes. Since the massive union victory in Los Angeles in 1999, in which 74,000 home care workers gained collective bargaining representation with the SEIU, making it one of the largest single union victories in modern labor history, momentum has continued to build. Current home care union membership tops 350,000, and Boris and Klein estimate that "discounting the underground economy of home health care aides, about thirty-five percent of the home health care labor force now belongs to unions."[32]

More recently, unionism has spread to child care workers. One of their first large-scale breakthroughs occurred in April 2005, when 49,000 Illinois family child care providers voted to unionize. Since then, some additional 100,000 have joined, creating new child care provider organizations in Washington, Oregon, New Jersey, and elsewhere. In March 2009, the SEIU alone claimed 200,000 organized child care workers.[33]

New intimate worker associations are cropping up as well. Domestic Workers United, for example, whose aim is to represent the 200,000 nannies, housekeepers, elder caregivers, and others working in New York City private homes—a largely immigrant female work force from Latin America, the Caribbean, and the Philippines—in 2003 helped secure passage of the Domestic Workers Bill of Rights, the first citywide ordinance in the country protecting the rights of domestic workers. In the spring of 2008, the first national convention of domestic worker associations gathered in New York City, making quite a stir.[34]

Workers providing intimate care to the bodies of women (and some men)—facials, bikini waxes, massages, manicures, and pedicures—may be the next group to organize nationally. In 2007, as Miliann Kang shows in this volume, nail salon workers, a group primarily Asian in background, formed a network in New York City, the Nail Salon Workers Network, to address the severe health and safety issues in their industry and the disrespect with which they are treated by their clients or salon owners. The Nail Salon Workers Network, part of a coalition of groups representing service-economy workers called "Justice Will Be Served," arose after Susan Kim, a fifty-three-year-old Korean manicurist, won a $182,000 class action lawsuit against a number of Upper East Side salons for overtime violations, back pay, and for "retaliatory termination." In Kim's case, she had been fired after she complained to her employer about the grueling ten-and-a-half hour work shifts and other illegalities.[35]

Although the exotic dancers union at Lusty Lady in San Francisco disappeared, sister unions and sex worker associations have emerged in Argentina, Australia, Britain, Europe, and elsewhere.[36] The largest union of prostitutes currently exists in India. Founded by a public health scientist in 1992 but now largely run by the prostitutes themselves, it has some 65,000 members concentrated in West Bengal. *Newsweek* credited the union with lowering the HIV infection rate in the Sonagachi or red-light district of Kolkata (formerly Calcutta) to 5 percent, a stunning achievement, particularly when compared to the higher and rising infection rates elsewhere. Seventy percent of Mumbai's prostitutes, for example, are estimated to be HIV-positive. The union asked its members to boycott customers who refused to wear condoms. It took considerable solidarity among the prostitutes to change their clients' behavior, but eventually safer sexual practices became more widespread.[37]

The majority of the intimate workers who have organized since the 1980s, it should be noted, do not fit the "factory paradigm" of who will turn to collective organization. Many work in scattered, isolated workplaces, often hidden from public view; their boss may be a family member or someone else with whom they have close emotional ties. Their primary employment relationship, for better or for worse, may be with their clients, customers, or patients. Indeed, the "factory paradigm" would have predicted that center-based child care workers would have organized because they are more likely to work in large, impersonal work environments and have adversarial relations with their employer. The United Child Care Union, an AFSCME-affiliate based in Philadelphia, has signed up a few center-based child care workers, as has the SEIU. But overwhelmingly it is home-based child and family care providers who have organized, as Ellen Reese details in this volume.[38]

More Intimate Unions

What will it take to grow intimate unionism? Certainly, there needs to be a greater commitment to organizing among current labor organizations: what many talk about as moving toward an "organizing" or a "social movement unionism."[39] But, just as importantly, there needs to be a transformation of union culture and values so that those who service the physical and emotional needs of others are welcomed and respected in the movement.

Most obviously, the intimate labor of sexual service remains in the shadows and, when mentioned in union circles, may elicit embarrassed silence or involuntary laughter. There are exceptions, of course, but the traditional labor movement is far from reaching a consensus over whether to organize sex workers and what specific political and economic policies would best serve their interests and those of the larger society. Here is an instance in which pressure from both inside and outside the union movement will need to be applied before much will alter. As sex workers "self-organize," creating their own networks, associations, and alliances, established unions will feel pressure to change. Unions who already represent workers in the sexual service sector also can help spearhead this transformation by responding aggressively to issues involving sexuality and erotic labor in their industries.

UNITE HERE (the merged garment and hospitality union),[40] for example, has a long and honorable tradition of representation in this sector, which they could turn into an asset in organizing. I've written elsewhere about how HERE (Hotel Employees and Restaurant Employees) organized Playboy Bunnies in the early 1960s under the guidance of the unstoppable Myra Wolfgang and how by 1969 they secured a national union contract covering all Hugh Hefner's Playboy Clubs. The national contract ended the employer's "no wage" policy (the bunnies had been expected to live solely on tip income), gave bunnies more control over the cut and style of their uniforms, set rules for customer behavior—"look but do not touch"—and challenged the club's rigid ideas of female beauty. Bunnies were fired, for example, on "loss of bunny image" or the first sign of "crinkling eyelids, sagging breasts, crepey necks, and drooping derrieres." After one arbitrator ruled in the union's favor and reinstated one group of "defective bunnies," Wolfgang quipped that not only had "bunnies bit back" but that Hugh Hefner had finally been "displaced as the sole qualified beholder of bunny beauty."[41]

Some locals of HERE have continued their union's historic willingness to challenge appearance standards and respond to the problems of those in sexual service jobs. In the 1990s, for example, Atlantic City's HERE Local 34 threatened the casinos with a "pantyhose arbitration" over the sheerness of the pantyhose that management required casino waitresses to wear; the local also considered a class-action suit against all twelve casinos, alleging sex discrimination. The waitresses preferred thicker, less sheer pantyhose because they experienced less harassment. Heavier "support" hose also were more comfortable, helped tired legs, and covered varicose veins.[42]

Yet problems with sexual harassment and appearance discrimination are widespread and increasing in hospitality, retail, and other sectors, and the labor movement has not made these issues a priority. Women workers are challenging these conditions in court: In *In Jespersen v. Harrah's Operating Co.*, for example, a case recently rejected by the Ninth Circuit, a female bartender protested Harrah's "personal best" grooming and appearance policy requiring women to wear makeup. Yet, so far, the large class action sex discrimination lawsuits in hospitality have not been brought by unions, as Avery and Crain note in their recent analysis of how service businesses are aggressively pursuing profit from "sexual commodification." Sex discrimination is a "collective harm," to borrow Marion Crain's phrase, and labor will not be able to respond effectively to the needs of its members until it recognizes the intimate and the erotic as economic and labor matters.[43]

In addition to taking sexual labor more seriously, the traditional labor movement has other things to learn from the new intimate unions that have arisen. Home care and child care unions put monetary matters at the center of their organizing: Not surprisingly, raising their own low wages and gaining some measure of economic security were top concerns for these workers. Yet their discourse about money was rarely just about money. The child care campaigns for "worthy wages" gained public support for raising the pay of providers by emphasizing the skill of their work as well as the *social* importance of care work. Put another way, theirs was a unionism that was challenging the distribution of wealth *and* of social prestige.[44]

Many intimate unions also have repeatedly made connections between raising wages and improving the quality of care. Like earlier campaigns among teachers, nurses, and other frontline service workers in health and education, child care providers are conscious of creating a unionism that could help solve the problems of both service producers and service consumers. The collective bargaining agreement between SEIU Local 925 and the state of Washington, negotiated in 2007, is remarkable for its attention to the dual needs of caregiver and care recipient. In addition to guaranteeing higher wages, training, and benefits to 12,000 family child care providers, it pledges increased access to quality child care for every Washington State family *and* specifies that the rights of consumers to select or change their child care provider will be protected.[45] This is a unionism that, in alliance with parents, is pushing for a virtuous circle in which organizing caregivers raises the value of their care labor, improves the quality of the care they provide, and advances the right of all to receive good care.

Yet, in far too many instances, unions remain prisoners of what Viviana Zelizer calls a "nothing-but" economic mentality; that is, they still see the marketplace and industrial relations as almost wholly about commercial exchange and economic maximization.[46] Rather, what intimate unionism demonstrates is that monetary or "standard of living" issues are a good place to begin in representing workers but not the place to end. Worker's psychological and relational needs must be addressed along with their economic needs.

The Harvard Union of Clerical and Technical Workers (HUCTW) has led the way in this regard, pioneering what founding organizer Kris Rondeau calls a "relational unionism." Like the nail salon workers, HUCTW members speak pointedly about the need to transform relationships—not just between worker and employer but between workers and those they serve. Transforming the point of consumption (which, in many ways, is also the point of production in service economies) is central to their mission.[47]

Customers can be allies in the process of improving service encounters, as has largely been the case with home care and family care unionism. They may also be adversaries, as was true for nail salon workers, the Playboy bunnies, and the Indian prostitutes' union, all instances in which collective pressure was necessary to change the behavior of clients. Indeed, in contrast to the child care unionists who sought to ensure the right of public access to their services, the Indian prostitutes' union did not seek to expand sexual services. Their goal, one spokewoman explained, was to ensure that they and their daughters had alternatives to sex work.[48]

Harvard clerical workers fall somewhere between these extremes in terms of their relationship to their "customers." When the Harvard administration offered "skills training" for clericals in how to handle "customer encounters" with irate and demanding faculty and students, HUCTW members found one lesson particularly galling. At this infamous session, the consultant hired by Harvard instructed attendees to "think of yourself as a trash can," a vessel that would simply fill up with everyone's ill humor throughout the day and then could be dumped after work. HUCTW decided it needed an alternative and insisted on setting up its own training program in "negotiating relationships." Its goal, the union explained, was to end management's "customer is always right" rule and develop more humane norms for clerical–customer interactions. The customer was neither right nor wrong, they decided, but certainly was "always interesting."[49]

HUCTW also tried to get management to understand that if the full complicated idiosyncratic lives of each worker were recognized and honored it would actually be to the advantage not just of Harvard but of everyone. As Kris Rondeau once explained, "as a mature union," we felt it was time to move "beyond economic man."[50] For HUCTW, that meant resisting the idea that people's desires can be reduced to the material and that selfishness and hyper-individualism are the best bases for prosperity and happiness.

Viviana Zelizer reminds us in this volume how much "mutual caring" occurs in the workplace and indeed how much occurs everywhere. It's time not only for unions to recognize and value the intimate labor that we all do but also to put transforming human relationships at the heart of their mission. In the new economy of the twenty-first century, the economic and the intimate converge. Intimate workers and their unionism have the potential to transform these new relations of exchange, making them into a world C. Wright Mills could not envision, one that was both more intimate *and* more personal. Ultimately, it is not the things that matter; it's the people. That's why we need more intimate unions and why they would benefit us all.

Notes

1. See, for example, Milkman, 1985; Baron, 1991.

2. For an introduction, Larrabee, 1993; and Tronto, 1993.

3. For discussions of nonworkplace organizing, see Kelley, 1993; and Kaplan, 1982.

4. The term *personal service* has been discarded in part because of its negative associations with servitude. But the stigmatization of service and its conflation with servitude is a cultural and intellectual legacy that should be challenged. The African American men who founded the Brotherhood of Sleeping Car Porters in the 1920s sought such a change. Their slogan was "Service not Servitude." See, among others, Arnesen, 2001; and A. Philip Randolph Institute (retrieved March 7, 2009).

5. For "interactive" service work, see Leidner, 1993; for "frontline," see Korczynski, 2009; for quote, see Benson, 1986: 258.

6. For example, Cobble, 1991a, 1999; Cobble and Merrill, 2009.

7. The term *emotional labor* is from Hochschild, 1983: 3–12, passim; for contrasting views on who does "care work," see England and Folbre, 1999; and Duffy, 2005.

8. Baxandall, Gordon, and Reverby: xx.

9. Mills, 1951: introduction and 161–188. See also Zelizer's expanded and ambiguous formulation of "intimacy" in *The Purchase of Intimacy,* 2005, 14–16.

10. On "deep acting" and "self-alienation," see Hochschild, 1983; on "surface" encounters and ritualistic performance, see Butler, 2006.

11. Mohanty, 2003: chapter 6.

12. For example, Collins, 2000, especially 173–201.

13. Brown, 1989; Kaplan, 1982; Cobble, 2004: 3.

294 Dorothy Sue Cobble

14. Macdonald and Merrill, 2002.

15. Ritzer, 2004.

16. Herzenberg, Alic, and Wial, 1998: 11–14, 42–43.

17. For a fuller development of these points, see Cobble, 1994.

18. Tomlins, 1979; Cobble, 1991b, 2005.

19. Cobble and Vosko, 2000.

20. Cobble, 2005; U.S. Department of Labor, "Union Members in 2008."

21. Boris and Klein, 2007.

22. Palmer, 1995; Mettler, 1998.

23. Cobble, 2004: 111.

24. Hart, 1994.

25. Cobble, 1994; U.S. General Accounting Office, 2002.

26. Compa, 2003; Freeman, 2007.

27. Lerner, 2007.

28. Bronfenbrenner, 2001.

29. Cobble, 1991a: especially chapters 2, 3, and 4.

30. Gordon, 2005. For nurse membership figures, AFSCME (retrieved February 2, 2010); MacDonald (retrieved February 2, 2010); SEIU (retrieved February 2, 2010).

31. Ketter, 1996; Furillo, 2007; Raine, 2009; Beyerstein, 2009. The other two organizations that amalgamated with CNA were the Massachusetts Nurses Association and the United American Nurses, a group founded in 1999 by activist nurses within ANA.

32. Delp and Quan, 2002; Boris and Klein, 2007, 2008: 33.

33. Smith, 2004; Whitebook, 2002; Cobble and Merrill, 2009: 157, 162–163; Reese, "But Who Will Care for the Children?" Chapter 16 in this volume; SEIU (retrieved February 2, 2010).

34. Fine, 2007; Boris and Nadasen, 2008.

35. Gonnerman, 2007; Nussbaum, 2007. See also Kang, "Manicuring Intimacies," Chapter 14 in this volume.

36. On organizing Lusty Lady and the exotic dancers alliance, see *Live Nude Girls Unite*; Friend, 2004; Kempadoo, 1998. On sex worker unions globally, see Gall, 2006: chapters 6 and 7; on Argentina, where AMMAR (the Argentinean Female Sex Workers Union) has been particularly successful, see Hardy, 2010.

37. MacKinnon and Piore, 2001; Mukerjee, 2006.

38. Smith, 2004; Whitebook, 2002.

39. On "social movement unionism," see Turner and Hurd, 2001; and Lopez, 2004.

40. UNITE HERE is in transition as an organization. As of July 2009, part of its membership, under the leadership of former UNITE (Union of Needletrades, Industrial and Textile Employees) President Bruce Raynor, organized a new union, Workers United, and affiliated with the SEIU. Another group, under the leadership of former HERE (Hotel Employees and Restaurant Employees) President John Wilhelm, remained in UNITE HERE.

41. Cobble, 1991a: 128–131.
42. Cobble, 1996: 347.
43. Avery and Crain, 2007; Crain, 2007.
44. Macdonald and Merrill, 2002; Boris and Klein, 2007.
45. Contract in possession of the author.
46. Zelizer, 2005: 29–32.
47. Rondeau, personal interview with author (November 8, 2008); Savage, 2007.
48. MacKinnon and Piore, 2001.
49. Eaton, 1996.
50. Rondeau, 1998.

Bibliography

AARP. Brief as *Amicus Curiae* in Support of Plaintiff-Appellant. *Coke v. Long Island Care at Home*, 03-7666 in the United States Court of Appeal for the Second Circuit. 2006.

Abdul-Alim, Jamaal. "Child care providers face reimbursement cut." *Milwaukee Journal Sentinel*, February 18, 2003, 3B.

ACORN-LA. "Los Angeles Childcare Providers Organize." Newsletter, 2001.

AFSCME, "Jobs We Do: Nurses," Retrieved on February 2, 2010 from: http://www.afscme.org/workers/68.cfm

AFSCME Works Online. "Child Care Providers Win with AFSCME in KS and PA!" AFSCME Works Online, 2007. Retrieved on September 13, 2007, from: www.afscme.org/publications/16129.cfm

The Aggressives. Daniel Peddle, director. Seventh Art Releasing, 2005.

Agustín, Laura. "Working in the European Sex Industry: Migrant Possibilities." *OFRIM*/Suplementos, June, 2000. Retrieved on February 12, 2010, from: www.nodo50.org/Laura_Agustin/working-in-the-european-sex-industry

———. *Sex at the Margins: Migration, Labour Markets and the Rescue Industry.* London: Zed Books, 2007.

Ahmed, Sara. "Affective Economies." *Social Text* 22, 2 (2004): 117–139.

Allison, Anne. *Nightwork: Sexuality, Pleasure, and Corporate Masculinity in a Tokyo Hostess Club.* Chicago: The University of Chicago Press, 1994.

Almeling, Rene. "Selling Genes, Selling Gender: Egg Agencies, Sperm Banks, and the Medical Market in Genetic Material." *American Sociological Review* 72 (2007): 319–340.

Altman, Dennis. *Global Sex.* Chicago: University of Chicago Press, 2001.

American Federation of Teachers. "New York Order Gives Green Light to Child Care Union Drive." American Federation of Teachers, 2007. Retrieved on September 13, 2007, from: www.aft.org/news/2007/ny-earlychild.htm

Amnesty International. "Amnesty International Report 2003: Paraguay." New York: Amnesty International, 2003.

———. "Stolen Sisters: A Human Rights Response to Discrimination and Violence Against Indigenous Women in Canada." New York: Amnesty International, 2004.

Anderson, Bridget. *Doing the Dirty Work? The Global Politics of Domestic Labour.* London: Zed Books, 2000.

Anderson, R. C., and D. M. Reeb. "Founding-Family Ownership and Firm Performance: Evidence from S&P 500." *The Journal of Finance* 58 (2003): 1301–1327.

Aneesh, A. "Spectres of Global Communication." *Frakcija*, 2008.

A. Philip Randolph Institute. Retrieved on March 7, 2009, from: www.apri.org

Apple, Rima D. *Perfect Motherhood: Science and Childrearing in America.* New Brunswick, NJ: Rutgers University Press, 2006.

Armstrong, Elizabeth M. *Conceiving Risk, Bearing Responsibility: Fetal Alcohol Syndrome and the Diagnosis of Moral Disorder.* Baltimore: The Johns Hopkins University Press, 2003.

Armstrong, Pat, and Hugh Armstrong. "Public and Private: Implications for Care Work." In *A New Sociology of Work?* edited by Lynne Pettinger, Jane Parry, Rebecca Taylor, and Miriam Glucksman, pp. 169–187. Oxford, U.K.: Blackwell, 2005.

Arnesen, Eric. *Brotherhoods of Color: Black Railroad Workers and the Struggle for Equality.* Cambridge, MA: Harvard University Press, 2001.

Arrington, Marie. "Community Organizing." In *Good Girls/Bad Girls: Sex Trade Workers and Feminists Face to Face*, edited by Laurie Bell, pp. 104–108. Toronto: Women's Press, 1987.

Asian American Legal Defense and Education Fund (AALDEF). "$17.5K Back-Wage Win for Nail Salon Worker," January 17, 2006. Retrieved on July 2, 2006, from: www.aaldef.org/article.php?article_id=28

———. "Asian Immigrant Nail Salon Workers Win Major Legal Victory: Manhattan Federal Jury Awards Back Wages and Reinstatement," 2007. Retrieved on October 30, 2007, from: www.aaldef.org/article.php?article_id=351

Asian Law Caucus and University of California San Francisco Community Occupational Health Project. "Oakland Healthy Nail Salon Project: Infection Protection." 2005.

Associated Press. 2005. "Abdul urges tough nail salon standards." Posted June 27, 2005. Retrieved on January 30, 2010, from: www.usatoday.com/life/people/2005-06-27-abdul-nail-salons_x.htm

"Aún En Busca De Los Niños Que La Guerra Se Llevó." SwissInfo, October 6, 2006.

Avery, Dianne, and Marion Crain. "Branded: Corporate Image, Sexual Stereotyping, and the New Face of Capitalism." *Duke Journal of Gender, Law & Policy* 14 (2007): 13–123.

Baker, Beth. *Old Age in a New Age: The Promise of Transformative Nursing Homes.* Nashville, TN: University of Vanderbilt Press, 2007.

Bakker, Isabella. "Social Reproduction and the Constitution of a Gendered Political Economy." *New Political Economy* 12 (December 2007): 541–556.

Bales, Kevin. *Disposable People: New Slavery in the Global Economy.* Berkeley: University of California Press, 1999.

———. "Because She Looks Like a Child." In *Global Woman: Nannies, Maids, and Sex Workers in the New Economy,* edited by Barbara Ehrenreich and Arlie Hochschild, pp. 207–229. New York: Henry Holt, 2002.

Baron, Ava, ed. *Work Engendered: Toward a New History of American Labor.* Ithaca, NY: Cornell University Press, 1991.

Barrett, Tom. "Takeover by Hookers Feared." *Vancouver Sun,* March 3, 1983, B5.

Barry, Kathleen. *Female Sexual Slavery.* Englewood Cliffs, NJ: Prentice Hall, 1979.

———. *The Prostitution of Sexuality: The Global Exploitation of Women.* New York: New York University Press, 1995.

———. "Introduction." In *Vietnam's Women in Transition,* edited by Kathleen Barry, pp. 1–18. New York: St. Martins Press, 1996.

Bauman, Zygmunt. "On Postmodern Uses of Sex." *Theory, Culture, and Society* 15: 3–4 (1998): 19–35.

Baxandall, Rosalyn, Linda Gordon, and Susan Reverby, eds. *America's Working Women: A Documentary History.* New York: Vintage, 1976.

Beck, Elizabeth. "The National Domestic Workers Union and the War on Poverty." *Journal of Sociology and Social Welfare* 28 (December 2001): 195–211.

Becker, Gay. *The Elusive Embryo: How Women and Men Approach New Reproductive Technologies.* Berkeley: University of California Press, 2000.

Benítez, Inés. "Guatemala: Whitewash for 'Adoption Paradise.'" *Inter Press Service,* June 5, 2007.

Benoit, Cecilia, and Alison Millar. "Dispelling Myths and Understanding Realities: Working Conditions, Health Status, and Exiting Experiences of Sex Workers." 2001. Available at: http://web.uvic.ca/~cbenoit/papers/DispMyths.pdf

Benson, Susan Porter. *Counter Cultures: Saleswomen, Managers, and Customers in American Department Stories, 1890–1940.* Urbana: University of Illinois Press, 1986.

Bernhardt, Annette, Siobhan McGrath, and James DeFilippis. "Unregulated Work in the Personal Services Industry in New York City." New York City: Brennan Center for Justice, 2007. Retrieved on December 20, 2007, from: www.brennancenter.org/page/-/d/download_file_49382.pdf

Bernstein, Elizabeth. "What's Wrong with Prostitution? What's Right with Sex Work? Comparing Markets in Female Sexual Labor." *Hastings Women's Law Journal* 10 (1999): 91–117.

———. "The Meaning of the Purchase: Desire, Demand, and the Commerce of Sex." *Ethnography* 2:3 (2001): 389–420.

———. *Temporarily Yours: Intimacy, Authenticity, and the Commerce of Sex*. Chicago: University of Chicago Press, 2007.

Beyerstein, Lindsay, "It's Official: Three Unions Merge to Form Nurses' 'Super Union'" *In These Times*, December 8, 2009, 4.

Bhattacharjee, Anannya. "The Habit of Ex-Nomination: Nation, Woman, and the Indian Immigrant Bourgeoisie." *Public Culture* 5:1 (1992): 19–44.

Biklen, Molly. "Note: Healthcare in the Home: Reexamining the Companionship Services Exemption to the Fair Labor Standards Act." *Columbia Human Rights Law Review* 35 (2003): 113–150.

"Birds of a Feather Flock Together . . . at Work." *Accountemps*, June 14, 2007. Retrieved on July 12, 2007, from: www.accountemps.com/portal/site/atus/menuitem .b368a569778a80c6cb42b21002f3dfa0/?vgnextoid=39a73468151e6010VgnVCM 100000e2aafb0aRCRD

Bittman, Michael, Janet E. Fast, Kimberly Fisher, and Cathy Thomson. "Making the Invisible Visible: The Life and Time(s) of Informal Caregivers." In *Family Time: The Social Organization of Care*, edited by Nancy Folbre and Michael Bittman, pp. 69–90. London: Routledge, 2004.

Blackman, Lisa. "Affect, Relationality and the 'Problem of Personality.'" *Theory, Culture & Society* 25:1 (2008): 23–47.

Bleidorn, K. Joan. "W-2 Needs Humane Replacement." *Milwaukee Journal Sentinel*, June 16, 1998, 13. Retrieved May 5, 2007, from: www.lexisnexis.com

Blomley, Nicholas. *Unsettling the City: Urban Land and the Politics of Property*. New York: Routledge, 2004.

Bluth, Alexa H. "Revised Budget Backs Off Cuts $103 Billion Plan Mostly Spares Health Services." *Sacramento Bee*, May 14, 2004, A1.

Boehner, Kirsten, Rogério DePaula, Paul Dourish, and Phoebe Sengers. "How Emotion Is Made and Measured." *International Journal of Human-Computer Studies* 65:4 (2007): 275–291.

Boei, William. "City Backs Crackdown on Hookers." *Vancouver Sun*, May 18, 1983, A3.

Bohn, Glenn. "City Bylaw on Hookers Upheld." *Vancouver Sun*, September 16, 1982, A3.

———. "Hookers: Lazy Crooks or Victims?" *Vancouver Sun*, July 7, 1983, B1.

Bombay Calling, DVD. Directed by Ben Addelman and Samir Mallal. National Film Board of Canada, 2006.

Boris, Eileen. *Home to Work: Motherhood and the Politics of Industrial Homework in the United States*. Cambridge, U.K.: Cambridge University Press, 1994.

Boris, Eileen, and Jennifer Klein. "'We Were the Invisible Workforce': Unionizing Home Care." In *The Sex of Class: Women Transforming American Labor,* edited by Dorothy Sue Cobble, pp. 177–193. Ithaca, NY: Cornell University Press, 2007.

———. "Labor on the Home Front: Unionizing Home-Based Care Workers." *New Labor Forum.* 17:2 (Summer 2008): 32–41.

———. *Caring for America: Home Health Workers in the Shadow of the Welfare State.* New York: Oxford University Press, forthcoming.

Boris, Eileen, and Premilla Nadasen. "Domestic Workers Organize!" *WorkingUSA: The Journal of Labor and Society,* 11 (December 2008): 413–437.

Bornstein, Kate. *Gender Outlaw: On Men, Women, and the Rest of Us.* New York and London: Routledge, 1994.

Bourgois, Phillip. *In Search of Respect: Selling Crack in el Barrio.* Los Angeles: University of California Press, 1995.

Boy I Am. DVD. Directed by Sam Sam and Julie Hollar. 2005.

Brennan, Denise. "Selling Sex for Visas: Sex Tourism as a Stepping Stone to International Migration." In *Global Woman: Nannies, Maids, and Sex Workers in the New Economy,* edited by Barbara Ehrenreich and Arlie Hochschild, pp. 154–168. New York: Henry Holt, 2001.

———. *What's Love Got to Do with It? Transnational Desires and Sex Tourism in the Dominican Republic.* Durham, NC: Duke University Press, 2004.

Brenner, Joanna, and Barbara Laslett. "Gender and Social Reproduction: Historical Perspectives." *Annual Review of Sociology* 15 (1989): 381–404.

Briggs, Laura. *Reproducing Empire: Race, Sex, Science and U.S. Imperialism in Puerto Rico.* Berkeley: University of California Press, 2002.

———. "Orphaning the Children of Welfare: 'Crack Babies,' Race, and Adoption Reform." In *Outsiders Within: Writing on Transracial Adoption,* edited by Jane Jeong Trenka, Julia Chinyere Oparah, and Sun Yung Shin, pp. 75–88. Cambridge, MA: South End Press, 2006.

Brock, Deborah. *Making Work, Making Trouble.* Toronto: The University of Toronto Press, 1998.

Brodsky, Rose. "Philosophy and Practices in Homemaker Service." *Child Welfare* 37 (July, 1958): 11.

Bronfenbrenner, Kate. "Uneasy Terrain: The Impact of Capital Mobility on Workers, Wages, and Union Organizing." Supplement to *The U.S. Trade Deficit: Causes, Consequences and Recommendations for Action.* Washington, DC: U.S. Trade Deficit Review Commission, 2001.

Brooks, Fred P. "What Differences Unionizing Teachers Might Make on Child Care in the USA: Results from an Exploratory Study." *Child & Youth Care Forum* 32:1 (February 2003): 3–22.

———. "New Turf for Organizing: Family Child Care Providers." *Labor Studies Journal* 29:4 (Winter 2005): 45–64.

Brown, Elsa Barkley. "Woman Consciousness: Maggie Lena Walker and the Independent Order of Saint Lake." *Signs* 14 (1989): 610–633.

Brown, Mareva. "Child Care Subsidy at Risk: Some Families Would Lose Aid Under the Governor's Plan to Shift Help to Those with Lower Incomes." *Sacramento Bee*, April 21, 2002a.

———. "Child-Case Subsidy Changes Dropped but a Proposal to Alter the Rules and Make Some Parents Pay Fees Could Pop Up Again." *Sacramento Bee*, May 26, 2002b.

Buckley, Cara, and Annie Correal. "Domestic Workers Organize to End an 'Atmosphere of Violence' on the Job." *New York Times*, June 6, 2008.

Budig, Michelle J., and Paula England. "The Wage Penalty for Motherhood." *American Sociological Review* 66 (2001): 204–225.

Burawoy, Michael. "The Extended Case Method." *Social Forces* 16 (1998): 4–33.

Burgess, Alison. "White Homonormativity and the Degenerate 'Other': The Elimination of 'The Steps' in Toronto's Gay Village." Unpublished paper presented at the Canadian Sociological Association Meeting, Vancouver, British Columbia, June 5, 2008.

Butler, Judith. *The Psychic Life of Power: Theories in Subjection*. Stanford, CA: Stanford University Press, 1997.

———. *Precarious Life: The Powers of Mourning and Violence*. London: Verso, 2004.

———. *Gender Trouble: Feminism and the Subversion of Identity*. New York: Routledge, 2006.

CAAAV Organizing Asian Communities. "Women Workers Project." Retrieved on January 30, 2010, from: www.caaav.org/projects/wwp

Cacchioni, Thea. "Heterosexuality and 'the Labour of Love': A Contribution to Recent Debates on Female Sexual Dysfunction." *Sexualities* 10 (2007): 299–320.

Callender, David. "Child Care Providers Want W-2 Fees Cut." *Capital Times*, April 22, 1998, 6A.

"Carers (Recognition and Services) Act 1995." Retrieved on July 12, 2007, from: www .hmso.gov.uk/acts/acts1995/Ukpga_19950012_en_1.htm

Carroll, Maurice. "Mediation Effort Is Set by Ginsberg." *New York Times*, May 1967, 79.

Castells, Manuel. "The Network Society." Paper Presented at the Center for Working Families. University of California, Berkeley, 2001.

———. "The Net and the Self: Working Notes for a Critical Theory of the Informational Society." *Critique of Anthropology* 16:1 (1996): 9–38.

Castilla, Emilio J. "Social Networks and Employee Performance in a Call Center." *American Journal of Sociology* 110 (2005): 1243–1283.

Center for Child Care Workforce and Human Services Policy Center. "Estimating the Size and the Components of the U.S. Child Care Workforce and Caregiving Population." Washington, DC: Center for Child Care Workforce, 2002. Retrieved on July 7, 2007, from: www.ccw.org/pubs/workforceestimatereport.pdf

Chalfie, Deborah, Helen Blank, and Joan Ethnmacher. "Getting Organized: Unionizing Home-Based Child Care Providers." Washington, DC: National Women's Law Center, 2007. Retrieved on July 31, 2007, from: www.nwlc.org/pdf/Getting Organized2007.pdf

Chandra, A., G. M. Martinez, W. D. Mosher, J. C. Abma, and J. Jones. "Fertility, Family Planning, and Reproductive Health of U.S. Women: Data from the 2002 National Survey of Family Growth." In *Vital Health Statistics* 23:25 (2005). Hyattsville, MD: National Center for Health Statistics, 2005. Retrieved on March 19, 2010, from: www.cdc.gov/nchw/data/series/sr_23/sr23_025.pdf

Chang, Grace. "Undocumented Latinas: The New 'Employable Mothers.'" In *Mothering: Ideology, Experience, and Agency,* edited by Evelyn Nakano Glenn, Grace Chang, and Linda Rennie Forcey, pp. 259–286. New York: Routledge, 1994.

———. *Disposable Domestics.* Boston: South End Press, 2000.

Chapkis, Wendy. *Live Sex Acts: Women Performing Erotic Labor.* New York: Routledge, 1997.

Cheever, Susan. "The Nanny Track." *New Yorker,* March 6, 1995.

Childress, Alice. *Like One of the Family: Conversations from a Domestic's Life.* New York: Independence Publishers, 1956.

Chin, Margaret. *In Service and Servitude: Foreign Female Domestics and the Malaysia Modernity Project.* New York: Columbia University Press, 1998.

Chodorow, Nancy. *The Reproduction of Mothering: Psychoanalysis and the Sociology of Gender.* Berkeley: University of California Press, 1978.

Choy, Catherine Ceniza. *Empire of Care: Nursing and Migration in Filipino Nursing History.* Durham, NC: Duke University Press. 2003.

Christiansen, Lars. *The Making of a Civil Rights Union: The National Domestic Workers Union of America.* Ph.D. dissertation, Florida State University, 1999.

City Manager's Reports. City of Vancouver Archives, Vancouver, Canada.

City of New York Department of Hospitals (DOH). *Annual Reports, 1940–1970.* New York.

Clark-Lewis, Elizabeth. *Living In, Living Out: African American Domestics and the Great Migration.* New York: Kodansha America, 1996.

Cleeland, Nancy. "9 Hotels in L.A. Region Made Lockout Pact." *Los Angeles Times,* June 2, 2004, C-1.

Clough, Patricia Ticineto. "Future Matters: Technoscience, Global Politics and Cultural Criticism." *Social Text* 22:3 (2004): 1–23.

Clough, Patricia Ticineto, and Jean Halley, eds. *The Affective Turn: Theorizing the Social.* Durham, NC: Duke University Press, 2007.

Cobble, Dorothy Sue. *Dishing It Out: Waitresses and Their Unions in the Twentieth Century.* Urbana: University of Illinois Press, 1991a.

———. "Organizing the Post-Industrial Work Force: Lessons from the History of Waitress Unionism." *Industrial and Labor Relations Review* 44 (1991b): 419–436.

———. "Making Postindustrial Unionism Possible." In *Restoring the Promise of American Labor Law*, edited by Sheldon Friedman, Richard W. Hurd, Rudolph A. Oswald, and Ronald L. Seeber, pp. 285–302. Ithaca, NY: Cornell University Press, 1994.

———. "The Prospects of Service Unionism." In *Working in the Service Society*, edited by Cameron Macdonald and Carmen Sirianni, pp. 333–358. Philadelphia: Temple University Press, 1996.

———. "'A Spontaneous Loss of Enthusiasm': Workplace Feminism and the Transformation of Women's Service Jobs in the 1970s." *International Labor and Working-Class History* 56 (Fall 1999): 23–44.

———. "Lost Ways of Unionism: Historical Perspectives on Reinventing the Labor Movement." In *Rekindling the Movement: Labor's Quest for Relevance in the Twenty-First Century*, edited by Lowell Turner, Harry C. Katz, and Richard W. Hurd, pp. 82–98. Ithaca, NY: Cornell University Press, 2001.

———. *The Other Women's Movement: Workplace Justice and Social Rights*. Princeton, NJ: Princeton University Press, 2004.

———. "A 'Tiger by the Toenail': The 1970s Origins of the New Working-Class Majority." *Labor: Studies in Working-Class History of the Americas* 2 (2005): 103–114.

Cobble, Dorothy Sue, and Michael Merrill. "The Promise of Service Unionism." In *Service Work: Critical Perspectives*, edited by Cameron MacDonald and Marek Korczynski, pp. 153–174. New York and London: Routledge, 2009.

Cobble, Dorothy Sue, and Leah Vosko. "Historical Perspectives on Representing Nonstandard Workers." In *Nonstandard Work: The Nature and Challenges of Changing Employment Arrangements*, edited by Francoise Carre, Marianne Ferber, Lonnie Golden, and Stephen Herzenberg, pp. 291–312. Ithaca, NY: Cornell University Press, 2000.

Coble, Alana Erickson. *Cleaning Up: The Transformation of Domestic Service in Twentieth Century New York City*. New York: Routledge, 2006.

Colen, Shellee. "'Just a Little Respect': West Indian Domestic Workers in New York City." In *Muchachas No More: Household Workers in Latin America and the Caribbean*, edited by Elsa Cheney and Mary Garcia Castro, pp. 171–194. Philadelphia: Temple University Press, 1989.

Collins, Patricia Hill. "Shifting the Center: Race, Class, and Feminist Theorizing about Motherhood." In *Mothering: Ideology, Experience, and Agency*, edited by Evelyn Nakano Glenn, Grace Chang, and Linda Rennie Forcey, pp. 45–66. New York: Routledge, 1994.

———. *Black Feminist Thought: Knowledge, Consciousness and the Politics of Empowerment*, 2nd ed. New York: Routledge, 2000.

Comisión para el Esclarecimiento Histórico. *Guatemala: Memoria del Silencio*. 12 vols. Guatemala City: Oficina de Servicios para Proyectos las Naciones Unidas, 1991.

Commission on Health Care Facilities in the Twenty-First Century. *Factors Book.* New York State Department of Health, July 2005. Retrieved on February 7, 2010 from: www.nyhealthcarecommission.org/materials/

Community Council of Greater New York, Citizens' Committee on Aging. "Systems Analysis of the Home Attendant Program." 1977. McMillan Library, New York.

Compa, Lance. "Workers' Freedom of Association in the United States: The Gap between Ideals and Practice." In *Workers' Rights as Human Rights*, edited by James A. Gross, pp. 23–52. Ithaca, NY: Cornell University Press, 2003.

"Comunidad Internacional Solicita a Guatemala Conceder Más Atención a Problemática Infantil." Prensa Libre/Archivo de Recortajes CIRMA/31.4 Niñez, October 13 1996.

Constable, Nicole. *Romance on a Global Stage: Pen Pals, Virtual Ethnography, and "Mail-Order" Marriages.* Berkeley: University of California Press, 2003.

Corbin, Alain. *Women for Hire: Prostitution and Sexuality in France after 1860.* Cambridge, MA: Harvard University Press, 1990.

Cornell, Angela, and Kenneth Roberts. "Democracy, Counter-Insurgency, and Human Rights: The Case of Peru." *Human Rights Quarterly* 12 (1990): 529–553.

Correll, Shelley J., Stephen Benard, and In Paik. "Getting a Job: Is There Motherhood Penalty?" *American Journal of Sociology* 112 (2007): 1297–1338.

Coser, Lewis. "Servants: The Obsolescence of an Occupation Role." *Social Forces* 52 (1973): 31–40.

Covington, Sharon, and William Gibbons. "What Is Happening to the Price of Eggs?" *Fertility and Sterility* 87 (2007): 1001–1004.

Cowan, Ruth Schwartz. *More Work for Mother: The Ironies of Household Technology from the Open Hearth to the Microwave.* New York: Basic Books, 1985.

Cox, Sarah, and Glen Schaefer. "Hookers Fight from Church." *Vancouver Sun*, July 21, 1984, A12.

Crain, Marion. "Sex Discrimination as Collective Harm." In *The Sex of Class: Women Transforming American Labor*, edited by Dorothy Sue Cobble, pp. 99–116. Ithaca, NY: Cornell University Press, 2007.

Cresson, Geneviève. *Le Travail Domestique de Santé.* Paris: L'Harmattan, 1995.

Crowley, Gregory. *The Politics of Place: Contentious Urban Redevelopment in Pittsburgh.* Pittsburgh: University of Pittsburgh Press, 2005.

Culbert, Lori, Neal Hall, and Jeff Lee. "An Emotional End to Pickton Trial." *Vancouver Sun*, December 10, 2007, A1 and A4.

Dalby, Liza. *Geisha.* New York: Vintage Books, 1985.

Dale, Holly, and Janice Cole. *Hookers on Davie.* Toronto: Spectrum Films, 1984.

Dalton, Juan José. "Cicatrices No Cerradas De La Guerra." *Proceso*, October 25, 2003a.

———. "El Salvador: La Deuda Con Los Niños Deaparecidos" *Proceso*, March 8, 2003b.

———. "Ante La Corte Interamericana." *Proceso*, March 22, 2005.

Das Gupta, Monisha. *Unruly Immigrants: Rights Activism, and Transnational South Asian Politics in the United States*. Durham, NC: Duke University Press, 2007.

Davidoff, Judith. "Child Care Programs Faces Huge Deficit; W-2 Problems Create Budget Challenge for Doyle." *The Capital Times*, January 24, 2007a, C1.

———. "Child Care Subsidies Get Boost; Joint Finance Panel Closes Funding Gap." *The Capital Times*, May 23, 2007b, C1.

"A Decade of Service," *The Welfarer* (July, 1961): 11.

Degiuli, Francesca. "A Job with No Boundaries: Home Eldercare Work in Italy." *European Journal of Women's Studies* 14 (2007): 193–207.

De la Rocha, Mercedes González. *The Resources of Poverty: Women and Survival in Mexico City*. Oxford, U.K., and Cambridge, MA: Blackwell, 1994.

Delp, Linda, and Katie Quan. "Homecare Worker Organizing in California: An Analysis of a Successful Strategy." *Labor Studies Journal* 27 (2002): 1–23.

Dembski. "Cleaning Up; Candidates for County Executive Address the Issues." *Milwaukee Journal Sentinel*, March 24, 2002, 01J.

D'Emilio, John. "Capitalism and Gay Identity." In *The Lesbian and Gay Studies Reader*, edited by Henry Abelove, Michele Aina Barale, and David M. Halperin, pp. 467–478. New York: Routledge, 1993.

Demleitner, Nora. "The Law at a Crossroads: The Construction of Migrant Women Trafficked into Prostitution." In *Global Human Smuggling: Comparative Perspectives*, edited by David Kyle and Rey Koslowski, pp. 257–293. Baltimore: Johns Hopkins University Press, 2001.

De Sa, Karen. "Health Care Would Be Hardest Hit by New Plan; Social Services." *San Jose Mercury News*, May 15, 2002, A17.

Devi, Mahasweta. *Breast Stories*. Calcutta: Seagull Books, 1997.

Devor, Holly [Aaron]. *FTM: Female-to-Male Transsexuals in Society*. Bloomington: Indiana University Press, 1997.

De Vries, Maggie. *Missing Sarah: A Vancouver Woman Remembers Her Vanished Sister*. Toronto: Penguin Canada, 2003.

Diamond, Timothy. "Nursing Homes as Trouble." In *Circles of Care, Work and Identity in Women's Lives*, edited by Emily K. Abel and Margaret K. Nelson, pp. 173–187. Albany: SUNY, 1990.

———. *Making Gray Gold: Narratives of Nursing Home Care*. Chicago: University of Chicago Press, 1992.

Dickson, Akeya. "There's No Business Like the Nail Business." *Nguoi Viet*, September 28, 2005. Available at: http://news.newamericamedia.org/news/view_article .html?article_id=4afb34e71cc7be9d530db2492070689c

Dill, Bonnie Thornton. "Our Mothers' Grief: Racial-Ethnic Women and the Maintenance of Families." *Journal of Family History* 13 (1988): 415–431.

———. *Across the Boundaries of Race and Class: An Exploration of Work and Family among Black Female Domestic Servants*. New York: Garland, 1994.

Domestic Workers United. *Home Is Where the Work Is: Inside New York's Domestic Work Industry.* New York: Domestic Workers United and DataCenter, July 2006. Retrieved February 10, 2010, from: www.datacenter.org/reports/homeiswherethe workis.pdf

Dorothy Bolden Thompson Collection. Auburn Avenue Research Library, Atlanta-Fulton Public Library, Atlanta, GA.

Downer, Lesley. *Women of the Pleasure Quarters.* New York: Broadway Books, 2001.

Dozier, Raine. "Beards, Breasts, and Bodies: Doing Sex in a Gendered World." *Gender & Society* 19 (2005): 297–316.

Ducey, Ariel. *Never Good Enough: Health Care Workers and the False Promise of Job Training.* Ithaca, NY: Cornell University Press, 2009.

Ducey, Ariel, Heather Gautney, and Dominic Wetzel. "Regulating Affective Labor: Communication Skills Training in the Health Care Industry." *Research in the Sociology of Work* 12 (March 2003): 49–72.

Duffy, Mignon. "Reproducing Labor Inequalities: Challenges for Feminists Conceptualizing Care at the Intersections of Gender, Race, and Class." *Gender and Society* 19 (2005): 66–82.

Duggan, Lisa. *The Twilight of Equality? Neoliberalism, Cultural Politics, and the Attack on Democracy.* Boston: Beacon Press, 2004.

Dworkin, Andrea. *Pornography: Men Possessing Women.* New York: Perigee, 1981.

Early Childhood Focus. "WI-Child care union forms," November 15, 2006. Retrieved on July 31, 2007, from: www.earlychildhoodfocus.org/modules.php?name=News& file=article&sid=3318

Eaton, Susan. "'The Customer is Always Interesting.'" In *Working in the Service Society,* edited by Cameron Macdonald and Carmen Sirianni, pp. 291–332. Philadelphia: Temple University Press, 1996.

Edelman, Lee. *No Future: Queer Theory and the Death Drive.* Durham, NC: Duke University Press, 2004.

Edwards, Susan. "Selling the Body, Keeping the Soul: Sexuality, Power, and the Theories and Realities of Prostitution." In *Body Matters: Essays on the Sociology of the Body,* edited by Sue Scott and David Morgan, pp. 89–104. London: The Falmer Press, 1993.

Ehrenreich, Barbara. "Maid to Order: The Politics of Other Women's Work." *Harper's Magazine,* April 2000: 59–70.

———. *Nickel and Dimed: On (Not) Getting by in America.* New York: Metropolitan Books, 2001.

Ehrenreich, Barbara, and Arlie Russell Hochschild, eds. *Global Woman: Nannies, Maids, and Sex Workers in the New Economy.* New York: Metropolitan Books, 2002.

Ellingwood, Susan. "The Collective Advantage." *The Gallup Management Journal,* September 2001. Retrieved on July 12, 2007, from: http://gmj.gallup.com/content/ default.aspx?ci=787&pg=1

England, Paula. "Emerging Theories of Care Work." *Annual Review of Sociology* 31 (2005): 381–399.

England, Paula, Michelle Budig, and Nancy Folbre. "Wages of Virtue: The Relative Pay of Care Work." *Social Problems* 49:4 (2002): 455–473.

England, Paula, and Nancy Folbre. "The Cost of Caring: Emotional Labor in the Service Economy." *Annals of the American Academy of Political and Social Sciences* 561 (1999): 39–51.

Erikson, Jane. "Doctors Mislabel Defects: Fetal Alcohol Misdiagnosed." *Arizona Daily Star*, November 27, 1995.

Evan B. Donaldson Adoption Institute. "Evan B. Donaldson Adoption Institute: International Adoption Facts," 2003. Retrieved on August 30, 2007, from www .adoptioninstitute.org/FactOverview/international.html

Experimental Chair on the Production of Subjectivity. "Call Center: The Art of Virtual Control." *Ephemera: Theory and Politics in Organization* 7:1 (2007): 133–138.

Fairclough, Terence John. "The Gay Community of Vancouver's West End: The Geography of a Modern Urban Phenomenon." Unpublished M.A. thesis, Department of Geography, University of British Columbia, 1985.

Faludi, Susan. *Backlash: The Undeclared War against American Women.* New York: Crown, 1991.

"Family, Inc.: Special Report." *BusinessWeek* online, November 10, 2003. Retrieved on July 10, 2007, from:www.businessweek.com/magazine/content/03_45/b3857002 .htm

Farley, Melissa. " 'Bad for the Body, Bad for the Heart': Prostitution Harms Women Even if Legalized or Decriminalized." *Violence against Women* 10:10 (2004): 1087–1125.

Farmer, Paul. *Pathologies of Power: Health, Human Rights and the New War on the Poor.* Los Angeles: University of California Press, 2004.

"Fast Action Urged on Hooker Problem." *Vancouver Sun*, May 14, 1982, A10.

Federal Register. "Employment of Domestic Service Employees, Record Keeping Definitions and General Interpretations," 39 (October 1, 1974): 35382–35385.

———. "Application of the Fair Labor Standards Act to Domestic Service, Extension to Domestic Service Employees," 40 (February 20, 1975): 7404–7407.

———. "Application of Fair Labor Standards Act to Domestic Service, Proposed Rule," 66 (January 19, 2001): 5481–5483.

———. "Application of the Fair Labor Standards Act to Domestic Service, Proposed Rule, Withdrawal," 67 (April 8, 2002): 16668.

Feinberg, Leslie. *Transgender Warriors: Making History from Joan of Arc to Dennis Rodman.* Boston: Beacon Press, 1997.

Fernandez, Manny. "Get Me to the Marriage Bureau on Time (45 Minutes Early)." *The New York Times*, July 10, 2007, B1, 5.

Férnandez, Roberto M., Emilio J. Castilla, and Paul Moore. "Social Capital at Work: Networks and Employment at a Phone Center." *American Journal of Sociology* 105 (2000): 1288–1356.

Fine, Janice. "Worker Centers and Immigrant Women,." In *The Sex of Class: Women Transforming American Labor,* edited by Dorothy Sue Cobble, pp. 221–230. Ithaca, NY: Cornell University Press, 2007.

Flanagan, Caitlin. "How Serfdom Saved the Women's Movement: Dispatches from the Nanny Wars." *Atlantic Monthly* 293 (March 2004): 109-28.

Flynn, Francis J. "How Much Should I Give and How Often? The Effects of Generosity and Frequency of Favor Exchange on Social Status and Productivity." *Academy of Management Journal* 46 (2003): 539–553.

Flynn, Patricia, and Mary Jo McConahay (Directors). *Discovering Dominga: A Survivor's Story.* Jaguar House Films, 2002.

Folbre, Nancy. "Nursebots to the Rescue? Immigration, Automation, and Care." *Globalizations* 3:3 (2006): 349–360.

Folbre, Nancy, and Jennifer Nelson. "For Love or Money—or Both?" *Journal of Economic Perspective* 14 (2000): 123–140.

Foner, Nancy. *The Caregiving Dilemma.* Los Angeles and Berkeley: University of California Press, 1994.

Fonseca, Claudia. "Transnational Connection and Dissenting Views: Intercountry Adoption in Brazil." In *International Adoption: Global Inequalities and the Circulation of Children,* edited by Diana Marre and Laura Briggs, pp.154–173. New York: NYU Press, 2009.

Foucault, Michel. *Discipline and Punish.* New York: Vintage Press, 1977.

———. *The History of Sexuality, Volume I.* New York: Vintage, 1980.

———. "Governmentality." In *The Foucault Effect,* edited by Graham Bruchell, Colin Gordon, and Peter Miller, pp. 87–104. Chicago: University of Chicago Press, 1991.

———. "17 March 1976." In *Society Must Be Defended,* edited by Mauro Bertani and Alessandro Fontana, pp. 239–264. New York: Picador Press, 2003.

Fraenkel, Marta. *Housekeeping Service for Chronic Patients.* New York: Welfare Council of New York, 1942.

Frank, Katherine. *G-Strings and Sympathy: Strip Club Regulars and Male Desire.* Durham, NC: Duke University Press, 2002.

Freeman, Joshua B. *Working-Class New York: Life and Labor Since World War II.* New York: The New Press, 2000.

Freeman, Lance. *There Goes the 'Hood: Views of Gentrification from the Ground Up.* Philadelphia: Temple University Press, 2006.

Freeman, Richard. *America Works: Critical Thoughts on the Exceptional U.S. Labor Market.* New York: Russell Sage Foundation, 2007.

Friend, Tad. "Letter From California: Naked Profits." *The New Yorker.* July 12, 2004.

Fung, K. K. "One Good Turn Deserves Another—Exchange of Favors within Organizations." *Social Science Quarterly* 72 (1991): 443–463.

Furillo, Jill. "From Patient Advocate to Social Advocate: The Work of Nursing." Keynote Address, Intimate Labors Conference, University of California, Santa Barbara, California, October 4, 2007.

Gall, Gregor. *Sex Worker Union Organizing: An International Study*. London: Palgrave Macmillan, 2006.

Geissinger, Steve. "$50 Million OK'd for Neediest Preschools." *Whittier Daily News*, September 7, 2006.

Giannarelli, Linda, and James Barsimantov. "Child Care Expenses of America's Families." Occasional paper number 40. *The Urban Institute* (December 1, 2000). Retrieved July 7, 2007, from: www.urban.org/url.cfm?ID=310028

Gilmore, Stephanie. "Strange Bedfellows: Building Feminist Coalitions around Sex Work in the 1970s." In *No Permanent Waves*, edited by Nancy Hewitt. New Brunswick, NJ: Rutgers University Press, 2010.

Glavin, Terry. "Hooker Defenders Tired of the Abuse." *Vancouver Sun*, January 16, 1984, A2.

Glenn, Evelyn Nakano. *Issei, Nisei, War Bride: Three Generations of Japanese American Women in Domestic Service*. Philadelphia: Temple University Press, 1986.

———. "From Servitude to Service Work: Historical Continuities in the Racial Division of Paid Reproductive Labor." *Signs* 18 (1992): 1–43.

———. "Social Constructions of Mothering: A Thematic Overview." In *Mothering: Ideology, Experience, and Agency*, edited by Evelyn Nakano Glenn, Grace Chang, and Linda Rennie Forcey, pp. 1–32. New York: Routledge, 1994.

———. "Creating a Caring Society." *Contemporary Sociology* 29:1 (January 2000): 84–94.

———. *Forced to Care: Dependency, Coercion, and Citizenship in Reproductive Labor*. Cambridge, MA: Harvard University Press, 2010.

Goad, Ann. "Prostitution Swells in the West End." *Province*, May 15, 1983, B1.

Goffman, Erving. *Stigma: Notes on the Management of Spoiled Identity*. New York: Simon & Schuster, 1963.

Goldberg, Gertrude. "Nonprofessional Helpers: The Visiting Homemakers." In *Community Action against Poverty: Readings from the Mobilization Experience*, edited by George A. Brage and Francis P. Purcell, pp. 175–207. New Haven, CT: College & University Press, 1967.

Golden, Janet. *Message in a Bottle: The Making of Fetal Alcohol Syndrome*. Cambridge, MA: Harvard University Press, 2005.

Gonnerman, Jennifer. "The Manicurists' Heroine: Susan Kim Took her Employers to Court, and Catalyzed a Movement for Salon-Workers' Rights." *New York Magazine* (2007). Retrieved on November 25, 2007, from: http://nymag.com/beauty/features/41281

Gonzalez de la Rocha, Mercedes. *The Resources of Poverty: Women and Survival in Mexico City*. Oxford, UK: Blackwell, 1994.

Gordon, Suzanne. *Nursing against the Odds: How Health Care Cost Cutting, Media Stereotypes, and Medical Hubris Undermine Nurses and Patient Care*. Ithaca, NY: Cornell University Press, 2005.

Gorman, Alexandra, and Philip O'Connor. *Glossed Over: Health Hazards Associated with Toxic Exposure in Nail Salons*. Missoula, MT: Women's Voices for the Earth, 2007.

"Governor says teen-age mothers will pay less for day care." The Associated Press State & Local Wire, August 22, 1998. Retrieved on May 5, 2007, from: www.lexisnexis.com

Grandin, Greg. *The Blood of Guatemala: A History of Race and Nation*. London: Duke University Press, 2000.

———. *The Last Colonial Massacre: Latin America in the Cold War*. Chicago and London: University of Chicago Press, 2004.

Graves, Scott. "California's Child Care and Development System. Budget Backgrounder: Making Dollars Make Sense." Sacramento: *California Budget Project*, 2005. Retrieved on September 1, 2007, from: www.cbp.org/pdfs/2005/0504bb_childcare.pdf

Green, Linda. *Fear as a Way of Life: Mayan Widows in Rural Guatemala*. New York: Columbia University Press, 1999.

Greenaway, Norma. "Government Rejects Decriminalization of Prostitution." *Ottawa Citizen*, February 7, 2008, 1.

Greenhouse, Steven. "At Nail Salons, Beauty Treatments Can Have a Distinctly Unglamorous Side." *New York Times*, August 19, 2007a, 22.

———. "Justices to Hear Case on Wages of Home Aides." *New York Times*, March 25, 2007b, 1, 31.

Grieco, Margaret. *Keeping It in the Family: Social Networks and Employment Chance*. London: Tavistock Publications, 1987.

Griffin, Susan. *The Book of the Courtesans: A Catalogue of their Virtues*. New York: Broadway Books, 2001.

Groves, Ethnie. 2005. "Governor Doyle Signs State Budget; Protects Education, Freezes Property Taxes." Governor's Office Press Release, July 25. Available at: www.wisgov .state.wi.us/journal_media_detail.asp?locid=19&prid=1241

Gubrium, Jaber F. *Living and Dying at Murray Manor*. New York: St. Martin's Press, 1975.

Guillermoprieto, Alma. "Letter from Lima." *New Yorker* October 29, 1990: 116–127.

Gupta, Akhil. "Narratives of Corruption: Anthropological and Fictional Accounts of the Indian State." *Ethnography* 6, 1 (2005): 5–34.

Guy-Sheftall, Beverly. *Words of Fire: An Anthology of African American Feminist Thought*. New York: New Press, 1995.

Guzmán, Genner Oswardo. "Casa Para Niños Pobres." Prensa Libre/Archivo de Recortajes CIRMA/31.4 Niñez, September 13, 1999.

Halberstam, Judith. *In a Queer Time and Place: Transgender Bodies, Subcultural Lives.* New York: New York University Press, 2005.

———. "Notes of Failure." Keynote address at the "Failure: Ethics and Aesthetics" Conference. University of California, Irvine. March 3, 2006.

"Harcourt Warns MPs on Hookers." *Province*, March 3, 1983, B1.

Hardt, Michael. "Affective Labor." *Boundary* 2 26:2 (1999): 89–100.

Hardt, Michael, and Antonio Negri. *Empire*. Cambridge, MA: Harvard University Press, 2000.

———. *Multitude: War and Democracy in the Age of Empire.* New York: Penguin Press, 2004.

Hardy, Kate. "Incorporating Sex Workers into the Argentine Labor Movement," *International Labor and Working-Class History 77* (Spring 2010).

Hardy, Lisa Allyn. "Sex in the City: Where to Learn about the Birds, the Bees, and Sexual Bliss." *San Francisco Bay Guardian*, May 23, 2001, 31.

Hart, Vivian. *Bound by Our Constitution: Women Workers, and the Minimum Wage.* Princeton, NJ: Princeton University Press, 1994.

Hartman, Chester, with Sarah Carnochan. *City for Sale: The Transformation of San Francisco.* Berkeley: University of California Press, 2002.

Harvey, David. *The Condition of Postmodernity: An Enquiry into the Origins of Cultural Change.* Cambridge, U.K.: Blackwell, 1990.

———. *A Brief History of Neoliberalism.* New York: Oxford University Press, 2005.

Hays, Sharon. *The Cultural Contradictions of Motherhood.* New Haven, CT: Yale University Press, 1996.

Held, David, and Anthony McGrew, eds. *The Global Transformations Reader: An Introduction to the Globalization Debate.* Cambridge, U.K.: Polity Press, 2000.

Held, Virginia. "Care and the Extension of Markets." *Hypatia* 17:2 (Spring 2002): 19–33.

Hendrix, Steven E. "Land Tenure in Guatemala." *GIS Law 7* (Winter 1997): 7–15.

Hennessy, Rosemary. *Profit and Pleasure: Sexual Identities in Late Capitalism.* New York: Routledge, 2000.

Herald staff. "Sex Bill Green Light for Prostitutes." *Calgary Herald*, June 24, 1983, 1.

Hershatter, Gail. *Dangerous Pleasures: Prostitution and Modernity in 20th-Century Shanghai.* Berkeley: University of California Press, 1997.

Herzenberg, Steve, John Alic, and Howard Wial, eds. *New Rules for a New Economy: Employment and Opportunity in Postindustrial America.* Ithaca, NY: Cornell University Press, 1998.

Higginbotham, Evelyn Brooks. "African American Women's History and the Metalanguage of Race." *Signs* 17 (Winter 1992): 251–274.

Hill, Suzette. "The Asian Influence." *Nails* Magazine. April 2007, 98–107.

Himmelweit, Susan. "Caring Labor." *ANNALS, AAPSS* 561:1 (January 1999): 27–38.

"Historic Election Will Improve Quality of Child Care for Thousands of Pennsylvania Working Families." *SEIU Press,* April 28, 2008. Retrieved on February 1, 2009, from: www.seiu.org/2008/04/20000-more-pennsylvania-child-care-providers-to-form-union.php

Hobson, Barbara Meil. *Uneasy Virtue: The Politics of Prostitution and the American Reform Tradition.* Chicago: University of Chicago Press, 1987.

Hochschild, Arlie Russell. *The Managed Heart: Commercialization of Human Feeling.* Berkeley: University of California Press, 1983.

———. *The Second Shift: Working Parents and the Revolution at Home.* New York: Viking, 1989.

———. *The Time Bind: When Work Becomes Home and Home Becomes Work.* New York: Metropolitan Books, 1997.

———. "Love and Gold." In *Global Woman: Nannies, Maids, and Sex Workers in the New Economy,* edited by Barbara Ehrenreich and Arlie Hochschild, pp. 15–31. New York: Henry Holt, 2002.

———. *The Commercialization of Intimate Life: Notes from Home and Work.* London: University of California Press, 2003.

Hodson, Randy. *Dignity at Work.* New York: Cambridge University Press, 2001.

Hollibaugh, Amber (interviewed by Leah Lilith Albrecht-Samarasihna). "Gender Warriors: An Interview with Amber Hollibaugh." In *Femme: Feminists, Lesbians, Bad Girls,* edited by Laura Harris and Elizabeth Crocker, pp. 210–222. New York: Routledge, 2002.

Holzman, Harold, and Sharon Pines. "Buying Sex: The Phenomenology of Being a John." *Deviant Behavior* 4 (1982): 89–116.

"Home Care Bill Would Undo DOL's 'Casual Basis' Interpretation." Occupational Health and Safety, September 24, 2007. Retrieved on August 6, 2008, from: www.ohsonline.com/articles/50525

"Homemakers Groups to Recognize Union." *New York Times,* May 16, 1967, 37.

Hondagneu-Sotelo, Pierrette. *Doméstica: Immigrant Workers Cleaning and Caring in the Shadows of Affluence.* London: University of California Press, 2001.

———. "Blowups and Other Unhappy Endings." In *Global Woman: Nannies, Maids, and Sex Workers in the New Economy,* edited by Barbara Ehrenreich and Arlie Hochschild, pp. 59–69. New York: Henry Holt, 2002.

Hondagneu-Sotelo, Pierrette, and Ernestine Avila. "I'm Here, but I'm There: The Meanings of Latina Transnational Motherhood." *Gender and Society* 11:5 (1997): 548–571.

Hoogvelt, Ankie. *Globalization and the Postcolonial World: The New Political Economy of Development.* Hampshire, U.K.: Macmillan, 1997.

"Hooker Ruling Appealed." *Vancouver Sun,* September 29, 1982, A10.

"Hookers Invited to Speak." *West Ender,* September 24, 1981, 13.

"Hookers Parade Over Proposals to Change Laws." *Vancouver Sun*, April 21, 1983, B6.

Hospital Council of Greater New York. *Organized Home Medical Care in New York City: A Study of Nineteen Programs*. Cambridge, MA: Harvard University Press, 1956.

Hoyme, H. E., L. Hauck, and D. J. Meyer. "Accuracy of Diagnosis of Alcohol Related Birth Defects by Non-Medical Professionals in a Native American Population." Paper presented at the David W. Smith Morphogenesis and Malformations Workshop, Mont-Tremblant, Québec, Canada, 1994.

Hubbard, Phil. *Sex and the City: Geographies of Prostitution in the Urban West*. Aldershot: Ashgate, 1999.

Hübinette, Tobias. "Comforting an Orphaned Nation: Representations of International Adoption and Adopted Koreans in Korean Popular Culture." Ph.D. Dissertation, Stockholm University, 2005.

Human Rights Watch. *Hidden in the Home: Abuse of Domestic Workers with Special Visas in the United States*. New York: Human Rights Watch, June 2001.

Hunter, Tera. *To 'Joy My Freedom: Southern Black Women's Lives and Labors after the Civil War.'* Cambridge, MA: Harvard University Press, 1997.

Huston, Margo. "W-2 Work or Else; County Falls Far Behind on W-2 Child-Care Aid; Officials Say Safeguards Delay Subsidies; Backlog May be Gone by January." *Milwaukee Journal Sentinel*, November 25, 1997, 1.

———. "Less than 40% of W-2 Families Use Child-care Subsidies. New Study Asks Businesses to Play Greater Role in Helping County's Children." *Milwaukee Journal Sentinel*, June 8, 1998a, 3.

———. "W-2 Work or Else; Payment Backlog Freezes Child Care; Some Centers, Stung by County's Delay, Reject Children of W-2 Clients." *Milwaukee Journal Sentinel*, April 20, 1998b, 1.

Ibarra, Maria. "Mexican Immigrant Women and the New Domestic Labor." *Human Organization* 59:4 (2000): 452–467.

———. "Emotional Proletarians in a Global Economy: Mexican Immigrant Women and Elder Care Work." *Urban Anthropology and Studies of Cultural Systems and World Economic Development*, 31:3–4 (2002): 317–350.

———. "The Tender Trap: Mexican Immigrant Women and the Ethics of Elder Care Work." *Aztlan: Journal of Chicano Studies* 28:2 (2003): 87–109.

In re Estate of Beecham, 378 N.W.2d. 800. (Minn. 1985.)

Instituto Latinoamericano para la Educación y comunicación. "Adoption and the Rights of the Child in Guatemala." Geneva: ILPEC for UNICEF, 2000, Retrieved on February 12, 2010, from: www.intern-kinderhulp.org/docs/ilpec-unicef_english _report_2000.pdf

Izquierdo, Marcelo. "Abuelas De La Plaza De Mayo: 25 Años De Búsqueda." *Proceso* (October 25, 2002).

Jacobs, Jane. *The Death and Life of Great American Cities*. New York: Random House, 1961.

Jenness, Valerie. "From Sex as Sin to Sex as Work: COYOTE and the Reorganization of Prostitution as a Social Problem." *Social Problems* 37:3 (August 1990): 403–420.

Jewish Family Service. "A Different and Economical Service to the Aged: Report on the Community Homemaker Service for the Aged Administered by the Jewish Family Service 1945–1950." New York, July 1950, pp. 2–3.

Jiwani, Jasmin, and Mary Lynn Young. "Missing and Murdered Women: Reproducing Marginality in News Discourse." *Canadian Journal of Communication* 31:4 (2006): 895–917.

Juffer, Jane. *At Home with Pornography: Women, Sex, and Everyday Life*. New York: New York University Press, 1998.

Kang, Miliann. *The Managed Hand: Race, Gender and the Body in Beauty Service Work*. Berkeley: University of California Press, 2010.

Kaplan, Temma, "Female Consciousness and Collective Action: The Case of Barcelona, 1910–1918." *Signs* 7 (1982): 545–566.

Katzman, David. *Seven Days a Week: Women and Domestic Service in Industrializing America*. Oxford, UK: Oxford University Press, 1978.

Kauffman, Sharon. *The Ageless Self: Sources of Meaning in Late Life*. Madison: University of Wisconsin Press, 1986.

Keller, Evelyn Fox. *A Feeling for the Organism: The Life and Work of Barbara McClintock*. San Francisco: W. H. Freeman, 1983.

Kelley, Robin D.G. "'We Are Not What We Seem': Rethinking Black Working-Class Opposition to the Jim Crow South." *Journal of American History* 80 (1993): 75–112.

———. *Race Rebels: Culture, Politics and the Black Working Class*. New York: Free Press, 1996.

Kellogg, Susan, and Steven Mintz. "Family Structure." In *Encyclopedia of American Social History, Volume III*, edited by Richard Williams, Peter W. Williams, and Mercy Kupiec Cayton, pp. 1925–1945. New York: Scribner, 1993.

Kempadoo, Kamala. "The Exotic Dancers Alliance: An Interview with Dawn Passar and Johanna Breyer." In *Global Sex Workers*, edited by Kamala Kempadoo and Jo Doezema, pp. 182–191. New York: Routledge, 1998.

———, ed. *Sun, Sex and Gold: Tourism and Sex Work in the Caribbean*. New York: Rowman and Littlefield Publishers, 1999.

Kempadoo, Kamala, and Jo Doezema, eds. *Global Sex Workers: Rights, Resistance, and Redefinition*. London: Routledge, 1998.

Kempadoo, Kamala, Jhoti Sanghera, and Banadana Pattanaik, eds. *Trafficking and Prostitution Reconsidered: New Perspectives on Migration, Sex Work, and Human Rights*. Boulder, CO: Paradigm Publishers, 2005.

Ketter, Joni. *A Seat at the Table: 50 Years of Progress*. Silver Spring, MD: American Nurses Association, 1996.

Keystone Research Center. "Unions and Child Care—A Brief Summary." Keystone Research Center, August 17, 2006. Retrieved on July 7, 2007, from www.wecanaeyc .org/uploads/media/Keystone_Research_Center-Brief_Summary_of_Unions_in _ChildCare.pdf

King, Deborah. "Multiple Jeopardy, Multiple Consciousness: The Context of a Black Feminist Ideology." *Signs* 14 (Autumn 1988): 42–72.

King, Russel, Tony Warnes, and Allan Williams. *Sunset Lives, British Retirement Migration to the Mediterranean*. Oxford and New York: Berg Press, 2000.

Kinsman, Gary. *The Regulation of Desire: Homo and Hetero Sexualities in Canada*. Montreal: Black Rose, 1996.

Kleinman, Arthur. *What Really Matters: Living a Moral Life Amidst Uncertainty*. New York: Oxford University Press, 2006.

Kleinman, Arthur, Veena Das, and Margaret Lock, eds. *Social Suffering*. Los Angeles: University of California Press, 1997.

Knorr Cetina, Karen. "Sociality with Objects: Social Relations in Postsocial Knowledge Societies." *Theory, Culture & Society* 14:4 (1997): 1–30.

Korczynski, Marek. "Understanding the Contradictory Lived Experience of Service Work: The Customer-Oriented Bureaucracy." In *Service Work: Critical Perspectives*, edited by Marek Korczynski and Cameron Macdonald, pp. 73–90. New York and London: Routledge, 2009.

Kornbluh, Felicia Ann. *The Battle for Welfare Rights: Politics and Poverty in Modern America*. Philadelphia: University of Pennsylvania Press, 2007.

Koven, Seth, and Sonya Michel. *Mothers of a New World: Maternalist Politics and the Origins of Welfare States*. New York: Routledge, 1993.

Kozol, Wendy. "Madonnas of the Fields: Photography, Gender, and 1930s Farm Relief." *Genders* 2 (1988): 1–26.

Krauthammer, Charles. "Crack Babies Forming Biological Underclass." *St. Louis Post-Dispatch*, July 30, 1989, 3B.

Lafer, Gordon. *The Job Training Charade*. Ithaca, NY: Cornell University Press, 2002.

Lara, Julio F. "Niños Son Vuilnerables a Problemas Sociales." Prensa Libre/Archivo de Recortajes CIRMA/31.4 Niñez, January 19, 1998.

Larra, Myriam. "Arzú Instó a Los Niños De Guatemala Cumplir Con Sus Deberes Familiares, Escolares Y Nacionales." Prensa Libre/Archivo de Recortajes CIRMA/31.4 Niñez, October 2, 1996.

Larrabee, Mary Jeanne, ed. *An Ethic of Care*. New York and London: Routledge, 1993.

Latour, Bruno. "How to Talk about the Body? The Normative Dimension of Science Studies." *Body and Society* 10: 2–3 (2004): 205–229.

Laumann, Edward O., John H. Gagnon, Robert T. Michael, and Stuart Michaels. *The Social Organization of Sexuality: Sexual Practices in the United States*. Chicago: University of Chicago Press, 1994.

Layzer, Emily. *Individual Providers in Home Care: Their Practice, Problems, and Implications in the Delivery of Homemaker-Home Health Aide Services.* New York: National HomeCaring Council, 1981.

Lazzarato, Maurizio. "Immaterial Labor." In *Radical Thought in Italy*, edited by Paolo Virno and Michael Hardt, pp. 133–150. Minneapolis: University of Minnesota Press, 1996.

Lechner, Frank J., and John Boli, eds. *The Globalization Reader.* Oxford, U.K.: Blackwell, 2000.

Lee, Charles T. "Tactical Citizenship: Domestic Workers, the Remainders of Home, and Undocumented Citizen Participation in the Third Space of Mimicry." *Theory and Event* 9:3 (2006). Retrieved on February 10, 2010, from: http://muse.jhu.edu .proxy.library.ucsb.edu:2048/journals/theory_and_event/v009/9.3lee.html

Lee, Chisun. "Women Raise the City—Domestic Disturbances: The Help Set Out to Help Themselves." *The Village Voice*, March 12–19, 2002.

Lee, Jennifer. "Former Nail Salon Owner Files for Bankruptcy." New York Times, June 17, 2009. Retrieved from: http://cityroom.blogs.nytimes.com/2009/06/17/former-nail-salon-owner-files-for-bankruptcy/#more-48705

Lefebvre, Henri. *The Production of Space.* Cambridge, MA: Blackwell Publishers, 1991.

"Legislative Changes May Make Child Care Subsidies More Available." *Wisconsin State Journal*, April 25, 2000. Retrieved on May 10, 2007, from: www.lexisnexis.com

Leidner, Robin. *Fast Food, Fast Talk: Service Work and the Routinization of Everyday Life.* Berkeley: University of California Press, 1993.

Leigh, Carol. "Inventing Sex Work." In *Whores and Other Feminists*, edited by Jill Nagle, pp. 226–231. New York: Routledge, 1997.

Lerner, Gerda. *Black Women in White America: A Documentary History.* New York: Vintage Books, 1972.

Lerner, Stephen. "Global Unions: A Solution to Labor's Worldwide Decline." *New Labor Forum* 16 (2007): 23–37.

"Letters," *New York*, August 16, 2004, 5.

Lev, Elianna. "For Those Selling Sex, Little Has Changed." *Globe and Mail*, December 31, 2007, A8.

Lever, Janet, and Deanne Dolnick. "Clients and Call Girls: Seeking Sex and Intimacy." In *Sex for Sale: Prostitution, Pornography, and the Sex Industry*, edited by Ronald Weitzer, pp. 85–102. New York: Routledge, 2000.

Lever, Janet, Gail Zellman, and Stephen J. Hirschfeld. "Office Romance: Are the Rules Changing?" *Across the Board* (March/April 2006): 33–41.

Levitt, Steven D., and Dubner, Stephen J. *Freakonomics: A Rogue Economist Explores the Hidden Side of Everything.* New York: Harper Collins Publisher, 2006.

Levitz, Stephanie. "Group of Sex Workers Seeking to Go Legit." *Globe and Mail*, March 24, 2007, 3.

Ley, David. "Liberal Ideology and the Postindustrial City." *Annals of the Association of American Geographers* 70:2 (1980): 238–258.

Liepe-Levinson, Katherine. *Strip Show: Performances of Gender and Desire.* London: Routledge, 2002.

Liga Guatemalteca de Higiéne Mental. "Todos Por el Reencuentro." (2008). Retrieved on June 4, 2008, from: www.ligatpr.org

Lim, Lin L. *The Sex Sector: The Economic and Social Bases of Prostitution in Southeast Asia.* Geneva: International Labour Office, 1998.

Lock, Margaret. "Displacing Suffering: The Reconstruction of Death in North America." In *Social Suffering,* edited by Arthur Kleinman, Veena Das, and Margaret Lock, pp. 207–244. Berkeley: University of California Press, 1997.

Live Nude Girls UNITE! Written and directed by Julia Query and Vicky Funari; produced by Julia Query and John Montoya. First Run Features, 2000.

Loe, Meika. "Dildos in Our Toolboxes: The Production of Sexuality at a Pro-Feminist Sex Toy Store." *Berkeley Journal of Sociology* 43 (1998): 97–137.

Lopez, Steve. "Hold the Pickles, Please: This Drive-Through Has a New Menu Item." *Time,* October 2, 2000, 6.

Lopez, Steven. *Reorganizing the Rust Belt: An Inside Study of the American Labor Movement.* Berkeley: University of California Press, 2004.

Love, Heather. *Feeling Backward: Loss and the Politics of Queer History.* Cambridge, MA: Harvard University Press, 2007.

Lowman, John. "Violence at the Outlaw Status of (Street) Prostitution in Canada." *Violence Against Women* 6:9 (2000): 987–1011.

Luker, Kristin. *Abortion and the Politics of Motherhood.* Berkeley: University of California Press, 1984.

Luong, Hy Van, ed. *Postwar Vietnam: Dynamics of a Transforming Society (Indochina Unit).* Oxford, U.K.: Bowman and Littlefield Publishers, 2003.

Lyon, Dawn. "The Organization of Care Work in Italy: Gender and Migrant Labor in the New Economy." *Indiana Journal of Global Legal Studies* 13:1 (2006): 227–242.

Macdonald, Cameron, and David Merrill. "'It Shouldn't Have to Be a Trade': Recognition and Redistribution in Care Work Advocacy." *Hypatia* 17 (2002): 67–83.

Mackie, John. "Anti-Hooker Group Thanks Friends." *Vancouver Sun,* August 30, 1984, A3.

MacKinnon, Ian, and Adam Piore. "The Other Aids Crisis." *Newsweek,* June 11, 2001.

Marcucci, Michele R. "Davis Reinstates Threatened Funds to Child-Care Program." *Alameda Times-Star,* December 6, 2001, 1.

———. "Child Care Subsidy Central to Funding Debate; Child Care Subsidy a Necessity for Working Poor." *Tri-Valley Herald,* May 27, 2002.

Marks, Stephen R. "Intimacy in the Public Realm: The Case of Co-Workers." *Social Forces* 72 (1994): 843–858.

Martin, Emily. *The Woman in the Body: A Cultural Analysis of Reproduction*. Boston, MA: Beacon Press, 1987.

———. *The Woman in the Body: A Cultural Analysis of Reproduction*, 2nd ed. Boston: Beacon, 1992.

———. "The Pharmaceutical Person." *BioSocieties* 1 (2006): 273–287.

Martinez-Buján, Raquel. *Bienestar y Cuidados: El Oficio del Cariño: Las Mujeres Inmigrantes y Mayores Nativos*. Ph.D. Dissertation, University of Coruña, Spain, 2007.

Massumi, Brian. *Parables for the Virtual: Movement, Affect, Sensation*. Durham, NC: Duke University Press, 2002.

———. "Fear (the Spectrum Said)." *Positions* 13:1 (2005): 31–48.

Mayoral Fonds. City of Vancouver Archives. Vancouver, Canada.

McClintock, Anne. *Imperial Leather: Race, Gender and Sexuality in the Colonial Contest*. New York: Routledge, 1995.

McCombs, Brady. "July Is Deadliest Month for Illegal-Entrant Women." *Arizona Daily Star*, August 3, 2007.

McDonald, Cameron Lynne, and David A. Merrill. "'It Shouldn't Have to Be a Trade': Recognition and Redistribution in Care Work Advocacy." *Hypatia* 17:2 (2002): 67–83.

MacDonald, Mary Lehman, "About AFT Healthcare." Retrieved on February 2, 2010, from: http://aft.org/yourwork/healthcare/about.cfm

McEachern, C. J. S. C. [Allan]. *Attorney General of British Columbia v. Couillard et al.* Judgment July 4, 1984, in *British Columbia Law Reports Vol. 59, Part I*. Calgary, Alta: Carswell Legal Publications, 1985.

McGeehan, Patrick. "For New York, Big Job Growth Is in Home Care." *New York Times*, May 25, 2007, A1.

McGuire, Gail M. "Intimate Work: A Typology of Social Support That Workers Provide to Their Network Members." *Work and Occupations* 34 (2007): 125–147.

McLaughlin, Emma, and Nicola Kraus. *The Nanny Diaries: A Novel*. New York: St. Martin's Press, 2002.

McMartin, Pete. "Can New Bylaw Hook the Hookers?" *Vancouver Sun*, March 14, 1984, A5.

Meagher, Gabrielle. "What Can We Expect from Paid Carers?" *Politics and Society* 34:1 (2006): 33–54.

Medical Care Administration Branch, Division of Community Health Services. *Directory of Homemaker Services, 1963: Homemaker Agencies in the United States with Selected Data*, Public Health Service Publication No. 928, Revised 1964. Washington, DC: U.S. Government Printing Office, 1964.

Menjívar, Cecilia. "The Ties That Heal: Guatemalan Immigrant Women's Networks and Medical Treatment." *International Migration Review* 36 (2002): 437–466.

Menyasz, Peter. "West End Hooker Furore Heard All the Way to Ottawa." *Vancouver Sun*, March 25, 1982, A2.

Mettler, Suzanne. *Dividing Citizens: Gender and Federalism in the New Deal Public Policy*. Ithaca, NY: Cornell University Press, 1998.

Meyerhoff, Barbara. *Number Our Days*. New York: Simon and Schuster, 1978.

Middlekauff, Tracey. "Maid in America." *Gotham Gazette Magazine*. Fall 2002. Available at: www.gothamgazette.com/commentary/46.middlekauff.shtml

Milfred, Scott. "Vetoes Called a Setback for W-2 Participants." *Milwaukee State Journal*, November 2, 1999, 3B.

Milkman, Ruth, ed. *Women, Work and Protest: A Century of U.S. Women's Labor History*. Boston: Routledge & Kegan Paul, 1985.

———. *L.A. Story: Immigrant Workers and the Future of the U.S. Labor Movement*. New York: Russell Sage, 2006.

Milkman, Ruth, and Rachel E. Dwyer. "Growing Apart: The 'New Economy' and Job Polarization in California, 1992–2000." In *The State of California Labor 2002*, edited by Ruth Milkman, pp. 3–36. Berkeley and Los Angeles: University of California Institute for Labor and Employment, 2003.

Milkman, Ruth, Ellen Reese, and Benita Roth. "The Macrosociology of Paid Domestic Labor." *Work and Occupations* 25:4 (November 1998): 483–510.

Mills, C. Wright. *White-Collar: The American Middle-Classes*. New York: Oxford University Press, 1951.

Mind If I Call You Sir? A Video Documentary on Latina Butches and Latino. Produced by Karla Rosales. StickyGirl Productions, 2004.

Mohanty, Chandra Talpade. *Feminism without Borders: Decolonizing Theory, Practicing Solidarity*. Durham, NC: Duke University Press, 2003.

Molina, Joshua, and Scott Hadley. "Editorial." *Santa Barbara News Press*. September 24, 2000, A14.

Mor, Vincent, Jacqueline Zinn, Joseph Angelelli, Moan M. Teno, and Susan C. Miller. "Driven to Tiers: Socioeconomic and Racial Disparities in the Quality of Nursing Home Care." *Milbank Quarterly* 82:2 (2004): 227–256.

Morlock, Maud. *Homemaker Services: History and Bibliography*. Washington, DC: U.S. Government Printing Office, 1964.

Mukerjee, Madhusree. "The Prostitutes' Union." *Scientific American*, April 2006, Retrieved from: www.scientificamerican.com/article.cfm?id=the-prostitutes-union

Munoz, Jose Esteban. *Disidentifications: Queers of Color and the Performance of Politics*. Minneapolis: University of Minnesota Press, 1999.

Nadasen, Premilla. "'Sista' Friends and Other Allies: Domestic Workers United and Coalition Politics." In *New Social Movements in the African Diaspora: Challenging Global Apartheid*, ed. Leith Mullings, pp. 285–298. New York: Palgrave Macmillan, 2009.

Nails Magazine. "Regional Analysis, Nail Techs and Nail Salons, 2006 and 2007," in *NAILS Big Book 2007–2008*. Torrance, CA: Nails Magazine, 2008. Retrieved from: www.nailsmag.com/pdfView.aspx?pdfName=NAILS20072008stats.pdf

National Domestic Workers Union (NDWU) Papers. Southern Labor Archives, Pullen Library, Georgia State University, Atlanta, GA.

National Research Council Staff. *Elder Mistreatment: Aging, Abuse, and Neglect in an Aging America*. Washington, DC: The National Academies, 2002.

National Women's Law Center. "Child Care Providers: Increasing Compensation Raises Women's Wages and Improves Child Care Quality." Washington, DC: National Women's Law Center, March 2008. Retrieved from: www.nwlc.org/pdf/ProvidersApril2008.pdf

Neville, Helen A., and Jennifer Hamer, "'We Make Freedom': An Exploration of Revolutionary Black Feminism." *Journal of Black Studies* 31:4 (March 2001): 437–461.

Newman, Zoë. "Whitening the Inner City: The Containment of Toronto's Degenerate Spaces and the Production of Respectable Subjects." Ph.D. dissertation, University of Toronto, 2002.

New York Academy of Medicine (NYAM). 1940–1970. Archives. New York City, New York.

New York City Law Department, Office of the Corporation Counsel. "U.S. Supreme Court Takes Case Impacting City Programs Providing Long-Term Home Health Care." January 8, 2007. Retrieved on April 17, 2007, from: nyc.gov/law

New York State. Department of Social Services, Metropolitan Regional Audit Office. "Audit of Home Attendant Services, New York City, Department of Social Services, #76-835-S-029-58, August." McMillan Library, New York City, 1977.

New York State. Division of Licensing Services. "Licensing of Nail Specialty, Natural Hair Styling, Esthetics and Cosmetology," Appearance Enhancement Law, Article 27, Sections 400–417 of the General Business Law. Albany: State of New York Department of State, July 5, 1994.

New York State Office of the Comptroller, Bureau of Audit and Control. "Report on the Quality of Care and Operating Practices of the Home Attendant Program: Summary of Significant Observations, October 25." Albany: New York State, 1976. Available from New York State Library.

New York Times. "Editorial: Lilly and Evelyn," January 29, 2010.

"No Se Protege a Los Niños." Prensa Libre/Archivo de Recortajes CIRMA/31.4 Niñez, October 13 1996.

Norberg, Kathryn. "Prostitution in Eighteenth Century Paris: Pages from a Madam's Notebook." In *Prostitution: On Whores, Hustlers, and Johns*, edited by James E. Elias, Vern L. Bullough, Veronica Elias, Gwen Brewer, and Joycelyn Elders, pp. 61–80. Amherst, MA: Prometheus Books, 1998.

Not a Love Story: A Film about Pornography. Directed by Bonnie Sherr Klein. Canadian National Film Board, 1981.

Nugent, Mary. "Parenthood Widens His World: In Inner View, Single Dad Mitchell White Learns about Support, and Lends a Hand Too." *Chico-Enterprise-Record*, July 24, 2006.

Nussbaum, Emily. "A Stranger's Touch." *New York Magazine*, November 25, 2007. Retrieved from: http://nymag.com/beauty/features/41280/

O'Callaghan, Sean. *The Yellow Slave Trade*. London: Anthony Blond, 1968.

"Officials of a Welfare Agency Discuss Union with Ginsberg." *New York Times*, May 9, 1967, 36.

Oishi, Nana. *Women in Motion*. Stanford, CA: Stanford University Press, 2005.

Olsen, Richard. "Families under the Microscope: Parallels between the Young Carers Debate of the 1990s and the Transformation of Childhood in the Late Nineteenth Century." *Children & Society* 14 (2000): 384–394.

Opdycke, Sandra. *No One Was Turned Away: The Role Of Public Hospitals in New York City Since 1900*. New York: Oxford University Press, 1999.

Opperman, Martin. *Sex Tourism and Prostitution: Aspects of Leisure, Recreation, and Work*. New York: Cognizant Communication Corporation, 1998.

"Opposition to Prop. 82 Duplicitous." *Inside Bay Area*, June 3, 2006. Retrieved on September 8, 2007, from: www.lexisnexis.com

O'Reilly, Karen. *The British on the Costa Del Sol: Transnational Identities and Local Communities*. New York and London: Routledge, 2000.

Orleck, Annelise. *Storming Caesars Palace: How Black Mothers Fought Their Own War on Poverty*. Boston: Beacon Press, 2005.

Ortner, Sherry B. *Life and Death on Mount Everest*. Princeton, NJ: Princeton University Press, 1999.

Ousten, Rick. "New Court Ruling Clears Hookers Out of West End." *Vancouver Sun*, July 5, 1984, A12.

Ovando, Olga López "Adopción Ayuda Al Niños: Sandoval." Prensa Libre/Archivo de Recortajes CIRMA/31.4 Niñez (October 24, 1999).

Oxfam. "Dumping without Borders." Briefing paper, August 2003.

Palmer, Phyllis. *Domesticity and Dirt: Housewives and Domestic Servants in the United States, 1920–1945*. Philadelphia: Temple University Press, 1989.

———. "Outside the Law: Agricultural and Domestic Workers Under the Fair Labor Standards Act." *Journal of Policy History* 7 (1995), 419–440.

Parreñas, Rhacel Salazar. "Migrant Filipina Domestic Workers and the International Division of Reproductive Labor." *Gender & Society* 14:4 (August 2000): 560–580.

———. *Servants of Globalization: Women, Migration and Domestic Work*. Palo Alto, CA: Stanford University Press, 2001.

———. "The Care Crisis in the Philippines: Children and Transnational Families in the New Global Economy." In *Global Woman: Nannies, Maids, and Sex Workers in the New Economy*, edited by Barbara Ehrenreich and Arlie Hochschild, pp. 39–55. New York: Henry Holt, 2002.

———. *Children of Global Migration: Transnational Families and Gendered Woes.* Stanford, CA: Stanford University Press, 2005.

Parrott, Sharon, and Jennifer Mezey. "New Child Care Resources Are Needed to Prevent the Loss of Child Care Assistance for Hundreds of Thousands of Children in Working Families." Center for Law and Social Policy/Center for Budget and Policy Priorities (July 15, 2003). Retrieved on July 1, 2007, from: www.cbpp.org/7-15-03tanf.htm

Pateman, Carole. *The Sexual Contract.* Stanford, CA: Stanford University Press, 1988.

Pear, Robert. "Unreported Abuse Found at Nursing Home." *New York Times,* March 2, 2002. Available at: www.nytimes.com/2002/03/03/us/unreported-abuse-found-at-nursing-homes.html?pagewanted=1

Peiss, Kathy. *Cheap Amusements: Working Women and Leisure in the Turn-of-the-Century New York.* New York: Temple University Press, 1986.

Perlmutter, Emanuel. "The Welfare Tangle." *New York Times,* January 25, 1965, 19.

———. "City and Welfare Unions Agree on Cut of 9,000 Jobs." *New York Times,* February 10, 1969, 79.

Pettinger, Lynne. "Friends, Relations and Colleagues: The Blurred Boundaries of the Workplace." *Sociology Review* 53:2 (2005): 37–55.

Pivot Legal Society. "Voices For Dignity: A Call to End the Harms Caused by Canada's Sex Trade Laws." 2004. Available at: http://pivotlegal.org/publications/reports/htm

———. "Beyond Decriminalization: Sex-Work, Human Rights and a New Framework for Legal Reform." 2006. Available at: http://pivotlegal.org/publications/reports/htm

Plantz, Margaret. "Indian Child Welfare: A Status Report: Final Report of the Survey of Indian Child Welfare and Implementation of the Indian Child Welfare Act and Section 428 of the Adoption Assistance and Child Welfare Act of 1980." Washington, DC: U.S. Department of the Interior, 1988.

Pogrebin, Abigail. "Nanny Scam." *New York,* July 26–August 2, 2004.

Poole, Mary. *The Segregated Origins of Social Security: African Americans and the Welfare State.* Chapel Hill: University of North Carolina Press, 2006.

"Poor Teens to Get Free Day Care." *Wisconsin State Journal,* June 9, 1998. Retrieved on May 5, 2007, from: www.lexisnexis.com

Portes, Alejandro, and Robert D. Manning. "The Immigrant Enclave: Theory and Empirical Examples." In *Comparaive Ethnic Relations,* edited by Susan Olzak and Joanne Nagl, pp. 47–68. New York: Academic Press, 1986.

Pratt, Geraldine. "Abandoned Women and the Spaces of Exception." *Antipode* 37 (2005): 1052–1078.

Pred, Allan. *Even In Sweden: Racisms, Racialized Spaces, and the Geographical Imagination.* Berkeley: University of California Press, 2000.

Rafkin, Louise. *Other People's Dirt: A Housecleaner's Curious Adventures*. Chapel Hill, NC: Algonquin Books, 1998.

Raine, George. "Nurses Unions to Combine." *San Francisco Chronicle*, February 19, 2009, C-1.

Ramberg, Lucinda. "Given to the Goddess: Devadasis, Kinship, Ethics." Ph.D. Dissertation, University of California at Berkeley, 2006.

Ray, Raka, and Seemin Qayum. *Cultures of Servitude: Modernity, Domesticity, and Class in India*. Stanford, CA: Stanford University Press, 2009.

Raymond, Janice. *The Transsexual Empire: the Making of the She-Male*. New York: Teachers College Press, 1994.

Razack, Sherene H. "Gendered Racial Violence and Spatialized Justice." In *Race, Space and the Law: Unmapping a White Settler* Society, edited by Sherene H. Razack, pp. 121–156. Toronto: University of Toronto Press, 2002.

Repak, Terry. *Waiting on Washington: Central American Workers in the Nation's Capital*. Philadelphia: Temple University Press, 1995.

Rio, Cecilia. "On the Move: African American Women's Paid Domestic Labor and the Class Transition to Independent Commodity Production." *Rethinking Marxism* 17: 4 (October 2005): 489–510.

Ritzer, George. *The McDonaldization of Society,*. Thousand Oaks, CA: Pine Forge Press, 1993.

Rivchin, Julie Yates. "Colloquium: Building Power among Low-Wage Immigrant Workers: Some Legal Considerations for Organizing Structures and Strategies." 28 *N.Y.U. Review of Law and Social Change* 397 (2004).

Roberts, Dorothy E. *Killing the Black Body: Race, Reproduction, and the Meaning of Liberty*. New York: Pantheon, 1997.

Roberts, Nickie. *Whores in History: Prostitution in Western Society*. London: Harper Collins, 1992.

Rollins, Judith. *Between Women: Domestics and Their Employers*. Philadelphia: Temple University Press, 1985.

Romero, Mary. *Maid in the U.S.A.* New York: Routledge, 1992.

Rondeau, Kris. "The Future of HUCTW." Talk presented at the Women Work Symposium, University of Southern Maine, Portland, 18 September 1998.

Rosen, Ruth. *The Lost Sisterhood: Prostitution in America, 1900–1918*. Baltimore: Johns Hopkins University Press, 1982.

Ross, Becki L. *Burlesque West: Showgirls, Sex, and Sin in Postwar Vancouver*. Toronto: University of Toronto Press, 2009.

Rubbo, Anna, and Michael Taussig. "Up off Their Knees: Servanthood in Southwest Colombia." *Latin American Perspectives* 10:4 (Autumn 1983): 5–23.

Rule, Sheila. "Couples Taking Unusual Paths for Adoption." *New York Times*, July 26, 1984.

Sahlins, Marshall. *Apologies to Thucydides: Understanding History as Culture*. Chicago: University of Chicago Press, 2004.

Salmi, Brian. "Hooker History: 125 Years of Illegal Sex and the City." *Georgia Straight* 34:1715 (November 2–9, 2000): 17–19, 21.

Samar Collective. "One Big, Happy Community? Class Issues Within South Asian Homes." *Samar* 4 (Winter 1994): 10–15.

Sanchez, Lisa. "Boundaries of Legitimacy: Sex, Violence, Citizenship, and Community in a Local Sexual Economy." *Law and Social Inquiry* 22:3 (1997): 543–580.

———. "The Global E-rotic Subject, the Ban, and the Prostitute-Free Zone: Sex Work and the Theory of Differential Exclusion." *Environment and Planning D: Society and Space* 22 (2004): 861–883.

Sandoval, Julieta. "Nuevo Código Del Niños a Discusión." Prensa Libre/Archivo de Recortajes CIRMA/31.4 Niñez. October 25, 2000.

Sassen, Saskia. *Globalization and Its Discontents: Essays on the New Mobility of People and Money*. New York: The New Press, 1998.

———. *Cities in a World Economy*. Thousand Oaks, CA: Pine Forge Press, 2000.

———. *The Global City: New York, London, Tokyo*. Princeton, NJ: Princeton University Press, 2001.

Savage, Lydia. "Changing Work, Changing People: A Conversation with Union Organizers at Harvard University and the University of Massachusetts Memorial Medical Center." In *The Sex of Class: Women Transforming American Labor*, edited by Dorothy Sue Cobble, pp. 181–216. Ithaca, NY: Cornell University Press, 2007.

Savner, Steve, Julie Strawn, and Mark Greenberg. "TANF Reauthorization: Opportunities to Reduce Poverty by Improving Employment Outcomes." New York: Center for Law and Social Policy, January 2002. Retrieved on March 11, 2002, from: www.clasp.org/publications/tanf_reauthorization_opportunities_to_reduce.pdf

Schneider, Pat, and David Callender. "Higher Child Care Co-Pay Under W-2 Threatens Centers." *Capital Times*, March 27, 1998: 2A. Retrieved on May 5, 2007, from: www.lexisnexis.com

Schor, Juliet. *The Overworked American*. New York: Basic Books, 1992.

Schover, L. R., S. A. Rothmann, and R. L. Collins. "The Personality and Motivation of Semen Donors: A Comparison with Oocyte Donors." *Human Reproduction* 7 (1992): 575–579.

Schroedel, Jean Reith, and Paul Peretz. "A Gender Analysis of Policy Formation: The Case of Fetal Abuse." *Journal of Health Politics, Policy and Law* 19 (1994): 335–360.

Schulman, Karen, and Helen Blank. "State Child Care Assistance Policies 2008: Too Little Progress for Children and Families." Washington, DC: National Women's Law Center, September 2008. Retrieved on January 19, 2009, from: www.aecf .org/~/media/PublicationFiles/statechildcare.pdf

Schultz, Vicki. "The Sanitized Workplace." *112 The Yale Law Journal* 2061 (2003).

Scott, James C. *Weapons of the Weak: Everyday Forms of Peasant Resistance*. New Haven, CT: Yale University Press, 1985.

Seidman, Steven. *Romantic Longings*. New York: Routledge, 1991.

Seifer, Nancy. *Nobody Speaks for Me! Self-Portraits of American Working Class Women*. New York: Simon and Schuster, 1976.

SEIU Kids First Maryland. "We Won the Freedom to Form a Union!" SEIU Kids First Maryland, July 3, 2007. Retrieved on September 13, 2007, from: www .kidsfirstmaryland.org/news/2007/7/3/we-won-the-freedom-to-form-our-union .html

Selman, Peter. "The Movement of Children for International Adoption; Developments and Trends in Receiving States and States of Origin, 1998–2004." In *International Adoption: Global Inequalities and the Circulation of Children*, edited by Diana Marre and Laura Briggs, pp. 32–51. New York: NYU Press, 2009.

Sengers, Phoebe, Kirsten Boehner, Michael Mateas, and Geri Gay. "The Disenchantment of Affect." *Personal and Ubiquitous Computing* 12:5 (2008): 347–358.

Sensenbrenner, Lee. "State Day Care Aid Limits Affect Many; Council Members Call For New Rate." *The Capital Times*, April 5, 2006, C4.

Serano, Julia. *Whipping Girl: A Transsexual Woman on Sexism and the Scapegoating of Femininity*. Emeryville, CA: Seal Press, 2007.

Service and Office Retail Workers Union of Canada. Papers. Rare Books and Special Collections. University of British Columbia.

Service Employees International Union (SEIU). "A Closer Look Inside Labor's Fastest-Growing Union," Retrieved on February 2, 2010, from: http://www.seiu.org.

Shapiro, Peter, ed. *A History of National Service in America*. 1994. Retrieved on July 29, 2007, from: www.academy.umd.edu/publications/NationalService/senior_service .htm

Sherman, Rachel. *Class Acts*. Berkeley: University of California Press, 2007.

Shick, Robert Alan. "The Contracting-Out of Local Government Services: New York City Home Health Care." Ph.D. Dissertation, New York University, 1989.

Shinjuku Boys. Directed by Kim Longinotto and Jano Williams. Twentieth Century Vixens, 1994.

Smith, Avril. "Over 2,000 Maine child care providers to vote in first-ever union Election." Press Release, SEIU (September 6, 2007). Retrieved on September 13, 2007, from: www.seiu.org/media/pressreleases.cfm?pr_id=1480&bSuppressLayout=1

Smith, Dorothy E. *The Everyday World as Problematic: Toward a Feminist Sociology*. Toronto: University of Toronto Press, 1987.

Smith, Neil. *The New Urban Frontier: Gentrification and the Revanchist City*. New York: Routledge, 1996.

———. "Giuliani Time: The Revanchist 1990s." *Social Text* 57 (1998): 1–20.

Smith, Peggie R. "Organizing the Unorganizable: Private Paid Household Workers and Approaches to Employee Representation." *North Carolina Law Review 79* (2000): 45–110.

———. "Caring for Paid Caregivers: Linking Quality Child Care with Improved Working Conditions." *University of Cincinnati Law Review 73* (2004): 399–431.

Snitow, Ann. "Mass Market Romance: Pornography for Women Is Different." In *Powers of Desire: The Politics of Sexuality*, edited by Ann Snitow, Christine Stansell, and Sharon Thompson, pp. 245-63. New York: Monthly Review Press, 1983.

Solnit, Rebecca, and Susan Schwartzenberg. *Hollow City: The Seige of San Francisco and the Crisis of American Urbanism*. London: Verso, 2000.

Sorrentino, Constance. "The Changing Family in International Perspective." *Monthly Labor Review* (March, 1990): 41–58.

Special Committee on Pornography and Prostitution (The Fraser Committee). *Report on the Special Committee on Pornography and Prostitution, Vols. I and II*. Ottawa: Department of Supply and Services, 1985.

Spivak, Gayatri Chakravorty. "Scattered Speculations on the Question of Value." *Diacritics* 15:4 (Winter 1985): 73–93.

Social Service Employees Union (SSEU) Members for a Militant Caucus. Records. M86-189, MAD 4/Unprocessed SC File. State Historical Society of Wisconsin, Archives, Madison, WI.

Statistical Abstracts of the United States. Washington, DC: U.S. Government Printing Office, 1975.

Steans, Jill. "The Gender Dimension." In *The Global Transformations Reader: An Introduction to the Globalization Debate*, edited by David Held and Anthony McGrew, pp. 455-62. Cambridge, U.K.: Polity Press, 2000.

Stearns, Peter N. *Anxious Parents: A History of Modern Childrearing in America*. New York and London: New York University Press, 2003.

Stern, Steve. *Remembering Pinochet's Chile: On the Eve of London 1998, The Memory Box of Pinochet's Chile*. Durham, NC: Duke, 2004.

Stetson, Damon. "Union Pickets Welfare Office to Protest City Talk Impasse." *New York Times*, December 22, 1966, 25.

———. "Welfare Strike Is Ended by Union." *New York Times*, January 19, 1967, 1, 24.

Stevens, Rosemary. *In Sickness and Wealth: American Hospitals in the 20th Century*. New York: Basic Books, Inc., 1989.

Stewart, Linda. "W-2 Allows Mothers Time to Find Child Care." *Milwaukee Journal Sentinel*, September 25, 1997, 17.

Stewart, William H., Maryland Y. Pennell, and Lucille M. Smith. *Homemaker Services in the United States, 1958: A Nationwide Study*. Public Health Service Publication No. 644. Washington, DC: U.S. Government Printing Office, 1958.

Stoler, Ann Laura. "Colonial Archives and the Arts of Governance." *Archival Science* 2 (2002): 87–109.

Stolley, Kathy S. "Statistics on Adoption in the United States." *Adoption* 3:1 (1993): 26-41.

Strasser, Susan. *Never Done: A History of Housework.* New York: Henry Holt, 2000.

Stryker, Susan. *Transgender History.* Berkeley, CA: Seal Press, 2008.

Stryker, Susan, and Stephen Whittle. *The Transgender Studies Reader.* New York: Routledge, 2006.

"Supreme Court Ruling Puts Hookers in 10-Day Limbo." *The Province*, January 26, 1983, A1.

Swedish Institute. "Telecommunications and Information Technology in Sweden." *Swedish Industry* no. 125, 2001.

Szymanski, Zak. "Out on the Web: Affirm Your Identity." *Curve Magazine* (February 2003): 14.

Tait, Vanessa. *Poor Workers' Unions: Rebuilding Labor From Below.* Boston, MA: South End Press, 2005.

Tales of the Night Fairies. Directed by Shohini Ghosh. Centre for Feminist Legal Research (New Delhi), and MAMACASH (Amsterdam), 2002.

Tate, Winifred. "Paramilitaries in Colombia." *Brown Journal of World Affairs* 8:1 (2001): 163–175.

Taylor, P., J. Hyman, G. Mulvey, and P. Bain. "Work Organization, Control, and the Experience of Work in Call Centers." *Work, Employment, and Society* 16, 1 (2002): 133–50.

Tench, Megan. "Care Provider Charged in Death at Nursing Home." *Boston Globe*, June 16, 2007. Retrieved on January 25, 2010, from: www.boston.com/news/local/ massachusetts/articles/2007/06/16/care_provider_charged_in_death_at_nursing _home/

Thai, Hung. *For Better or for Worse: Vietnamese International Marriages in the New Global Economy.* New Brunswick, NJ: Rutgers University Press, 2008.

Thomas, June. *Redevelopment and Race: Planning a Fine City in Postwar Detroit.* Baltimore: Johns Hopkins University Press, 1997.

Thompson, Joey. "Hookers Ousted from Zone." *Province*, July 5, 1984, A3.

Thompson, John D. "Nursing Service in a Home Care Program." *American Journal of Nursing*, 51 (April 1951): 233–234.

Tilly, Chris, and Charles Tilly. *Work under Capitalism.* Boulder, CO: Westview, 1998.

"To Book a Hooker" (editorial). *The Province*, January 26, 1983, B1.

Tomlins, Chistopher. "AFL Unions in the 1930s: Their Performance in Historical Perspective," *Journal of American History* 4 (1979): 1021–1042.

Toosi, Nahal. "Ailing NYC Woman at Center of Supreme Court Home-Care Case" (2007). *Newsday.com.* April 13, 2007. Retrieved on April 17, 2007, from: www .newsday.com/news/loca/newyork/ny-bc-ny

"Transition for W-2 Families Studied; Results Show Problems with Child Care and Economic Hardships." *Wisconsin State Journal*, April 28, 2000. Retrieved on May 10, 2007, from: www.lexisnexis.com

Tronto, Joan C. *Moral Boundaries: A Political Argument for an Ethic of Care*. New York and London: Routledge, 1993.

Tucker, Richard. *Insatiable Appetite: The United States and the Ecological Degradation of the Tropical World*. New York: Rowman and Littlefield, 2007.

Tucker, Robert C., ed. *The Marx-Engels Reader*. New York: W. W. Norton & Co., 1978.

Turley, William, and Mark Selden. *Reinventing Vietnamese Socialism: Doi Moi in Comparative Perspective*. Boulder, CO: Westview Press, 1993.

Turner, Lowell and Richard Hurd. "Building Social Movement Unionism: The Transformation of the American Labor Movement." In *Rekindling the Movement: Labor's Quest for Relevance in the 21st Century*, edited by Lowell Turner, Harry C. Katz, and Richard W. Hurd, pp. 9–26. Ithaca, NY: Cornell University Press, 2001.

Ungerson, Clare. "Whose Empowerment and Independence? A Cross-National Perspective on 'Cash for Care' Schemes." *Ageing & Society* 24 (2004): 189–212.

Ungerson, Clare, and Sue Yeandle. *Cash for Care in Developed Welfare States*. New York: Palgrave Macmillan, 2007.

Union Labor News of the South Central Federation of Labor (adapted from a report compiled by the Wisconsin Early Childhood Association). "Symposium Acknowledges Need for Worthy Wages." August 2000. Retrieved from: www.scfl.org/?ulnid=555

U.S. Bureau of Labor Statistics. "A Profile of the Working Poor." Washington, DC: Department of Labor, 2000.

———. "Employed Persons by Detailed Occupation, Sex, Race and Hispanic Origin." Washington, DC: U.S. Department of Labor, 2007.

U.S. Census Bureau. "Studies in Marriage and the Family." Current Population Reports, pp. 23–162. Washington, DC: U.S. Government Printing Office, 1989.

———. "Marriage, Divorce, and Remarriage in the 1990's." Current Population Reports, pp. 23–180. Washington, DC: U.S. Government Printing Office, 1992.

———. "Household and Family Characteristics: Summary Tables." (June 13, 2000a) http://www.census.gov/population/www/socdemo/hh-fam-sum98tab.html

———. "Santa Barbara, Santa María, Lompoc, Metropolitan Statistical Area files." Washington, DC: U.S. Government Printing Office, 2000b.

U.S. Central Intelligence Agency. "CIA—The World Factbook—Country Comparison: Infant mortality rate." Retrieved on August 3, 2009, from www.cia.gov/library/publications/the-world-factbook/rankorder/2091rank.html

U.S. Children's Bureau (USCB). Records. RG102. National Archives and Records Administration. College Park, MD.

———. *Supervised Homemaker Service: A Method of Child Care: Publication 296*. Washington, DC: U.S. Government Printing Office, 1943.

U.S. Department of Health, Education, and Welfare (HEW). "Human Resources Issues in the Field of Aging: Homemaker–Home Health Aide Services." *Administration on Aging Occasional Papers in Gerontology* 2, DHEW Publication No. (OHD) 77-20086 (1977): 1–32.

U.S. Department of Labor. *Dictionary of Occupational Titles*, Vol. II, *Occupational Classification and Industry Index*, 2nd edition. Washington, DC: U.S. Government Printing Office, 1949.

———. Wage and Hour Division. "Opinion Letter: FLSA," WH-174, 1972 WL 34917, August 20, 1972.

———. "New York City Spas and Nail Salons Agree to Pay More Than $222,000 in Back Wages and Interest to Settle U.S. Labor Department Lawsuit." Wage and Hour Division Release Number: 06-1581-NEW / BOS 2006-288. October 12, 2006. Retrieved on November 12, 2006, from: www.dol.gov/esa/whd/media/press/whdpressVB2.asp?pressdoc=Northeast/20061588.xml

U.S. Department of Labor. Bureau of Labor Statistics. "Union Members in 2008." Press Release, January 28, 2009. Retrieved on March 8, 2009 from: www.bls.gov/news.release/union2.nro.htm

U.S. Department of State. "Immigrant Visas Issued to Orphans Coming to U.S." Washington, DC: U.S. Department of State, June 12, 2002a. Retrieved on July 16, 2002, from http://travel.state.gov/orphan_numbers.html

———. "Trafficking in Persons Report." Washington, DC: U.S. Government Printing Office, 2003.

———. "Trafficking in Persons Report." Washington, DC: US Government Printing Office, 2004.

———. "Trafficking in Persons Report." Washington, DC: U.S. Government Printing Office, 2005.

———. "Immigrant Visas Issued to Orphans Coming to the U.S." Retrieved on January 19, 2006, from: http://travel.state.gov/family/adoption/stats/stats_451.html

U.S. Division of Public Health Methods. *Homemaker Services in the United States, 1958: Twelve Statements Describing Different Types of Homemaker Services*. Washington, DC: U.S. Government Printing Office, 1958.

U.S. General Accounting Office. "Collective Bargaining Rights: Information on the Number of Workers with and without Bargaining Rights." GAO-02-835 (September 2002). Washington, DC: U.S. Government Printing Office.

U.S. House Committee on Education and Labor. *Fair Labor Standards Amendments of 1973: Hearings Before the General Subcommittee on Labor of the Committee on Education and Labor on H.R. 4757 and H.R. 2831*. 93rd Congress, 1st Session. Washington, DC: U.S. Government Printing Office, 1973.

———. "H.R. 3582, the Fair Home Health Care Act." Hearings held on October 25, 2007. Retrieved on August 15, 2008, from: http://edlabor.house.gov/hearings/2007/10

U.S. House Committee on Ways and Means. *Independent Contractors*. Hearings on H.R. 3245, 96th Congress, 1st Session; June 30, July 16, and July 17, 1979. Washington, DC: U.S. Government Printing Office, 1979.

U.S. House Select Committee on Aging. *New York Home Care Abuse*. Hearing, February 6, 1978, 95th Congress, 2nd Session. Washington, DC: U.S. Government Printing Office, 1978.

U.S. Senate Committee on Labor and Public Welfare. *Legislative History of the Fair Labor Standards Amendments of 1974 (Public Law 93-259)*. Vol. I, 94th Congress, 2nd Session. Washington, DC: U.S. Government Printing Office, 1976.

U.S. Supreme Court. *Long Island Care at Home, LTD., et al., Petitioners v. Evelyn Coke*, No. 06-593. Transcript of Oral Testimony (April 16, 2007). Washington, DC: Alderson Reporting Company, 2007.

———. *Long Island Care at Home v. Evelyn Coke*, 551 U.S. 158, 2007.

Urban Justice Center. Brief, Brennan Center for Justice et al as *Amici Curiae* Supporting Respondent in *Long Island Care at Home, LTD, et al., v. Evelyn Coke*, No. 06-593 in the Supreme Court of the United States. 2007.

Van Raaphorst, Donna L. *Union Maids Not Wanted: Organizing Domestic Workers, 1870–1940*. New York: Praeger, 1988.

Veblen, Thornton. *The Theory of the Leisure Class*. London: Penguin, 1994.

Venning, Rachel. "How To Suck Dyke Cock." *On Our Backs*. December/January 2002: 11.

Walkowitz, Daniel J. *Working with Class: Social Workers and the Politics of Middle-Class Identity*. Chapel Hill: University of North Carolina Press, 1999.

Walkowitz, Judith R. *Prostitution and Victorian Society: Women, Class, and the State*. Cambridge, U.K.: Cambridge University Press, 1980.

Walters, Steven. "Severe Cuts Loom For State Child Care: Agency Handling Subsidies for Needy is Facing Deficit of $187 Million; Co-pays, Who Qualifies Might Change." *The Milwaukee Journal Sentinel* (January 29, 2007). Retrieved on July 31, 2007, from: www.lexisnexis.com

Warner, Michael. *The Trouble with Normal: Sex, Politics, and the Ethics of Queer Life*. New York: The Free Press, 1999.

Weber, Florence. "Peut-on rémunérer l'aide familiale?" In *Charges de Famille*, edited by Florence Weber, Séverine Gojard, and Agnès Gramain. Paris: La Découverte, 2003.

Weeks, Jeffrey. "Inverts, Perverts, and Mary-Annes." In *The Subcultures Reader*, edited by Ken Gelder and Sarah Thornton. London: Routledge, 1997.

Weitzer, Ronald, ed. *Sex for Sale: Prostitution, Pornography, and the Sex Industry*. New York: Routledge, 2000.

"Welfare's Homemakers Honored with Ten-Year Service Awards." *The Welfarer* (August, 1959): 3.

West, Candace, and Don Zimmerman. "Doing Gender." *Gender & Society* 1 (1987): 125–151.

When Mother Comes Home for Christmas. Directed by Nilita Vachani. The Greek Film Centre and FilmSixteen, 1996.

Whitebook, Marcy. *Working for Worthy Wages: The Child Care Compensation Movement, 1970–2001.* Berkeley, CA: Institute of Industrial Relations, Center for the Study of Child Care Employment, 2002.

Whitebook, Marcy, Carollee Howes, and Deborah Phillips. "Who Cares? Child Care Teachers and the Quality of Care in America." *The National Child Care Staffing Study.* Washington, DC: Child Care Employee Project, 1990. Retrieved on July 1, 2007, from: www.ccw.org/pubs/whocares.pdf

Whitebook, Marcy, Laura Sakai, Emily Gerber, and Carollee Howes. "Then and Now: Changes in Child Care Staffing, 1996–2000. Technical report." Washington, DC: Center for the Child Care Workforce, 2001. Retrieved on July 1, 2007, from: www .ccw.org/pubs/Then&Nowfull.pdf

Williams, Christine L., Patti A. Giuffre, and Kirsten Dellinger. "Sexuality in the Workplace: Organizational Control, Sexual Harassment, and the Pursuit of Pleasure." *Annual Review of Sociology* 25 (1999): 73–93.

Williams, Harrison. "Remarks on Introducing S. 682." *Congressional Record.* (February 19, 1971): 3287–3288.

Williams, Joan, and Zelizer, Viviana. "To Commodify or Not to Commodify: That Is Not the Question." In *Rethinking Commodification: Cases and Readings in Law and Culture,* edited by Martha M. Ertman and Joan C. Williams, pp. 362–382. New York: NYU Press, 2005.

Winiecki, Donald J. "Subjects, Subjectivity, and Subjectification in Call Center Work." *Journal of Contemporary Ethnography* 36:4 (2007): 351–377.

Wissinger, Elizabeth. "Always On Display: Affective Production in the Modeling Industry." In *The Affective Turn: Theorizing the Social,* edited by Patricia Ticineto Clough and Jean Halley, pp. 231–260. Durham, NC: Duke University Press, 2007.

Wolfe, Alan. "Democracy versus Sociology: Boundaries and Their Political Consequences." In *Cultivating Differences: Symbolic Boundaries and the Making of Inequality,* edited by Michele Lamont and Marcel Fournier, pp. 309–26. Chicago: University of Chicago Press, 1992.

"Women's Work." *New York Times* editorial, June 8, 2008.

Wonders, Nancy, and Raymond Michalowski. "Bodies, Borders and Sex Tourism in a Globalized World: A Tale of Two Cities—Amsterdam and Havana." *Social Problems* 48:4 (2001): 545–571.

Wong, Sau-ling. "Diverted Mothering: Representations of Caregivers of Color in the Age of Multiculturalism." In *Mothering: Ideology, Experience, and Agency,* edited by Evelyn Nakano Glenn, Grace Chang, and Linda Rennie Forcey, pp. 67–91. New York: Routledge, 1994.

Wrigley, Julia. *Other People's Children*. New York: Basic Books, 1995.

Xiao, Suowei. "China's New Concubines? The Contemporary Second-Wife Phenomenon." Ph.D. Dissertation, University of California, Berkeley, 2009.

Yancy, Dorothy Cowser. "Dorothy Bolden, Organizer of Domestic Workers: She Was Born Poor but She Would Not Bow Down." *Sage* 3:1 (Spring 1986): 53–55.

Zelizer, Viviana. *Pricing the Priceless Child: The Changing Social Value of Children*. New York: Basic Books, 1985.

———. "Circuits within Capitalism." In *The Economic Sociology of Capitalism*, edited by Victor Nee and Richard Swedberg, pp. 289–322. Princeton, NJ: Princeton University Press, 2000.

———. *The Purchase of Intimacy*. Princeton, NJ: Princeton University Press, 2005.

———. "Caring Everywhere." Keynote presented at "Intimate Labors: An Interdisciplinary Conference on Domestic, Care, & Sex Work." University of California, Santa Barbara. October 4–6, 2007.

———. "Intimacy in Economic Organizations." In *Economic Sociology of Work*, edited by Nina Bandelj, pp. 23–55. Bingley, U.K.: Emerald, 2009.

Zinn, Maxine Baca, and Bonnie Thornton Dill. "Theorizing Difference from Multiracial Feminism." *Feminist Studies* 22 (Summer 1996): 321–331.

Index

CPSIA information can be obtained
at www.ICGtesting.com
Printed in the USA
LVHW041040220120
644408LV00001B/8